HISTORY
of
CHRISTIANITY
1650-1950
Secularization of the West

JAMES HASTINGS NICHOLS

Professor of Church History
University of Chicago

THE RONALD PRESS COMPANY   •   NEW YORK

2

Library of Congress Catalog Card Number: 56-6268

PREFACE

This volume is directed to the student of Christian history—the college undergraduate, the seminary student, the clergyman, and the interested layman—who wishes to understand the development of Christian life during the crucial period of the last three centuries: the most complicated and least generally known of the major divisions of church history. The long series of crises during this period can now be seen as a revolution in the relation of Christianity to Western culture. A knowledge of the events of these three hundred years and a clear grasp of their significance are of capital importance to the responsible Christian believer. The author has conceived this book, therefore, as an orientation to the present state of Christianity.

Even where doctrine and church life have remained very conservative, the place of Christian doctrine and church life in the minds and practice of Christians has radically changed. Even where confessions, liturgies, and institutions seem substantially what they were early in the seventeenth century, they do in fact represent something significantly different. And yet little effort has been made, at least in histories in the English language, to comprehend this transformation of modern Christianity. There are valuable histories of various particular churches, or the churches of this or that country, but few if any which interpret comprehensively the developments which lie behind the present state of Christianity as a whole. This volume undertakes to survey these developments.

Many separated church traditions are treated in this account as if they were all part of the Christian society, the church, or as if the church were to be found in significant measure within them. This is in fact the premise of this history. It is not to assert that all are equally parts of the church, or in the same way. But the historian who believes in the church ecumenical must strive to keep it all in vision, even if only in representative and survey fashion.

Our story begins with the close of the Religious Wars, when the confessional map of Europe was stabilized. It is marked out into epochs by the French Revolution, the several crises about 1870, the World War (1914-18). These periods are progressively shorter in years, but this is inevitable because of the growth of population and the greater political and cultural complexity in the more recent generations.

Through four periods are traced the events and tendencies of four great cultural and religious divisions of the West: the Latin and Roman Catholic (France, Italy, Spain, Latin America); the Germanic and Lutheran (Germany and Scandinavia); the Orthodox Slavic and Greek (Russia, the Balkans, the Near East); and the English-speaking world with its distinctive family of related "denominations." This basic scheme is qualified, of course, by important exceptions, minorities, and border areas. In addition some reference is made in the more recent periods to a fifth area, that of the Younger Churches in non-European cultures. The central theme throughout is the changing relation of Christian faith to society, culture, and the state.

The exposition presupposes an acquaintance with general European and American political and cultural history. Readers unfamiliar with this background will find it convenient to have at hand one of the standard accounts. A good historical atlas will also be useful for a careful reading.

The plan and substance of this book grew out of a course taught jointly for some years with Sidney E. Mead, Professor of American church history, at the University of Chicago. At one stage it was intended to write the book jointly, and it still bears the marks, at more points than the author could identify, of Professor Mead's insight and scholarship. Chapters 6, 15, and 21, in particular, are based upon Professor Mead's lectures, although he is not to be held responsible for their present organization and emphasis. The author is also indebted to his Dean, Jerald Brauer; to Luther A. Weigle, formerly Dean; and to Clarence P. Shedd, Professor Emeritus at Yale University Divinity School, for their very valuable criticism. Special thanks are due to his former colleague, Professor Wilhelm Pauck, who criticized an earlier version with a discernment and learning difficult to match.

James H. Nichols

Chicago, Illinois
    February, 1956

CONTENTS

PART I

WESTPHALIA TO THE FRENCH REVOLUTION

PART II

FROM THE FRENCH REVOLUTION TO 1870

PART III

1870 TO WORLD WAR I

PART IV

FROM WORLD WAR I TO THE MID-CENTURY

Part I

WESTPHALIA TO THE FRENCH REVOLUTION

Chapter 1

MAIN THEMES OF MODERN CHURCH HISTORY

Our task is a delineation of the development of Christianity in the last three hundred years. This period since the Peace of Westphalia has been the most complicated and least generally known of all the major divisions of church history. It was not primarily distinguished by creative personalities of monumental stature, such as Augustine, Hildebrand, Luther, or Calvin. Men such as Zinzendorf, Wesley, Schleiermacher, Maurice, and Leo XIII, and there are many others, must be given due acknowledgment, but such men did not in this period create great new institutions like the medieval papacy, or the Reformation. They were, on the whole, content to work within existing structures. Some significant new groups, such as the Moravians and the Methodists, have arisen, but, on the whole, the denominational map of Europe has changed remarkably little since 1648.

GEOGRAPHICAL EXPANSION. But this is true only of Europe; the first great theme of modern Christian history is its geographical expansion outside Europe. Christianity in the Middle Ages had suffered notable losses in its Eastern centers and had become largely confined to Western Europe. Numerically this displacement evened out. The number of Christians in 1500 was about the same as in A.D. 500, a millennium before. Politically and culturally, however, the new center in Western Europe occupied no such world pre-eminence as had the fifth-century Roman Empire. In wealth, size, political power, and in some respects, civilization, Christian Western Europe in 1500 was inferior to Hindu India, the Ottoman Empire, and the Ming

3

Dynasty. Europe was one of the smallest major cultural areas, containing only 10 or 15 per cent of humanity.

The four centuries after 1500, however, witnessed an unprecedented expansion of this Cinderella among the world's cultures. A startling increase in exploratory and commercial activity coincided with a great increase in population. The population of Europe itself increased seven or eight times, so that in 1914 Europeans numbered 25 per cent of all humanity.

Meanwhile, European peoples had migrated, as had no known earlier civilization, and had formed new nations. Overseas territories wholly unknown to Europeans in 1500 were thoroughly explored and all of the inhabitable continents were pre-empted by Western economic and political imperialism by 1914. This unprecedented European expansion was the major factor in the spread of Christianity in this same period, although Christianity had also in various ways contributed to the expansion. Geographically, the Western hemisphere had become equally important with Europe. Since 1914, however, the gain of non-Western groups has been so notable that the prospect is raised of a possible future return of the center of political and cultural gravity to the non-Western peoples.

The first expansion of the sixteenth and seventeenth centuries was largely under the aegis of the Counter Reformation. Spain and Portugal were the chief colonial powers, and their most striking achievements were the colonizing and missionizing of Latin America and the Philippines. In the seventeenth century the leadership of the Roman Catholic world passed to France, whose monks were most active in the West Indies and the St. Lawrence and Mississippi basins. The Portuguese Catholics and the Dutch Reformed, meanwhile, scattered missions around the coasts of Africa, India, Ceylon, and the East Indies. The highly Erastian pattern of these missions, however, produced enervated churches. Latin America, for example, has never to this day produced enough clergy for her own needs or experienced a "Great Awakening." Only the British colonies of North America, although weaker in wealth and nominal membership than those of Latin America, developed from the beginning a Christianity of expansive power.

After a brief recession in the second half of the eighteenth century, the migrations and missions resumed on an enormous scale. Beginning in Great Britain and the United States during the Napoleonic Wars, and passing to Roman Catholic and Lutheran countries, an unprecedented movement arose. The English-speaking Protestant churches dominated this next century as the Counter Reformation Spanish and French had shaped the earlier movement. The most considerable result was the creation of new Western peoples in Australia, New Zealand, South Africa, Canada, and particularly the United States, which by 1914 had a population equal to that of all Europe in Cromwell's day. Missions to non-Western peoples continued, meanwhile, especially in Africa, Madagascar, India, Indo-China, Japan, China, Korea, and the East Indies, so that by 1914 Christianity, if not yet firmly rooted among nearly all the major non-Western peoples, was at least being offered to them. Since 1914 the chief gains have been among these peoples.

Despite the tremendous emigration from Europe, chiefly to North and South America, population increased nearly three times in Europe itself during the "Great Century." The increase was due first to medical control and secondarily to the technological revolution, which made possible a new type of urban society. Beginning in France and Ireland and the United States, however, the practice of birth control spread during the century, so that the population of Western culture seemed to be approaching stability if not decline. The forces which released the great increase, meanwhile, as well as those which made for Western political supremacy, are today operating in Russia and Asia, which bid fair to return Western society to its earlier smaller ratio to humanity as a whole. Eastern Orthodoxy and the Younger Churches thus may acquire more strategic significance.

When we turn to the inner history of the Church in these three centuries, we must deal with the perennial ebb and flow in the relation of the faith to culture. The life of the Church is always shaped by two concurrent movements, the penetration and transformation of cultural life by faith in Christ, and the secularization of relations and areas once converted. The second movement predominated during this period, but the process has been a complicated one.

CIVILIZATION OF THE ENLIGHTENMENT. In order to obtain a somewhat schematic view of the distinctively "modern" relation of the Christian faith to Western culture, this relationship will be presented first from a cultural viewpoint. The opening of our period of "modern" church history is defined by the end of the medieval and Reformation pattern of a church-dominated state and society. It is easier to begin with the negative definition of modern culture as a culture emancipated from Christian control and integration. In the seventeenth century, for the first time in a thousand years in Western history, a deliberate attempt was made on a grand scale to organize a religiously neutral civilization—a political, economic, ethical, and intellectual structure independent of Christianity. This great transformation was effected in the seventeenth and eighteenth centuries by the movement sometimes described as the *Enlightenment*. And although the positive dogmas of the Enlightenment were themselves to undergo radical criticism and often rejection in the nineteenth and twentieth centuries, nevertheless by and large the negative side of the work of the Enlightenment endured. Modern Western culture, whatever its positive meaning, may be distinguished from that of earlier phases by its emancipation from explicit Christian direction.

THE MODERN STATE SYSTEM. The Peace of Westphalia (1648), which ended the Thirty Years' War, is as good a date as any to represent the transition to the new phase in politics. In the preceding warfare, the various states of Europe had acted in what they thought were the interests of the religious group to which they belonged. The Peace signified a stalemate—that neither the Reformation nor the Counter Reformation had succeeded. The acceptance of this situation (over the strenuous protests of the papacy) meant that major political alignments and questions of war and peace were to be settled by criteria other than those of theological conviction. The fundamental political structure of modern Western culture thus came into existence—the family of Western states with its shifting "balance of power." This is the political framework in which the modern church has lived, in contrast to medieval Christendom or the Reformation confessional alliances. The basis for political decisions in this modern system was to be dynastic or national power and glory.

The actual practice of these states in their relations has not been exclusively a Machiavellian pursuit of *raison d'état*, although this phrase describes much of it. The pursuit of power and glory has been conspicuous in political life in all periods. And in the modern West there has been maintained also a tradition of certain ethical criteria or limits for state action. These norms were in essence those of medieval and Reformation (and ultimately Roman Stoic) "natural law." But now they were taken out of their theological context and set on their own feet as findings of the supposed universal moral sense. The liberal Dutch Calvinist, Hugo Grotius, for example, codified them in his great early classic of "international law." It is hard to say whether in practice the Christian political code of the Middle Ages was any more of a restraint or guide than international law has been in the modern period. But the point that concerns us here is that the international law has been conceived as independent of Christianity, and that with certain exceptions, the states inhabited by Christians have thus made their decisions on avowedly a-Christian grounds in this modern period.

In their domestic policies also, these modern Western states have no longer recognized Christian criteria for policy. Most of them, to be sure, at least in the early modern period, thought of themselves as "Christian states" and maintained established churches. But the emergence and prevalence of the theory of "sovereignty" show that in fact the modern state has insisted on its independence of and superiority to Christian direction. The actual criterion has been the military, commercial, and general economic welfare of the state. The modern state has generally declined to serve as the "secular arm" of a Christian society, and the political influence of the Christian churches has been confined to secondary and indirect manifestations. Modern political thought has found the governing sanctions for political association in the nature of man in general, without benefit of biblical revelation or ecclesiastical authorities. The established churches, Roman Catholic, Anglican, Lutheran, and Reformed, contested this development and relinquished their control of state power and social discipline only under constraint, but the governmental elites and the dominant social classes have admitted ever less religious interference in politics. Modern Christians have generally thought and acted in politics independently of their faith.

The modern state, again, has widely claimed a moral basis for its law and authority, and the substance of this, again, has been derived from the Christianized tradition of natural law, but has been taken out of its religious context. Theories of natural law and rights have been used to support different forms of government—monarchical and constitutional. And the states shaped by Lutheran, Anglican, Roman Catholic, and Reformed communities have taken significantly different attitudes toward such questions. Whichever way they turned, however, these states have generally conceived their decisions as having been formed by natural reason apart from any specifically Christian direction.

The substitution of dynastic or state interest for religious conformity as the principle of political organization led in most cases to a greater or lesser degree of religious toleration. This came earliest in the predominantly Reformed Dutch and English-speaking countries. Lutheran and Roman Catholic princes were slower to renounce attempts to enforce confessional uniformity. By the latter half of the eighteenth century, however, toleration was becoming the prevailing policy of the enlightened despots of Europe. And the nineteenth century continued the trend toward the religious neutrality of the state.

AUTONOMY OF ECONOMICS. The growth of toleration was also furthered by the growing strength of commercial preoccupations. Commerce and industry had been regulated in the Middle Ages and the Reformation in the interests of community welfare and social justice with religious sanctions, and involved price-fixing, and regulation of quantity, quality, and conditions of production. In the early modern period much the same devices were adopted for the political aims of mercantilist absolutism. Holland and England again pioneered the theory and practice of economic freedom from such restraint. The theory reached its classic formulations with Adam Smith and Francois Quesnay in the late eighteenth century, whereby business operations were to be made subject only to the "natural laws" of supply and demand in a free market. In such fashion as this, most modern Christians persuaded themselves not to let their Christian tenets interfere with their business.

COSMOLOGY AND THE NEW SCIENCE. Modern natural science and cosmology, meanwhile, were radically reshaping the relation of the Christian faith to man's understanding of his world. The old "common-sense" Ptolemaic cosmology and Aristotelian physics had left room for purposive and moral aspects to the workings of nature, and could be adjusted without too great difficulty to the cosmology of the Bible. But the new mechanical physics and astronomy, from the seventeenth century on, largely eliminated purpose. Men came to think of God increasingly less in concrete patriarchal images, and more impersonally, abstractly, and remotely. Sometimes the effort was made to preserve certain areas of nature, especially human nature and history, from the sweep of mechanistic thought, but the prestige resulting from the practical technological success of the new science gave it strength to override all barriers. The prevailing cosmology on the popular level came to be ever more clearly a mechanistic atomism, of which the natural tendency was atheism. Numerous efforts at a Christian metaphysics have not succeeded in checking or materially modifying this prevailing drift of the last four centuries. The modern Christian has been forced to nourish his faith in archaic forms of thought about the world, forms which he could not use for everyday life nor readily re-interpret into the world-view which he was in fact using.

Only in slightly less degree did the new geographical and historical knowledge undercut the traditional Christian view of the story of man's fall and redemption. Knowledge of hitherto unknown cultures made such classical schemes of Christian history as Daniel's four kingdoms and the panoramas of Augustine and Bossuet seem provincial. The assumption of a common humanity and unchanging natural laws made biblical miracles and special revelations increasingly problematical.

The educational curriculum provides a convenient epitome of the dominant ethical and religious assumptions of a culture. The history of Western education since the seventeenth century exhibits an emancipation both from clerical control and from a religious orientation. Instead of being a preparation for man's communion with God, education came to be dominated by utilitarian motives and political preoccupations, both disciplined by "natural" rather than Christian morality. The period has been characterized by great faith in education as the chief means of progress. Theological instruction and worship, meanwhile, have occupied an ever smaller place in the curriculum, and their relevance to the other subjects of study has been ever less obvious. One would judge from the prevailing pattern of education that Christian faith has become a minor and somewhat irrelevant factor in the cultural tradition.

Looked at thus from a cultural viewpoint, the Christian faith would seem to have played a progressively declining role in the lives of modern Christians. And we do speak of this period as one of the "secularization" of the culture. But from the viewpoint of the faith, as we have suggested, this "secularization" is a very complicated and even ambiguous process.

ROMAN AND ORTHODOX CATHOLIC SECULARIZATION. The nature of secularization is seen in its simplest form in Orthodox and Roman Catholic societies. With the Orthodox, especially in Russia, the new forms of religiously emancipated culture burst from the West with revolutionary force. These forms had not developed in association with the life of Orthodoxy and were generally hostile to it. The Bolshevik conquest of Russia illustrates this process of secularization in its crudest and most violent form.

Roman Catholicism in Western Europe had more relations with the development of modern civilization, but, on the whole, these relations were passive where not negative. In Roman Catholic countries the medieval tradition of a priest-controlled society, state and culture, on a static hierarchical pattern, remained normative and was compromised only grudgingly. We may trace here a steady emancipation of various elements of the common life from clerical control and medieval patterns from the seventeenth into the twentieth centuries. This loss of extensive influence has been countered by a corresponding tightening of the lines of internal discipline, for the Roman Church conceived itself to be on the defensive throughout. From this perspective, as certain Roman Catholic and Orthodox historians give evidence, the whole of modern church history is to be read as a progressive secularization and rebellion against the faith.

PROTESTANT SYNTHESIS.   Such an image of progressive apostasy, however, cannot be imposed on the modern history of most Protestant countries without violence.   And these are precisely the countries where the leadership in shaping Western culture has been found from the seventeenth to the twentieth centuries.   Leadership in the intellectual as well as in the political and economic spheres passed in the seventeenth century from southern Roman Catholic Europe to Holland, Great Britain, Protestant Germany, and English-speaking North America.   And in these countries the Christian faith exerted a powerful influence in the shaping of such new cultural movements as political democracy and humanitarianism, modern technology and capitalism, and modern philosophy and history. This influence was more indirect than direct, more lay than clerical, more unconscious than intended; yet it produced a new synthesis of faith and culture not unworthy of comparison with that of the thirteenth century.   With particular reference to social teachings, Ernst Troeltsch compared the cultural impact of what he called "ascetic Protestantism" (referring to the Puritan, pietist, and sectarian tradition) to the medieval synthesis. "Along with medieval Catholicism," he wrote, "it constitutes the second great main type of Christian doctrine."   For most of modern history, consequently, "secularization" cannot be applied to the leading Protestant countries of the West in the same sense as to the Roman Catholic countries.

The second sense of the term "secularization" can be used for the relationship of modern Protestantism to culture.   As we have already suggested in reference to the emancipation of the spheres of modern culture from biblical or ecclesiastical authority, the criteria which were retained were borrowed largely from the Christian tradition of natural law.   It was quite possible, for example, for a Protestant to support political liberalism on the conviction that the ethical principles on which it rested were compatible, if not identical, with those of the Ten Commandments. It was on this type of confidence that Protestantism generally maintained an openness to modern culture far exceeding that of Roman Catholicism, and, in turn, was able to penetrate and to discipline this culture more than proved possible in Roman Catholic countries. Puritan Protestantism has been the great upholder of the moral law of nature in modern civilization and has transferred to it the energies which built theocracies in the Reformation epoch. Modern Protestant culture has been secularized in the sense that it has specifically renounced efforts toward biblical theocracies, but its pursuit of the moral law of nature has been conceived as a goal harmonious with God's revealed will. And where the contrast between cultural norms discerned by the natural reason and Christian faith has been obvious and painful, Christians have often satisfied themselves by a faith in "progress," which in the future would perfect the imperfect harmony.

THE DENOMINATION AS MODERN CHURCH FORM. The effect of this synthesis of faith and culture on ecclesiastical institutions must also be observed. Instead of the "church" and "sect" as the classical forms of ecclesiastical institution, modern church history is characterized by the "denomination." Even bodies like the Roman Catholics, who have wished to remain churches, or the Mennonites, who have intended to be sects, have been forced to become, for most practical purposes, "denominations." It was the free-church Calvinists of seventeenth-century England and Holland, on the other hand, who first deliberately shaped this new form of ecclesiastical life. Two features are particularly important. On the one hand, the denomination does not make exclusive claims. It purports to be one alternative form of Christian organization among others, often in the same community. It is not in itself *the church*, but rather only one denomination of the church. A plurality of organizations within the church is thus presupposed, as is the fact that they recognize each other as parts of the church.

Equally striking is the second feature of the denomination. The denomination restricts itself to but one or two of the traditional functions of the church. It is an institution for worship, for theological education, and for a degree of ethical discipline, usually very general and ineffective outside the area of family and personal relations. The denomination entrusts the remaining functions of the church, such as guidance in the major ethical decisions of life, to nonecclesiastical organizations, the state, public school, and the business corporation. Thus the denomination implies that the church is to be found, not merely in other denominations, but also in various nonecclesiastical institutions. And, in fact, the church history of the modern period must extend its scope far beyond the activities of all the denominations. For these activities do not include all, or even always the most important part, of the life of the people of God. This life of the community of believers in the modern period is thus in part hidden, or religiously anonymous, in a fashion very baffling for its historians.

The ethical and social initiative of the modern church, to take an example, has been largely anonymous. The nineteenth century was the great age of moral causes pursued by individuals, voluntary societies, or committees, and much or most of this belongs to the history of the modern church. The denominational institutions, however, were involved only to a slight extent, and gave a general impression of indifference. Much the same could be said of the activities of the people of God in higher culture and in education, for which the church received little recognition.

DISINTEGRATION OF THE PROTESTANT SYNTHESIS. Since the last generation of the nineteenth century, the whole modern synthesis of faith and culture has often seemed to be in dissolution. Non-Christian religious movements of various sorts, especially nationalist and Marxist, have attempted to re-integrate the modern West into new pagan theocracies, purging incompatible elements such as Christianity. The Christian church, likewise, has shown some symptoms of a desire to reconstitute itself as a total faith, a community. There has been a mutual permeation of ideas and practices among the denominations, and a concern to give greater institutional expression to the unity of the one church in its denominations.

In European Protestantism, at least, the twentieth century

has seen a widespread rejection of the whole program of a synthesis of faith and culture. Against all cultural norms and "natural laws," appeal is again being made directly to the living Word as known in the church through the Bible. Here and there, at least, one finds bold concepts of a new conquest of society and culture from this basis, although the Roman Catholic counterattack seems to be more successful. In the English-speaking world, however, where the modern synthesis was earliest and most thoroughly worked out, it still endures in measurable degree. Everywhere a new responsibility is felt to manifest the life of God's people more directly and unmistakably in the world.

Chapter 2

EASTERN ORTHODOXY, PARTICULARLY IN RUSSIA

Our theme is the history of Christianity in the last three centuries. The history of the churches outside the culture of Western Europe shows the extent to which the shape and periodization of our story are determined by events in Western Europe and her colonies. The development of the churches under Moslem rule and in Russia cannot be fitted easily into the same pattern as that of Christianity in Western culture. Their history, nevertheless, has been profoundly influenced by the impact of Western civilization as well as Western Christianity, for Western forces have increasingly dominated the world through most of these three centuries. Both at the beginning and at the end of our survey, however, we should remind ourselves that Christianity cannot be identified with Western culture, and that in non-Western cultures it has been developing along largely independent lines.

THE MOSLEM CONQUEST. We may begin with Christianity in its ancient homeland—Asia Minor, Syria, and the Eastern Mediterranean basin in general. It is hard for Westerners to realize that Christians in these lands have been under steady Moslem pressure and occasional persecution until within the last century and, in some areas, until this very moment. Christianity's greatest losses to Islam came in the early Middle Ages. The attacks of the Arabs, Mongols, and Ottoman Turks swept over about half the chief Christian territories. The successive surges left Christianity in desperate straits in its Asiatic and African homelands. Everywhere, the Christians were constricted into little cultural and religious islands and there slowly strangled. Every one of the four ancient Patriarchates has

15

lived for generations in our period under sufferance of the Ottoman Empire, and the mentality of Eastern Orthodoxy bears the marks of subjection. In the last three centuries, only the Orthodox mission territory among the Slavs above the Black Sea has been able to develop in some measure according to its own genius. We must look, consequently, first at the history of the Orthodox under the control of the Crescent, and then at the development of Christianity in the new state and culture of Russia, where today are to be found the large majority of all Orthodox Christians.

Beside the Orthodox churches of the Near East, there were a number of lesser Eastern churches considering themselves Orthodox, but not in communion with the ancient Patriarchates, who rather considered them schismatics and heretics. In general character, however, as in hierarchical organization, liturgy, doctrine, and ethos, all these Eastern churches displayed a family resemblance. The greatest of them was the Church of the East (Nestorian), which at one time had apparently comprised a larger community than all the medieval Western Christians in communion with the Roman Pope. From a base in Persia the Church of the East had extended down into India and up across Central Asia into China. This great Church was decimated by Islam. It was completely wiped out in China, but it survived in enclaves in Persia, South India (the St. Thomas Christians), and Turkey. Similarly, groups of the ancient Monophysites and Monothelites survived in Armenia, Syria (Jacobites), Egypt and Ethiopia (Copts), and in the Maronites of Mount Lebanon. All these communities were now small and fossilized, doubly isolated from the rest of the Christian Church by their doctrinal peculiarities and by the surrounding sea of Islam. In neither the Orthodox nor the lesser Eastern churches was there any hope of winning converts from Islam, which punished apostasy by death, and which placed various advantages in the way of those who would leave Christ for the Prophet.

THE CHURCH OF BYZANTIUM. The cultural nationalism of the various provinces of the ancient Roman Empire had been a significant force in the rupture of the Monophysite and Nestorian Churches from the church of the Byzantine Empire. Sometimes these Churches had even supported the Arabs and

the Turks against Byzantium, and their growth had left the
ancient Patriarchates of Jerusalem, Antioch, and Alexandria as
mere centers of Greek-speaking minorities among Arabic and
Syriac or Coptic churches. The Moslem armies had swept
over each of these Patriarchates and pressed on up the Balkan
Peninsula to capture Budapest and to lay siege to Vienna itself.
The desperate Patriarch of Constantinople, the last bastion of
Christianity in the East, had been willing to bargain even with
the heretical Pope of Rome at the Council of Florence (1439),
hoping for a crusading force of "Franks" (i.e., Latin Christians). But all was in vain. Constantinople also fell. And
after the first massacres of the conquest, the Ottomans elaborated a system of governing their Christian subjects which was
to last into the nineteenth century.

THE TURKISH SYSTEM. The system was well calculated to
corrupt Christianity. The Turks organized the Christians as
a semiautonomous community—the "Rum Millet" as the Moslems referred to them—and made the clergy responsible for
them. This in some ways increased the power of the clergy,
but it also made them bear the onus of collecting extortionate
taxes and the infamous tribute of children. Every four years
the pick of Christian boys was taken from their families to be
trained in Moslem military schools. They emerged as fanatical
Moslems and formed the backbone of the crack troops of the
Ottoman Empire, the famous Janissaries and Spahis. The Orthodox clergy became instruments of slavery and extortion
and experts in intrigue and fraud.

Periodically the very exercise of Christian worship was
threatened, since most churches were converted to mosques
and no new ones could be built. The habit of churchgoing
perforce declined. Monasteries remained the only effective
centers of Christianity. It is understandable that many communities voluntarily left Orthodoxy for Islam. The Greeks
of Constantinople, moreover, became willing parasites on the
Ottomans and extended their private interests. They persuaded the Sultan to put the hierarchy of the Serbians and Bulgarians in their hands and in the eighteenth century also
captured the Patriarchate of Antioch and fought for control of
Jerusalem. In all these cases they substituted Greek language

and liturgy for the various national languages. At the disintegration of the Ottoman Empire in the nineteenth century, the Greeks reaped the well-earned hatred of their Orthodox cousins, the Bulgarians, Serbians, and Rumanians.

The romantic career of Cyril Lukar illustrates both the desperate situation of Orthodoxy in the early seventeenth century and its relations with the Western churches. Lukar had been born in Venetian Crete, had studied in the West, and had adopted many Calvinist views in Geneva. He taught for a time in a Russian seminary, was elected Patriarch of Alexandria about 1602, and was then transferred to Constantinople in 1621. In Constantinople the Turks confiscated one after another of his churches until he had moved successively from four, and was left with but one in the capital. Twice Christianity was threatened with complete extermination. Patriarch Cyril himself had the added disadvantage of his evangelical sympathies. The French embassy was the base of Roman Catholic operations in Turkey, and the Jesuits intrigued with the Sultan against Cyril. Five times he was deposed, and five times reinstated. Finally the Sultan condemned him for alleged high treason, and in 1638 he was strangled by the Janissaries and thrown into the sea. The Jesuits had also managed to destroy the printing press Cyril had secured to print his creed and catechism.

ORTHODOX DOCTRINAL STATEMENTS. In reaction partly to Cyril's Calvinist innovations and partly to the Roman Catholic pressure around Kiev and at Constantinople, the Orthodox church of the seventeenth century defined its relation to both these Western systems. In Cyril's time, the Russian church officially recognized no distinction, grouping them together as "Latin heresy." The Metropolitan of Kiev, Peter Mogila, drew up a confession in 1640 which, after certain revisions, was signed by the four Eastern Patriarchs and sanctioned by the Council of Jerusalem in 1672 as the creed of all Orthodoxy. The latter Council is the most important in modern Orthodox history, publishing, in eighteen articles, the "Confession of Dositheos," which was later accepted in Russia (1838) with some toning down of Roman Catholic concepts and terms. These two seventeenth-century doctrinal statements are the most definitive elaboration of Orthodoxy in general over and above the canons of the Seven Ecumenical Councils, which alone, of course, are authoritative.

UNIATES. Roman Catholics have actively proselyted in the East all through the modern period, working from Poland and the envoys of France. Latin monasteries and Jesuit and Capuchin teams have been scattered widely. France has been given an official protectorate over the Holy Land and Roman Catholic interests in the Levant by the "capitulations" of the Ottoman Empire. Ecclesiastically the result has been the formation of a number of "Uniate" churches. So long as they acknowledge the jurisdiction of the pope of Rome, Uniate churches are permitted various Eastern rites and practices, although there is a tendency, where expedient, to assimilate them gradually to the Latin customs.

Let us now turn from the Orthodox of the Mohammedan occupation to the free Orthodox of Russia.

The fall of Constantinople in 1453 to the Turks left only the Russian diocese of the Patriarch of Constantinople free from Ottoman control. The Russians, organizing around the Grand Duke of Moscow, proceeded to eliminate the Mongol threat from their frontier. In the second half of the fifteenth century Moscow was the only major city in all the East which was ruled by a Christian prince.

THE THIRD ROME. The meaning of these events from a theological viewpoint was much pondered in the East, where all assumed that a Christian Empire was a necessary and divinely appointed aid to the Church, and where the Empire of Charlemagne and his successors had always been viewed as an usurpation. The destruction of the Byzantine Empire seemed to some to portend the coming end of the world, and the end was widely expected for 1492. In Russia the fall of Constantine's city was widely understood as a divine judgment on the Patriarch for the concessions he had made to Roman Catholic heresy at the Council of Florence. At that time he had been so desperate in seeking aid from the West against the Turks that Orthodox emissaries made doctrinal concessions which were later repudiated at home. And instead of meaning the end of all history, this destruction of the Byzantine Empire, together with the concurrent rise of Muscovy, might signify the transfer of the divine election to another dynasty. The monk Philotheos formulated this theory of Moscow, the "Third Rome," at the beginning of the sixteenth century. "The first Rome collapsed owing to its heresies, the second Rome fell a victim to the Turks, but a new third Rome has sprung up in the north, illuminating the whole universe like a sun . . . the third will stand till the end of history, for it is the last Rome. Moscow has no successor; a fourth Rome is inconceivable." This consciousness of an inherited commission was strengthened by the marriage of Ivan III of Moscow to Sophia of the Byzantine dynasty of Paleologus (1472), after which the Muscovite princes adopted the two-headed eagle of Byzantium. In the sixteenth century the title Tsar (Caesar) came to be used regularly. Thus was shaped the concept of the Holy Orthodox Tsardom of Moscow, appointed to preserve the true faith until the Second Coming.

THE PATRIARCHATE OF MOSCOW. The Dukes of Moscow found this theory of the Third Rome convenient for their aggrandizement over the other Russian territorial princes and their internal consolidation. In the church this close involvement with civil power developed some opposition. The policy found its chief support in the Volokolamsk monastery, the "nursery of bishops." Abbot Joseph defined the Tsar as "the Vicar of God on this earth, the supreme head of the State and of the Church." He had the greatest reverence for ritualistic piety and wished the church to have the financial means to maintain it. He was ready to use the civil power against heresy. In opposition, however, the "elders from across the Volga," headed by Nil of Sorsk, urged a view of Christianity akin in some ways to that of the Spiritual Franciscans of the Western Middle Ages. They denied the right of monasteries to hold great lands and serfs. They protested persecution of heretics. And in general they refused to put all church tradition on an equal level of authority with the Gospel. These "nonpossessors" were violently suppressed in the second quarter of the sixteenth century, leaving control of the church in the hands of the party of Joseph. This triumph reached its climax in a series of councils (1549-1551) summoned by Ivan the Terrible, in which over a score of Russian "Fathers" were canonized as credentials and ornaments of the "Third Rome" and anathema laid down against various heretics. Various legends appeared, similar to those of the Donation of Constantine in the West, to create a past for the authority of the Tsar. And in 1589 the fugitive Patriarch Jeremiah of Constantinople, being grateful for the protection of the Muscovite Tsar, was induced to preside over the consecration of an independent Patriarch of Moscow and Russia.

Of all these Patriarchs, Nikon is best known to history, for his career was to have great consequences. When the first Moscow Patriarch was consecrated, the installation acknowledged to the Tsar the theory of the Third Rome: "all other Christian kingdoms are merged in thy kingdom. Thou art the only Christian Sovereign in the whole world, the master of all the Christians." In the seventeenth century Orthodox Christians from many areas made pilgrimages to Moscow or fled as refugees for aid. Nikon, elected Patriarch in 1652, set out to actualize this leadership of the Tsar over all Orthodox everywhere. This called for the development of closer relations and unity among the five Eastern patriarchs and involved bringing the Russians also out of their isolation to awareness of the other Orthodox. To accomplish this, Nikon set out to correct the Russian service books to conform with the Greek.

NIKON'S LITURGICAL REFORM. But the proud consciousness of unchanging fidelity to the Orthodox faith, on which the theory of the Third Rome was built, stood in the way of any compromise for the sake of the unity of all Orthodox. Whereas the Greeks viewed the Russians as barbarians, innocent of the great tradition of classical culture and Christian theology, the Russians were impressed with the moral degradation, intrigue, and trickery of the Greeks and suspected them of truckling to Moslems and Romanists. Ritual and worship were the sum of religion to most of the Russians. There was no preaching, very little knowledge of the Creed, the Commandments, or the Lord's Prayer. The priesthood included many illiterates. Piety focused on religious art, liturgy, icons, and music. Consequently, changes in ritual touched the core of the religion. The specific issues of the great controversy, matters of words or gestures, or the direction of processions in the liturgy, seem trivial today. But the Russian Council of 1551 had already condemned the Greek usage of three instead of two fingers in making the sign of the cross. A triple instead of double "Hallelujah" was "Latin heresy," as was shaving the beard. The "rule of the Apostles" had been that church burial must be denied to one who shaved his beard. It was only natural that the greater part of religious Russia arose in horror when the Tsar supported the innovations and corrections of Patriarch Nikon. When Nikon's opponents were condemned by Councils in 1666 and 1667, in which the Patriarchs of Antioch and Alexandria were represented, it was felt widely among the church folk that these Councils had "abolished the ancient faith of the fathers and established the impious heterodoxy of Rome."

SCHISM OF THE "OLD BELIEVERS." The last third of the seventeenth century was the generation of the schism, a generation marked by hysterical apocalyptic fervor. The apostasy of the hierarchy was taken by many as the opening of the prophesied reign of Antichrist, which should end in two and one-half years. In 1668 the fields were unplowed and unsown over wide areas, and early in 1669 great assemblies gathered, and the faithful lay at night in white shrouds in coffins waiting for the Day of Judgment. When 1670 passed as usual some took it as an augury that the old ritual would be returned. Others recalculated the prophecies of the Book of Revelation and settled on 1699. It was rather hard to believe in the former opinion after the decree of 1684, which threatened all "Old Believers" with the stake. The Archpriest Avvakum is typical of the martyrs of those years, "Come, Orthodox People," he cried, "suffer tortures for the two-finger sign of the cross. . . . Although I have not much understanding—I am not a learned man—yet I know that the Church which we have received from our Holy Fathers is pure and sacred. As it came to me, so shall I uphold my faith until the end." Such men preached group suicide, by drowning or by fire, as a way of winning the martyr's crown. Perhaps 20,000 immolated themselves, mostly in the decade after 1684. As one cried, "I wish that all Romanov [his native village], every man, wife, and child would come to the banks of the Volga, throw themselves into the water, and sink . . . and what is even better, that I might set fire to and burn down the entire city . . . so that none could receive the stamp of Antichrist."

The prophecy about 1699 proved to be more accurate. Five days before the dreaded New Year, Tsar Peter the Great returned from his travels in Europe. He escaped the assassination plot of the royal guard, which included many Old Believers, and then amused himself for some days cutting off the beards of the nobility and the heads of the guardsmen, and in general playing the role of Antichrist in full. Once more the "liers in coffins" were heard. But again the reign of Antichrist did not end but only grew more lenient in time. What were the Old Believers to make of it, and how were they to organize their own lives?

Once the problem of organization arose, the Old Believers split apart. The radicals among them had become convinced that no existing body was the true church and waited for a new miraculous dispensation. They denied that there were true sacraments anywhere, save those available to all the laity, namely baptism and confession. They formed the so-called "priestless" wing and flourished in the frontier swamps and forests of the White Sea littoral or of Siberia, where people were used to living without regular clergy or sacraments. The larger section of the Old Believers, however, was terrified by the concept of life without the sacraments and preferred to believe that their own clergy still held the sacraments of the true church. They were concentrated in the Ukraine and the southwest. The two wings of the Old Believers went through periods of persecution and toleration and internal dissension down to the Bolshevik Revolution. They numbered about one-sixth of the population, except that a larger number would doubtless have adhered to them if the price had not been so high. Possibly the better part of the religiously concerned people of Russia have for the last three hundred years been inclined to the Schism and have shared the schismatic attitude of hostility to the established church-state. A strain of eschato-logical nihilism and anarchism, of rejection of state, property, and family life has run through this history. Berdiaev finds in this traditional messianic hope of the disaffected masses a psychological spring of Russian communism today.

THE SECTS. On the fringe of the Old Believers with their chronic apocalyptic attitude there grew up, especially in the eighteenth century, sects which accepted new bases of community life. As with left-wing Protestantism these sects oscillated between Word and Spirit, God's redeeming work in history, and the testimony of the Spirit within as their sources of authority. Toward the evangelical pole were the "Judaizers," the Molokans, the Stundists, and the Baptists. Toward the spiritualist pole were the flagellant, ecstatic Khlysty (from the 1690's) and their offspring, the Skoptsy ("castrated") from about 1790, and more important, the Dukhobors ("wrestlers by the Spirit") from about 1750. The last held Gnostic views on pre-existence, transmigration of souls, the dualism of flesh and spirit, and practiced "free love," and communism in property. After a period of degeneration in the nineteenth century, they revived at its close under persecution and with the championship of Tolstoy. Their misadventures in Canada are also well known. The Molokans, on the other hand, arose by way of a reaction from Dukhobor inner light to biblical bases. They grew more rapidly.

Late in the nineteenth century, the Stundists and Baptists, both influenced by Western Protestantism, replaced the Molokans as the leading evangelical sect. The intellectual leaders of the various groups worked for merger, and at length the Stundists, Molokans, and Pashkovists joined in a "Union of Evangelical Christians." From the beginning the various Russian sects had tended to intermingle, and this tendency increased in the nineteenth century when the contributions of various intellectuals had been shared by many groups. From the beginning also, the sects had shown radical social tendencies, some of them being pacifists and opposed to oaths and taxes, and the Dukhobors, Molokans, and Stundists organizing communist communities. All suffered under various legal disabilities, and simply belonging to the Khlysty or Skoptsy was a felony entailing exile to Siberia.

PETER'S WESTERNIZING. The hostility of these sectarians and schismatics to the state church was heightened by the reorganization of church and state under Peter the Great (1682-1725). With him began a forced Westernization of Russia, a Westernizing which was in time to mean also secularization after the emerging pattern of the Western Enlightenment. Peter left Holy Moscow for the new capital of St. Petersburg. He put off the ecclesiastical vestments and daily religious exercises of the Tsar. He adopted Western dress and the use of the razor. He developed a Western type of bureaucracy. From his day there were to be two cultural strata in Russia, differing in language, dress, and especially in religion, with little or no understanding of each other. The religion of the great masses was early medieval, untouched by Scholasticism, classical humanism, the Reformation, rationalism, or modern science. The religion of the aristocracy was to be an imitation of French and German deism and rationalism. Whether the former should be viewed as essentially one with early Western medieval culture, or a distinct sister culture and religion may be debatable. But the Westernization which occurred, like the Westernization of the other non-European cultures since, was expedited by the hope that Western sciences and technology might be adopted quite apart from Western religion. To a great extent the influence of modern Western civilization on non-Western peoples has been effective insofar as that civilization has become apparently religiously neutral. But whereas in the West itself this Enlightenment culture has maintained contact and significant, if unacknowledged, indebtedness to a continuing Christian tradition and community, in Russia and other non-Western societies, secularization has come in as a foreign element intruded into the natural course of development.

With regard to the Orthodox Church Peter carried through such a reorganization as to preclude any rival center of authority in the patriarch, such as Nikon had represented. Patriarch Nikon had struggled to achieve independent constitutional status for the clergy as against the state. His personal force of character had enabled him to be the second ruler of

Russia in the time of a weak tsar. But the Council of 1667 which condemned the Old Believers also condemned Nikon's ideal of the independence of the episcopate. A generation later Peter seized the opportunity to swing the pendulum to the other extreme. When the patriarchate became vacant, he announced, "Henceforth I will be your Patriarch." He also abolished the sobors or councils, and in 1721 his famous *Religious Regulation* set up an appointed committee of clergy which was described as the "Holy Synod" and was perforce greeted by the other Orthodox patriarchs as "Brother." Peter was adopting the Prussian Lutheran consistory both on the local and national levels, and this system of political control of the church lasted through the eighteenth and nineteenth centuries to the Bolshevik Revolution. Peter's lay observer in the Synod, the High Procurator, did not, however, become a lay-pope who tyrannized over the church, as was to happen in the nineteenth century. The Crown took over the management of the churches' revenues, which came from something like one-third of the lands of Russia, with serfs attached. The clergy were organized as a sort of auxiliary police force and were made to use the confessional to search out political disaffection. The parish church was the official place of publication of laws and decrees, and all enemies of the Muscovite state fell under the anathema of the church.

POSITION OF THE CLERGY. The Russian Orthodox church was held in this kind of captivity for two centuries after Peter the Great. At the end of his reign the church was again permitted to manage its own properties. But the state was not to be long denied; in 1764 Catherine II nationalized the bulk of the church lands and put the clergy on subsidies which amounted to but a fraction of the former church revenues. The resultant economic hardships of the priests impelled them to a chronic struggle with their parishioners for maintenance. Toward the end of the eighteenth century the old custom of nominating to the parish priesthood by election had lapsed, and parishes were assigned by inheritance or as gifts. The priesthood became a caste with little or no sense of vocation, comparing poorly with the ministry of the Old Believers and the sects.

The nobility despised the "ploughmen in cassocks," who were subject to flogging as late as the nineteenth century. The government burdened the priests with the registry of vital statistics and used them in espionage. The peasants resented them as extortioners.

THEOLOGY. There was some theological activity in eighteenth-century Russia, centering around the theological academy in Kiev, but it was largely derivative from the West, was carried on in Latin, and had little influence on the Russian church as a whole. Iavorsky borrowed from the Roman theologians on the relations of Scripture and tradition, and on the role of human effort in earning redemption, while Prokovich commended the Reformation position on both points. The general attitude of the Russians was to use the arguments of each of the Western churches to refute the other, although the balance lay on the Roman Catholic side.

The outstanding ecclesiastic of the century was Platon, Archbishop and, later, Metropolitan of Moscow. His catechisms were the chief textbooks of theology for two generations, and he began the collecting of documents for Russian church history, publishing a history of the Russian church himself in 1805. He was active in drafting a compromise scheme for bringing Old Believers back into the Orthodox communion.

In general, however, the Russian church avoided systematic theology, resting content with the liturgical presentation of the faith. When Russians did write about religion, they were more interested in its devotional, practical, and moral aspects. Their monastic life did not serve the church at large in theological scholarship as did that of the Latin church, although the most influential religious leaders of the people were usually monks, like Tikhon of Zadonsk, in the eighteenth century. For the understanding of Russian spirituality, one must study such charismatic figures, on the one hand, and seek to penetrate the meaning of the icons and the liturgical chant, on the other. Of fresh theological or institutional expression, Russian Orthodoxy at this period had little more to show than the Orthodoxy captive to the Turk. And indeed this suited the Orthodox concept of the faith as once given, completed, and unchangeable. No church body had the right to tamper with doctrine or the sacraments; hence institutional matters were merely administrative or executive and theology was simple exposition. Neither was expected to touch the central issues, as they were in the West.

Chapter 3

THE ROMAN CHURCH AND THE CATHOLIC PRINCES

Of the churches in the West in the seventeenth and eighteenth centuries, the largest was the Roman Catholic as reconstituted at Trent in defense against the Reformation and finding its chief political bases in Austria, France, and Spain. This Roman half of Europe, although it had been unable to reconquer the reformed regions in the Wars of Religion, nevertheless held a political and military predominance. Spain, which had been the military spearhead of the Counter Reformation, relinquished her hegemony after 1648, and the Empire centered in Vienna now also yielded to France in political and cultural leadership. France, as the spiritual, political, and cultural center of the Roman Catholic sphere, provides the best focus for a survey of these centuries.

ULTRAMONTANISM VS. DECENTRALIZED AUTHORITY. Constitutionally this period was characterized by the struggle between "ultramontanism," or the advocacy of papal supremacy in the church, and the programs of decentralized authority in the hands of the episcopate and the Roman Catholic princes. The former concept was always advocated at Rome itself, and found its chief champions generally in the Jesuit order. In the church at large, however, the seventeenth and eighteenth centuries exhibited the predominance of the opposing tendency, called "Gallicanism" in France.

The Counter Reformation had been unable to restore, even within its shortened lines, the papal theocracy of the high Middle Ages. On the contrary, in order to combat the Reformation, the Roman Church had found it necessary to grant even greater powers over the church to Roman Catholic princes.

29

The Council of Trent (1545-63) had not dared to carry out the item on its agenda called the "reform of princes." Even so its decrees were promulgated by the chief Roman Catholic powers only with qualifications, and France never officially accepted the decrees at all. On every side, the papacy faced the threat of national Catholic churches and had to adapt itself to the demands of the princes. The Holy League against the Turks could not be held together. The Roman Catholic sovereigns continued dealing with Queen Elizabeth of England even after Pius V had "deposed" her. When the papacy tried to impose an interdict on Venice, even the clergy declined to observe it. The Roman Catholic rulers simply refused to permit the papacy to control their policies.

The actual pattern of church-state relations in the strongest powers was caesaropapism qualified by a minimum recognition of papal authority. Philip II of Spain provides the illustration for the sixteenth century. He controlled the finances of the church and its patronage. And through his Inquisition he also controlled theological and moral issues, at times in defiance of the pope, for political ends. The great sixteenth-century Jesuits, such as Suarez and Bellarmine, tried to come to terms with this increasing independence of the Catholic kings by the theory that the pope's civil power was not direct, but indirect.

THE FOUR GALLICAN ARTICLES. But for the seventeenth century, even the indirect power of the papacy was too much, as Louis XIV of France inherited the role of Philip II. The prevailing view came to be such a concept of sovereignty by divine right as precluded correction either by people or by pope. In 1612 and 1613 the Jesuits in France were forced solemnly to repudiate the thesis that popes could release subjects from allegiance, even to heretical or schismatic kings, or could invade the royal power under pretext of religion. What was to become the classical formulation of Gallicanism for all Roman Catholic Europe was drawn up by Bishop Bossuet in 1682 on the basis of an earlier declaration by the theological faculty of the Sorbonne. Of the famous "Four Propositions," the first declared that kings were not subject in temporal matters to any ecclesiastical power, and that the pope could not depose them directly or indirectly, or release subjects from their oath of

allegiance. The second reasserted the decrees of the Council
of Constance on the superiority of councils to the pope. The
third maintained the right of local and national church canons
and usages against the papacy. The fourth denied that papal
decisions in faith were infallible without the consent of the
church. These four articles were accepted by the Assembly
of French prelates and Louis XIV and were ordered to be
taught in all universities and seminaries.

It will be seen that these articles maintained two distinguish-
able strains of Gallicanism. First there was the conciliarist
heritage of the Council of Constance and the Pragmatic Sanction of Bourges (1438), which placed ultimate authority in
the bishops gathered in council rather than in the pope alone,
and which defended the right of provincial and national usages
and canons. Secondly there was the claim of the territorial
prince to rule the church, as a "bishop for external affairs." Although episcopal Gallicanism and royal Gallicanism were thus
in league against ultramontanism, they might also at times be in
tension with each other.

The Roman Court protested vigorously against the Four
Articles, refusing to institute as bishops those clergy who had
had a part in the Assembly of 1682. In a few years some thirty
bishoprics were vacant. The King seized the papal palace, imprisoned the nuncio, threatened a schism, and appealed to a new
ecumenical council. He was at least as bold with the pope as
had been Henry VIII of England, and it was not his fault that
"Gallican" does not today signify an independent church as
does "Anglican." The French clergy, however, shied away
from actual schism, and a compromise was finally achieved in
1693; the papacy conceded to the King controverted revenues
from vacant bishoprics in return for his relaxation of insistence
on the Gallican Articles. These articles could still be held and
taught, however, and were widely taught over Roman Catholic
Europe. Royal control of the French church increased after
Louis XIV until the French Revolution.

CHURCH ORGANIZATION. The general organization of the
French church remained the same up to the Revolution.
Church and state were organically related at every level. The
king was anointed with consecrated oil at his coronation, a cere-

mony which had much of the character of ordination. The clergy were the first estate of the realm. They had an income about half that of the entire state; they were exempt from taxation; and they were economically independent of the crown. The main sources of income were: (1) rent from very extensive landholdings, (2) tithes, and (3) a great aggregation of fees and alms. One half of the wealth was nominally in the hands of the monastic clergy, although four-fifths of the monasteries were held as benefices for secular clergy. The low morale of these monasteries was notorious and some were being suppressed even before the Revolution.

The secular clergy were sharply divided by caste lines. The 140 bishoprics and archbishoprics were reserved for the nobility and enjoyed a princely share of the revenues. Some sixty thousand parish clergy, meanwhile, lived in a poverty which drove them to continued bickering with the peasants over tithes. Some were forced to beg. These lower clergy were also helpless against the arbitrary rule of their bishops. It is easy to understand that they desired a more equitable disposition of church revenues and would have liked to break the caste system of preferments by having the bishops elected. Such hopes as these led them to support the Revolution in its early stages.

The church had a monopoly, not only of public worship, but also of marriage, education, and charities. Primary education was under episcopal control, yet in 1789 the vast majority of the nation were illiterate. The universities, about twenty in number, had no intellectual distinction and exerted little influence on the thought of the nation.

GREAT PERSECUTION OF THE PROTESTANTS. Despite the profound irreligion of Louis XIV and his courtiers, and even various leading prelates, rigorous formal orthodoxy was made a matter of political loyalty as well as of etiquette. At a time when Protestant Holland and England had found even religious reasons for toleration, Louis XIV revived the sixteenth-century policy of persecution, but now as a requirement of his absolutism. In 1685 the Edict of Nantes was revoked and the attempt was renewed to exterminate French Protestantism. Protestant schools and churches were closed and pastors banished.

Troops were quartered on Protestant families and encouraged to abuse and to outrage women, children, and old people until they were converted to the faith of the "Sun King." Some thirty thousand "conversions" were thus achieved, while a quarter of a million or more of the better educated and more skillful subjects of the king fled for refuge to Prussia, England, and England's American colonies. This persecution firmed the purpose of the English to get rid of James II, who was conspiring with Louis, and to call William from the Netherlands. England thus turned decisively toward constitutionalism, toleration, and Protestantism, while France intensified her absolutism, Roman Catholicism, and persecution.

As was the case with the Spanish Inquisition, Louis' requirements of conformity were more political than religious and were derived more from internal policy than from papal initiatives. The Pope publicly approved the great Protestant persecution but expressed private reservations. In similar fashion, however, he was pushed into doctrinal decisions on controversies within the Roman Catholic fold by the French king. The condemnations of Quietists (Miguel de Molinos and Fénelon) and of Jansenists were more political in their inspiration than impartial judgments of a doctrinal tribunal.

JANSENISM.   Jansenism provided the chief doctrinal controversy of the second half of the seventeenth and the first half of the eighteenth centuries—a controversy which was intermixed with the constitutional debate over Gallicanism. The name was taken from Professor Cornelis Jansen of Louvain, whose posthumous work *Augustine* (1640) became a manual of the Augustinian party in the French church, a party which had its center in the convent of Port Royal. The leader was the Abbot of St. Cyran, who was imprisoned for maintaining that genuine repentance arising from love of God, rather than mere fear of punishment, should be a condition of sacramental absolution. Arnauld, religious director at Port Royal, similarly argued against the Jesuit practice of frequent communion, stating that communion should be taken only after serious spiritual preparation. As a reforming movement of deep piety and ethical earnestness, Jansenism had a considerable appeal among the middle class, the country clergy, the intellectuals,

and the Dominicans and Augustinians. It was also remarkably
successful in bringing many of the high nobility from dissolute
lives to genuine and enduring repentance. This influence
aroused the jealousy of the King and of the Jesuits of the court,
who encouraged a merely decorative Christianity there. Doctrinally the Jesuits also preferred the near-Pelagian tradition of
Luis Molina to the Augustinian emphasis on God's sovereignty
and grace. They secured repeated condemnations of Jansenist
ideas from the Vatican, which did not, however, succeed in
suppressing the movement.

In the French church much of the controversy centered
around the institution of the confessional. It was the Jesuits,
especially, who had led in the new emphasis on penance and
the confessional, to a degree unknown before the Reformation.
The centrality of the Eucharist was in practice often lost, and
the confessional had become as important an element in church
equipment as the altar. Seminaries now laid most weight on
training in "moral theology," which was the system of applied
casuistry associated with the administration of penance. It was
the body of Roman Catholic moral theology which Pascal attacked in his *Provincial Letters*. He blamed the Jesuits, but it
was not their creation. Casuistry, probabilism, mental reservation, and laxism all had a long history. After the hierarchy
condemned probabilist errors, however, it was the Jesuits in
particular who evaded the condemnations and continued to
practice and to teach the system.

PROBABILISM. According to the probabilists, a confessor
must permit a penitent to perform with a good conscience any
act for which he can find any respectable warrant, even if it is
contrary to the confessor's opinion, and even if, to the penitent
himself, it is probably less right than another course. If there
is any probability for it, even the lesser probability, it is per-
fectably acceptable to Christ. This system was the result of
the effort to take from the individual priest, who might not be
competent for it, the responsibility of decision on the ethical
issue. It had also the recommendation that a penitent was
rarely lost from formal relations with the church through severity. And the astounding indulgence which the probabilists
often showed made them highly popular confessors around

courts and in worldly society generally. The confessor must grant absolution even if in his own judgment the act that the penitent was committing was a mortal sin. And in the vast literature of opinions as to what was mortal and what venial, one could usually find an author to taste. Thus on the question of petty thefts by servants, Molina considered them no sin, Escobar venial, and Sanchez mortal. The casuists analyzed with bureaucratic thoroughness everything from cheating on taxes to depth of décolletage. The chief exponent of the system in its maturity was St. Alphonsus Liguori. In the nineteenth century Liguori was made a "Doctor of the Church," a dignity which had not been awarded since Bonaventure was so honored. In many ways Liguori gives a better key to the actual operation of modern Roman Catholicism than any other writer, even Aquinas.

UNIGENITUS AND THE SCHISM. Louis XIV, whose sympathies were for obvious reasons with the Jesuit theory of the Christian life, increased the pressure on the Jansenists. A new condemnation was secured in 1705, and in 1709 Port Royal was razed to the ground and the tombs of the dead were violated. The climax came in 1713 when, under pressure from the King's Jesuit confessor, Pope Clement XI condemned 101 propositions from the *Moral Reflexions on the New Testament* by Quesnel, the leader of the Jansenists. The book had been in general use and in high regard for twenty years. The bull of condemnation, *Unigenitus*, aroused most of the French theologians and lawyers and the religiously active laity in opposition. A party of "Appellants" (to a future general council) was created, and under the whip of excommunication a schism occurred. The Archdiocese of Utrecht, where the chapter still retained the right to elect its archbishop, became the refuge of Jansenists from France and continued as a separate Catholic church. The church of France also continued to be distracted by debate over the *Unigenitus* up to the Revolution. Jansenism and Gallicanism made common cause in this Church of Utrecht. In the controversies over the rights of the chapter in election, appeal was made to the leading canonist of the age, Professor van Espen of Louvain. Van Espen had approached the development of canon law historically rather than scholastically in his *Jus ecclesiasticum universum* (1700), and perceived the ultramontane distortions effected by the use of the false decretals. He revived the conciliarist tradition of church government. Although his name was put on the Index in 1734, he still had the support of much of the episcopate and dominated canon law in many countries in the second half of the century.

FEBRONIUS. Nicolas von Hontheim, Coadjutor Bishop of Trier, and a student of van Espen, became even more influential. Writing as "Justinus Febronius," he published a volume in 1763 on the *State of the Church and of the Legitimate Power of the Roman Pontiff*. Febronius argued that the power of church government belonged to the whole body of the faithful in principle. It was exercised in their behalf by the bishops, among whom the pope was chief, yet was subject to the whole episcopate in council. The ultramontane claims for papal jurisdiction had been built up on the basis of the forged decretals and, he contended, should be relinquished for the sake of reunion with the Protestants. Febronius was no longer merely making a case for the privileges of one national church, like most French Gallicans, but was arguing for a conciliarist structure of the universal church on the basis of Scripture and tradition.

Clement XIII and the Index promptly condemned Febronius' work in 1764, but bishops and princes disregarded the Curia and encouraged distribution of the book in Germany, Italy, Portugal, Spain, and France, and in as many languages. Everywhere in the Roman Catholic world there seemed to be a conciliarist party to support Febronius. After fifteen years Hontheim was finally driven to a formal recantation, but the Chancellor of the Holy Roman Empire himself wrote Hontheim's family that, despite the recantation, the intelligent Catholic world still believed in the truth of his work.

In the Germanies the views of Febronius did not rest upon any general conviction in the church. They were taken up chiefly by the prince-bishops of the ecclesiastical territories, each of whom desired to be as absolute as Louis XIV in his own realm. The courts of Fulda, Würzburg, and Mainz also sought to imitate the pleasures and splendor of Renaissance Italy or of Versailles. These prince-bishops resented the efforts of the popes to interfere in their domains. In 1769 representatives of the three Archbishop Electors of the Empire drew up thirty "Articles of Coblenz" based on Hontheim's ideas, and in 1785 much the same program was set forth in the "Ems Points." Among other things, they demanded abolition of the jurisdiction of papal nuncios and that of foreign ecclesiastical superiors over religious orders, and release from the episcopal oath to persecute heretics.

JOSEPHISM. At the central court in Vienna, one found some influence of Febronianism, but even more of the enlightened theory of the state. The Empress Maria Theresa and her son Joseph II considered themselves Catholics, but they did not recognize the political and disciplinary powers of the church as essential to the faith. The state was to be the promoter of enlightened civilization, and the church and clergy should assist the state in this task. The Queen thus required all seminarians to study canon law in the law faculty, where the natural law theory of the state was taught, rather than in the theological faculty. Under Joseph II the state set up seminaries for the clergy. This "sacristan king" issued an Edict of Toleration (1781), permitting the private exercise of "non-Catholic" worship. Similarly in the interests of social utility he closed half the two thousand monasteries and used their revenues for the expenses of the rural clergy or for new churches. He set up his own censorship of books and sermons, commending useful moralism and mocking or punishing "superstition" and "fanaticism." The Emperor thus interfered freely in the life of the church, using it as an agency of the state and for the purposes of the state.

In Tuscany, similarly, which was ruled by Joseph's brother Leopold, major church reforms of Jansenist and Febronian character were encouraged. Bishop Ricci convened a Synod at Pistoia in 1786, which adopted conciliarist views of the nature of the church, defended Quesnel on sin and grace, and commended several liturgical reforms which have been taken up again by the contemporary liturgical movement. The proceedings were condemned in 1794 by the bull *Auctorem Fidei*. All these various conciliarist programs in the Empire were to be abortive because of the great upheaval of the French Revolution and the Napoleonic Wars, but they illustrate the prevailing tendencies of the eighteenth century.

The enlightened ideas of educational, judicial, and religious reform which governed Joseph II found their most vigorous expression in France. Here the *philosophes* dominated the cultured classes in the last two generations of the eighteenth century. Their whole tendency was to encourage the state to the type of reforming humanitarian manipulation of the church which Joseph illustrated. The structure of the church was retained, on the whole, but the real confessional character of the society evaporated.

RISE OF TOLERATION. This transition from the confessional state to the state based on natural law can be seen in the relaxation of the great persecution of Louis XIV. French Protestantism was defending itself by guerrilla war "in the desert" deep into the eighteenth century. An edict of 1724 made Protestant ministers liable to death and sent those harboring them to the galleys. Hundreds of Protestants bore witness to their faith as galley slaves, while their women were imprisoned in convents and their children reared as Roman Catholics. But persecution dropped off sharply in the second half of the century, although Pastor de la Rochette was hanged for administering the sacraments as late as 1762. Agitation by intellectuals of Roman Catholic background for toleration evidenced major change in the attitude of the French Catholic laity. To the end the clergy called for persecution, but the laity no longer believed in their authority in such matters. In 1787 France joined Austria in permitting Protestants to worship privately and to be married legally.

Another indication of the changing character of French mentality is to be seen in the contrast between the universal preoccupation with the Jansenist controversy at the end of the seventeenth century and the general approval of the banishment of the Jesuits at the end of the eighteenth century as champions of obscurantism and reaction. For while the Jesuits had largely won their battle for moralism against the Augustinians, they went down under the tide of royal absolutism conjoined with conciliarism in the church.

DISSOLUTION OF THE JESUITS. The courts of Roman Catholic Europe resented the Jesuits in the eighteenth century as constituting a quasi-autonomous body qualifying royal sovereignty. Jesuits claimed the right to control education in every country—appointing faculties and determining textbooks—without permitting the civil authorities so much as a glimpse into the inner management of their educational institutions, or giving any guarantee that their methods or subjects of instruction were related to state interests. By the eighteenth century their schools had everywhere deteriorated and were viewed as antiquated reactionary forces by the educated classes. The Jesuits pushed the miserable Jansenist persecution to the point of discrediting all theology. Similarly the Jesuits resisted civil authority in judicial and financial matters. The Order was not liable for the misdemeanors and felonies of its members. Despite its tremendous wealth it paid no taxes. And then the diplomatic intrigue of the Jesuits tended to set the concerns of the Counter Reformation over dynastic interests, however discreetly, and the courts were no longer ready to sacrifice themselves to this program.

In the second half of the eighteenth century all the Bourbon courts turned on the Jesuits. They were suppressed in Portugal in 1759, in France in 1764, and in Spain in 1767. And the Bourbons together intrigued at the papal conclave of 1769 to secure a pope who would suppress the Order everywhere. The papal lands at Avignon and Benevento were held as hostages. The loyalty and reputation of the Order were already questioned at the Curia because the Jesuits had opposed the pope and supported the French king, had defied regulations on probabilism, and had repeatedly sought to evade regulations against participation in ancestor worship in China. The backstairs controversies at Rome were ferocious, but in 1773 Clement XIV crossed the Rubicon. In the bull *Dominus ac redemptor noster*, for reasons stated, the Pope irrevocably suppressed the Society of Jesus "forever." The effect was felt promptly in both education and on the mission field and in some respects crippled the Roman Catholic Church just as it was entering the severe trials of the French Revolution and Napoleonic Wars. The fall of the chief champions of papal jurisdiction in church and state also symbolized the decline of papal power in the Roman Catholic states.

Chapter 4

LUTHERANISM IN STATE AND SOCIETY

Lutheran Germany and Scandinavia suffered from many disadvantages in the period under consideration. Through the Reformation and religious wars, when France, England, and Spain were consolidating into centralized monarchies, the Germanies had remained a loose federation within the forms of the old Holy Roman Empire. The Peace of Westphalia weakened this structure even further. Confessional diversity was legally established and the member states retained even the right of making war independently. The Diet was a gathering of envoys, rather than a parliament. From a political viewpoint, "Germany" was now a Balkanized crazy quilt, containing besides the two kingdoms of European significance, Austria-Hungary and Brandenburg-Prussia, the realms of nine Electoral princes, about one hundred other spiritual and lay princedoms, another hundred duchies, some fifty free towns, nearly as many minor church territories, and two or three thousand virtually autonomous petty nobles and their estates. The general drift of the times to centralized monarchical absolutism produced hundreds and thousands of petty provincial despots in Germany and Scandinavia, exhibiting in miniature all the disadvantages of the system, with few of the compensating virtues.

In addition to this political fragmentation and despotism, Germany had been left behind economically in the opening of the Atlantic trade routes. The wealthy towns which had shared in the Italian trade with the Levant in the sixteenth century, such as Augsburg and Nürnberg, now petrified, and the Hanseatic League no longer counted beside the English and the Dutch in world trade. Germany was left a landlocked back-country, where the tolls and tariffs of the innumerable political subdivisions added to the rigidities of the guild system of artisans and medieval land tenure in keeping the economy far behind the Roman Catholic and Reformed peoples to the West. The chief German export at this period was mercenary soldiers, enlisted by press gang methods, and sent abroad to fight; only half of the thirty thousand "Hessians" sent to fight the American rebels, e.g., came home. The general economic backwardness, with the weakness in communications and the lack of large centers, made for a provinciality and mediocrity also in many aspects of cultural and religious life.

In addition to these long-term unfavorable trends, Germany suffered as no other country from the religious wars. A population of eighteen million had been reduced to ten million. The fields were barren, cattle stolen or killed, homes destroyed, and commerce paralyzed. The cultural and moral degradation was comparable. A whole generation grew up in the lawlessness of warfare. Wild children roamed in packs; thousands of women were debauched; education virtually disappeared. The brutalizing of manners and morals can be sampled in von Grimmelshausen's *Simplicissimus*. And while the general respect for pastors probably rose through their fidelity in danger, yet their situation and task were made infinitely more difficult by the devastation.

PARTISAN ORTHODOXIES. But not even the deadly danger of the Thirty Years' War had conquered the particularism and prejudice of the Lutheran churches. In the mid-sixteenth century the churches of the Augsberg Confession had split in bitter controversy, chiefly over Eucharistic doctrine. A revolt was mounted against Melanchthon as a "crypto-Calvinist" by those who would make all Luther's *obiter dicta* canonical. Territorial jealousies and rivalries between universities were involved. Eventually the largest, strictly Lutheran party consolidated around the *Formula* (1577) and the *Book of Concord* (1580). The chief principalities in this group were the two Saxonies, linking Württemberg on the south to Mecklenburg and Prussia on the north. The only out-and-out Melanchthonian territory was the Palatinate, which was driven to form its closest relations with the Reformed to the West. But a significant group of other states declined to endorse the anathemas of "Concord" against the Melanchthonians. Most important of these were Pomerania, Schleswig-Holstein, Brunswick, and Hesse. Denmark and Sweden had similarly omitted to subscribe at this period. Each of these states had its own church administration and usually its own theological faculty, jealous of its prerogatives and distinction. Of the latter the most famous on the exclusive Lutheran side were Wittenberg, Leipzig, and Jena in Saxony, while the leaders of the more irenic tendency were Brunswick's Helmstedt, Heidelberg in the Palatinate, and Marburg in Hesse. Controversy over "pure doctrine" played a larger role here perhaps than in any other period of church history, and the stage was filled with a fanatical race of scribes and pharisees abusing each other over mint and anise and cummin.

The exclusive Lutherans, who contended that Calvinists were not even Christians, refused to lift a finger to help Frederick of the Palatinate in the first round of the Thirty Years' War, just as they had refused aid to William of Orange in Alva's terror. They remained unconcerned while Protestantism was stamped out in Bohemia and the balance of the confessions in the Empire was changed by the substitution of Bavaria for the Palatinate. "Sooner papist than Calvinist" was a popular view in Saxony. In the second round of the war, Brandenburg again supported the Emperor and the Roman cause against Denmark. Even Gustavus Adolphus, who came from Sweden to rescue the Protestant cause, could not unite the Protestants of Germany. And at the peacemaking the exclusive Lutherans, led by Saxony, were still trying to deny legal rights to the Reformed. It was only the Great Elector of Brandenburg (1640-1688) who forced Saxony to yield and admit the Reformed to the benefits defined by the Treaty. The leadership of Protestant Germany was now passing from Saxony to Brandenburg, however, in power as in policy, and the Great Elector opened a new epoch, forbidding his subjects to study at Wittenberg, the school of intolerance, and welcoming the Huguenot refugees from the great persecution of Louis XIV of France who were banned by Württemberg.

LIMITS OF TOLERATION. In Germany the system of the confessional period, *cuius regio eius religio*, was affected by the political pluralism. In contrast to England, for example, where the system meant denial of all religious liberty while it lasted, the mosaic of states in the Germanies meant that one might hope to find a church of his beliefs within a reasonable distance. This was true, of course, only for the three legal confessions. Other religious organizations were banned, in contrast to legal nonconformity in England after 1689. Numerous edicts all over Germany prohibited pietist meetings, for example. And when the Moravians formed a community, they had to do it under the auspices of a Lutheran landholder and a Lutheran state pastor. The Moravian system of colonies, when transplanted to the relative freedom of England and America, soon became dissipated into another denomination. And the mystics, spiritualists, chiliasts, and other unusual figures, who might crop up anywhere in the English system, were in the Germanies herded together in one or two political asylums, as in Berleburg. The community organized in the second half of the century around the writings of Swedenborg, chiefly in Stockholm and London, arose when the system was already well loosened. That loosening in Lutheran areas, however, came not as in England and in America, by the recognition of legal rights for nonconformity, but by the free grace of despots who had lost personal religious conviction.

SOCIAL STRATIFICATION. Among the divisions in the Germanies which were heightened by the Thirty Years' War, the geographical were outweighed by those between social classes. At the time of the Reformation the prosperous upper merchant classes in Germany had promised to fuse with the lower nobility, as actually happened in England. The war, however, together with the decline of German trade and industry, cut off this promised development. All power was concentrated in the hands of the nobility, save in a few great commercial centers like Hamburg and Bremen, and the lines between social classes hardened into unbridgeable caste barriers. In church records, consequently, one might find the nobility referred to as "der gnädige Herr," "die gnädige Frau," while upper middle-class officials, professional men and the like would be "Herr," and "Frau." The mass of artisans, farmers, and the rest were not even "Mr." At the end of this period Mme. de Staël found French society on the eve of the Revolution less rigidly segregated than the German.

After the Thirty Years' War the class which monopolized political power in the Germanies was estranged from the great body of the people. This was less true of the country gentry who managed their own estates, but the tone was set by the five hundred or so courts where the fashionable nobility gathered in little imitations of the court of the French "Sun King." This court life represented a distinct moral code, taste, customs, even language. The education of a nobleman now differed from that of the middle class. Latin and religion gave way to French, fencing, riding, dancing, shooting, some politics, and geography. Most important of all was a stay at the French court during the "grand tour." Unlike the nobility of France, Italy, and England, this German aristocracy played almost no intellectual role in cultural life. It was beneath a noble's dignity to be educated, just as it was bad form in most courts (save those affected by pietism) to be "virtuous." The prevailing pattern of these rulers in the Germanies, with many local variations, was that of ignorant boors and sots, who spent most of their time gambling at cards, hunting, and drinking.

BAROQUE MUSIC. In architecture, the drama, and music, however, these courts made significant cultural contributions. Particularly the last found noble religious expression under these auspices. For this was the age of Bach and Handel, whose works rank among the greatest productions of religious art in modern church history. Bach's "Passions" and masses leave no doubt of the religious depths of stiff Saxon orthodoxy. They also attest to a concentration of musical resources made accessible for the church by an age of despotism which has not been since equalled.

POLITICAL ETHICS. The rulers of these petty despotisms operated by standing armies, a bureaucracy of more or less efficient officials to raise the finance for them, and Lutheran preachers to teach constantly the duty of unquestioning submission to authority. Johann Gerhard, the patriarch of Lutheran scholasticism, had elaborated the doctrine of the three God-given "orders" of society so as wholly to frustrate that of the priesthood of all believers. He had no fault to find with his Elector, Johann George, who was drunk daily. After the war it was particularly the court preachers who gave Christian coloration to the servile adulation required. Calov compared his Elector to Josiah, Jehoshaphat, Constantine, and Theodosius. Wrote the Prussian court preacher Jablonski on Proverbs 24:21, "God is a heavenly king, and the king an earthly mortal God—yet both are Gods and both kings, and both to be feared and honored." When two Brunswick court preachers wished, even against the desires of the court, to warn a fourteen-year-old princess against a marriage which would entail her becoming Roman Catholic, an opinion was requested from Thomasius, the leading jurist of the period. Thomasius recommended extended imprisonment and banishment for the impertinent ministers. Thomasius was the chief ornament of the law faculty at Halle, where nearly all of the officials for the eighteenth-century Prussian bureaucracy were trained. The faculty held that princes were responsible only to God, that even in their grossest sins they were not to be judged by men or pastors, and that their mistresses were beyond reproach as participating in the glory of their noble lovers. The idea of church discipline on the person of the prince was pure absurdity, and on the part of the minister involved, shameless disobedience.

THE PRINCE BISHOPS. This relationship of the prince to the church had developed out of the emergency system of Luther's day. By the end of the religious wars the emergency system had become established, and the princes claimed the rights and functions of the pre-Reformation Catholic bishops as their due prerogative. Sometimes the argument was specifically made that in Protestant areas these rights had legally devolved upon them. But these Protestant "bishops" were now above the limitations of canon law. The theologians of orthodoxy, such as Calov and Quenstedt, by stressing the purely "spiritual" character of the church, left all actual decisions in the hands of the civil ruler. And the princes saw to it that the Lutheran churches should have no bishops, synods, or other organs of

independent self-government, just as they discouraged territorial diets in this period, and overruled the law courts with
the star chamber proceedings of *Kabinettsjustiz*. Through his
appointed "consistory" the prince settled all financial questions,
appointed the clergy, and arranged discipline. Usually a general superintendent was chairman or vice-chairman, and each
diocese had superintendents to execute the regulations of the
consistory.

One might take Friedrich Wilhelm I of Prussia as an instance of a prince "bishop" in the first half of the eighteenth
century. This rough, honest vulgarian was typical of the German prince in his anti-intellectualism. His purposive energy
and military preoccupation, on the other hand, were distinctively Prussian. The king was also atypical in that although
he was Reformed, he ruled over overwhelmingly Lutheran
populations. But he took his episcopal functions seriously.
Just as the crown prince was required to execute his private devotions by the clock, so the king set a fine for all pastors who
preached longer than one hour. Another order commanded a
specific style of preaching. Another (1733) forbade candles,
copes, chasubles, Latin hymns, and the sign of the cross. "If
any . . . wish to make it a matter of conscience . . . they can be
relieved by dismission from their parishes." And one pastor
was so relieved.

ECUMENICAL AND IRENIC EFFORTS. The king had little patience with confessional differences and encouraged his court
preacher Jablonski in his negotiations with Leibnitz and Abbot
Molanus in Brunswick and Chancellor Pfaff of Württemberg
toward a union of Lutherans and Reformed. The scheme was
at length reduced to certain churches in Prussia. The king's
confessional openness was revealed in the asylum he gave to
the thousands of evangelicals driven out of the Tyrol by the
Emperor and prelates of Austria in the 1720's and 1730's. Discharged without pay, with homes and lands confiscated, often
abused and outraged personally, these witnesses to the evangelical faith marched across Germany from Protestant city to city
on the way to Berlin. (One hundred of these "Salzburgers"
eventually found their way even to South Carolina.) By 1740
a full quarter of the subjects of Frederick the Great were im-

migrants or their descendants, chiefly Huguenots and Salzburgers. They changed the mentality of Prussia as well as its
industries, and prepared Berlin to become the center of the
German version of the Enlightenment in the latter part of
the eighteenth century.

POSITION OF THE CLERGY. The social position of the Lutheran pastor was an important factor in this shaping of the life
of the church. In contrast to French or German Roman Catholicism, or Anglicanism, there was, as a rule, no place for the
aristocracy in the Lutheran clergy. Ministers were generally
of lower-class or even peasant background and were despised
by most courtiers. There were no prince prelates or fox-hunt-
ing parsons. In the universities the one graduate faculty open
to sons of the poor was theology. The ministry that was produced from this socially restricted background had less breed-
ing and capacity for affairs than their Roman Catholic
equivalents, but more book learning. The pedantry and dogmatic temper of the Lutheran clergy may also have been influenced by these social factors. In any case the tendency, as
generally in German society, was to form a caste of clerics.
By the eighteenth century most pastors had had at least one or
two years at a university. Thereafter they had usually spent
a period as schoolteachers or tutors until some patron had given
them a post. Village pastors normally had to supplement their
income by farming, taking boarders, beekeeping, or brewing.
The local nobility used them as part-time tutors or grooms.
And as with many guilds, a frequent condition of entering the
office was that one should marry his predecessor's widow. In
order to protect them, the clergy of one district were actually
required to state on oath that they had not been required to
marry certain women in order to receive their charges.

The city pastors ranked much higher, often before the civic
senators. And at the top, of course, were the court preachers
in their posts of dangerous eminence, and the theological professors in the universities. The last have always been more
highly esteemed in Lutheran areas than elsewhere in Protestantism, where other aspects of the church's life are considered as
important as "pure doctrine." In the eighteenth century the
theological faculties were ever less consulted by the prince's

consistories, and the rulers of the church grew increasingly contemptuous of the disputes of the theologians. But most pastors and the unfashionable devout still respected the faculties highly. And out of this religious reverence for the universities came the nineteenth-century heritage of academic freedom, so remarkable in Germany in contrast to the generally low level of civil and political liberty there.

The congregations which were served by this clergy were almost purely passive. They had no organization, no rights, no relation to the minister except purely official ones, unless he were affected by pietist views of his office. The congregational "call" or even veto were eliminated, as well as all share in discipline, as forms of "crypto-Calvinism." The true "Lutheran" system as set forth by the orthodox theologians such as Gerhard or Calov was caesaropapism, the territorial despot as Lutheran pope. In general the church was viewed as an affair of the state and its clergy, in which the people had no say.

Some exception must be made for Württemberg. Here the Landtag survived as a genuine representative assembly and maintained its rights against the duke. In the Landtag the clerical estate was represented by fourteen prelates and maintained a sense of the church as a continuous living body intrinsically independent of the civil power. And Chancellor Pfaff maintained the rights of the congregation *in sacra*, in contrast to the legal and financial *jus circa sacra*, which inhered in the civil ruler. Historically, he argued, even those matters of dogma, worship, and church government had been assigned to the state in the sixteenth century. In practice, consequently, he justified the same civil control as did the defenders of the prince-bishop theory. But here there at least existed a consciousness of the church as resting on voluntary adherence and covenant rather than political coercion, and intrinsically capable of self-government.

FREDERICK THE GREAT. But the strongest Lutheran state and the most influential in policy was Brandenburg-Prussia. And here, under Frederick II, was worked out that view of the church as a cog in the bureaucracy of the secular state, a view that was to have imitators all over the Germanies by the end of the eighteenth century. Thomasius, as we have seen, had al-

ready laid down much of the theory in the time of Frederick
William I. Boehmer similarly argued that the civil sovereign
had absolute power over all overt acts of religion. The church
had no rights, legal authority, or powers of self-government.
Ministers of religion were responsible not to the congregations,
but to their sovereign, and had no more claim to independence
than any other clerk in a bureaucracy.

This system reached its fullest expression under Frederick
II. Regarding all positive religions and revelations as equally
bogus, he tolerated all equally. Mennonites, Socinians,
Schwenckfelders, and Eastern Orthodox who were banned
elsewhere found aslyum under Prussian indifference. He considered importing Mohammedans for an army reserve, like
General Franco. "All religions are equally good," he said, "if
the people who profess them are honest; and if Turks and
heathen came and were willing to populate the land, we would
build mosques and temples. . . . False religious zeal is a tyrant
that depopulates provinces; toleration is a kind mother that
cherishes and advances their prosperity." Here we see materialistic and in this case militaristic utilitarianism operating for
religious toleration.

Frederick gave to Roman Catholics greater liberty than they
had ever before enjoyed, building a school for the children of
Roman Catholic soldiers and protecting the construction of the
great Roman Catholic church in Berlin, since, as he said, "in this
country every one must be saved after his own fashion." But
he had no respect for canon law or liberty of conscience. He
forbade subjects to take monastic vows without permission.
He appointed higher clergy, such as the Bishop of Breslau, and
the pope felt constrained to institute his appointees. He punished controversial preachers and defied the papal suppression
of the Jesuits. Frederick wanted to keep them for the schools
and would not allow the bull *Dominus ac Redemptor Noster*
to be published. The Society of Jesus was thus maintained in
Orthodox Russia and Protestant Prussia when it was abolished
perpetually and eternally by the pope.

Unlike his father, who had laid down rules about liturgy and
ritual, Frederick the Great told the clergy to do as they pleased.
"As to the hymn-books, let every one be free to sing 'The

duteous day now closeth' [Gerhardt's much-loved hymn], or any other such nonsense he pleases. But the preachers must not forget tolerance, for no persecution by them will be allowed." Anti-Christian writings were also punished. Like Voltaire, the King considered religion necessary as a discipline of the masses. Scepticism was for the elite only. Lessing had some justification when he complained that Prussia, despite all the toleration, was the "most slavish" land in Europe.

THE PRUSSIAN LANDRECHT. The contemptuous and qualified freedom which Frederick permitted Christianity was codified in the *Landrecht*, first published after his death in 1794, although compiled by his jurists, (II, xi deals with religion). This code was the first since the Reformation to recognize any notable amount of freedom for individuals and congregations. While under it the church had latitude in calling or judging pastors, or in liturgy, all changes had to be approved beforehand by the government. All officers were to be either appointed or approved by the state. Buying or selling of property or building of new churches required permission. Ecclesiastical discipline could not touch the person, property, or honor of a subject. This self-government was so limited that no religious society could exclude members "for mere opinion deviating from the common confession of faith provided that there was no occasion of scandal or interruption of worship." The church was not defined, in fact, by a common faith or discipline. Legally it was supported by the state much as a public school system might be, to teach loyalty and obedience and the fear of God.

The tenuous character of the limited liberties established by the jurists of Frederick the Great is illustrated by the Inquisition set up by his successor in the famous Religious Edict of 1788. The notoriously immoral Frederick William II had made a worthless favorite named Wöllner virtual premier. Wöllner was disturbed by the rationalist and deist movement now well established especially in the universities, and without even consulting the clergy, had issued a decree seeking to enforce orthodoxy. Biblical criticism was declared heretical and, along with natural religion, deism, and Socinianism, could be taught only on penalty of certain dismissal. A vigorous press censorship was set up. All ecclesiastical and academic appointments were to be closely regulated. All ministers and teachers were to adhere to the letter of the confessions of the sixteenth century, whatever their private opinions might be. A commission was established to draw up lists of orthodox and suspected clergy. The purge was largely ineffectual and the students even ran the commission out of Halle. Yet till the end of the reign in 1797, there was continual pressure and exercise of force from the throne toward orthodoxy. Despite the *Landrecht*, the Lutheran church was subject at any time into the twentieth century to a theological, liturgical, or disciplinary revolution depending on the opinions of the court.

By the end of the eighteenth century, the churches had become tools of secular policy in the absolute states of Germany. The ministers had more security than when they were subject to local patrons, but their spiritual freedom was gone. Especially in the countryside, the minister kept the registry of vital statistics, the recruiting office, served as superintendent of the schools and poor relief, and made from the pulpit all the announcements thought useful by his superiors, about taxes, public health, or the roads. As General Superintendent Herder summed it up, "A minister is only entitled to exist now, under state control and by authority of the prince, as a moral teacher, a farmer, a list-maker, a secret agent of police."

Even more significant for the future was to be the alienation of the educated middle class from the churches. This had proceeded throughout the century as higher education generally rejected the Aristotelian-Lutheran pattern stemming from Melanchthon. Halle, founded in 1694, first broke radically with the old Lutheran university system. Thomasius was the first professor to refuse to lecture in academic garb and in Latin. Halle adopted a pragmatic curriculum for the training of civil servants, pushing aside Latin and theology for mathematics, the natural sciences, modern languages, geography, and history. After Wolff's return to Halle in 1740, his type of textbook spread widely, appealing always to reason rather than revealed authority. With the founding of Göttingen, in the mid-century, a more humanist literary emphasis was set up beside the hard utilitarianism of Halle. That literary idealism which was

to sweep educated Germany by the end of the century was
foreshadowed. And the German universities in the second
half of the century now at last equalled the Dutch and English
and French and looked forward to their nineteenth-century
pre-eminence. But the nearly universal attitude of the leaders
of this intellectual movement in the universities toward religion
and theology was disdain. It was viewed as an anachronism, a
symptom of stupidity or backwardness. Those who still supported the churches did so for their moral by-products. But
for the whole "enlightened" class, the rejection of theology
was precisely the basis of their self-consciousness and sense of
superiority.

Chapter 5

THE REFORMED TRADITION, ANGLICANISM, AND FREE CHURCH CALVINISM

International Calvinism bore the chief burden of the religious wars in Holland and France, and much of it in Germany, and not until 1648 was the Reformed Church recognized beside the Roman and the Lutheran in the Empire. Geographically the Reformed peoples occupied the no man's land between the Lutheran and the papal territories, and they perforce developed a militant ethos. They were also the most international and ecumenical of the Protestant communions. With an international refugee center as their capital, crowded with French, Italians, Germans, Dutch, English, Scots, and Swiss, it was the Reformed who labored hardest for Protestant unity in the sixteenth century. Into the seventeenth century interchange was continuous and normal among their universities. Until they were ruined by the Thirty Years' War, Marburg, Heidelberg, and Herborn welcomed Dutch, Scottish, and French scholars. Until they were closed by Louis XIV, French Reformed "academies" often had Scottish professors and German and Swiss students. Some of the founders of New England had studied at these Continental Reformed universities. In contrast to Anglicans and Lutherans, the Reformed developed, at least in some countries, a form of church life and government which could act, like Roman Catholicism, in some independence from the civil power. And alone of the Protestant communions, the Reformed had succeeded in convoking an international synod, at Dort in the Netherlands (1619), whose canons were accepted by Anglicans, Swiss, Scots, and French, as well as by the Dutch.

CHURCHES UNDER THE CROSS. For the next century and a half after 1648, the period we are to consider, the Reformed tradition can be studied in two different types of situations. There are first the "churches under the cross," whose existence was so far determined by the mere struggle to survive persecution or war that internal development was scarcely possible. This was true of Magyar Calvinism in its long agony under the Hapsburg Counter Reformation, and of those parts of Switzerland and Germany devastated by the Thirty Years' War or by the scorched earth policy of Louis XIV in the Palatinate. It was especially applicable to the Huguenot community of France under the persecution of Louis XIV and his successors. This attempt to exterminate a highly cultured community of a million Protestants, with their "temples," "academies," industries, and commerce, led to the desperate Camisard wars in the Cevennes mountains in the eighteenth century and the long annals of martyrdoms of the "Church in the Desert." The stream of refugees to Germany, Holland, England, and America carried people with irreplaceable skills and character out of France, and they, with the escaped galley slaves, were a perpetual warning to Protestants of the continuing danger of the Counter-Reformation spirit. Religiously the strains of the struggle produced eccentric hysterical manifestations, the influence of which was felt also in Germany and England in the eighteenth century and contributed to the American "Shakers." The Scottish Covenanters similarly endured a purgation in the "killing-times" under the restored Stuart kings. Anglican oppression was only less grievous in Ulster. The Reformed in all these lands depended especially on Holland and England, where there was enough security for the development of thought and church life.

FREE-CHURCH CALVINISM. The Reformed in Holland, England, and England's American colonies had sufficient margin of energy for new developments. At various times and in differing degrees all three of these areas passed from the Genevan, Scottish, and Massachusetts Bay pattern of a Calvinist church-state—uniform and authoritarian—to free church Calvinism colored by spiritualist and sectarian tendencies. In this tradition was created a new type of Christian organization, and the way opened to a penetration of modern culture unparalleled in Lutheran or Roman Catholic lands. What Troeltsch called "ascetic Protestantism" has had, of all Christian traditions, the most pervasive influence in Western life in the last three hundred years.

The beginnings of this new formation are found in Holland at the turn of the seventeenth century; the results are seen in seventeenth- and eighteenth-century England and her American colonies. The Dutch were to the seventeenth century what the English were to the eighteenth and the Americans to the nineteenth—the working model of free institutions. Fundamental to this liberalism throughout society was the acceptance by Calvinists of what they had considered the "Anabaptist heresy" of toleration. In this regard William the Silent and Cromwell were crucial figures, as men of political power who first insisted on religious liberty as a right. Roman Catholic *politiques*, Lutherans, Anglicans, and Orthodox Catholics have all been willing under pressure to concede toleration as a measure of expediency, but it has usually meant a concurrent weakening of religious conviction. The modern heritage of liberty of religion as a right, with all the derivative civil liberties of speech, press, and assembly, is the peculiar legacy of free church Calvinism, which first demanded it not out of a weakened but a more intense religious conviction. There were also *politiques* and latitudinarians, such as Dutch Arminians and deistic Anglicans in Holland, England, and America, and these were willing to water down doctrine for the social and moral utilities of a comprehensive state church. But it was the support of separatist and spiritualist views among the more intensely religious groups which changed the equilibrium of forces from the general type common to Lutheran, Roman Catholic, and Orthodox Catholic societies.

Seventeenth-century Holland, we should remember, numbered about the same population as England, and was vastly wealthier. And in the first half of the century Holland was the "University of Europe." Here was the best of Europe's intellect, in philosophy, science, law, classical scholarship, and art, while most of the rest of the Continent was either at war or suffering under ecclesiastical censorship. Politically Holland was an oasis of constitutional liberties in the great waste of Romanist and Lutheran despotisms. Here Grotius and Althusius pioneered the construction of the modern state and international relations on natural law. And here, out of the struggle of theocratic predestinarians and Arminian Erastians, was evolved at last the confessional neutrality of the state. Episcopius, the spokesman of the Remonstrants, was the earliest to develop this "collegialist" view of free churches within the state. And from Utrecht, the chief intellectual center of international Calvinism in the second half of the century, Voetius' influence made for such a free church version of Calvinism. For the fullest illustration of this transition, however, we should turn to England.

One of the striking contrasts between British Christianity and that of Lutheran countries is the emphasis on issues of polity and the doctrine of the church. Lutheran countries, as we have seen, rarely exhibited any feeling that a particular form of visible church was an essential matter. And this was also the predominant view in sixteenth-century England. Elizabethan England was just one Protestant country among others. Her retention of episcopacy was viewed as a matter of the royal preference rather than as a theological distinction. It was not related to the validity of sacraments. Sixteenth-century Anglicans were classical Protestants, both in holding to such views of redemption as are set forth in the Thirty-nine Articles, and in holding that a church should define itself and the terms of its communion with other churches on faith rather than organization. Hooker and Whitgift defended episcopacy as traditional, expedient, and established by the crown, but also recognized the Scots and French Reformed, and the German Lutherans as full and legitimate churches with valid ministry and ordination. Such ideas lie behind the method of extending episcopacy to Scotland in 1610, when Presbyterian ministers who had never been episcopally confirmed or ordained to the diaconate or priesthood were consecrated to the episcopate simply on the basis of their Presbyterian orders. Other non-episcopally ordained ministers were accepted as ministers in the Church of England.

PURITANISM. RISE OF LAUDIANISM. A more doctrinaire attitude toward polity, however, was growing in England. The Puritans began it by insisting that one particular form of church government was specified in Scripture and was essential to the faith. Soon presbyterian synods and congregational independency were each being urged as the sole justified forms of polity for the Church of England. And episcopalians began to defend themselves in kind. The Laudian divines discovered Eastern Orthodoxy and the fathers of the fourth and fifth centuries, which gave them more pride in their episcopal government. They stopped being apologetic about their peculiarities among the Reformed churches and started to make virtues of them. They did not yet go so far as to unchurch those churches without bishops, but they now regarded this lack as a defect on the part of the other Reformed churches. The Romanist Queen provided pressure to conceive Anglicanism as different from the other Reformed churches in kind as in degree. Archbishop Laud, however, still accepted Lutheran superintendents as the thing without the name, and most explained the loss of bishops at the Reformation as the unfortunate necessity of the crisis. But while divine-right episcopacy was rarely asserted in its modern sense, the Laudians rested their whole case on divine-right monarchy, whose agents were the king's bishops. And they used recklessly such agencies of absolutism as the Court of High Commission. For this identification of episcopacy with divine-right absolutism they paid in 1643, when Parliament, largely supported by the Puritans in religion, abolished absolutism, and episcopacy as an integral part of it.

PURITAN REVOLUTION. With the Puritan Revolution and Civil War we reach the crucial turning point in Protestant history and the origin of "modern" church history as we use the term. It was, on the one hand, the second heroic age of Protestantism, with a richness and vitality and exaltation of religious life comparable to that of the Continental Reformation. As such, it was the last attempt on a great scale to establish the thousand-year-old aspiration of a confessional state and culture. But from our viewpoint, the significance of these efforts was their failure, or at least their transformation into a new type of relationship of church and culture. With the creation of a whole family of free churches, i.e., the emergence as denominations of the English Presbyterians, Congregationalists, and Baptists in the 1640's, the old type of church establishment was no longer possible. Politics and economics were now released in principle from ecclesiastical regulation; toleration became the basis of a common life, and ethical issues were to be determined henceforth with reference to "moral law," conceived as identical with Christian morality, and yet independently ascertainable.

COMPREHENSION VS. PERSECUTION. Although the Restoration which succeeded Cromwell's Puritan theocracy was not enduring in its political aspects, it has more significance ecclesiastically, for the denominational structure of England was then definitely settled more or less as we have it now. There were two chief possibilities for an ecclesiastical settlement. On the one hand there was the plan of a comprehensive national church originally favored by the new king as well as by the Presbyterian Anglicans who had done the most to bring him back. A constitutional episcopate like that earlier proposed by Archbishop Ussher, together with greater flexibility in the use of the liturgy, might well have brought nearly all of the Presbyterians and perhaps some Independents into the establishment. But the Savoy Conference of 1661 chose the other possibility. The Laudian party determined, by imposing their party formula, rather to define the Church of England more narrowly than had ever been done before.

The failure of the Savoy Conference was followed by the Act of Uniformity of 1662, designed to humiliate or to unchurch all of Puritan sympathies. For the first time episcopal ordination was made an indispensable requirement of ministry in the Church of England, a stipulation which would have forced many to repudiate their orders and seek reordination. Similarly all were required to yield unfeigned assent to all things in a forthcoming revision of the liturgy. And lastly, all ministers had to swear that the Solemn League and Covenant, which many of them had subscribed, had been unlawful. The result was the "Great Ejection" by which about one-fifth of the ministry of the church, including many of the abler and more dedicated, was deposed. A large number who agreed with them conformed outwardly. The very size of the purge, however, defeated the Laudians and made toleration necessary. Had the plan of comprehension succeeded, the joint weight of presbyterian and episcopal persecution would have rested heavily on all dissenters. But with so large and respectable a body driven from the church, it would not be possible to maintain monopoly and persecution long.

To be sure, the following generation under the savage "Clarendon Code" was not an easy age for nonconformists. The Corporation Act and the Test Act required communication according to the state liturgy as a qualification for office in corporations, or civil or military functions; the University Test Acts required subscription of the Thirty-nine Articles and compulsory attendance at the state's liturgy at the universities; penalties under the Conventicle Acts included banishment and death for common worship other than the state's; and the Five Mile Act denied former Puritans the right to come within five miles of an incorporated town, or to teach anywhere. In the generation of persecution under the restored Stuarts, William Penn estimated that five thousand died in bonds for conscience's sake and thousands were exiled to America. This was the time of meetings in cellars and haylofts, a time of the "long rows of tarred and gibbeted Dissenters along the roadside," a time when a John Bunyan spent twelve years in jail. The killings in Scotland were even worse, approaching the savagery of Louis XIV, and James II observed them with frank enthusiasm. But the attempts of the Stuarts to model England on the despotism of Louis XIV finally came to disaster when the appeal went out to William of Orange, Louis' worst enemy, to come to the throne of England.

THE GLORIOUS REVOLUTION. From the perspective of church history the Glorious Revolution had European significance. The 1680's had seen a last effort on the grand scale to put down Protestantism by force. Louis XIV, the most powerful prince in Europe, made this program his own in international affairs as well as in France. In these years the Palatinate fell into Roman hands, the attempt was again made to wipe out the Waldenses, while thousands of Huguenot refugees brought chilling tales to England, Holland, and Prussia of Roman Catholic ferocity in France. James of England was in the pay of the French king also, and only the Netherlands and its prince, William, stood firm in the pass. William accepted the invitation to England, not primarily for the sake of England, but as a major stroke in the Europe-wide struggle for Protestantism and for political liberty. The result, however, was to put England decisively and permanently in the Protestant camp. Papist intrigues like those of James II were henceforth to be precluded by the constitutional requirement that the crown be Protestant.

The Revolutionary settlement of 1689 also brought toleration again to England, this time permanently. "Nonconformists" were now granted legal protection for their public worship, while still suffering the civil and social disabilities of the Test and Corporation Acts. The censorship was abrogated. The full meaning of the defeat of comprehension at the Savoy Conference now began to appear. The Church of England was no longer in the old sense the national church. It was simply the largest denomination in England and endowed with many privileges, but it was accompanied by other legal self-governing, self-maintained free churches—the Presbyterians, Independents, Baptists, and Quakers. The English state, on the other side, was by the logic of this situation already on the road to confessional neutrality, as Locke suggested in his *Letters on Toleration*.

The new position of the nonconformists as an integral part of the nation raised again the possibility of comprehension as thirty years before. Leading bishops like Tillotson, Burnet, and Stillingfleet were ready to recognize the validity of non-episcopal orders. But the bulk of the clergy were hostile to the government and the bishops and opposed to toleration or comprehension. Toward the end of Queen Anne's reign, in fact, legislation was actually passed to end toleration. The "occasional conformity," which had originally arisen out of the religious concern of Dissenters like Baxter to recognize the established church by attending its worship occasionally, was now forbidden. And the Schism Bill would have barred all dissenters from teaching and would have prevented the notable contribution of the eighteenth-century dissenting "academies" to English education. Queen Anne, however, passed to her reward opportunely and both laws were repealed in 1718.

THE NONJURING SCHISM. The problem created for the Laudian party of Episcopalians by the Glorious Revolution is dramatized by the "nonjurors." Their most sacred principle was divine-right monarchy. At the Restoration they had inserted two political holy days in the church calendar, one for King Charles "the Martyr," and one for the Restoration. The clergy had sworn their oaths to King James II. How could they swear another to William and Mary while James was still alive at the court of Louis XIV? And was not the Glorious Revolution precisely a manifestation of those theses of the supremacy of parliament and government under law for which the Puritans had fought? Could the Episcopalian Church of England accept the theses of the Puritan Revolution after triumphing over them? The pulpits had been ringing for a generation with divine, indefeasible, hereditary right and the duty of passive obedience. Could High Anglicans so easily turn from Filmer to Locke? Archbishop Sancroft, five suffragans, and some four hundred clergy did not think so and declined to take the oath to a parliamentary elective king. Thus the Laudian principle of divine right was now driven into schism and into schemes of insurrection with Irish and Scottish Jacobites and papists around the Pretender.

Since the Scottish Episcopalians as a group took the nonjuring position, whereas the great Presbyterian majority were ready to accept a Dutch Presbyterian king, it was the Presbyterian Kirk which was now established north of the border. Thus was prepared that curious arrangement whereby the British crown is Presbyterian in Scotland and Episcopal in England. In 1707 England and Scotland united as the kingdom of Great Britain.

HIGH CHURCH–LOW CHURCH CONTROVERSY. Within the Church of England tension ran high between the pro-Laudian clergy, who were for persecution and thus were called "high church," and the bishops appointed by the new government, who were for toleration and therefore called "low church."

Controversy between rebellious presbyters and their bishops was scandalous in the opening years of the eighteenth century and led finally to the prorogation of convocation in 1717 for more than a century. This silencing of convocation has often been deplored as a denial of self-government in the church. But had the Tory clergy been able to use the lower house much longer as their organ, they would probably have publicly involved themselves in Jacobite sedition in a degree very damaging to the church.

The character of the political involvements of the church had been significantly affected by the establishment of constitutional monarchy. The center of decision had passed from the crown by itself to the crown in Parliament and the balance of parties there. The political significance of the church was no longer manifested in the use of great ecclesiastics as ministers by the prince directly, but rather in party politics both in and out of Parliament. The bishops sat in the House of Lords, where they constituted about one-fifth of the total, a voting strength of considerable importance to the rival parties. The manipulation of the bench, by promotions and translations, was a significant aspect of politics by ministers of the government. One implication of toleration, moreover, was that both parties had church support or that the church transcended the political divisions. In Roman Catholic countries such as France, by contrast, where there was no toleration, the only possible church party was the government party, and political opposition would be forced to be also anticlerical.

The Anglican tradition remained the majority and socially dominant one. The ancient church structure continued, with its centuries-old abuses of pluralism and nonresidence. The higher grades of preferment in the church were reserved for the aristocracy, usually younger sons, while the poorer parish curates suffered from insufficient salary and insecurity of income. Preferment in the eighteenth century was a matter of party patronage, and therefore of party regularity and personal connections within that club of landed gentry, the eighteenth-century Parliament.

THEORY OF ESTABLISHMENT. The established church was coming to understand the religious basis of the state, and its own nature, in a fashion much closer to Locke than to that of seventeenth-century Anglicanism. Warburton, for example, (*Alliance between Church and State*, 1736), adumbrated the modern confessionally neutral state. With Locke he maintained that the state must support a minimum theism or deism as a basis of morality and must exclude Romanism as a political threat. But within these limits the state is not concerned with the truth of religious doctrines, only with their social consequences. With Locke also, and as against Lutheran and Roman Catholic theorists of natural law, he argued that the church must have powers of self-government up to excommunication. Such powers, however, must be devoid of coercive power and civil penalties. Where Locke drew from all this the consequence of separation of church and state, Warburton argued that the state could ally itself with any church on grounds of social utility, but that the church which accepted such support and privileges must expect to yield its liberties in the same proportion. Paley, who justified an established church on the same grounds of social utility, went beyond Warburton to urge equality of civil status for dissenters. Thus Anglican spokesmen rested their case now on utilitarian rather than theological grounds so far as the state was concerned, but they generally held that the church must still have an integrity and basis of its own apart from the state.

DOCTRINE OF THE CHURCH. Bishop Hoadley, to be sure, created great controversy by arguing that the true church was wholly invisible and that all church government was mere machinery which must recognize unlimited private judgment. William Law had no difficulty in showing that this view made any organized church impossible. And Hoadley's views were not typical even of most "low" churchmen, although many, both conformists and nonconformists, approached Hoadley in their lack of feeling for the visible Christian society. From very shortly after the Revolutionary settlement, in fact, the bitter struggles over polity, which had defined much of the seventeenth-century controversy, had become a dead issue, leaving only a group of churches variously organized but maintained more by institutional inertia and social class than by theological conviction.

Owing partly to the lack of concern for confessional peculiarities, perhaps, the churchmen of the eighteenth century engaged in numerous explorations in interconfessional relations. Archbishop Wake, especially, negotiated with the Gallican Appellants (see above, p. 35), with the Russian Orthodox, and with the Lutheran church of Prussia. The last scheme was the most promising, involving the Moravians, headed by the Prussian court preacher Jablonski, who possessed another "apostolic succession" of bishops, and hoped thereby to establish intercommunion and closer similarity between Lutherans and Anglicans.

NONCONFORMISTS. The nonconformists, meanwhile, were left to suffer the slow penalties of social snobbery, economic boycott, and intellectual isolation. In the 1690's the leaders of the Presbyterians and Congregationalists drew up some "Heads of Agreement," which for a time promised a merger, and which contributed to Connecticut Presbygationalism. But theological controversy precipitated at the Salter's Hall Conference of 1719 prevented any effective ecclesiastical union. The rapid spread of rationalist and pietist views of the visible church was enough to prevent solution in this area in the eighteenth century. The pietist and evangelical view made the church a missionary society. The rationalists made it a voluntary association on the basis of private judgment. Neither view could make sense of the grounds on which Episcopalian, Presbyterian, and Congregationalist polity had been devised and had been defended in the seventeenth-century struggles. For their common political defense, however, the "Three Old Denominations" were able to organize a committee, the "Dissenting Deputies" (1732). And the long battle against their disabilities confirmed the nonconformists' tendency to champion civil and political liberty in general.

POLITICAL AND CULTURAL INFLUENCE. Most significant was that general disposition referred to in the nineteenth century as "the nonconformist conscience." The various seventeenth-century attempts at a church-controlled society had failed, yet they left a sense of obligation to submit the whole common life to moral law. This obligation, moreover, had been brought home to the generality by the Puritans. Their enduring legacy was to be the consciences of common men as a political force. Here is the basis of the Anglo-American tendency to political moralism, which contrasts so sharply with the Lutheran approach to public questions. It produces a sense of personal responsibility and the habit of initiative in organizing social action, together with a strong sense of law. The result in politics has been the conservative democracy of the English-speaking world, whereas in Lutheran and Roman Catholic countries democracy was forced into revolutionary and antichurch attitudes.

While nonconformity made the major contribution to political democracy in this period, Anglicanism also had increasingly taken over Puritan and Whig views of the state. When George III attempted to restore Stuart ideas of royal prerogative, there was a large section of English opinion which considered that the Americans were defending true English tradition. The nonconformists supported the Colonial cause almost to a man. Price and Priestley developed the Lockean tradition and laid the foundations of Benthamite utilitarianism. What was even more striking was to see Anglican bishops like Hoadley also defend'ng the right of rebellion.

The Puritan theocratic urge to master the common life according to a higher mandate had a similar indirect effect in economic life. In England, especially, the closing of public life and the professions to dissenters forced them into trade and industry, while their exclusion from the universities led them to develop mathematics and the natural sciences in their academies. In technology and economic life, consequently, nonconformity did more than Anglicanism to shape modern England. The late seventeenth century saw economic life organized on a supposed natural law independent of theology. But the assumption of providential order lay behind it, as is clear in Adam Smith, and the ascetic discipline of Puritan energy furnished a new impetus. The relation between Calvinism and Puritanism and the "capitalist" mentality has been much debated. There does seem to be a correlation of Lutheran, Roman Catholic, and high Anglican ethics with economic traditionalism. Commercial, technological, and industrial leadership, by contrast, have rested with the Calvinist and Puritan Dutch, English, and Americans. Free church Calvinism penetrated and became identified with democracy, capitalism, and applied science to a degree unequaled by the other major Christian traditions. And whereas this tradition was secondary to Anglicanism in England, everywhere else in the English-speaking world free church Calvinism has been vastly more numerous and influential than the Anglican communion.

THE EVANGELICAL SYNTHESIS. The largest part of the religious history of eighteenth-century England is the story of the Evangelical Awakening. That story we will postpone until a later chapter. Here, however, we may observe how Evangelicalism accepted the emerging pattern of church and culture, which we have been describing, and became the most characteristic religious formation of it. In contrast to the original Puritan intention, the Evangelical accepted unquestioningly the organization of state and economic and cultural life on religiously neutral "moral" and "natural" standards. He assumed the compatibility of these standards with Christian ethics and thus turned to their promotion by voluntary agencies the energies which the Puritan would have used to build a theocracy. Evangelicalism stressed the individual even more than Puritanism, dissolving the sense of history, of the church, and of the state as communities, and thus, incidentally, making predestination ever less credible. Thus was prepared a transition to a personalism and moralism in which the Puritan ethos might survive, especially in its emotional pattern and its secondary cultural effect, but with very little of its metaphysical bases.

Chapter 6

BRITISH PURITANISM OVERSEAS

As against the communions of the European continent—Roman Catholic, Orthodox Catholic, Lutheran, and Reformed—the religion of the North American English colonies was predominantly Puritan. It was the overseas extension of Puritan Anglicanism and of what came to be called the three denominations of "old dissent," the Presbyterians, Congregationalists, and Baptists. The colonial foundations of the first half of the seventeenth century generally conformed to the medieval and Reformation pattern of a uniform authoritarian state church. The founders intended no contribution to religious liberty or even tolerance, except insofar as they found liberty from European restrictions for the purification of the Church of England to a genuinely biblical church. But the experiences of the Puritan Revolution, the Restoration, and the Glorious Revolution, together with certain developments peculiar to the American scene, progressively broke down the original state-church pattern in favor of free church Puritanism.

The colonies organized in the first half of the seventeenth century on the state-church basis were of two types, namely, those in Congregationalist New England, and secondly, those Episcopal settlements from Virginia and Maryland south, which we may call the "Southern colonies." The third main group, the "Middle colonies," Pennsylvania, New York, and New Jersey, represent on the whole a different and later concept, arising out of the experiences of the English Civil War, the Commonwealth, and the Restoration. All three of these colonial areas were to come at various times and for various reasons to a system of religious liberty and of a separation of church and state.

RELIGIOUS INTENTIONS IN VIRGINIA. Of the Southern colonies with established Anglicanism, Virginia was the most important and the best example. The first two charters of 1606 and 1609 brought out clearly the anti-Roman motive which was significant with nearly all the colonies. They were conceived in part as Protestant outposts against the forces of the Counter Reformation so recently defeated in England, the Spaniards in Mexico and Florida, and the French in the St. Lawrence Valley. And indeed there were to be legal disabilities on Roman Catholics in most of the colonies for most of the colonial period. All settlers in Virginia were required to subscribe to the Anglican Oath of Supremacy. The religious provisions of "Dale's Laws" of 1611 were as rigorous as was to be the case in New England. Attendance at religious services was required twice daily of all; the penalty for blasphemy was death, and that for disrespect to the Anglican clergy was whipping. To be sure, these laws, which were probably written in England, could not be strictly enforced, but they show something of intentions.

The defeat of these intentions came largely from physical difficulties. The very existence of the colony was long in doubt. Virginia was one of the most expensive beachheads ever established. Many of the first immigrants were gentlefolk, unaccustomed to the brutal labor necessary to establish themselves in the wilderness. They were decimated by disease and Indian warfare as rapidly as they came over. By 1624, when the London Company at last turned over Virginia as a royal colony, it had spent five or six million dollars, and sent over 14,000 emigrants. Almost 13,000 of them had already perished.

In 1619 the first Negro slaves were brought to Virginia in a ship ironically named the *Jesus*, and gradually was evolved the plantation system by which the colony learned how to survive. The character of the immigration also changed to a more rough-and-ready type, including bankrupts and pirates, better suited to the life. Complaints were heard that Virginia was developing a population without honor, honesty, or religion. And indeed, how could the Anglican parish system be adapted to the plantations of Virginia, stretched out along the navigable rivers? A clergyman would have from thirty to one hundred miles to travel to call on his parishioners. In 1661 the suggestion was actually made that to save the church the government should build villages around churches and require the population to come in off the plantations to spend the week ends there. These difficulties did not attract the best clergy to Virginia. And there were other handicaps. A system of congregational control by vestries grew up—a system by which a clergyman would be reappointed from year to year. While his formal induction was thus postponed, he could not claim the parson's freehold and he remained under the thumb of the laity. Thus in actual practice Virginia was as congregationalist as New England. And for the first generation or so it was dominantly Puritan and "low church" in tone. There were no bishops in the colonies, and discipline from England was nearly impossible to enforce. In 1638 Archbishop Laud completed arrangements to send a bishop and troops to New England, but the outbreak of the Civil War forestalled him. Until the 1660's there was no tie between the colonial Episcopal churches and their nominal episcopal overseers in England.

The missionary motive, so prominent in the early literature of the colonizing movement, was also largely frustrated. John Rolfe's account of the reasons for marrying Pocahontas brings out this evangelistic concern. But in fact the English Protestants were less successful than the Roman Catholic French. In contrast to the French fur traders, the English brought their women along, cleared the forests, and spoiled the hunting grounds by the initiation of an agricultural economy. The Indians, who had no concept of private property in land, naturally grew resentful and there were savage conflicts, in Virginia in 1623 and in New England in 1675-1676, after which the missionary enterprise languished until the Great Awakening of the eighteenth century.

MASSACHUSETTS BAY. Massachusetts Bay, the strongest of the New England colonies, suffered much less than Virginia from the difficulties mentioned. The colony was compact and homogeneous in contrast to Southern plantation life, and its clerical leadership was as conspicuously strong as Virginia's was weak. "Probably no colony in the history of European emigration was superior to that of Massachusetts in wealth, station, or capacity." These were the pick of the Puritan party in England who could not stomach the measures of Archbishop Laud. They were not separatists, but Congregationalist Anglicans who would establish in America a biblical church order, free of the gathered corruptions of Stuart Anglicanism, and together with it, a community regulated throughout by divine and natural law, the Canaan of the new covenant. That order was defined in the *Cambridge Platform* of 1648. The church was composed of the regenerate and their children who should "own the covenant." Only church members had political rights. Nonchurch members, to be sure, had to pay church taxes and attend services. And the civil magistrate enforced orthodoxy. Nathaniel Ward in his *Simple Cobbler of Agawam* (1647) defined the limits of toleration in terms which would suit a Leo XIII. The true church, he said, "must connive in some cases, but may not concede in any."

And yet heresy and schism were not stamped out in New England. The colony of Massachusetts Bay was constantly sloughing off dissenting groups, such as the founders of Rhode Island and Connecticut. And Quaker missionaries, seeking the martyr's crown, refused to heed all warnings from the Puritan magistrate. They made their way repeatedly to the Puritan capital to prophesy against the churches, and were escorted over the border or punished. And the second generation of Puritans felt the strain of maintaining the system under frontier conditions. Famine and plague and Indian wars took their toll and were interpreted by the clergy as evidence of God's wrath with the growing laxity in New England. The Reforming Synod of 1679 sought to return church and state to the high requirements of God's law, but the extension of the "half-way covenant" traced across the map of New England the subsiding of the fire of conviction. The rising generation could no longer give evidence of that personal conversion which was the first qualification for full church membership in classical Congregationalism.

THE MIDDLE COLONIES. In contrast to the Southern and New England colonies generally, the Middle colonies represented on the whole a post-Civil War view of toleration. With them must be classed the New England colony of Rhode Island, which stood for such concepts even earlier. Roger Williams championed in America the religious liberty and democracy espoused by such radical Puritans as John Lilburne in the Civil War. When theocratic Massachusetts Bay drove Williams out, he founded Rhode Island on these principles. After the restoration of the Stuarts a similar religious freedom was provided in the Quaker colonies, Pennsylvania, New Jersey, and Delaware. In Dutch New Amsterdam economic motives were more conspicuous in the achievement of toleration. The Dutch directors scolded Governor Stuyvesant for persecuting Quakers in 1663. There were already some fourteen languages being spoken in the city of New York, and the character of a cosmopolitan trading center could not be maintained along with religious conformity. Similar business considerations undoubtedly played some role in the Quaker colonies and with the proprietors of Virginia and Maryland. They contributed to the gradual conversion of the Southern and New England colonies to the system of religious liberty represented by Rhode Island and the Middle colonies.

ENGLISH INFLUENCE TOWARD TOLERATION. The Southern and New England colonies somewhat tardily and ungraciously followed the example of the mother country with regard to the toleration of nonconformity. Even earlier there had been restraining pressure from England on persecution. When the Baptist Obadiah Holmes was whipped in 1651 in Boston, ten London Congregationalist clergy protested to their New England colleagues that such intolerance was very injurious to their cause in England. In 1661 King Charles himself protested when four Quakers were hanged in Boston. And after the passage of the Toleration Act in 1689, dissenting groups in the colonies learned to appeal to it; the Presbyterian Makemie used it as a defense in Virginia in 1699 and won his case. As a consequence dissenters were tolerated in New England and the South in the eighteenth century. Toleration, in a rapidly expanding population, opens the possibility to the minority of coming to outnumber the original majority. And this is precisely what happened. At different times the old state churches of the Southern and New England colonies were consequently disestablished by political majorities composed of dissenters.

SCOTS AND GERMAN IMMIGRATION. Two developments in particular contributed to this increase of dissenters in New England and the Southern colonies. The role of the "Great Awakening" in turning numbers of nominal Anglicans and Congregationalists into dissenting Baptists and Presbyterians and, later, Methodists, we must describe later. It was one highly important factor. A second factor was the character of the eighteenth-century immigration, which was no longer dominantly Episcopal or Congregationalist. The two most considerable groups of immigrants of the eighteenth century were the Germans and the Scots, each consisting of about one hundred thousand. The Scots and Scots-Irish were solidly Presbyterian. Like the Baptists, the Presbyterians found their surest initial foothold in the Philadelphia area, under Quaker freedom, and from there spread west and south into the inland sections of the Southern Anglican colonies. In contrast to the Scots, the Germans were ecclesiastically very diverse. Lutherans were most numerous, but there were also Reformed, Taüfer, Mennonites, Moravians, and Schwenckfelders. Over two-thirds of them settled in Pennsylvania, where Count Zinzendorf unsuccessfully attempted to unite them all into one "Church of God in the Spirit."

The Southern colonies were more affected by this immigration of dissenters than was New England, but one curious development in New England in this direction was the creation there of a dissenting faction made up from the Church of England. We mentioned the difficulties of Anglicanism in the South without episcopal supervision. In the eighteenth century this problem was partly solved by a series of "commissaries," who exercised some tenuous control of the clergy of Virginia and Maryland on behalf of the bishop of London. But they were still unable to perform the functions of confirmation and ordination. The real vigor of the Anglican Church in eighteenth-century America was shown rather by the three hundred missionaries sent to the colonies by the Society for the Propagation of the Gospel (S.P.G.), organized in 1701. Conditions were such that more of these missionaries went to

New England than to the Anglican South. The conversion of the President of Yale College, Timothy Cutler, and other members of the faculty, together with five Congregationalist ministers, in 1722, illustrates the success of this propaganda in New England and the demoralization of Congregationalism in its very strongholds. Thus was formed another minority to support Baptists, Quakers, and others against the privileges of the state church in Connecticut and Massachusetts.

By the end of the third generation in America the difficulties of frontier life had brought culture and religion to a low ebb. The Church of England, although theoretically established in half of the colonies, had little real influence outside Virginia and Maryland. And even in Virginia not more than 5 per cent of the population were members of that church. Zinzendorf found that in the extraordinary mixture in the Middle colonies the most important group belonged to "the Pennsylvania church," i.e., no church at all. And although the New England colonies gave the impression of greater cultural and religious power, and although their clergy were able to strengthen their organization defensively, nevertheless the general conviction which had been the basis of the theocracy of the Puritans disintegrated. There seemed to be an actual danger of collapse into barbarism. For centuries no group of European peoples had had so little to do with Christian traditions and institutions.

THE GREAT AWAKENING. The incipient nation was rescued from this danger by a new movement which began in the 1730's, the movement usually called the "Great Awakening." It appeared in New England with Edwards, in the Middle Colonies with Frelinghuysen and Tennent. George Whitefield was the chief agent in consolidating the many local revivals into one great movement. He completed seven tours, traveling from Georgia to Massachusetts and preaching conversion to Congregationalists, Presbyterians, Anglicans, Dutch Reformed, Baptists, Methodists, Lutherans, Quakers—to everyone who would give him a hearing. Other itinerant preachers followed his example and fused in the Awakening a common consciousness through the separate colonies. "Whitefield, Edwards, and

Tennent preceded Franklin and Washington as rallying names for Americans irrespective of local distinctions."

The Awakening bore fruit in educational and evangelistic enterprises. Among the numerous academies and colleges which owe their origin to the Awakening, the best-known survivors are the Universities of Pennsylvania and Princeton. The latter grew out of Tennent's "Log College." Dartmouth College, on the other hand, developed from a school for the Indians. Edwards wrote his greatest works at the Indian mission at Stockbridge; his daughter's fiancé, David Brainerd, gave his life in missionary work among the Indians in New Jersey and Pennsylvania. Anglicans, Presbyterians, and most of all the Moravians, labored similarly among the aborigines. David Zeisberger, Moravian missionary, was perhaps the most successful.

The greatest intellect of the Awakening, and probably of colonial America generally, was Jonathan Edwards of Northampton. Edwards was startled at the response to his own preaching and could only explain it as God's ratification of the evangelical doctrines of grace and justification. His *Narrative of Surprising Conversions* was reprinted many times and was distributed in England by John Wesley. This, with his treatise on "Religious Affections," constituted a manual of the psychology of religious conversion. And indeed there were psychological manifestations of note. New England had never experienced such extravagances and has not since. Laymen rose to exhort the congregation in Edwards' church, sometimes three or four at once. Itinerant evangelists invaded settled parishes, and attempts were made to ordain uneducated exhorters. This uproar led in 1742 to a law for the regulation of abuses in Connecticut, and the churches were split in many districts into "New Lights" and "Old Lights." The Presbyterians of the Middle colonies, similarly, were split for a time into "New Side" and "Old Side" schisms.

In general the effect of the Awakening was to strengthen the churches numerically, especially the minority churches. About 150 new Congregational churches were gathered in New England. But the Awakening also led to the breaking off of separatist Congregational churches, or to Baptist separation.

Baptist congregations grew from six to thirty in Massachusetts, from four to twelve in Connecticut, and began to form a significant opposition to the standing order of the Congregational establishment. In the Middle and Southern colonies it was the Baptists and Presbyterians who profited most. The effects in Virginia were to be especially significant, as we shall see.

At the middle of the eighteenth century colonial Christians were generally divided for or against the revivals. The revivalists were strongest in the back country; the "old Calvinists" and Anglicans were rather concentrated among the prosperous and politically influential classes on the coast. Each party developed a distinct element of the Puritan heritage, while both relinquished the comprehensive theocratic program. Those of the Awakening retained the central evangelical convictions and religious intensity but, with the great exception of Edwards, tended to abandon the rational discipline of Puritanism and its cultural responsibility. The old Calvinists and Anglicans rather preserved the political and cultural vocation, while their grasp of the gospel itself grew superficial and moralistic.

THE CHURCHES AND THE REVOLUTION. It was especially the "old Calvinists" and rationalizing Anglicans who brought their political ethic to bear on the struggle for colonial home rule. When considering the intellectual preparation for the American Revolution, one must remember that the clergy were still as a rule the best-educated men in the community, and that the pulpit was the strongest single influence in forming public opinion. The most powerful body of clergy in all the colonies was the Congregationalists, and after them came the Presbyterians of the Middle colonies. Among both groups the prevailing tendency among those who interested themselves in political ethics was the philosophy of natural law, political contract, and the right of revolution. Locke, Milton, and Sidney were the theorists most appealed to in the election and fast-day sermons of New England in the mid-eighteenth century. The ideas of the Preamble to the Declaration of Independence had been pulpit commonplaces for a generation or so before.

Charles Chauncy of the First Church in Boston was the defender of the colonial cause most widely read in Europe. Jonathan Mayhew of the West Church in Boston attacked the high Anglican party, as represented in New England especially by the S.P.G., as the spokesmen for the political authority of canon law and the divine right of the "apostolic succession" of bishops. Mayhew stood on the ground of his Puritan predecessors and would have none of the attempt to kindle the cult of Charles I as "saint and martyr."

The endeavors of the S.P.G. to establish an Anglican episcopate in the colonies occasioned a series of conjoint annual assemblies of Congregationalists and Presbyterians from 1766 to the outbreak of the Revolution. The sons of the Puritan revolution understood episcopacy still as the ecclesiastical tool of absolute monarchy, and the old affiliation of constitutionalism and presbyterianism made itself felt again. This Puritan political ethic of government based on covenant was taken up directly by the political leaders from Congregationalist and Presbyterian preachers. And whereas the Baptists, because of their emphasis on the lay ministry, produced fewer outstanding ministers, their whole church tradition built a solid popular support for the same political ethic in the tradition of the English Civil War and John Locke.

While the prevailing tendency in the leading churches thus supported the Puritan ethic of natural law and political compact, two divergent currents might have been observed. The "low church" and Puritan Anglicans, who had generally opposed the plan of establishing an episcopate in the colonies, also sympathized generally with the colonial cause. This was the general temper of the Anglicanism of the Southern colonies. Two-thirds of the signers of the Declaration of Independence were Anglicans of this stamp. In New England, on the contrary, Anglican clergy and laity tended to be High Church and Tory. The Anglicans of the Middle colonies were divided. Consequently, when war actually came in sight, there was a migration of Anglican and Methodist clergy back to England, for in this tradition one found the assertion of the duty of passive obedience to constituted authority, as it was generally taught also by the Lutheran and Roman Catholic clergy.

The second minority was composed of the pacifist churches, the Quakers, the Moravians, the Church of the Brethren, the Mennonites, and some Methodists. These groups were naturally strongest in the former Quaker colonies, especially Pennsylvania. The Quakers themselves had voluntarily abdicated from political control in Pennsylvania and New Jersey in the Seven Years' War, twenty years before, as they realized the necessity of military action by the colony in which they were now only the strongest minority. During the Revolution these pacifists were misunderstood and often abused by both sides. Perhaps the most pathetic fate of all was that of the Christian Indians converted by the Moravians, who were cut down in cold blood by the colonial troops.

Another ecclesiastical consequence of the Revolution, little noticed at the time, is worth mention in the light of later history. This was the legal and political emancipation of the colonial Roman Catholics. The colonies were ninety-nine per cent anti-Roman Catholic, and the handful of Roman Catholics were concentrated chiefly in Pennsylvania and Maryland as a result of legal disabilities elsewhere. But during the Revolution Roman Catholic Spain, France, and Canada were wooed as allies against England. General Washington forbade the traditional Guy Fawkes Day celebrations in the army, and anti-Roman Catholic laws in several states were revoked. In the new constitution American Roman Catholicism, then consisting of not more than 25,000 members, received a new prospect of freedom of movement.

RELIGION IN THE CONSTITUTION. In the organization of a new political society out of the former colonies after the Revolution, religion proved one of the more difficult problems. The several new states were too diverse both as to denominations and as to church-state relations to agree on any common pattern. The new Federal Constitution perforce left matters of religion to the several states. In the actual drafting, the example of Virginia was most influential. Just before national independence, the movement for religious liberty in Virginia, led by Madison and Jefferson and backed chiefly by Baptists and Presbyterians, had won its victory. Now it became the model for the Federal Constitution. The Middle colonies had adopted this solution a century earlier. And although New England generally was to hold to state church Congregationalism for a generation or so longer, even here the pietism of the revivals and its rival rationalism had weakened the determination to insist on legal privileges. The new nation entered upon the nineteenth century with its church life shaped by a prevailing tendency toward free church Puritan denominationalism.

Chapter 7

PIETISM AND EVANGELICALISM

We have been surveying the patterns of ecclesiastical administration and of church-state relations. In most cases we observed an astonishing tenacity of formal structure throughout while the inner meaning of the institutions had radically changed. The seventeenth century began with the ideal of a uniform state church and Christian culture and, nearly everywhere, the end of the eighteenth century presented states and cultures emancipated from the control of the ecclesiastical bodies associated with them. The state, law, commercial and industrial life, science, philosophy, literature, and art had ceased to be aspects of an ecclesiastical civilization and were rather constituted on standards and aims supposedly derived from the "nature" of man and of society. What did this mean for the churches, and for the Christians who must spend part of their time in these nonecclesiastical activities of the common life? What could that "Christianity" be which was not the standard and the motive of the whole living of the Christian?

PIETISM AS A SOCIOLOGICAL TYPE. In a word, we may call it "Pietism." Pietism has served different meanings in different contexts. Here we mean an individualization and internalization which takes for granted or ignores the structure of church and state, seeking to build within it the significant religious fellowship. Pietism often expressed a reaction against orthodox formalism. The concern was not so much for new institutional expressions, as for personal appropriation of religious truth, subjective religious "experiences," and personal devotional and ascetic discipline. The larger relations of church and state and culture were discounted, sometimes because of apocalyptic expectations, or as religiously neutral. Or sometimes the pietist was himself a rationalist in these matters, accepting their emancipation from the church. In some way pietism involves the segregation of a certain sphere of life as peculiarly "religious," and concentration on it. This general tendency can be recognized with many variations in every major communion and in every country in the seventeenth and eighteenth centuries.

So defined, of course, pietism covers a great variety of concrete religious views and attitudes. The main stream of Lutheran, Reformed, and Anglican pietism, as with Roman Catholic Jansenism, may be described as evangelical. But there were also important mystical currents. From Jakob Boehme, the greatest modern German mystic, stemmed a theosophical mysticism which passed over into Roman Catholicism with Angelus Silesius, into nonjuring Anglicanism with William Law, and formed the basis of the "Philadelphians" and "Behmenists" in Protestant England. The quietistic mysticism of Madame Guyon found Protestant counterparts in Poiret and Tersteegen and many others. Some groups were primarily determined by millenarian expectations. Some were moralist and legalist, others, antinomian to the point of scandal. In every case, however, these religious attitudes now had to express themselves through voluntary associations or conventicles, within, even if sometimes little respectful of, the general framework of church and state. It has been argued with some justice that pietism was essentially the revival within the Reformed, Lutheran, and Anglican state churches of the sectarian, spiritualist, and mystical motifs of the medieval and Reformation periods. Ecclesiastical Protestantism was thus penetrated and disintegrated by a nonecclesiastical religiosity.

REFORMED PIETISM. Although the word "pietism" was first used in 1689, and then to ridicule a Lutheran manifestation of the movement, the beginnings are to be traced in the Reformed communion. And there it was closely associated with the transition from state-church to free church Calvinism. English Puritanism and Dutch precisianism alike had embodied many of the emphases which were to characterize pietism. They stressed personal conversion and practical holiness both in preaching and in their literature. Spiritual diaries and biographies, as well as devotional and ascetic manuals, were common. Such intensified religious practice was cultivated in voluntary conventicles, "prophesyings," and prayer meetings. At the beginning of the seventeenth century, however, the movement still hoped to shape the national community after its own pattern. It was only after the Puritans and precisians had become reconciled to the impossibility of this program that the introversion characteristic of pietism became apparent. And Anglo-American nonconformity even in its later pietist phase never quite relinquished the old Puritan sense of responsibility for the whole community.

This close relation of Puritanism and pietism may be illustrated by the case of William Ames, the architect of New England Congregationalism. Although Ames in this setting is to be viewed as a Puritan, in Holland, where he was very influential but never able to order church and state as a whole, he is rather honored as a pietist. Teelinck, known as the father of Dutch pietism, also had close relations with English Puritanism. In England Puritanism passed into its pietist phase under the persecution of the Restoration and the galling disabilities of the Restoration settlement. Watts and Doddridge provide the most attractive representatives of the first generation of the eighteenth century, still exhibiting much of the breadth of the seventeenth-century vision, which was to be narrowed in the Evangelical revival. In Holland Voet was the leader of the pietist party. Rigidly orthodox, he rated theology below practical Christianity and stressed the use of devotional literature, moral rigor, church discipline, pastoral care, and catechizing. The more easygoing and Erastian party in the Dutch church was led by Koch, the founder of biblical theology and the chief Dutch exponent of the theory of the biblical covenants as embodied also in the *Westminster Confession*. Outside Holland, however, the Reformed pietists widely adopted Koch's covenant theology. This was the case with the pietism of the Lower Rhine, for example, where Neander anticipated Watts and Doddridge in persuading Calvinists to use hymns along with their psalms. The theologian, Lampe, was to develop further this pietist hymnology in the generation of Watts and Doddridge.

Another aspect of the close relation between Puritanism and pietism arose from the fact that even classical Calvinism, as distinct from Lutheranism, contained motifs which could readily be developed in a pietist direction. There was here much more sympathy for lay participation in congregational life, for church discipline, and for ascetic rigor. And in fact pietist movements in Reformed countries rarely led to serious difficulties with the authorities. The chief exception was the separatist movement of the Labadists in Holland and the Lower Rhine region. Jean de Labadie was a French Jesuit who was converted to Calvinism and preached for a time in Geneva. He taught a contemplative mysticism, not unlike that of Guyon or Poiret, and won a very considerable following. Under increasing opposition he came to organize a separate community with a common purse like a monastic order. The movement prospered briefly, making itself felt even in the American colonies, but died out by the end of the century.

LUTHERAN PIETISM. The group to whom the name "pietist" was first specifically attached was the movement within Lutheranism initiated by the Alsatian pastor Philipp Jacob Spener. Spener was influenced by the Reformed pietists Leger and Labadie in Switzerland, where the church discipline also impressed him. He read English Puritans. In 1675 Spener challenged the Lutheran territorial church system with the Puritan and precisianist religious fellowship. His *Pia Desideria* of that year urged an awakened ministry, reform of the pastorate and seminaries, prayer meetings where the laity might share in Bible study, and increased devotional and charitable activity. He formed his *collegia pietatis* to realize this program. He had a strong expectation of the Second Coming, and his emphasis was on escape from a sinful world rather than its conquest. For devotional reading he could draw on good Lutheran mystics, especially Arndt's *True Christianity* (1606), long a classic in Europe and America, Arndt's pupil Gerhardt, and Grossgebauer's *Wächterstimme*. Spener was called to Dresden as court preacher in 1686 but soon found himself in a row with the academic theologians. A. H. Francke began *collegia* at nearby Leipzig the same year. These conventicles were forbidden by the theological faculty, and both Spener and

Francke were forced out of conservative Saxony at the beginning of the 90's. Between territorialism and the conventicle there was a much sharper tension than between the latter and the Reformed church system.

Frederick III offered them asylum in Brandenburg, the haven of religious refugees from all over Europe. The University of Halle, founded in 1694, gave Spener a chance at forming a center. For ten years he built the school, but after his death in 1705 it was even more successful under Francke for the two decades until his death in 1727. The University was surrounded with other institutions: a pauper school, a boy's boarding school, an orphanage, a Latin school, a printing press, a pharmacy, a Bible Institute. Thousands of children were taught there; many became missionaries, and some six thousand pietist clergy were trained in the Halle theological faculty, which was the largest divinity school in Germany. Bogatzky was one of the most influential of the devotional writers of Halle, and Freylinghausen the chief hymn writer. Even the Reformed pietists on the Lower Rhine contributed regularly to Halle. Colonial Lutheranism in America was largely evangelized and organized from Halle.

In the second third of the eighteenth century, however, Halle pietism was growing stale and stereotyped. Leadership passed to two other movements, the pietism of Württemberg, with the New Testament scholar J. A. Bengel as its most distinguished figure, and the renewed church of the "Unitas Fratrum" with Count Zinzendorf as its patron. Württemberg pietism was more of a popular movement than other Lutheran pietism, which tended to attract aristocratic coteries and showed none of the social and political radicalism of English Puritanism. As a bishop and member of the Supreme Church Council, Bengel was able to domesticate pietism into the parish system. Württemberg pietism was closely akin to the pietism of German Switzerland across the river, and Basel, especially, remained into the nineteenth century a famous center of pietism among its republican aristocracy.

All this Lutheran pietism had more difficulties than the corresponding and earlier movements in Reformed countries. There was a series of intrigues, heresy charges, court trials, pamphlet wars. In 1695 the theological faculty of Wittenberg, the citadel of scholasticism, charged Spener with 264 errors. The orthodox did not relish the demand for a converted ministry. They considered creedal orthodoxy sufficient and insisted on the authority of the clergy over the pretensions of laymen in conventicles. Private confession and absolution were preferable to the mutual confessions of the pietists, and baptismal regeneration must not be devaluated by the emphasis on conversion. Sanctification of life and perfectionism must not be so urged as to obscure the orthodox doctrine of justification by faith. And the puritanical reaction against sports, theater, and other amusements was most distasteful to the Old Lutherans. They were fond of comparing the pietists to Anabaptists, Quakers, and the Rosicrucians.

THE MORAVIANS. The Unity of the Brethren, or Moravians, is a distinct denomination arising from the pietist movement. Count Zinzendorf, godson to Spener and student at Francke's grammar school, and dedicated to pietistic enterprise from youth, permitted a group of refugees from Roman Catholic oppression in Moravia to settle on his estate at Herrnhut in 1722. He became increasingly interested in the constitution and life of the Bohemian church and fused it with his own Lutheran pietism to form a "society of friends" within the Lutheran church, much as the early Quakers had sought to bridge over denominations in a "society." Like the Quakers the Herrnhuters thus drew on sectarian and spiritualist motives. Zinzendorf, however, injected a dominant note of passion-mysticism, of the sort familiar in Angelus Silesius or the Roman Catholic cult of the Sacred Heart. The language of early Moravian hymns is highly sensuous and sentimental, full of blood, wounds, nail-prints of Jesus, mixed with the sexual imagery of the Bride and Bridegroom metaphor. The Moravians developed a rich liturgy and music, with love feasts, foot washing, the kiss of peace. They had their own costume and language like the Quakers. The Christ-mysticism was carried to the point of declaring Christ the "Chief Elder" of the brotherhood and having him decide, by means of the lot, such questions as ministerial appointments, marriages, or missionary assignments. It was a highly evangelistic movement, as were the first generation Quakers, and the Moravians soon spread over Germany to Holland, England and Ireland, Denmark, Norway, and North America.

This missionary urge, incidentally, spread through the Protestant churches with pietism. It began in Holland with Teelinck and Lodenstein, in England with the Society for the Propagation of the Gospel, and within Lutheranism, first at the Danish court, then at Halle. But of all this Moravians probably supplied the better part, perhaps over half of all Protestant missionaries in the eighteenth century. The missionary zeal may have been related to their concept of universalism and free grace, as with the Methodists. Within the territorial system of Germany the Moravians were concentrated in colonies where permission was granted, but in the religious freedom of the English-speaking world their communities tended to disintegrate. For the latter situation Methodism found the appropriate method of organization.

EVANGELICAL AWAKENING. Methodism was but one phase of a tide of awakenings which appeared with strange similarity in many parts of the English-speaking world in the 1730's and 1740's. In England it was especially the work of the Wesleys and Whitefield, in the American colonies of Edwards and Tennent, in Wales of Griffith. Methodism was to be the most considerable institutional consequence of the whole pietist movement; indeed, the most important ecclesiastical development in Protestantism since Puritanism. It was created by the organizational genius of John Wesley and came to bear the idiosyncrasy of synergism, which distinguished him among the preachers of the awakening generally. Beginning as a society within the Church of England, it grew into a separate church far larger than its parent, and is today the largest single Protestant church in the English-speaking world. At the risk of distorting the picture of the Evangelical awakening as a whole, we will concentrate on Methodism.

METHODISM. Methodism was peculiar among pietist developments in two respects. It was not so much a reaction against a sterile orthodoxy as was the case with Lutheran pietism. Methodism rather arose at a time when the leading churches in

England had already succumbed to rationalism and deism. It was more of a reaction against rationalism than against orthodoxy, in so far as it was polemically determined. It was characteristic of Methodism, however, not to attempt to compete with rationalism in the cultured class. Rather, Methodism consciously directed itself to the poor and unchurched; it was a great home missions movement. And it began just in the middle of the eighteenth century, when the revolution in agricultural, medical, and industrial methods had begun the transformation of English life. The English yeoman class was being swept off the land and concentrated without schools or churches around factories and mines in the great warrens of the Industrial Revolution. Methodism was the means by which this barbarian invasion from within was in great measure evangelized and civilized. In both these latter particulars, consequently, Methodism found its parallels on the Continent in the nineteenth-century "Awakening" rather than in the pietist developments which were contemporary with it. On the Continent rationalism and the Industrial Revolution both made themselves felt later than they did in England.

RELIGIOUS BACKGROUND OF THE WESLEYS. Methodism derived most of its peculiar emphasis and structure from the leadership of the two Wesley brothers, Charles and John, especially the latter. Their development up to 1739 provides an illustration of the currents of eighteenth-century pietism and mysticism. They grew up in a high-church Tory parsonage under the care of a very remarkable mother, Susannah Wesley, who not only bore nineteen children, but also supervised their education and religious development to an extraordinary degree. The boys formed a religious group as students at Oxford, which was called in derision "The Holy Club." They read the Bible and devotional literature, practiced frequent communion, and made a point of charitable visits to the poor and sick. This was a churchly and sacramental pietism, which seems to have been a continuation of the impetus which had led to the foundation, at the beginning of the century, of such societies as the "Society for the Reformation of Manners" (1692), the "Society for the Propagation of Christian Knowledge" (1698), and the "Society for the Propagation of the Gospel" (1701) among high

Anglican Caroline clergy. The group took as their counselor the writer William Law, who lived not far from Oxford. Law was a High Churchman who held to the divine-right tradition of Laud and refused to take the oath to the new Hanoverian line. Law's treatise on *Christian Perfection* (1726) commended an institutional Catholic piety, emphasizing fasting, charities, and self-denial in almost monastic austerity. Wesley took Law as spiritual counselor, consulting him at various times. Impressed by Law's manner of life, Wesley even briefly considered retreat "to the desert" to live the life of contemplation as a recluse. Here was an individualistic quietism in some ways akin to that of Fénelon. And Wesley read the mystics, especially Tauler, Molinos, and the *Theologia Germanica*, which Law had recommended to him. He decided finally to become a missionary to the American Indians, consulting Law again before his departure.

WESLEY'S CONVERSION. From 1735 to 1738 Wesley labored in Georgia with almost complete lack of success. His rigid churchmanship and his attempts to enforce all the canons in the impromptu circumstances of the frontier led to a virtual revolt of his parishioners. He lost confidence in individualist mysticism in such a situation. Even deeper, however, was Wesley's discovery of the inadequacies of his institutionalist piety in crises. On the Atlantic crossing he had traveled with a group of Moravians. In the midst of dangerous storms their quiet trust in God had made a profound impression on Wesley. For Wesley had discovered that with all his strenuous religious exercises, he was still afraid to die. And the secret of the Moravians, he discovered by talking with them, was their experience of salvation by faith. They were sure that they were forgiven and accepted by God even though they had not earned such acceptance and were not worthy of it. John Wesley returned from Georgia in 1738 convinced that man cannot face the crises of life by his own efforts but must look for his rescue to God alone in trust. And even before he felt that he himself had saving faith, he began preaching justification by such faith early in 1738. At an Aldersgate Street prayer meeting in 1738, after hearing read Luther's exposition of Paul on justification by faith, he became assured of his own salvation. Thus he had passed from quietistic mysticism to evangelical pietism. He broke with Law and went to Germany to learn from the Moravians, although in his emphasis he was really more akin to Halle than to the Moravians.

Wesley now found himself buttressed by the Puritan tradition in his own Anglican church. He reacted against the spokesmen of the dominant rational supernaturalism, considering Bull and Archbishop Tillotson to be apostates and Pelagians. The general stream of writers and preachers had gone in this direction, and the Wesleys now stood isolated within Anglicanism. They were told: "You have gone back into the old and exploded Calvinistical expositions of the Christian faith." And indeed John Wesley himself considered that Calvinism was within a "hairsbreadth" of the truth, far closer than the moralistic and rationalistic Anglicanism of his day.

FIELD PREACHING. The most distinctive characteristic of Methodism, however, in contrast to Continental pietism, was the field preaching which began in 1739. Whitefield and Wesley found themselves increasingly barred from Anglican pulpits as their Evangelical enthusiasm became known. Several interviews with the bishops produced little result. It was Whitefield who first broke with the parish system and in February 1739 began to preach in the open to the miners' colony near Bristol, just as he would to the American Indians. In two to three weeks he was preaching to thousands at every appearance. On March 25, for example, he claimed that he had been heard distinctly by twenty-three thousand at once. Overwhelmed by this response he appealed to Wesley to come and help him with the problem of organization, for he had recognized Wesley's remarkable gifts in this capacity. Wesley hesitated for a month before accepting. As a gentleman and an Oxford fellow, his sense of the proprieties was outraged. He felt that it was almost a sin to save a man outside a church. But he finally went to Bristol, where he spent most of 1739 organizing the new converts into "bands" on the pattern of the Moravians.

WESLEY'S CONTROVERSIES. Wesley's strength of mind was such that he soon came to controversy with his associates in the revival. Wesley had apparently carried over synergistic views from his Laudian upbringing, and the teaching of predestination in the growing Methodist societies provoked him to attack. His famous Bristol sermon of 1740 on "Free Grace" opened the public discussion which separated him from Whitefield. Whitefield, however, was to win much more support among Anglican clergy than Wesley, and Anglican Evangelicalism was to be generally Augustinian.

Similarly Wesley came to break in the same year with the Moravians, whose London society he had attended up to 1740. Here the issue was rather churchmanship. The London Moravians moved away from the practices of the Christian life, public worship, sacraments, and the like, arguing that the Spirit alone could save and that the Spirit must be waited upon. They were holding silent meetings like those of the Quakers. Wesley would not thus dispense with the historical and institutional means of grace and took nearly a score with him when he left the Fetter Lane Society to establish a separate group in the Foundry in July 1740.

Thus was Wesley launched on a lifelong mission to the religiously neglected poor of England, the miners, navvies, and factory workers, for whom there was no provision in the state church. Wesley deliberately turned from the class to which he belonged to devote himself to this untouched social frontier. Thereafter he preached an average of three or four sermons a day, the first usually at 5:00 A.M. for over forty years, and, especially in the first decade, at real peril to life and limb. He must have been the center of fifty to a hundred riots, often instigated by a local parson. Some of his assistants were badly hurt, some killed. Wesley himself, however, had an iron will and the complete poise to face down a mob of drunken rowdies. He was a small man, only 5 feet 6 inches tall and weighing about 120 pounds, but his absolute fearlessness carried him through situations which would have unnerved professional soldiers. The accounts in his *Journal* make dramatic reading.

WESLEY'S ORGANIZATION. Wesley was not, like Whitefield, merely a great orator. His genius was for administration. His preaching was always followed by organization. His converts were gathered after six months of probation into bands of about ten members, each with a leader, for regular weekly meetings. Cards of membership were given and every quarter the ranks were rigorously purged of the halfhearted. Wesley raised up a new class of lay readers as helpers, and in time developed a group of itinerant evangelists like himself. The whole system he ruled with autocratic personal authority. When he died in 1780 there were about 136,000 members of the Methodist societies in England and America, but at least a million were associated with the movement.

METHODIST THEOLOGY. The peculiar doctrinal originality of Wesley lay in his view of Christian perfection. Wesley taught his people to expect a real increment of spiritual grace from the Holy Spirit, a "second blessing" after conversion, which would lead them toward perfection in Christian love. This was Wesley's most peculiar and most debated doctrine. This emphasis on perfect love and holiness is perhaps the most characteristic note of Methodist hymns, and hymns were the theological texts and devotional manuals of the Methodists. The Methodist hymns were written mostly by Charles, who, after Watts, was probably the greatest English hymn writer, and one of the greatest in all Christian history.

RUPTURE WITH ANGLICANISM. It is difficult to state the precise moment at which the Methodist societies left the Church of England. Wesley himself to the end insisted that the Methodists were, and should remain, good Anglicans. But he had already moved far to found a new church. The state church made it very hard for him, and if he must choose he would rather see the gospel preached than church order followed. The bishops refused to ordain the preachers he had developed. Many clergy refused the sacraments to parishioners who were known to be Methodists. If the Methodists separated from the Anglican church, they would be free of such persecution and could claim the legal toleration for dissenters. Wesley first broke the canons by ordaining clergy for missions in America and Ireland in the 1780's. Two of them, Coke and Asbury, later assumed the title of "bishop" in America on their own authority. The rupture was made irreparable shortly after Wesley's death. The Conference of one hundred preachers, to whom he had deeded his authority, decided in 1795 to let local societies administer the sacraments independently of the parish church if they so wished. Thereafter it was only a matter of time until separation would be complete.

The history of British Methodism in the century after Wesley's death is a history in the democratization of the authoritarian system Wesley left. From the 1780's to the 1850's there was a long series of schisms in Methodism, virtually all over questions of broadening the centralized clerical control. At the same time the movement as a whole was growing with extraordinary rapidity, both in America and in Britain. At length the structure of the whole was so far democratized that reunion of the various divisions on such a basis became possible.

POLITICAL AND SOCIAL ETHIC. The social and political impact of Methodism passed through a corresponding cycle. Wesley himself never gave up his Toryism. He was opposed to the American and French Revolutions, in contrast to the Presbyterians and Congregationalists and Baptists, the old Puritan denominations. And it was quite in his spirit that early nineteenth-century Methodism earned the hatred of the rising trade-union movement. To this socially and politically conservative impact of Methodism the historian Lecky attributed the fact that England escaped the contagion of the French Revolution. That conclusion is probably overdrawn, but the character of the Methodist influence is clear. It is interesting to note the gradual transfer of Methodism in the nineteenth century from the Tory to the Liberal camp, eventually to become a mainstay of the Labour Party. This development was correlative with the liberalization of the ecclesiastical structure itself, which we have already mentioned.

Methodism, and even more the Evangelical party which remained within the Church of England, made a major contribution to the humanitarian reforms of the eighteenth and nineteenth centuries. We shall have occasion later to notice the contribution to the antislavery movement, prison reform, popular education, and the temperance movement. In all these Methodism carried still further the individualistic tendency of late Puritanism. Attention was concentrated on personal rather than social morals, and sensuality was more feared than selfishness. In this sense Methodism was always a middle-class movement, even though the great majority of its original adherents were from the lower classes. Most modern criticism of "Puritanism" for its asceticism and its individualism has really been occasioned rather by Methodism and similar pietist movements, which broke with Puritanism in these matters. The original Methodist spirit was to live again at the end of the nineteenth century in the work of the Salvation Army.

Chapter 8

ENLIGHTENMENT CHRISTIANITY

We have observed how all across Western Christianity the orthodox systems of the sixteenth and seventeenth centuries were challenged by a new current of intense, personalized, and often anti-intellectualist piety. Orthodoxy had come to seem formal, empty, and sterile; pietism was a revival of the central themes of justification and sanctification, but in practice it tended to simplify and reduce the range of orthodoxy.

RELATION TO CHRISTIAN HUMANISM. About the same time and in the same places another movement of thought and life was also coming to rival orthodoxy in another way. This was the religion of the Enlightenment. In many respects the religion of the Enlightenment was a resumption of the religious humanism of the Renaissance, of men like Ficino, Erasmus, More. In contrast to the disillusionment with which the Reformers viewed natural man and his culture (a disillusionment which found its doctrinal expression in the concept of original sin), the humanist tradition placed a positive estimate on human nature and on the universe generally. It also sought to furnish a religious basis for the broad range of cultural activities. It was an ethical theism, moved to reverence and worship by the ordered magnificence of nature and the capacity of man. Although this ethical theism diverged sharply from Christian orthodoxy, and especially Augustinianism, on such crucial issues as sin and grace, or the uniqueness of biblical revelation, it did not generally attack Christianity. The general disposition, as with the Christian humanists of the Renaissance, was to work within the church, seeking to broaden and spiritualize Christian dogma and to shift the focus of religious interest.

REACTION TO PERSECUTION. Perhaps the most widespread factor in the growth of Enlightenment religion was the mood of revulsion against the embattled creeds. Europe had been ravaged and brutalized by a century of religious warfare. In the shifting tides of battle, in England and Scotland, for example, both sides had tasted persecution. And although a Bossuet still proclaimed for French Roman Catholicism the intention to force an outer conformity at the point of the sword, the toleration which was adopted in England and Holland won the support of an ever-increasing segment even of Roman Catholic laymen. It was necessary in the name of common humanity and mercy to set limits to the power of fanatical clerics. The continuing persecution of such groups as the Salzburgers and Huguenots, as performed in the name of Christ, increasingly turned the stomachs of decent people. The burning or drowning of elderly women accused of witchcraft aroused increasing disgust. From the seventeenth into the nineteenth century the strongest argument for Enlightenment religion was the general experience that religious orthodoxy in power meant massacre, crusades, and persecution. From the days of the great persecution of the Huguenots to the time of French Revolution, religious prejudice and superstition seemed a worse and greater danger than atheism.

In place of persecution Enlightenment religion, with certain exceptions, stood for tolerance. On the negative side this implied a degree of scepticism or relativity with regard to rival theologies. Especially among intellectuals, merchants, and soldiers, who were thrown into frequent contact with other forms of religion, there was an increasing disposition to try to distinguish the elements on which all agreed and to hold to these, while viewing all distinctive tenets with a degree of suspicion. Everywhere the effort was to simplify and standardize, to find a uniform and universal pattern of thought and life, which would be according to "reason" and "nature." Claims to special revelation were increasingly subjected to the arbitrament of common moral standards and religious awareness, and what remained from the sifting was generalized ethical theism in all varieties of the faiths.

NATURAL RELIGION. The geographical discoveries and the

experiences of the colonial powers, especially Holland, England, and France, widened this conversation and comparison of rival faiths outside Christianity altogether. In the Middle Ages and the Reformation, Christendom had seemed to stand in the center of history, with Judaism and Islam on the fringes, each with a particular relation to Christianity. But now the traders and also the missionaries flooded Europe with stories of hundreds of millions of Chinese, Indians, Persians, and other peoples who had never even heard of Christ. The world of historical life expanded tremendously, and the place within it of Christian history contracted to one minority movement. As a result there was an increasing tendency to try to establish the common elements, not merely of the Christian churches, but of all religions. One of the earliest of such efforts was made in the first half of the seventeenth century by the diplomat and soldier, Edward, Lord Herbert of Cherbury, but his work (*De Veritate*, 1624) had its chief influence only when it was translated into English at the beginning of the eighteenth century. By that time there was a considerable literature on the "religion of nature," much strengthened by the syncretistic stoicism of such classical authors as Cicero and Seneca. The substance of it usually consisted of the recognition of a Supreme God, creator and overseer of the universe, who desired of men worship of Himself and justice to their neighbors, and who enforced these desires with rewards and punishments in this world or the next. Here was common ground for the laymen among Roman Catholics, Lutherans, Anglicans, Reformed, and even, apparently, with ancient stoicism or what was then known of Asiatic religions. It was also the beginning of modern philosophy of religion conceived as a substitute for theology.

Free will was an almost universal dogma of Enlightenment religion, and in order to assert it the doctrines of depravity and predestination were almost universally rejected. Man had generally the possibility of ethical achievement and needed chiefly to exert himself to live rationally for the common good. Jesus was venerated, consequently, primarily as a moral example. To think of him as atoning Savior, as did the pietists, did not make sense in this outlook. The loss of the ideas of atonement and justification also took the central meaning from the sacraments, and the whole sacramental concept suffered in all confessions. Sermons were occupied chiefly with philosophizing about Providence, or with prudential morality. Religion came to be less a way of reconciliation with God and more the path to virtue and happiness, whereas the church existed less to glorify God than to make good and useful citizens.

An important source for the construction of such a religion of nature was orthodoxy itself. Many schools of orthodox theology, such as Thomism, made large room for natural or philosophical theology. Even Calvin would have granted that unregenerate man might infer something like Lord Herbert's principles by reason and observation apart from revelation. Late orthodoxy made an ever larger place for such natural theology as an apologetic device. All that was needed to pass to Enlightened theology was to shift the emphasis, to treat this method of thought no longer as a supplement to revealed theology, but as an independent and correlative mode of saving religious knowledge. Much of the debate of the first half of the eighteenth century was between the large majority who still insisted that revealed theology was essential in addition, and those radicals, often called "deists," who considered "natural religion" sufficient.

THE NEW COSMOLOGY. But something new had happened in natural theology in the seventeenth century. This was the century of giants in physics, mechanics, cosmology—the century of Kepler, Galileo, Descartes, Newton. These men evolved a new cosmology, mechanistic and materialistic in tendency, replacing the Ptolemaic scheme with the Copernican. Most of these scientists and philosophers were sincere Christians and had no desire to attack the faith. It may well be, as has been suggested, that the motives for advocating the new cosmology were at first aesthetic and religious, and that it was urged in the face of greater empirical support for the older Ptolemaic view. But in a short time the mathematical mechanistic approach proved itself by the new control over nature, and the practical interest of manipulative power became the strongest support of the new science. So great was this pragmatic interest that the high abstractions of the mathematicians were increasingly taken as the adequate account of reality.

Modern man came to believe in what the scientists told him was nature, "a dull affair, soundless, scentless, colorless; merely the hurrying of material, endlessly, meaninglessly," but predictably.

Now the natural theology built on such a cosmology, as by a Descartes, Newton, or Locke, was intrinsically much less congruent with the world view of the Bible than had been the old cosmology and natural theology. In Aristotelian teleological physics one could find room for frequent divine interventions and for the agency of demons and witches. But against the mechanical regularity of the new world image, the biblical miracles stood out with a stark exceptional irrationality they had never before possessed. Time and space, again, had now exploded to such vast dimensions that the story of salvation from the creation to the Last Judgment contracted to an imperceptible spasm on a grain of sand on the cosmic seashore. Not all these tensions were at once apparent, and the philosophical theologians of this movement, Descartes and Malebranche in France and Holland, Locke and Newton in England, Leibnitz and Wolff in Germany, all honestly undertook to maintain the old parallelism of revealed and natural theology. In the succeeding generations, however, the preponderance of intellect was to be devoted to natural theology, shaped by the peculiar emphases of the new science, and the intrinsic discrepancies with the biblical image of history and the universe were to become ever more distinct. But even the pietists who objected to the Enlightenment view of religion had no alternative world image which they could seriously urge. Pietists too became men of the Enlightenment in significant aspects of their minds and lives.

HOLLAND. Enlightenment religion, much like pietism, began in the Reformed churches of England and Holland in the seventeenth century, and passed thence to Roman Catholic France, Lutheran Germany, and to the British colonies of North America. Holland was the tolerant refuge of the seventeenth century. From France came Descartes and Bayle, from England Locke, while Spinoza grew up in the Jewish refugee colony. Bayle's *Dictionary*, (1695-1697) the "arsenal of all Enlightenment philosophy," marshaled the arguments against persecution and popularized a rational approach to Scripture, explaining away the miracles. Bayle was more of a sceptic than a deist, and Voltaire was to prove his best disciple. The *Encyclopédie* of Diderot and his friends was modeled on Bayle; some of it, indeed, was little more than a rewrite. The *Allgemeine Deutsche Bibliothek* was to be a similar effort in Germany. Another, although less extensive, Dutch publication, which attacked the ideas of demonic possession, witches, magic, miracles, and even the devil himself, was Bekker's *Bewitched World*.

ENGLAND. Across the Channel, meanwhile, the Cambridge Platonists showed the development of natural theology in late Puritanism. The representative figure in England, however, was John Locke, who dominated the whole eighteenth century in this, as in so many other respects. His *Reasonableness of Christianity* (1695) argued that the essence of Christianity lies in its ethics, and its excellence as a religion consists precisely in the fact that it coincides with the findings of reason unassisted by revelation. On the other hand Locke had no intention of dispensing with the corroboration of revelation. When John Toland, the deist, sought to push Locke's arguments to the point of saying that the revealed elements were superfluous (*Christianity not Mysterious*, 1696), Locke repudiated him sharply. For Locke the findings of natural theology remain somewhat uncertain and are in any case beyond the grasp of the common people. It is still essential to accept Jesus Christ as Messiah and King, to acknowledge thankfully the further religious knowledge he gives us, and to obey his ethical teachings. In this position Locke was followed by the moderate clergy and the majority of the laity. Archbishop Tillotson, the most renowned preacher of the day, similarly maintained that virtually all the substance of Christianity was identical with natural religion save the two sacraments and praying in Christ's name, and these were less important than the moral elements.

DEISM. The so-called "deist" literature which followed the writings of Locke and Toland was written largely by amateurs in theology who found the weight of scholarship and general opinion against them. On the other hand they forced into the open the internal tensions of the reconciliation, which men like Locke and Tillotson were seeking to effect. Toland and Tindal argued in effect that natural theology was an adequate basis for religion apart from Christian revelation. The second generation of deists opened an attack on revelation by beginning to apply to the biblical material the laws and standards of the new cosmology.

In this debate, which ran through the first third of the eighteenth century, the deists had one advantage. Both sides viewed revelation mechanically and literally, as a body of propositions of the same character as scientific findings. Revelation was information about things of which we would otherwise be ignorant. Immortality, for example, to which even the defenders of the faith had generally reduced eschatology, is not contrary to natural knowledge. It can be neither proved nor disproved by science. It can only be proved, consequently, in terms of the credentials of the authority who maintains the proposition. Thus the debate turned chiefly on the credentials for the authority of Jesus. These external evidences of religion were agreed to be twofold—the fulfillment of Old Testament prophecies, and the miracles which seemed to demonstrate superhuman powers.

It had never occurred to Locke, apparently, to doubt the inspiration of the Bible. And because Jesus Christ had fulfilled the messianic prophecies of the Old Testament, and because he demonstrated miraculous cures, raised the dead, turned water into wine, therefore we should believe that he was the Messiah and do what he teaches, especially since it is also what reason teaches. In fact accepting him as the Messiah may even compensate for some of our moral inadequacies.

This kind of accreditation of Jesus' authority, however, was undermined in the 1720's and 1730's by deist criticism. Anthony Collins, who became after Toland the most representative deist, launched a furious debate on the prophecies. Collins' contention was that when one interprets the Old Testament prophecies literally and exactly, one finds that they were not in fact fulfilled by Jesus. Many of the "rational supernaturalists" virtually gave up the argument from prophecy after this debate, staking everything on miracles. But just at this time a popular pamphleteer named Woolston was publishing half a dozen acute and very irreverent pamphlets against the argument from miracles. The miracles, he said, were the marks rather of a sorcerer or wizard, if they were to be believed at all, and prove nothing as to Jesus' messiahship. In all this debate the possibility of miracle was hardly ever denied on the basis of the universality of natural law. But such doubt was thrown on the evidence that the miracles had occurred, and on the contention that an unexplained phenomenon must be taken as a proof of God's intervention, that the value of miracles as a proof of the Christian revelation was largely destroyed. David Hume's *Essay on Miracles* (1748) was the climax of this discussion. A later generation is most struck in this debate by the extent to which the authority of the biblical account was still assumed by both sides, and by the wooden literal-mindedness with which both sides read mythical language as if it were the scientific observations of a member of the Royal Society.

By the 1740's the deist controversy was virtually over in England. In the popular mind the defenders of revelation had won the battle. In a sense they had. They had not answered satisfactorily all the critical attacks of the deists, but they had demonstrated that in the Christian revelation there was still a secret of vitality not to be found in natural religion freed of revelation. They had also shown that ethical theism needed such support, for deism failed not in its critical aspects so much as in the effort to constitute a substitute faith. It was a paper construct and the more acute minds had found it out. David Hume's *Dialogues on Natural Religion* demonstrated that the "religion of nature" had assumed everything that needed to be proved and had, in fact, no better case than the religion of revelation. Bishop Butler, in a somewhat different way, argued also that natural religion is as impenetrable and as mysterious as positive Christianity. The mystic William Law, much influenced later in life by Jakob Boehme, repudiated all natural theology. Man is rather in the position of Job, he said, and scarcely qualified to tell his Creator what is and what is not reasonable. Henry Dodwell's *Christianity not Founded on Argument* (1742) contested the whole enterprise of rational demonstration, referring Christianity rather to inner illumination. And from the other side the sceptical Epicurean Mandeville cut the nerve of deism and attacked even Christian morals. What was happening in England, at least with the ablest, was that deism was proving an untenable stopping place. The real choices were between Christian revelation and a real scepticism. The Evangelical Awakening caught up most of the serious religion of the second half of the century, and those inclined to scepticism, like Hume, turned attention rather to more practically useful activities.

FRENCH DEISM. But just as the debate over deism was dying out in England, it was again resumed in France. Voltaire had visited England and was pleased to find it the "most irreligious country" in the world. Back in France he became the chief exponent and popularizer of deist ideas, sharpened by his malice. None of the English critics of revealed religion had possessed the abilities of Voltaire or secured a comparable success. But in France the defenders of revelation were to be as obscure as had been its English attackers, and the champions of natural religion were to be the fashionable writers of the day. The political, economic, and cultural power of the Roman Church aroused more hostility than was occasioned by Christianity as organized in Great Britain. The rigidity of the Roman system also precluded the hope held by "Christian deists" in England and in Germany of expurgating Christianity. To Voltaire, who had been brought up by Jesuits, the pattern held together —priestly exploitation, superstition, intolerance, persecution. "I am no Christian," he said, "but only because I can love God better without being one." He hoped to see the last king strangled in the bowels of the last priest. Such hatred and violence were virtually unknown in Protestant countries.

In Roman Catholicism, however, there were theologians comparable to such "rational supernaturalists" as Locke and Tillotson, who were seeking to accommodate the new cosmology and the new worldly ethics. Chief among them were the Jesuits. Already at the beginning of the eighteenth century Massillon, the great preacher, had observed how Christianity was being toned down and made more "reasonable." As has been said, the Roman Catholics required a constitution of God before they did of the king. The sovereign God of Christian tradition was reduced in Molinist theology to a limited amiable power, the architect of a perfect universe, and the somewhat indulgent judge of men. The Fall was so interpreted as effectually to interpret it away, and an ethics was built on what amounted to free will and man's natural goodness. To the Jansenists, for whom the ancient dimensions of glory and abasement, terror and ecstasy were still real, the Jesuits were brothers under the skin to the deists, and it was indeed true that very little separated Rousseau from the "enlightened" Roman Catholic and Reformed clergy of his day. The Jesuits seemed to the Jansenists willing to reduce religion to merely one sacramental sphere, whereas in most matters a man might think and act as "natural" man alone, without reference to Christianity. They did insist on the authority of the church, and they wanted men in the confessional. To scare people to the latter they went in for sensational hell-fire preaching. A minimum of ritual conformity was extracted from many by the fear that there *might* be something to the church's teaching about hell. But few were thus brought to the love of God. A comparable criticism would apply to many Protestant revivalists of the eighteenth century.

CRITICISM OF TRADITION. The locus of what was left of revelation differed significantly in its Protestant and Roman Catholic forms. In practice Protestants showed ever less sense for tradition and rested their case on "the Bible and the Bible alone." We have seen how the deists then treated the Bible. The Roman Catholics, on the other hand, moved away from the unstable dualism of Trent. In practice the "equal" authority of Bible and tradition in Roman Catholicism came to mean ever less room for any independent norm in Scripture. And now "tradition" also, in the hands of theologians like Hardouin and Berryer, came to change meaning. It was increasingly less of an appeal to the actual mind of the ancient church as historically ascertainable—this could be embarrassing—and increasingly more the reference to what the hierarchy now teaches. This present teaching authority tended to be exalted beyond correction by either Scripture or actual tradition, and the way to the Vatican decrees of 1870 was already opening.

GERMAN NEOLOGY. The systematic exploration of the questions occasioned by the tensions between traditional dogmatics and the new natural theology and cosmology took place chiefly in Germany. German theological scholarship took over leadership from the English and Dutch about the middle of the eighteenth century. In Germany Leibnitz' popularizer, Wolff, played the role Locke had exercised in England in providing a philosophical apologetic conceived as parallel to revealed theology. Wolff's banishment only added luster to his triumph in the academic world in the 1730's. The optimistic affirmation of the spacious firmament on high as the proclamation of the divine architect was popularized by Gellert, the most widely read poet of the day. Mosheim, the "German Tillotson," represented the new style in preaching and opened new paths for church history, freeing it to a large extent from miracles and divine interventions, and treating it as of one texture with general history.

The same process was now applied to the Bible itself by Semler, Ernesti, and Michaelis. The doctrine of inspiration was retained, but the theory that the Holy Spirit had "accommodated" his revelations to the mentality and capacities of his human agents gave occasion for careful historical and literary analysis of the biblical writings in their human setting. The definitive substitution of this method of interpretation for the old allegorical and typological exegesis was finally initiated by these scholars. The discipline of biblical theology thus came into existence as a corrective to the old dogmatic exegesis. In similar fashion, a new discipline of historical theology challenged dogmatics with a reinterpretation of the dogmas and doctrines of church history. The "neologians," as these theologians of the German Enlightenment were called, were often quite conservative in their personal religious life. Semler, for example, opposed the deist attempt to dispose of revelation, and supported Wöllner's edict (see above, p. 51f).

The preachers were, if anything, more radical than the theologians. From the 1770's members of the Enlightened school felt themselves to have the initiative in church life. Men like Spalding and Sack stressed in the pulpit the view that the teaching of the Bible was natural theology and morals. With the minimizing of any distinctive revelation, worship came to be dominated by a didactic sermon. Attendance at communion declined. Church discipline vanished. The authority of the ministerial office was greatly weakened, and church attendance tended to depend upon the personality of the preacher. Relics of medieval Catholic customs—exorcism, vestments, private confession, the eternal lamp—passed away. There was widespread experimenting with new "creeds" for liturgical use and much revision of hymnals, partly for form and language, partly for content. That this type of utilitarian ethical theism was very popular can be seen from the success of the devotional writings of such men as Spalding and Zschokke. Zschokke's *Hours of Devotion* passed through more editions than any comparable writings save those of Arndt. For that matter, only Luther and Paul Gerhardt have by their hymns exceeded the popularity of Gellert.

DEISM IN GERMANY. There were also real deists in Germany. Young Frederick II of Prussia idolized Voltaire and brought him to his palace at Potsdam, where he became the center of a circle of "Berlin Frenchmen." In the 1740's also English deist writings, such as Tindal's *Christianity as Old as the Creation*, were translated. The critique of biblical miracles and prophecies was represented in Germany by a Hamburg schoolteacher, Reimarus, some of whose work was published by Lessing under the title, *The Wolfenbüttel Fragments*. Lessing himself was a Christian deist, and the Christian deist program is expressed by Kant's title, *Religion Within the Bounds of Reason Alone* (1793), although Kant pushed the whole discussion to a new phase. For Kant Christianity was the perfect natural religion, possessing in Jesus Christ the ideal example. It needs no fulfillments of prophecy or miracles as evidences, nor do any other religious duties beyond the moral belong to it. But Kant rejected the popular natural theology with its demonstrations of God. And he gave up also the eudaemonism and optimism. Men should do right because it is right, not for the sake of reward or fear of punishment.

EARLY IDEALISM. At the other extreme, meanwhile, pietists were striking a new alliance with orthodoxy against deists and rational supernaturalists alike. But they lacked an alternative cosmology and philosophy and were unable to fight on the whole front. The striking new development in Germany, however, which was not paralleled in Great Britain or France, was the rise of just such a new metaphysics and a new total view of life and culture. Even before the French Revolution a remarkable group of poets, musicians, artists, and philosophers was bringing into existence what we may call the mental world of German idealism. Goethe, Schiller, Klopstock, Lessing, Hamann, Herder, and Jacobi opened in various ways the movement which reached its philosophical climax in Kant, Fichte, Hegel, and Schelling. The movement was religiously syncretistic, with complicated relations to Christianity. It did continue the relation of religion to culture which the Enlightenment theologians had attempted in their way, but in its understanding of the nature of religion itself, idealism learned more from the pietist tradition than from the enlightened moralizers. As we shall see (Chapter 13), German idealism brought about the greatest revolution in Christian thought in modern history, superseding or transforming the old debates of Enlightenment theologians, pietists, and orthodox biblicists.

THE RELIGION OF PROGRESS. In France and Great Britain, meanwhile, interest shifted, as we have seen, from the discussion of natural religion. Among the ablest thinkers confidence in the rational construction of religion had been shaken. In France as in England deism ceased to be a serious option, and the focus of debate by the 1770's was rather between revealed theology and the out-and-out materialism and atheism of Helvetius and Holbach. The *philosophes* also turned, as in England, from philosophy and theology to more directly practical subjects, political theory, economics, education, and history written as reforming propaganda. In place of the complacency of the early Enlightenment, optimism was increasingly turned to the future, in a secularized eschatology of "progress." In contrast to the views of history of the Asiatic religions, or even those of the Greeks and Romans, the *philosophes* kept the Judaeo-Christian sense of history as an irreversible forward movement toward a fulfillment. In place of the new Jerusalem, however, they looked forward to a social Utopia on this earth. The desire for the gratitude of posterity replaced the hope of immortality as a sanction for service to humanity. Such eschatological optimism fired the crusading spirit, which built up to the French Revolution. American deists like Franklin and Jefferson were partly influenced by these French developments.

In the French Revolution, however, certain significant sociological shifts became apparent. It is important to remember that the theological and philosophical discussions of the eighteenth century were carried on in a society dominated by the cultured aristocracy. Even a deist like Voltaire believed orthodoxy good for the lower classes and built a chapel for them on his estate. But when fashions of thought change, they tend to work down the cultural levels. The intellectual leaders and the aristocracy might abandon deism and natural religion, but the Revolution showed that these ideas were now become a living force in the middle classes generally. A figure like Tom Paine, for example, seemed like one of the forgotten deist pamphleteers of the early eighteenth century come again to the birth. And for the first half of the nineteenth century the middle classes were to be the chief bearers of rationalism, natural religion, and deism, whereas the aristocracy, terrified by the Revolution, were become as punctiliously devout in public as their fathers and grandfathers had been sceptical. The revolutions of 1848, again, were to mark another major shift in the movement of Enlightenment ideas down the social and cultural scale, this time to the working classes where they were to live on into the twentieth century.

Part II

FROM THE FRENCH
REVOLUTION TO 1870

Chapter 9

THE FRENCH REVOLUTION

Although it does not constitute a period in the English-speaking world, the French Revolution, in its total implications and its sporadic recurrences, defines the greatest crisis since the Reformation in modern Continental history, as well as in Roman Catholicism. It marks the emergence in power in the Roman and Latin world of liberalism and nationalism. Those two forces were to spread from France over all the Continent and Latin America and to dominate much of the history of the nineteenth century. As we have seen, the former of these, at least, had for a century and a half before the French Revolution, been in fruitful interplay with the Puritan denominations of the English-speaking world. Roman Catholicism, however, was to find political liberalism unassimilable, and from the French Revolution into the twentieth century the Roman Catholic lands have been generally divided by a profound antagonism which has dominated their political and cultural development. Similarly, the internal development of Roman Catholicism proper was primarily shaped in the century after 1789 by the defensive reaction of the Church against liberalism. As the greatest nineteenth-century Roman Catholic historian, Döllinger, put it, the spirit and structure of modern Roman Catholicism are to be understood primarily in terms of its reaction to two movements—the Reformation and the Revolution.

Estates-General to National Assembly. The immediate cause of the French Revolution was the bankruptcy of the French state. The French nobility drove the government of Louis XVI to desperation on the fiscal problem, and the king, "handing in his resignation," convoked the Estates-General for the first time in 175 years. The elections of this assembly and the "reports of grievance and advice" collected at the same time caused great popular excitement and were interpreted in the light of the theories of the American Revolution of the preceding decade. These ideas altered in character and gained tremendously in scope as they were translated from a little backwoods rebellion to become the ideology of revolution in the greatest state of Western civilization. As a result the "rights of man" were to spread over all Europe and, in the twentieth century, over Asia.

In its first phase, the Revolution was the work of the *bourgeoisie* of the Third Estate, the representatives of the financial, commercial, industrial, and professional class (with the temporary but indispensable help of town artisans and peasants) against the political, legal, and economic privileges of the nobility in church and state. Their original intent was to emulate the constitutional monarchy which the Puritan bourgeois revolution had given England. The two great achievements of this first phase were the repudiation of feudal dues on the famous night of August 4, 1789, and the "Declaration of the Rights of Man," which cleared the ground for a new constitution based on civil and fiscal equality. The unwilling king, virtually a captive, was constrained to consent to these changes.

This first stage of the Revolution could not have been accomplished without the support of the parish priests. It was the curés who broke the united front of the two privileged Estates and enabled the Third Estate to make good its claim to represent the nation. The Assembly showed its gratitude and respect for the clergy. The abolition of feudal dues in August, to be sure, deprived the pope of his annates. At the same time the whole clergy was deprived of tithes, which were the source of nearly half of the church income. The bishops, who were all nobles, were displeased with the loss of privileges, but many of the lower clergy looked forward to the greater security of the money commutations. "Te Deums" were ordered in all churches.

The religious provisions of the "Declaration of the Rights of Man" occasioned more debate than any other articles. No one dreamed of a separation of church and state; even the *philoso-*

phes took a Roman Catholic establishment for granted. The Assembly acknowledged only one national religion, the Roman Catholic. There could be no full religious liberty, consequently, among human rights in France, although liberty of conscience was probably the basic liberty in the Anglo-American countries. Protestants were, however, granted the right of public worship for the first time. The *cahiers* had shown a mixed reaction on this point, some urging toleration, others intolerance.

PAPAL CONDEMNATION OF THE RIGHTS OF MAN. For reasons of his own Pius VI delayed for months any indication as to his attitude to the loss of his annates, or to the "Declaration of the Rights of Man." He foresaw that popular sovereignty, if it won its way, would deprive him of his feudal holdings in French lands, Avignon and Venaissin. On March 29, 1790, however, he delivered himself at some length in a secret consistory on the "Declaration of the Rights of Man." This pronouncement is interesting as the first in the long list of papal condemnations of liberalism and democracy in the nineteenth and twentieth centuries. The Pope rejected several of the Rights in particular, for example, that the law represented the general will; that all citizens should be represented in the formation of legislation; that religious opinion should have any rights; and that non-Roman Catholics should have equal right to municipal, civil, and military offices. The ideas of popular sovereignty and government responsible to the people were condemned along with toleration of non-Roman Catholics. The papal court aligned Roman Catholicism with the traditions of absolutism and inherited rights of rule, as well as with the traditional social classes.

NATIONALIZATION OF CHURCH LANDS. The National Assembly, in the meantime, had passed other legislation which profoundly changed the relation of the church to the nation. As we have seen, the clergy lost nearly half of their revenues with the renunciation of tithes and fees in August of 1789. In the following months the other main economic basis of the church, its landed property, amounting to about a fifth of that of all France, was nationalized. In November Mirabeau's bill, declaring all church property at the disposal of the state, became law; on this new security the Assembly at once issued the *assignats* by which it hoped to stave off financial collapse. The parish clergy were promised a decent living from state salaries to replace the pitiful recompense from church revenues they had hitherto been assigned by their prelates. Most of them welcomed the change, which meant perhaps a doubling of income. The ecclesiastical nobility, however, resented their conversion from the mastership of independent wealth to the status of a civil bureaucracy on salary. In December the Assembly ordered the sale of extensive church holdings and the bitterness of the prelatical nobles ran high.

RESTRICTIONS ON MONASTICISM. Over half the churches' wealth was held nominally by the monks and nuns, who were notoriously inferior to the parish clergy in morality and industry. For two or three decades before the Revolution a commission had been at work closing down moribund orders of monastics. In February 1790, the Assembly declared monastic vows taken after October 28, 1789 suspended, and refused to allow any more to be taken. Individuals were permitted to leave with liberal pensions, and houses were provided for those who could not leave. This decree conformed to a widespread opinion as revealed in the *cahiers* and occasioned no great stir. In April 1790, complete expropriation made all the clergy salaried functionaries. Nuns, however, were not affected by these laws. The Assembly, reflecting national opinion, was inclined to help the overworked and underpaid parish clergy at the expense of the wealthy and idle monks and the prelatical nobility.

CIVIL CONSTITUTION OF THE CLERGY. In May of 1790 came the report of the *comité ecclésiastique* appointed in August 1789 by the Assembly to arrange church affairs in accordance with the new constitution of the state. The members of this commission, in conformity with most of the *cahiers*, were strongly Gallican, and in some respects the "Civil Constitution of the Clergy" which was finally voted in July 12, 1790, was a return to the system of the fifteenth-century "Pragmatic Sanction." The committee conceived that without touching dogma, it was returning from innovations to "the discipline of the early Church." The most important provisions of the Civil Constitution were the following:

1. The French state assumed all stipends and pensions and lodgings from tax funds. The level of salaries was relatively high for upper clergy and very fair for the lower—a real gain.

2. The personnel and offices of the clergy were reduced. The number of dioceses was cut from 139 to 83 to conform with the political divisions of the nation into *départements*. These were grouped into ten metropolitan areas. The number of parish clergy was also considerably reduced. It is understandable that some fifty prelates were opposed to this reform.

3. The government of the church was notably presbyterianized. Bishops and curés, for example, were henceforth to be elected rather than appointed. All civil voters were eligible to share in these elections which were to take place after the parochial mass. This provision assumed that all French voters were Roman Catholic and the Assembly did not recognize how its toleration of Protestantism qualified this assumption.

Newly elected bishops, moreover, were to be canonically instituted, not by the pope, but by one of the metropolitans. They should write the pope in token of communion, but not to apply for confirmation. Thus the patronage which king and pope had shared by the Concordat of Bologna since 1516 was returned to the election of the body of the faithful. The lower clergy were given a chance of advancement on merit. *Vicaires*, also, were given a certain protection, since they could be removed only by showing of cause.

The debates over this Constitution in the Assembly had lasted six weeks and when it was passed the clergy was divided on it. A considerable majority of the lower clergy accepted it at first, but only 5 of 135 bishops paid attention to it. The rest held onto their old dioceses as if there were no law. The pope also urged Louis XVI to refuse his authorization to the Constitution, but the king felt obliged, against his own desires, to accept it. On October 30, 1790 a manifesto was issued by a cardinal and twenty-nine bishops, holding that the civil power could not change the constitution of the church, and that although metropolitan institution of bishops was traditional, it had not been followed since the sixteenth century, and that the election of priests was schismatic. Here was a conflict of jurisdiction, a denial of the Assembly's right to reorganize the church. The Assembly now undertook to force the issue by requiring an oath "to the law and constitution," first from all its own clerical members in November 1790, and, two months later, from all French clergy. Whether or not this oath included the specific provisions of the "Civil Constitution of the Clergy" was ambiguous. Apparently about three-fifths of the clergy took the oath.

SCHISM OF JURORS AND NONJURORS. The pope was slow to express himself, as he had been on the "Declaration of the Rights of Man." In the spring of 1791 he complained of the Civil Constitution, implored the bishops not to take the oath, and reprimanded Bishops Talleyrand and Lomenie de Brienne for doing so. In February Talleyrand, Gobel, and another bishop had consecrated two "constitutional" bishops. In April the pope annulled all elections to clerical office, called the Constitution "heretical and schismatical" and ordered signers to retract within forty days. Many who had taken the oath now felt constrained to retract it, and the church was sharply divided into "jurors" and "nonjurors"—a schism which was to last, in fact, for a decade. Diplomatic relations between France and the Vatican were broken off and the pope's effigy was burnt at the Palais Royal. The oath to the "Civil Constitution of the Clergy" was proving to be the major occasion of civil war. And the liberal lower clergy were given the hard choice between their political sympathies and church discipline. Many felt obliged to fight constitutionalism for the liberty of the church. Talleyrand later described the Civil Constitution as "the greatest political mistake of the National Assembly."

The laity were divided in support of jurors and nonjurors, although the proportion of papalists among the laity was apparently much smaller than among the clergy. In many towns the revolutionary governments were more antipapalist than the Assembly. Popular opinion in Paris also did not allow the papalists to hold parish churches. Lay supporters of the papalists, however, crowded into the chapels of the convents where nonjurors could still officiate, and sacraments were occasionally performed in the fields and woods. The royal family, with its preference for the papalists, caused that group to be identified more closely with the counterrevolution, especially as a result of the king's attempted flight in July. In August 1791, the Assembly put an article guaranteeing freedom of worship into the Constitution, but popular passions were not to be restrained by law, and there was in fact less and less liberty for nonjurors during the course of 1791. In November parish churches were decreed closed to all but official worship, and although the king refused his sanction the decree was enforced in most of the *départements*. Clerics who refused the normal civic oath could now be temporarily banished from their residence.

WAR, DEPOSITION OF THE KING, NATIONAL CONVENTION. The second great phase of the Revolution began in 1792 and ran through the Convention and the Terror of 1793-1794. This period is to be understood primarily in terms of war psychology. France found herself attacked in the spring of 1792 and involved in desperate struggle for survival against a diplomatic and military coalition whose moving spirit was popularly conceived to be Pius VI. The king was deposed and the republican Convention organized. In May a more severe decree had provided that nonjurors could be banished on a petition signed by twenty names. In August a new oath, "I swear to maintain liberty and equality," was required of all priests. This oath, without reference to the "Civil Constitution of the Clergy," let many in. But those who refused it were given fifteen days to get out of France, and all over the country there were abuse and even lynching of *emigrés* at the end of August and the beginning of September. A large portion of the one thousand to two thousand victims of the "September massacres" were nonjuring priests. About forty thousand priests were driven out and many became propagandists against the Revolution outside of France. The government of the National Convention was inaugurated at the end of September 1792 and proceeded to extend the August decree to monastic clergy and lay brothers.

The Convention began with the intention of continuing the Gallican establishment. It rejected motions at the end of 1792 to abolish the budget of worship and, in the spring of 1793, clergy were exempted from military service. The Constitution of 1793 proclaimed religious liberty. The single most important cause of the radical switch of policy to the attempt to wipe out Christianity was the counterrevolution in La Vendée in the spring of 1793. Nonjuring priests were some of the most active leaders in the "Royal and Catholic Armies," as they called themselves, who attacked the Convention in the rear while it was threatened with invasion. Without the revolt in La Vendée there might have been no "worship of Reason." Savage penalties were now decreed. All nonjurors were to be shipped to Guiana and death sentences were stipulated for any priests involved in the uprising.

It was in the late summer and autumn, however, that the great persecution of the church came. This persecution made manifest for the first time in the modern world that revival of pagan tribalism which is today, perhaps, the real religion of the majority of men in all Western culture. If Continental liberalism is the enduring heritage of the first phase of the Revolution, that of the second is nationalism.

RELIGION OF NATIONALISM. The religion of patriotism had been progressively penetrating and dominating Roman Catholicism through the earlier stages of the Revolution, despite the Gallican establishment. In 1790, for example, the anniversary of the taking of the Bastille was everywhere celebrated by ceremonies in which the French nation consciously covenanted as a religious community. In every commune on that day the oath to *la patrie* was taken, often around an open-air altar, and generally preceded by a mass.

The Church of St. Genevieve was converted into a civil Pantheon, to hold the ashes of Voltaire. In 1792 the Paris police did not require the usual decoration of houses for the Corpus Christi procession in June. Shops could stay open and the National Guard was not to be used. The Legislative Assembly decided that its members might take part, but only in their capacity as private individuals. Here was a virtual secularization of the state, at least in the capital, despite the constitutional establishment, and the substitution of a cult of *la patrie*.

Conscious substitution of the new faith for the old began in the provinces in the summer of 1793. The first purely civic festival came in August of that year, when libations were poured out to a statue of "nature." In the Ile de France Brutus replaced St. Blaise. Similarly, busts of Marat and Le Peletier replaced those of saints in homes. Various district representatives now began to parade to the bar of the Convention to announce their apostasy from Christianity. Bishop Gobel and eleven priests took off cross and ring and put on red cap in the Convention. Most ecclesiastical members of the Convention, including the Protestant pastors, did the same. Pastor Marron brought in four silver communion chalices, condemned theology, and paid tribute to the "eternal and immortal principles of fact and morality." The abbé Grégoire alone conspicuously resisted the hysteria of abdications in the Convention. Numerous resignations of vicars and curés occurred all over France. The Convention printed Chenier's speech which recommended: "one universal religion . . . the altar of our country, our mother and our deity."

The report of the Committee on the Republican calendar revision in October 1793 was partly anti-Christian. They recommended the elimination of saints days and Sundays as symbols of the Christian philosophy of history, and the substitution of holidays for purely naturalistic objects of "true national wealth." Foreigners were horrified.

STATE EDUCATION. The center of anti-Roman Catholic propaganda was now the Committee of Public Instruction, which was organizing a national system of education and which recommended that no more clergy or nuns were to be appointed as teachers. With this organization of a national school system began what has become the hottest single issue of church and state controversy in nearly every Western country.

The culmination of this movement came with the conversion of the churches into "temples of reason" which could with equal accuracy be called "temples of nationalism." The movement took its cue from the famous ceremony at Notre Dame in Paris. The statue of the Virgin was replaced by an actress in blue and to her Chenier's hymn was addressed:

> Come holy liberty, inhabit this temple
> Become the goddess of the French people.

When the Paris commune asked to have Notre Dame permanently converted to a "Temple of Reason," the Convention gave its permission. The whole ceremony was repeated for the Convention, whose president and secretary embraced the "Goddess of Liberty." Some two thousand towns similarly turned their parish churches into "temples of reason" and even the rural communes followed suit. In Paris the ceremony had been rather playful, but in the provinces it was a sincere affirmation of deism and patriotism, and the Goddesses of Reason were the flower of the *bourgeoisie*. The Convention followed rather than led the movement.

Roman Catholic worship continued over the winter in private chapels, and when these were closed in the spring of 1794, it was largely secret. Sometimes country people met with the schoolmaster to sing hymns. In March 1794 mass was still said openly in 150 parishes. But the greater part of the French nation had broken the habit of Christian religious observance and seemed indifferent to its loss.

In June of 1794 occurred another pageant of religion, Robespierre's *Fête de l'être suprême*. A certain reaction from atheism was expressed in this deistic celebration of (1) God and providence, (2) immortality, (3) rewards and punishments, and (4) sanctity of the social contract and the laws. But the people did not distinguish between the worship of reason and that of the Supreme Being. In either case the real object of devotion was *la patrie*. A new inscription was placed in the "temples": "The French people recognize the existence of the Supreme Being and the immortality of the soul." During the famous festival staged by the artist David, the statue of atheism was burned and Robespierre pontificated amid sarcastic mutterings by his Jacobin colleagues. The closing of Christian churches increased after this festival. In the Convention Grégoire alone dared defend the religion which a few months before had been that of the nation.

"DISDAINFUL TOLERATION." Late in 1794 the direct attack on Christianity by doctrinaire deistic nationalism passed into a new phase which shortly came to resemble the American system of separation of church and state with religious liberty. As was to be the case with the U.S.S.R. in the twentieth century, the Convention found it advantageous in its foreign negotiations not to seem too irreligious. A new policy of killing Christianity off by cultural strangulation was devised. Clerical salaries, which had been paid during the Terror, were cut off in September 1794. The crucial pressure now was to be in the field of education, in which the new free and compulsory elementary schools were purged of religious teaching. Instead was substituted the study of the "Declaration of the Rights of Man," the Constitution, and "Republican morals." Normal schools and a polytechnical school had been organized to complete the system. Thus it was hoped that by a monopoly on indoctrination of the new generation, something like Rousseau's "civic religion" could replace Christianity. This policy of "disdainful toleration" was indicated by the speech presenting what was to become the Law of Separation in February 1795. According to this policy there should be no more subsidy of the churches, nor any more insults to public worship. In September liberty of religion and separation were reaffirmed, and provision made against the dominance of any one church. The new Constitution of the "Year III" also defined the Separation in Article 354. This system lasted for seven years, with some persecutions on the part of an anticlerical Directory, but not enough to prevent the flourishing of religion. One of the chief impositions on religion was the *culte decadaire*, a reorganization of the calendar introducing a ten-day week and requiring Sunday work.

RELIGIOUS REVIVAL. Under this regime there was a startling revival of religion, beginning in the winter of 1794-1795. Grégoire gave the signal by making a long speech for liberty of worship in the Convention, and churches in his diocese reopened on New Year's of 1795. An almost spontaneous revival of Catholicism appeared everywhere, both among the Constitutional clergy as led by Grégoire, and among the nonjurors, who were, on the whole, more zealous and better supplied with funds. Grégoire again was the first bishop to dare resume episcopal functions and his pastoral letter announcing a reconciliation of Christianity and the Revolution created a sensation. The Constitutional clergy reorganized on the basis of the Civil Constitution and the four Gallican Articles, but without state support. They convoked a national Council in 1797. Whereas the *bourgeoisie* favored the Constitutional clergy, the people, especially the peasants, preferred the papalists, and emigrant priests came back in crowds. The Protestants also resumed public worship. By 1797 most of the old parishes were restored.

The papalist Roman Catholics, however, were split again between the supporters of Louis XVIII, and those prepared to accept the Revolution. Thus there were under the system of separation three distinct groups of Roman Catholics, as well as Reformed, Lutherans, Jews, "theo-philanthropists," and the organized freethinkers. Above all and free of all was the laic neutral state maintaining a rationalistic and nationalistic ideology in the new primary schools. This was the system Bonaparte inherited and destroyed after seven years to re-establish a pope whom he expected to make his personal chaplain.

Chapter 10

NAPOLEON AND THE CONCORDATS

The French Revolution had violently ruptured the organic unity of the Roman Catholic Church and the most powerful state in the Roman Catholic orbit. It was Napoleon, however, who was to add two further dimensions to this great transformation. First, by his attempts at the conquest of all Europe, he established many of the ideas of the French Revolution in numerous other states; what had happened in France thus became a model for the reorganization of much of the Continent. Secondly, Napoleon effected the reconciliation of the revolutionary program with the system of the old regime into a kind of *modus vivendi* which, in many respects, was to endure for generations after him. No epoch of modern European history has been so overshadowed by the achievements of one man as the first half generation of the nineteenth century. Napoleon was, as Tocqueville said, "as great as a man can be without virtue."

EXTENSION OF THE REVOLUTION. The diffusion of revolutionary ideas, to be sure, had begun before Napoleon's *coup d'état* in 1799. The very success with which the French governments of the Convention and the Directory waged war singlehanded against most of Europe showed that they represented ideas and forces effective outside France. Even militarily the new type of conscript citizen army was a far more formidable machine than the paid troops of the embattled princes. The French were fighting governments, but governments whose peoples were not always completely hostile to the revolutionary ideas. A considerable section of Western Europe had passed through a social and cultural development similar to that of France. The intellectuals of Italy, the Rhine-

123

lands, the Low Countries, and Switzerland were largely under the spell of French Enlightenment even before the Revolution. Where there were in these countries influential commercial and manufacturing classes, and peasants who were not serfs, there was considerable sympathy with the attack on feudal privileges —social, economic, and civil—in church and in state. Several of these districts, especially Italy and Belgium, were badly governed by foreign princes.

The French armies, consequently, were able to present themselves with some success as liberators, and their generals established a cordon of satellite revolutionary states around France. The Austrian Netherlands and the German states on the left bank of the Rhine were annexed outright into France, as was Piedmont later. In addition, Holland was converted into the "Batavian Republic," Switzerland into the "Helvetic Republic," and in Italy, "Cisalpine" and "Ligurian" Republics were established in the north, and in the south another republic of the old kingdom of Naples and Sicily. In all of these countries indigenous forces were making for constitutional change, and the French impact only accelerated and extended what probably would have happened anyway in some fashion. Little was stable, however, in the new state systems, until they were consolidated by Napoleon.

BELGIUM. The process of annexation may be illustrated by the case of Belgium. There had been trouble over religion in the Austrian Netherlands even before the French intervened. The Belgians had little enthusiasm for the rationalistic reforms of their Emperor Joseph II and little sympathy for Jansenism. They had objected to the Imperial Edict of Toleration in 1781. (See above, p. 37.) The next year Joseph had added fuel to the flames by approving of mixed marriages and ordering the *curés* to perform them. He had also intervened in theological education, suppressing the diocesan seminaries and establishing a central seminary at Louvain under government supervision. In 1789, consequently, a curious alliance of ultra-Romanists and liberals from Liège, held together by the liberal Archbishop of Malines, drove out the Austrians. They were unable to agree, however, and Leopold won control again in 1790. In 1795 the French, at war with the Hapsburgs, overran the Austrian

Netherlands and incorporated them outright into the French Republic.

The Directory applied French church legislation to their new Belgian province. They suppressed monastic orders (except those for teaching and nursing), and disestablished the church financially. Under resistance they closed all seminaries, chapters, and the University of Louvain, and gave priests the choice of testifying their hatred of royalty under oath or of being banished. The bishops fled to England. A peasant rising of 1798, in which clergy were implicated, led to a banishing of some four hundred more priests.

ITALY. In Italy, meanwhile, the revolutionary movement confronted the Pope himself. Gallican canonists and Jansenists were strong in the church, especially in the north, on the eve of the Revolution. The universities and many intellectuals belonged to the Enlightenment and honored Voltaire and Rousseau. The great jurist Beccaria had attacked the Inquisition and the use of torture. The most wretchedly misgoverned states in Italy, on the other hand, were the territories of the pope. We have seen how Pius VI pronounced on civil liberties and the Rights of Man and became the soul of the antirevolutionary coalition. The papal secretary of state informed the French ambassador that the papacy did not approve of his replacing the fleur-de-lis over the embassy with the device of the "so-called Republic." The ambassador was lynched in the streets in 1793 by a mob apparently egged on by one or two priests. In the northern papal states, on the other hand, there were popular risings in sympathy with the Revolution.

The General of the Army of Italy was Bonaparte. When he won his notable successes against Sardinia and Austria in 1796, the Directory instructed him to take the city of Rome and despoil the Pope. The papal court called for terms. The Directory required, however, not merely an indemnity, but an explicit retraction of all the violent expressions in bulls and briefs about the Revolution. This Pius VI could not agree to, and he broke the truce by appealing to Austria to attack the French. Napoleon at once moved further into the papal states and set even more stringent terms. By these France took the better half of the papal states and a large indemnity. This

seizure of the papal lands was the beginning of the end of the
Temporal Power, an ending which was to be a focus of
Roman Catholic interest throughout the nineteenth century.
General Bonaparte reorganized part of north Italy into the
"Cisalpine" and "Ligurian" Republics.

Now came another riot in Rome, in which a general of
the French Embassy was killed. The Directory was infuriated
and the French army marched on Rome. With this support in
the offing, a group of Roman radicals proclaimed the abolition
of the pope-king and the reign of liberty and equality. They
set up a tree of liberty on the Capitol and invited Pius to abdi-
cate and recognize the "Roman Republic." He refused.
They occupied the Vatican and in February 1798 gave him
forty-eight hours to get out of Rome. So the Pope left and a
Te Deum was sung in St. Peter's over the deposition, at which
some of the cardinals assisted. The Pope made his way north
into exile, dying at Valence in 1799. In the civil registry of
the French Republic his death was noticed as follows: "Citizen
John Braschi. Trade: pontiff."

Pius VII and Napoleon. The Conclave to elect his successor was held in Austrian territory (Venice) and at Austrian
expense. While Bonaparte was away on his Egyptian expedi-
tion, the Austrians had occupied the papal states, and now
wished for a new pope who would accept this situation. On
the eve of the meetings, however, General Bonaparte returned
to France and seized power in a virtual military dictatorship,
the so-called "Consulate." Realizing that Napoleon might be
the power to deal with, rather than Austria, the cardinals at
length chose a "religious" pope with a pro-French reputation,
Pius VII. And before the new pope had gotten back to Rome,
Napoleon had in fact entered Italy and won the battle of
Marengo.

Napoleon now indicated a startling turn of policy. He expressed his desire for reconciliation with the pope, and his conviction that the Roman religion was the only one to lay firm
the foundations of government. The papacy quickly responded and the negotiations were promptly undertaken which
were to result in the Concordat of 1801. This reconciliation
was to be the key to Napoleon's stabilization of a new *modus*

vivendi in the Roman Catholic world, and deserves analysis from that point of view.

NAPOLEON'S RELIGIOUS POLICY. Napoleon's policy signi-fied no conversion to Christianity. He was personally a Vol-tairian, with no belief in any of the historical religions. But he had a shrewd eye for the political uses of religion. A year or two before in Egypt, while he was caught up in his romantic dream of carving out an empire in Asia and Africa, he had flirted with Islam. He agreed with Henry IV that Paris was worth a mass: "Would not the dominion of the East, perhaps the subjection of the whole of Asia, be worth a turban and a pair of slippers?" He discussed the conversion of the French army to Islam at a conference with the sheiks in the great mosque. Polygamy, slavery, circumcision, and abstention from wine presented difficulties in an ascending order for Frenchmen. Whether they could be overcome for the sake of a restoration of the empire of the Caliphs, however, was a ques-tion which political changes made it unnecessary to explore. Napoleon returned to Europe ready to make similar adapta-tions. He would be Moslem in Egypt, Protestant in England, Roman Catholic in France or Italy. Religion was a necessary opiate of the people. Society cannot exist without inequality of wealth, nor inequality of wealth without belief in an author-ity who ordains it and who promises compensation after death.

At least three considerations influenced Napoleon's ap-proach to the Pope. He must preclude a royalist restoration by detaching the papacy from "Louis XVIII." The conclave of cardinals at Venice had written to Louis as "King of France," and the chief strength of the royalists both inside and out of France lay in the support of the church. Napoleon was an adventurer, a usurper; nothing could give him such claim to legitimacy as religious support. And indeed, he was looking ahead to his own establishment on the throne. Lafayette guessed shrewdly when he heard of how "the old fox" had now become to Napoleon "the Most Holy Father." "Con-fess," he said, "you want the little flask broken over your head."

For internal stability it was also essential for Napoleon to end the schism of the Constitutional and the Nonjuring churches. When he did, he would have the patronage of the whole church at the service of his policies. If necessary, he might try to use the Constitutional church, and to keep this possibility before the Vatican he permitted a national council of that church to meet in Paris during the negotiations for the Concordat. But this was a poor second choice, since such a church would be only a French church and Napoleon's private plans ranged far wider. As he later put it, he felt called of God to be Emperor of Europe. The majority of the people in Spain, Italy, and South Germany acknowledged the Roman pope, who might thus be a very useful "lever." Napoleon admired the quasi-political organization of the Roman Catholic church as an instrument of control. And so he forced the Concordat singlehanded on his reluctant generals, civil administrators, and the legislature.

A concordat entered into with such motives from the side of the state, however, was something essentially new in church history. Earlier concordats, like those of the fifteenth century, had determined arrangements between the papacy and Catholic princes, regarded as two sets of officers within the one Christian community. But this state was no longer Christian or Roman Catholic. The document itself defined the position of the Roman Church neither as the "religion of the state" nor even "the dominant religion," but only as "that of the great majority of French citizens," a mere statistical identification. The fiction was maintained, to be sure, that the head of the state adhered to the Roman Catholic Church, but in reality this was a treaty between the non-Christian postrevolutionary state and the church. Alexandre Vinet, the most distinguished French-speaking Protestant writer of the first half of the century, described it as a "marriage of convenience" between the Revolution, no longer very young, and old France, represented by its old religion. Such was to be the status of the church in the nineteenth century, in contrast to its organic unity with the state in the old regime.

The Concordat of 1801 regularized the alienation of church property and the government's responsibility to pay the salaries of the clergy. The whole financial basis of the church as transformed by the revolution was thus stabilized for the next century. The constitutional position of the clergy as an "estate" of the realm was also gone forever; now they were simply citizens and equals before the law of the religiously neutral state. Liberty of worship was established. The papacy, moreover, despite the protests of "Louis XVIII," now accorded to the dictator the rights and prerogatives of the old regime in nominating to the episcopate. An oath of loyalty was also now required of all clergy, not merely, as before, of the bishops.

To heal the schism, Napoleon asked the Pope to require the resignation of the entire episcopate. This meant the sacrifice of the nonjuring bishops who had, in many cases, endured great sufferings out of loyalty to the pope. From the papal point of view, however, such a deposition of the whole episcopate of a national church, being without canonical precedent, was a very welcome strengthening of the ultramontane program. Nearly half of the nonjuring bishops declined to resign their sees in the event, but these were all among the exiles. They formed the schismatic "*petite église*," but within France Napoleon secured a clean slate. To the new episcopate, moreover, he was to nominate ten from the constitutional clergy, who were instituted by the Pope after an equivocal recantation. From the papal point of view the schism had been ended and the church of France was once more free to do its work in unity with the papacy. Only through its relations with Napoleon, moreover, could the papacy hope to play a role in the reorganization of Western Europe generally.

ORGANIC ARTICLES. As a surprise for the Pope, Napoleon accompanied the publication of the Concordat with some administrative regulations which substantially changed the character of the settlement. The addition of these "Organic Articles" indicated that from the viewpoint of the postrevolutionary state, a concordat with the Vatican was not really a treaty between equals, but a body of church legislation open to revision unilaterally by the sovereign state. These articles provided for the teaching of the Four Gallican Articles in all seminaries, required government permission for all church meetings—diocesan, metropolitan, or national—and government approval of all papal letters, legates, or even decrees of ecumenical councils before promulgation in France. Provision was made for appeal from church discipline to the civil power.

The monastic orders were still radically curtailed. Civil marriage was to be prior to ecclesiastical. The Pope protested against the substance of the Organic Articles and even more against the way in which they had been unilaterally decreed, but he was not ready to push his protest to the point of upsetting the whole settlement, and was unable to do much about it.

There was no doubt that the Concordat was initially popular, despite the coolness of the bulk of government officials. Napoleon was given credit for the restoration of the Roman Catholic Church in France. Thus he capitalized on the incoming religious tide of which one symptom was the great success of Chateaubriand's *Génie du Christianisme*, published at about the same time as the Concordat. The effect of the Concordat in the church, however, was just the opposite from that which Napoleon had intended. He wished to restore a Gallican establishment with a minimum of papal power. But the pressure of the state was such on the French episcopate that they turned increasingly toward the pope for support. And several of the provisions of the Concordat effectively strengthened the position of the ultramontanes.

EXTENSION OF NAPOLEON'S EMPIRE. Napoleon's imperialism now became more apparent. In Italy Piedmont was incorporated as a French province in 1802 and thus subjected to the Concordat. The year before, Napoleon had drawn up a new constitution for the "Cisalpine Republic" which put all power in his hands. For this republic a new concordat was negotiated (1803) which was more favorable to the Vatican because it made Roman Catholicism the religion of the state. It was also accompanied, however, by Organic Articles of a Josephist character. In 1805 Napoleon was crowned king of Lombardy, and from that time until his fall Italy was wholly subject to him.

In Holland, similarly, French intervention had become steadily more open. In 1795 William V had fled and a National Assembly had drawn up a republican constitution, disestablishing the State Reformed Church and granting equal civil and political rights to Roman Catholics. A "Directory" on the French model succeeded from 1798 to 1801, and then Napoleon engineered a *coup* which put power more directly in his hands. Finally, in 1806, he installed his brother Louis Bonaparte. A state school system was established, as in France, where morals and history of religion were taught in primary schools, but no more instruction in faith.

In Switzerland, as in Holland, it was primarily the Reformed church which was affected by the revolutionary changes in the character of the state. Here the eighteenth-century regime had been a league of sovereign cantons, like the American states under the Articles of Confederation. The cantons were ruled by aristocratic cliques. The more populous and progressive cantons were Reformed, whereas the so-called "forest cantons," with some two-fifths of the total population, remained Roman Catholic. During the 1790's the revolutionary movement produced a "Helvetic Republic" which provided for civil equality and liberty of conscience, and which abrogated most of the old feudal burdens. The Directory intervened and exploited the country outrageously. Napoleon encouraged the misgovernment and confusion until it gave him occasion to intervene further in 1803. His "Act of Mediation" provided an adroit compromise of the old federal and the new unified systems, which made Switzerland in any case a mere satellite from that time until his fall.

GERMANY. In the crazy quilt of Germany, again, Napoleon's intervention was to mark the greatest changes since the Peace of Westphalia. The German Rhenish provinces on the left bank had gone the way of Belgium, being incorporated into France until 1814. They had little German patriotism and rather welcomed the ending of feudalism and the economic prosperity which was their fortune. They were subject to the same religious developments we have outlined for France. The Treaty of Lunéville (1801), however, also established the principle that German princes who had lost territory by this French annexation might compensate themselves east of the Rhine at the expense of the ecclesiastical principalities. Napoleon hoped thus to bind allies to himself in Germany. The Diet accepted the principle, over the protests of the ecclesiastical princes. The actual division of the loot, however, took place in Paris in a kind of auction, with Napoleon drafting individual treaties with each of the territorial princes as they received their cut. The deal came before the Diet in 1803 and was voted through as the *Reichsdeputationshauptschluss.*

The effect of this arrangement was to redistribute a sixth of the population of Germany and some seventeen hundred square miles. A population of over three million (greater than that of the United States at that time) was transferred to nonclerical, and for the most part Protestant, governments. The Archbishoprics of Cologne and Trier were abolished altogether, as were twenty-nine bishoprics and many monasteries. By 1806 some two hundred states were gone from the map, leaving less than one hundred in the Germanies. Chief among the gainers were Bavaria, Baden, Württemberg, and especially Prussia, which acquired half a million new subjects in Westphalia. The predominance of the Hapsburgs was thus reduced, and Protestants now held a majority of the imperial electors. Most of the old independent nobles lost their petty states along with the church states, and the structure of medieval Germany was in large measure transformed.

The culmination of the process came in 1806 when, at Napoleon's prodding, the states now indebted to him drew together in a secular "Confederation of the Rhine," with a Diet at Frankfurt. They withdrew from the Holy Roman Empire, and there was little for the Emperor to do but to dissolve that ancient creation of Charlemagne which had bound the Roman Catholic Church into the political system of Germany.

Because of these political changes the ecclesiastical reorganization of Germany became necessary. The addition of religious minorities in both Protestant and Roman Catholic states required modification of *cuius regio, eius religio* in the direction of toleration and equal rights. The Roman Catholic church-states disappeared, and along with them the Febronianism of the great prince-bishops. As in France, the ultimate effect after some years was to be the growth of ultramontanism. Roman Catholic dioceses had to be remapped and arrangements made with the new governments. The problem of negotiating concordats, however, was held up by the issue of whether each state should negotiate separately, or whether there should be one concordat for the whole Empire. Bavaria, which was strongly Josephist, wished a concordat like that of France, "a formal alliance between philosophy and religion." Dalberg, the former Elector Archbishop of Mainz and Napoleon's candidate for German primate, wished a concordat for all Germany. The Austrian Emperor, however, contended that he alone could treat for the princes of Germany. The Pope feared the possible independence of a national church as well as the character which the influence of Napoleon would probably give to a German concordat. But since Napoleon's was the only real power in Germany, no alternative to his proposals could be carried through. Because of this tangle of interests negotiations were delayed for years.

In Latin America, finally, we may just mention a last extension of the revolutionary tradition under Napoleon's rule. The series of declarations of independence from Spain manifested in their church policy the characteristic reaction against the Roman Catholic Church, as inextricably bound up with the aristocracy and monarchy of the old regime (see below, p. 324).

Back in France, meanwhile, Napoleon had himself proclaimed as hereditary emperor in 1804. By "emperor," however, he meant more than the ruler of France, as was indicated by his pilgrimage to the tomb of Charlemagne. He persuaded Pius VII to come and crown him, to the resentment of Hapsburg Francis and the scandal of the royalist de Maistre. Even then, however, Napoleon deprived the Pope of the symbolic honor of conferring the crown on him, by taking it out of his hands and crowning himself. And when the Pope refused to grant the annulments Napoleon desired for dynastic reasons, he had them declared, like Henry VIII, by prelates of the national church.

SEIZURE OF PAPAL STATES AND THE POPE. Napoleon's effort to control the whole Continent, moreover, brought him to absorbing the papal states like so many others. When Pius refused to close the ports of the papal states to the British, Swedes, and Russians, French troops closed them. Then Civita Vecchia, the port of Rome itself, was seized. Finally, in 1809, the Papal States were annexed entirely and the pope's temporal power was brought to an end. Napoleon had been trying to push the Pope in this direction, arguing that although he would recognize the pope's spiritual supremacy, in civil matters "I am your Emperor." He wanted the Pope to reside by his side in Paris, directing European Roman Catholic affairs under his supervision. He would be to the church a new Constantine or Theodosius.

When Pius replied to this French occupation by an excommunication, he was spirited away to confinement in France. His one weapon as a prisoner of Napoleon was to refuse to do any ecclesiastical acts, in particular to refuse to institute the Emperor's nominees to vacant episcopal sees. For nearly five years (1809-1814) the old man withstood the Emperor. More than once he yielded on crucial issues, but always he would think better of it and retract his concessions. Napoleon had been able, meanwhile, to terrorize a council of over one hundred French and Italian bishops (1811) into giving him his way. This spectacle of the superior power of resistance to the state in the papacy raised it from the moral mediocrity to which it had sunk in the eighteenth century and contributed to the new ultramontanism of the nineteenth. When Napoleon fell in 1814 and 1815, the papacy emerged with a prestige it had not possessed since the sixteenth century. In the relation of the Roman Catholic Church to the states of Europe, however, despite all efforts at restoration, the old regime was gone and the Concordat was the symbol of the new.

Chapter 11

REFORMED CHURCHES AND
THE STATES

The Reformed Churches resembled the Roman Church more than either the Lutherans or the Anglicans in the extent of their efforts in the nineteenth century to free themselves from the secularizing pressures of the state. Perhaps partly because of this preoccupation with church and state problems, the Reformed Churches, like the Roman, were not marked by great theological achievements in this period.

At the end of the eighteenth century the Reformed Churches had reached perhaps their lowest ebb in religious vitality and those on the Continent were in a peculiarly vulnerable condition when the French Revolution burst upon them. Their recovery was largely made possible by the Awakening of the early nineteenth century, which passed from country to country, building sometimes on Moravian cells but finding its chief stimulus in British Evangelicalism. Pulpits, professorships, and church administration were generally in the hands of moralizing rationalists, and in most cases the revival had to win its way against the sort of petty persecution which Wesley had met in England. Theological liberalism in power does not seem to display more toleration or respect for conscience than does theological conservatism. Protestant as well as Roman Catholic governments attempted to regulate and administer church affairs without regard to the spiritual sources of church authority freshly cultivated by the Revival, and conflicts of church and state occurred almost everywhere. In most places a disruption or separation from a state establishment took place, leaving free churches and state churches side by side. But even in the remaining state churches the principle of spiritual independence generally gained ground.

In this survey we will not discuss the Reformed Churches of Germany and German-speaking Switzerland, which may be more conveniently treated in connection with German Lutheranism. As for the Reformed bloc in Hungary and Transylvania (which was probably larger than that in Scotland, Holland, France, or Switzerland) its story in our period is still largely the grim record of Roman Catholic persecution. Under Maria Theresa this persecution had been so severe that even the Pope, fearing possible retaliation, sought to restrain her. The reaction under Joseph gave the Protestants a brief taste of toleration and enough Catholics were affected by the Enlightenment so that even under Metternich and the Restoration, Catholic laymen protested against the government's policy toward Protestants. Protestants, however, were made to bear the chief punishment for the unsuccessful Hungarian nationalist revolt of 1848. In the ensuing clerical regime of the 1850's and 1860's Protestants were again abused as in the days of Maria Theresa. Only at the very end of our period, after the Austrian defeat at Sadowa (1866), was there again a beginning of religious liberty for Hungarian Protestants. Under these circumstances, when Protestant books could not be printed and theological students studied abroad (if at all) and when there was no unified organization of the church and, except briefly in the 1840's, no periodical, the church could do little more than survive. In Hungary, as in France, the Reformed Church has the longest annals of persecution and martyrdom of any major body in modern church history. Nearly every village and congregation has memories of confessions for the faith, of galley slaves, kidnaped children, extortions and confiscations, lynchings and judicial murder. In contrast to Ireland, where a considerably milder persecution reduced a Roman Catholic population to squalid degradation, in Hungary and France the oppressed Reformed consistently excelled their Roman Catholic neighbors in industry, education, culture, and wealth.

EFFECTS OF THE FRENCH REVOLUTION AND NAPOLEON. The Reformed Churches of France, Switzerland, and Holland had all been influenced by the French *philosophes* and then suffered with the Roman Catholics through the religious policies of the French Revolution and Napoleon.   The first effects of the Enlightenment had made for toleration and disestablishment.   In 1787 certain concessions were made to French Protestants with regard to marriages, burials, and private worship, and then in 1789 the Revolution brought them eligibility to civil office.   The same rights were conceded in the Revolution to Roman Catholics in Geneva and in Holland, where hitherto such offices had been reserved to members of the Reformed state churches.   This principle of religious equality before the law and of the confessional neutrality of the state was to remain in French law thereafter, although it was not always observed in practice.

In the antireligious phases of the terror, Protestants suffered as much as Roman Catholics in proportion to their numbers. In Holland, the "Batavian Republic," they were made to feel the anticlericalism of the Revolution even more, since they were in the majority in that country.   In France, moreover, Protestants were made the victims of the "White Terror" at the time of Napoleon's defeat.   For several months the government allowed mobs to riot in massacre and rape against Protestants in the south of France, and all Protestant worship ceased.

In all these countries the dominant current in the Reformed Church was rationalistic moralism.   Recovery, consequently, was slow and unimpassioned, and the dominant desire seemed to be for peace.   The temper of the churches can be judged from what they were willing to accept from the state.   Napoleon's Concordat and Organic Articles were applied to the Reformed Church as well as to the Roman Catholic.   The dictator feared an independent church.   He suppressed congregational organization, prohibited regional or national synods, and left the church without any confessional basis.   Instead of being a self-governed community with its own basis of authority, the Reformed Church of France was henceforth to be a passive constituency of laity, administered by certain boards of well-to-do individuals nominated by the state.   The pastors were put on state salary, and in the absence of congregational organization, were more dependent on the French government than on their own people.   What is perhaps most revealing about the whole arrangement is that French Protestants accepted it without protest, even gratefully, as at last putting them on a legal equality with the Roman Church in France. It was to be some years before they awoke from their paralysis and discovered how they were bound hand and foot by the Concordat.

In the Netherlands, similarly, an enervated Reformed church offered no significant resistance to state intervention in its affairs. For twenty years after 1795, Paine and Priestley were popular authors in the Netherlands while a succession of French governments handled the churches cavalierly. The Congress of Vienna brought back the House of Orange and combined Belgium with Holland under King William I to provide a strong buffer state against another French aggression. And King William, although nominally Reformed, proceeded to handle church affairs as arbitrarily as had Napoleon. In 1816 he took it on himself to present the Reformed Church with a new constitution. This "Reglement" in effect substituted the Lutheran consistories, appointed by the state, for Reformed synods elected by the church. And the first Synod under the new constitution adopted a formula of subscription to the confessions by pastors which seemed calculated to admit the evasion of any responsibility to the stated faith of the church. The classis of Amsterdam protested against the intrusion of the state, but unsuccessfully; the Ministry of Worship retained virtually unlimited powers over all churches except the Roman Catholic. As in France, a system of state control was established which was to be a subject of contention for generations.

SWITZERLAND. In Switzerland, similarly, the Reformed churches emerged from the Revolutionary and Napoleonic period with little or no independence from the several states, especially in the French-speaking cantons. The government was a federation of sovereign states and the churches had not gained such country-wide organization as was effected by the General Synod of the Netherlands. Geneva had become the center of Reformed rationalism. The Calvinist confessions had been pruned of sin and grace early in the eighteenth century, and Rousseau and Voltaire had greatly embarrassed the Genevese clergy by calling them "shame-faced Socinians." During the Revolution respect for the church disappeared. In

1805 Geneva distinguished itself by publishing a rationalistic version of the Bible, which the French Protestant churches declined to use. The Venerable Company, now a self-perpetuating oligarchy, also sought to replace the lost religious content in Genevese worship by a more elaborate liturgical form. And yet it was precisely in this center of Unitarianism that the Awakening began on the Continent.

THE AWAKENING: SCOTLAND. Since a significant impetus to the Awakening in Geneva and France came from Scotland, we may begin a survey of the Awakening with that country. In Scotland the Evangelical revival may be dated from the 1790's. The Haldane brothers, wealthy laymen, were leaders in the work of evangelism, founding chapels, Sunday schools, and "Conventicles" here and there over Scotland. In 1799 the "Moderates" passed an act barring the pulpits to itinerants. As in England, vested interests made it next to impossible to create new parishes in the Established Church of Scotland to take care of population movements and, again as in England, various dissenting bodies consequently profited more from the Awakening than did the State Church. The greatest preacher and church administrator of the Revival, Thomas Chalmers, was converted from moralistic "Moderatism" in 1811, and in 1815 was called to the foremost pulpit in Glasgow. He was a champion of Sunday schools, but even more famous for a system of parish poor relief which he developed in two later slum parishes in Glasgow and Edinburgh, and which he proved to be more efficient than state relief. His system was based upon a large-scale revival of the institution of deacons and the development of real community and mutual aid in the slum areas. The German Inner Mission was to be influenced by Chalmers' work. Foreign missions, which had been voted down in the 1790's by the predominantly "Moderate" General Assembly, were cordially endorsed in the 1820's, and Alexander Duff began a distinguished line of Church of Scotland missionaries. Sunday schools, the temperance movement, and the Y.M.C.A. followed the Evangelical tide. By 1834 the control of the General Assembly by the "Moderates" was broken and Evangelicalism had become the dominant current in Scottish Christianity.

GENEVA. In Geneva, meanwhile, the first signs of a stirring
had appeared in 1810, when some of the university students, influenced by a Moravian fellowship, organized a religious society. They were further stimulated in 1813 by the visit of
Mme. Krudener, the Russian princess who had become a traveling evangelist and who was largely responsible for Tsar Alexander's "Holy Alliance." Most important, however, was a
series of visiting British Evangelicals, one of whom, Robert
Haldane, held a seminar for the theological students and introduced nearly all of them to Evangelical doctrines which had
never even been mentioned by their Pelagian teachers. A generation of ministers was raised here which was to dominate the
next decades in France as well as French Switzerland, and to
make itself felt also in Belgium, Holland, and Germany.
Caesar Malan, converted in 1817, became the most famous
evangelist and hymn writer of the Revival. Dismissed, partly
for founding a Sunday school, he moved over the frontier to
Ferney and founded an Evangelical church there with English
and Scottish aid. Deposed from the ministry, he was received
by the Secession church of Scotland founded by Erskine in the
eighteenth century. His tours in the 1820's and 1830's carried
him across France, Holland, Germany, England, and Scotland.
Another famous convert was the soldier, Felix Neff, who was
ordained in London and became a home missionary in the savage terrain of the French High Alps. There, like Oberlin in
Alsace, he civilized and educated as well as converted his parishioners, killing himself by prodigious exertions at the age of
thirty-one.

The Evangelicals were forced to seek ordination abroad by
the Venerable Company, which tried to stop the revival by requiring all ministers and ordinands to promise not to preach on
the divinity of Christ, sin and grace, or predestination. Ministers who would not sign this resolution organized in 1817 the
Free Evangelical Church of Geneva. They were attacked in
riots and labeled "Moravians," "Methodists," and "Mummers."
But British and French Protestants were sympathetic to the
Evangelicals, and the French refused to accept as pastors any
ministers who had signed the resolution of the Venerable Company. Missionary societies were organized, and even within

the cantonal church an Evangelical society came into being in 1831. In 1841 an Evangelical was even admitted to the university theological faculty and began to turn the tide there, but the Evangelicals did not win a majority of the Venerable Company till the very end of the nineteenth century.

FRANCE. In France, meanwhile, the Revival made itself felt under the restored Bourbons. Malan, Neff, A. Monod, and various pupils of Haldane were influential. The writings of Scottish and English Evangelicals, such as Scott, Chalmers, and Erskine, were widely read, and the works of older French Reformed writers were reprinted. The new voluntary associations of Evangelicalism also appeared. In 1819 a French Bible Society was constituted, and in 1821 a Religious Tract Society. In 1822 the first society for Evangelical missions was formed when the Protestants, forbidden to convert their neighbors, sent emissaries to South Africa. Leading laymen became active in many of these societies, as in Britain and America, among them the "French Wilberforce," Baron August de Staël, and Admiral Ver-Huell. By the time of the July Monarchy, French Protestantism, like the Swiss, was divided into two parties, called respectively (by their opponents) the "Methodists," and the "Rationalists."

THE NETHERLANDS. In the Netherlands the Revival was partly indigenous and partly stimulated from Geneva. It first appeared in the aristocratic and cultured circles of Amsterdam and The Hague. The poet and historian Bilderdyk rediscovered the heroic Calvinist days of the past. Two converted Jews, da Costa and Capadose, eloquently criticized the state of the church in the early 1820's. And through Genevan influence the man who was to be the political leader of the Revival, Groen Van Prinsterer, was converted. The philanthropy of the Dutch Evangelicals equaled that of the English, expressing itself through various charitable agencies, five missionary societies, a Bible society, and the Inner Mission. The movement was largely led by laymen, since the great majority of pastors, trained in the state universities, were opposed to the Revival, even after the middle of the century. The General Synod and other governing bodies of the church under the

"Reglement" were predominantly rationalist. The scattered Evangelicals among the clergy, however, found a warm welcome, especially in the country, where there was much resentment against the intrusion of "unbelieving" pastors by the government.

By the 1830's the Reformed Churches of Switzerland, France, Scotland, and Holland were all agitated by animated controversy over two issues—the faith and the discipline of the church. In every case the rising Evangelical party insisted that the church must have some specifiable faith and that it must have its own organs of government apart from the state bureaucracy. And in every case the church was actually controlled by a party which denied both claims. The Evangelicals were not all agreed on theology; for example, in Britain there were differences among them on predestination, on the atonement, on inspiration. Some wished to restore the ancient confessions, such as the Decrees of Dort, in full force; most were content with the central Evangelical doctrines of sin and redemption through the Cross and Resurrection. They were also divided on church-state relations between those who sought separation in principle, and those who demanded the independence of the church and accepted separation as a last resort, if at all. These differences may be illustrated in a brief survey of the church and state controversies of these decades.

DISRUPTION. The first large-scale revolt of Evangelicals against the rationalist church bureaucracy occurred in Holland in the early 1830's. A young pastor named de Cock won a great following by preaching high Calvinism, and baptized and confirmed children brought to him from other parishes. Also he attacked the *Hymnal* put out by the authorities in 1807. As in Scotland, most of the Dutch country folk still held only to psalms. De Cock was suspended and, when he proved obdurate, deposed. His congregation seceded with him from the state church in 1834, and was soon followed by others. The movement was strengthened by a refusal of the General Synod in 1834 to accept even a qualified form of subscription to the confession for ministers, a refusal which seemed to prove the case of the separatists. As in Prussia at the same time (see below, p. 156), the state at first tried to deny the right of separation and attempted to suppress the movement with fines, imprisonment, and the quartering of troops in offending communities. Under such persecution the separatists increased to over fifty thousand. When the separatist leaders quarreled, Scholte and Van Raalte led substantial migrations to Iowa and Michigan, to found churches which today occupy much the same relation to other American Reformed bodies as the Missouri Synod does to other American Lutherans. The leaders of the Revival, however, such as Groen Van Prinsterer, did not favor separatism, and most of those affected by the Awakening remained within the State Church in the hope of reforming it. The state at last recognized the Seceders in 1839.

Far more influential was the next crisis, the Scottish "Disruption" of 1843. Like most of the earlier divisions of Scottish Reformed, the Disruption was occasioned by controversy over patronage. In contrast to practice in Anglicanism or Lutheranism, an essential element to a valid ordination in the Reformed Church is the "call," involving the free acceptance of a minister as their pastor by a congregation. The high Anglican government of Queen Anne had, out of spite, imposed on the Church of Scotland in 1712 the Anglican Erastian pattern of patronage. The form of the call was retained through the eighteenth century, but in practice it was subordinated to the incompatible system of appointing ministers at the pleasure of the local patron. When the Evangelicals captured the General Assembly in 1834, they undertook a partial reform of the patronage system. The "Veto Act," passed by this Assembly, specified that a congregation might reject the patron's nominee, thus forcing him to present to them another candidate. This church law was promptly put to the test when a miserable nominee, rejected by a parish vote of 287 to 3, appealed to the civil court to install him as minister. The Court sustained his case, and when it was appealed to the British House of Lords, they decided in 1838 that neither congregation nor presbytery had the right to pass on the fitness of nominees to a parish charge. With this precedent other clergy defied the rules of the church, and soon a rain of injunctions was pouring from the civil courts, debarring the church from disciplining or deposing irregular clergy. Thus in Britain the judiciary sought to overrule the independence of the church just as the state executives were doing in France and Holland and Switzerland.

In 1842 the General Assembly of the Church of Scotland issued a solemn "Claim of Right" against the "unconstitutional and illegal encroachments of the Court." The British Parliament, however, being unsympathetic to the Scots and fearing to give the Anglican Tractarians (see below, p. 185) any precedents for church independence, declined to consider any legislative relief. As a result the church was faced with a clear choice of submission or disestablishment, and on this issue were chosen the delegates to the crucial General Assembly of 1843.

At the opening of that Assembly the moderator announced that the position of the government made it impossible to constitute a free assembly of the church. Bowing to the representative of the British queen, he laid a formal Protest on the table and left the hall, followed by a lengthening file of nearly one thousand commissioners. Almost five hundred ministers sealed their decision by signing a deed renouncing all claims to salary, manse, and security. They weighed the risk to their dependents against the right of the Church of Christ to conduct its own discipline under His leadership, and made their decision. An even larger number of congregations adhered to the Disruption. Seven hundred and twenty-nine ministers remained in the Establishment, but knew that their best ministers and the best portion of their people were gone. Every one of the foreign missionaries of the church went out with the Disruption, as did four hundred teachers of parish schools.

The Disruption was prepared for carefully. For months the administrative genius of Chalmers had been employed in organizing a system of finance for the Free Church. The Church was constituted in 1843 with six hundred congregations and not a single church building or manse. Fortunately the weather was pleasant that summer. In five years they built and opened seven hundred churches. A central "Sustentation Fund" was organized to guarantee a certain minimum to each minister. By 1868 the Free Church had a ministry just short of 1,000, with 800 churches, 650 manses, 600 schools, and 3 colleges.

The Disruption was not animated by the theory of separatism ("voluntaryism" in Scotland), as represented by the Secession Church since the 1790's and by minor bodies such as Congregationalists and Baptists. "We are not Voluntaries," said Chalmers. "We quit a vitiated establishment, but would rejoice to return to a pure one." He had previously defended eloquently the principle of establishment, on the ground that, so long as the spiritual autonomy of the church was preserved, an establishment with its parish system assigned ministerial responsibility for every soul and for the shape of the community as a whole. To accept free churchism on principle would be to disavow these responsibilities. The separatists, on the other hand, denied that the state had any business in subsidizing any religious ministrations. It was over these issues that negotiations for union of the Free Church with the United Presbyterians, which seemed so promising for a time in the 1860's, were, in 1873, defeated for a generation. A still longer time was to elapse before reunion with the established church would be possible, but a great barrier was removed by the passage by Parliament of the Patronage Act of 1874. Thereby, with some compensation to patrons, the choice of ministers was assigned to members of congregations in the classical Reformed pattern.

The example of the Disruption was very influential in the 1840's. Even the Church of Sweden was influenced by it to grant more religious liberty. And in Switzerland and France the Disruption was almost at once emulated. The canton of Vaud, for example, had been persecuting "conventicles" of Evangelicals since the 1820's. At least one important result of this persecution was the driving of Alexander Vinet to a series of masterly defenses of religious liberty. In 1830 the democrats had taken power, but they soon showed that a democracy can be as despotic as any monarch. In 1839 the government arbitrarily overturned both the doctrine and discipline of the church. The Helvetic Confession was abolished, as was the whole connectional structure of the church, leaving only the isolated parishes, each under state control. Vinet resigned but few followed until, in 1845, the state made further impositions, such as forbidding pastors to hold revival meetings. The Council declared bluntly that the Vaud establishment "implied the subordination of the Church to the State." At the showdown 140 ministers went out, leaving only 89. Many of the theological faculty at Lausanne, and nearly all the theological students also resigned. But in contrast to events in Scotland, most of the laity declined to follow their pastors out of the establishment. The state then tried to forbid all religious meetings outside the state church, and mobs sometimes broke up Free Church services. A synod of the Free Church was convened, nevertheless, and a constitutional committee under Vinet's leadership reorganized the church. In 1847 confession and constitution were adopted, and an appeal for funds brought substantial help, even from outside Switzerland. Letters of sympathy came from the Free Church of Scotland, from Germany, from France, even from some four hundred members of the Church of England. By 1851 religious liberty was secured in fact, if not yet in law.

Separations also took place in Geneva and in France in these years, chiefly over the doctrinal issue. When the Council of Geneva abolished the confession of faith, the leaders of the Evangelical school there, Merle d'Aubigné and Gaussen, led in the organization in 1849 of the Free Evangelical Church of Geneva. In France, meanwhile, the ideas of Vinet had been widely influential throughout the July Monarchy through the Evangelical Society and the pages of *Le Semeur*. At the Revolution of 1848 a conference of French pastors arranged for the first national synod of the Reformed Church of France since the secret meeting of 1763 in Languedoc. The Synod drew up a new constitution for the French church while the National Assembly was discussing the constitution for the Second French Republic. As against the Napoleonic organization, the Synod proposed to reconstitute the parish with its presbyterial council, the latter to be elected by all communicants. Also it proposed that there should be regional and general synods, the latter to convene every three years. The majority, however, were not ready to relinquish the salaries of the state. On the doctrinal question, the Synod was so divided that, at last, the question of a confession of faith was tabled. Disappointed on this last point, some of the Evangelicals, led by the Count de Gasparin, E. De Pressensé, and Frederick Monod, withdrew and organized a free synod, the "Union of Evangelical Churches of France." It was virtually congregational in polity, but with a permanent central committee and specifically Evangelical doctrine.

CONSTITUTION OF 1852. The government had never recognized the actions of the Synod of 1848, and under the existing organization of the church neither it nor any other synod could be regularly representative of the church. The Synod's work was not wholly in vain, however, for in 1852 the government of Louis Napoleon startled the church by announcing a new church organization. The new constitution embodied the recommendation of the Synod of 1848 as to reconstituting the local congregations with their councils, and basing the selection of these councils and the regional consistories on the suffrage of communicants. These consistories were to hold chief authority over worship and finances, and were also made responsible for the scattered Protestants of their region. All this was a substantial improvement over the Napoleonic administration of the church by a little self-perpetuating corporation of wealthy members. No provision was made, however, for a common voice and organ in a general synod. Instead a "Central Council" was to be appointed by the state, to represent Protestant interests to the state. And the question of the faith of the church remained problematical. In contrast to the lack of reaction in 1802 there was now vigorous protest against the infringements on the liberty of the church, evidencing a new self-consciousness on the part of church members.

Throughout the following two decades of the rule of Louis Napoleon, the attitude of the church swung increasingly toward separation, and the demand for a general synod continued. There was petty persecution from local officials and the state: schools were closed arbitrarily, Bibles could not be sold, Protestant meetings were banned under the Penal Code, to convert a nominal Roman Catholic was a penal offense. Yet Protestants prospered in numbers and in such good works as Sunday schools and the Inner Mission. And at length, in 1872, after the fall of Napoleon "the Little," a national synod was convened. The shift of sentiment now became clear. A substantial majority voted to adopt again the Confession of La Rochelle, and favored separation. The liberal minority opposed both an effective and independent church organization and a statement of faith, and contested the legitimacy and authority of the synod. The division was so sharp that no further national synod was to be called for some years.

EDUCATION AND CHARITIES. In Holland, as in France, the Revolution of 1848 brought in its train some slight liberation from state shackles, although it was as nothing compared to the gains of Dutch Roman Catholics. A new "Reglement" in 1852 gave congregations more voice in calling their pastors, and the synods more independence from the state bureaucracy. The laity still had most inadequate representation and the effect was to retain control firmly in "liberal" hands. Under these conditions a steady seepage to the seceded free churches continued.

A unique and most interesting development in these years in Holland was the organization of a Reformed political party which struggled to retain education and social welfare in the hands of the church. In this program, so similar to that of the Roman Catholics in France, Germany, and the Low Countries, the leader was Groen Van Prinsterer. Groen Van Prinsterer accepted the decision of 1795 on civil liberties and the equality of religious rights in the nation. Like Chalmers, he wished an independent church with its own discipline and confession. He did not desire separation as such, since he felt a strong responsibility to maintain the heritage of Holland as a "Christian nation." The state, he argued, should be nonconfessional and laic but, nevertheless, generically Christian. And, like Chalmers, he considered that charity and education were properly functions of the church rather than of the state.

In Scotland the Disruption itself was a decisive step in the transfer of poor relief and education from the church to the civil power. Up to the 1840's relief had always been handled from the contributions left at the door of the parish Kirk. Urbanization put an increasing strain on this method, but even in the big-city slums Chalmers had still made it work more efficiently than the municipal system. But the Poor Law Report of 1844 made plain that a compulsory state system was a necessity, since the church had become so divided. In education the transfer came later and less conclusively. The Free

Church ran hundreds of parish schools in addition to those of the established church, and their results were far better than those of England. In 1847 grants-in-aid were assigned to all schools up to standard. The "voluntaries," however, urged a state system which would leave religious instruction to church and home. In 1872 the Education Act effected a compromise. All parish schools, those of the established church, and most of those of the Free Church, were incorporated into a national system. By this system, instruction in Bible and "Catechism" was given at a special hour, and pupils with scruples could be excused from attending. Public education, in accordance with general opinion, thus remained also "Christian."

Groen Van Prinsterer, however, faced the already existing state monopoly of education created by the French Revolution and supported by the "Liberal" party. Only such religious views could be expressed here as were common to Jews and Christians; that is, deism. In 1842, private schools, religious or otherwise, were permitted for those who could afford them, although many "Liberals" would have required attendance at state schools whether the parents liked it or not. The Revolution of 1848 extended the franchise to about 2 per cent of the population, permitting "Liberal" merchants and bankers to vote for representatives in the Second Chamber. Civil liberties and "liberty of education" were also proclaimed. The conservative church groups argued that this should mean freedom for religious instruction in the schools. In 1857 a compromise was adopted which, in contrast to the Scottish system, kept the public schools secular, but permitted private schools at private expense. This solution was attacked by the Christians as involving "double taxation" and they began a campaign for public subsidy of their schools which was to continue for two generations and, finally, to triumph in 1917.

In the 1840's and 1850's the Reformed political party, the "Antirevolutionaries," in Parliament often consisted of Groen Van Prinsterer and one or two others. But the attention given him by the dominant Liberals indicated their recognition that he represented a very substantial body of opinion in the as yet unfranchised masses. Despite *mirari vos* (below, p. 207), the Roman Catholics sided with the Liberals against Groen Van

Prinsterer in the 40's and 50's, but school policy put increasing strains on this alliance. The Syllabus of 1864 left little room for co-operation with liberalism, and in 1868 the Dutch bishops issued a letter on the dangers of secular public education. In the 1870's a liberal education act denied state subsidy to the confessional schools and the Roman Catholics reversed their policy. They struck a "monstrous unity" with the "Antirevolutionary" Protestant conservatives, a unity which was to win a majority in 1887 and secure subsidy for church schools. Thus arose the pattern by which today the great majority of Dutch school children attend confessional schools.

Chapter 12

LUTHERANISM: COURT-CHURCH OR PEOPLES' CHURCH?

The French Revolution as carried abroad by Napoleon marked a major epoch in the history of predominantly Lutheran Germany and Scandinavia. Major political shifts in the area necessitated ecclesiastical reorganization. In this area, as in France and the English-speaking world, there followed a revival of Christianity. It became associated with conservative political tendencies by way of reaction from the excesses of the Revolution and the French occupation in Germany. Within Lutheranism, however, this revival did not move generally toward a new independence and concentration of Christian forces as against the non-Christian movements. In Germany, at least, the chief result was the increasing subordination of the church to the civil power and its increasing alienation from the people.

SCANDINAVIAN PEOPLES' CHURCHES. The experience of Scandinavian Lutheranism demonstrated that this development was not necessary to Lutheranism as such. Denmark, for example, suffered more from the Napoleonic Wars than did Prussia. She had supported Napoleon to the end, and as reward lost Norway at the peace. The Awakening in Denmark, as in Germany, was closely related to a new national consciousness, but in Denmark it was not captured for the political uses of the court, as was the case in Prussia. One wing was pietistic, but another, inspired by the historian and hymn writer Grundtvig, signified a great rebirth of church consciousness. Grundtvigianism had a high-church and sacramental tendency, but unlike most contemporary movements of the sort, such as Anglican Tractarianism, it was opposed to clerical pretensions. It

151

thus formed a genuinely popular churchly revival, and had an astonishing influence, through its folk-schools, in converting a sodden depressed peasantry into an alert, patriotic, and progressive community of farmers. Grundtvigian Lutherans were able, moreover, to absorb liberal constitutional ideas without the blind hatred shown by Prussian Lutheranism. To a lesser degree the lay pietist "reader's movement" stimulated by Hauge in Norway similarly nurtured the sense of the church as a community of the faithful.

The Scandinavian churches, however, were small and relatively uninfluential within Lutheranism generally. Germany set the type for Lutheranism, and there the church struggles of the Restoration period defeated all efforts to establish a peoples' church with general participation and loyalty. On the contrary, the whole tendency was to continue and increase the eighteenth-century absorption of the church into the civil bureaucracy. In sharp contrast to Roman Catholicism, which drew its lines tighter as state and society became more secularized, German Lutheranism was further stripped of organs of self-expression. The only substantial countertendency came, as in Anglicanism, from the emergence of a crypto-Roman Catholic claim for clerical authority among various Lutheran churches.

PRUSSIA: THE AWAKENING. The Awakening came to life in Prussia, the leading Protestant state of Germany, during the Napoleonic occupation. Then began the moral and physical regeneration of the country, led by the greatest of Lutheran statesmen, Baron Stein. The University of Halle had been closed by the occupation and Friedrich Schleiermacher, a young member of the theological faculty, had moved to Berlin. There, as preacher of Trinity Church under the occupation, he suddenly was revealed as the first great political preacher Germany had seen since the Reformation. From that pulpit he championed Stein's reforms and became the greatest single factor in building among the people the will to resist. Men began to pray again; they searched their Bibles and found more congenial the older hymns which had been laid aside by the rationalists as too crude and enthusiastic. And when the French army came to disaster in Russia, these Prussians saw the defeat as the judgment of God upon the satanic despotism of Napoleon. Once again Prussia took up arms, and this time she was successful. Most of the generals had only the humanist code of Kant and Fichte for their sense of duty, but for many the war of liberation was literally a crusade. Weapons were blessed by the church, and the old chorales rang out on the battlefield. Many who fought at Leipzig would remember always the God who had brought them out of Egypt and the house of bondage.

At the Congress of Vienna Prussia was awarded more territories than she had lost at the Peace of Tilsit, including large blocks of Roman Catholic areas. She also faced the problem of integrating the several provincial Protestant churches thus brought under Prussian jurisdiction. Stein had already set Schleiermacher to devising a new church constitution for Prussia. The principle, as with Stein's political reforms, was to adapt the constitutional structure of the Westphalian province in both church and state for all the Prussian territory. Stein would have ended the old consistory control and wished to have presbyteries and synods set up everywhere to engage the laity more actively in church life. But the system seemed ill-adapted to the great proportion of illiterates east of the Elbe. It was even less well adapted to the absolutist views of Friedrich Wilhelm III, and especially those of his Hegelian Minister Altenstein. After the peace a political reaction set in against such reforms as those undertaken by Stein and Schleiermacher.

The occasion which brought to an issue the diverse views of church organization and church-state relations was the attempted merger of Lutherans and Reformed in Prussia. Such a union was much in the air in this generation. Pietism and rationalism had alike made the old confessional issues seem secondary or even unreal. In any case, changes in physical theory made the language in which the old debate about the mode of Christ's presence in the Eucharist had been formulated seem archaic. In every German state where both confessions were substantial in numbers, the union was carried through. In Nassau, the Palatinate, Baden, Hesse, and Württemberg, the prevailing rationalism of most church officials facilitated the merger. In overwhelmingly Lutheran areas such as Saxony and Bavaria, on the other hand, union was not a live proposal. The great controversies arose in the diverse parts of newly enlarged Prussia.

THE EVANGELICAL CHURCH OF PRUSSIA. King Friedrich Wilhelm III of Prussia declared his desire for a consummation of the union at the celebration of the centenary of the Ninety-five Theses (1817). He proposed that the anniversary be marked by joint communion services. The Berlin ministers, with Schleiermacher as moderator, fell in with the royal proposal, and such services were held in Berlin and in the garrison church at Potsdam. The ministers were ready to drop the names "Lutheran" and "Reformed," and to use only "Evangelical." But when the king produced a new liturgy, he was shocked to encounter almost unanimous disagreement on the part of the clergy. Wrapping himself in his "episcopal" prerogatives, the king forbade the clergy to criticize his liturgy either in synod or in print. In 1821 the royal liturgy was published for the military churches and, in 1822, for the rest.

The king was disturbed by the liturgical anarchy and religious triviality of much preaching in the wake of theological rationalism. His solution, however, was largely ritualistic antiquarianism. The sermon was to be shorter and free prayer eliminated. Congregational participation similarly would be replaced by professional choral performances. The basis of the royal liturgy was the church order of Brandenburg (1640). In contrast to the great variety of Reformation worship, one order was now to be imposed by force on all congregations. The theological issues, meanwhile, on which everything had depended during the Reformation, were now treated as secondary and optional. Few Prussian ministers shared the king's hope that religious differences could be surmounted or spiritual life deepened by such devices.

The crucial issue, however, was the constitutional one. How far was the king justified in this personal intervention in such matters? The king's minister, Altenstein, recognized no limits to the royal prerogative. The king claimed to be exercising episcopal rights in the church which needed no confirmation by the estates or other political bodies. His chief opponent in the first stage was Schleiermacher, who, despite the king's ban, wrote (under a pseudonym) an attack on this episcopal right of the territorial prince. With a number of Berlin clergy he sent a petition to the monarch, who annotated it with such comments as "Insolence!" and "Twaddle!" For over a year judicial measures hung over Schleiermacher and, at length, he accepted the liturgy when variant forms were permitted.

REFORMED RESISTANCE. In the Rhinelands provinces, meanwhile, resistance was maintained even longer. Not that there was opposition to the idea of union. On the contrary, Protestants in these provinces were largely Reformed; they were generally stronger for union than Lutherans, and had been much influenced by pietism. But they cherished their ecclesiastical self-government under Christ. In the duchies of Jülich, Berg, Mark, and Cleve they still retained presbyterian and synodical institutions akin to those of Reformed Holland. Should they yield these up to the personal rule of the prince of Prussia in the church? In addition, as minorities in a Roman Catholic area they did not share the king's enthusiasm for such trappings of medieval ceremonial as vestments, genuflexions, and coffin altars. Elberfeld, under the leadership of G. D. Krummacher, declined to enter the union as denying the very nature of the church. This was exceptional, but the synods of this area objected to the king's liturgy throughout the 1820's. At length they were conceded alternative forms and, in 1829, accepted these only on the threat that otherwise their synods would be abolished altogether as they had been in the Eastern provinces. The synods they retained, however, were by the new Rhenish-Westphalian church constitutions of 1835 reduced to a consultative role under consistories and superintendents coming from the court. Thus the state church or, as Schleiermacher more accurately called it, the "court-church," was imposed by police power.

LUTHERAN OPPOSITION. There was resistance also on the Lutheran side. It had come first from outside Prussia (Kiel), from Harms, the foremost popular preacher of North Germany. Harms had published "Ninety-five theses" against the Union, arguing in substance that if Luther balked at Marburg, his followers should do likewise in 1817. Some hundreds of pamphlets took up the discussion, and Harms found some applause in the old Lutheran areas of north and east Germany. Here, where there were few if any Reformed, men could see little reason for the Union. In Saxony and Silesia there was a peculiarly doctrinaire brand of Lutheran orthodoxy which still considered all Calvinists heathen in the bitter tradition of the seventeenth century. Lutherans in these areas had discovered that synods were "forbidden by the Holy Ghost." All the ministers of Breslau refused flatly to use the king's liturgy. The chief Lutheran church of Breslau asked permission to separate from the state church in 1830 when its pastor was suspended for refusing to use the liturgy. Permission was denied. Other congregations were denied permission to emigrate. Pastors were jailed or fled. Troops were used to hunt down the "Old Lutherans" until after the accession of Friedrich Wilhelm IV in 1840, when they were permitted to emigrate. Most of the history of "Old Lutheranism" in the century following must be pursued in the United States, where it has come to constitute the Buffalo, Ohio, and Missouri Synods. In Germany the Old Lutheran resistance could never make much headway against the court church. The one outcome of the long struggle against both Reformed and Lutheran resistance had been the setting up of a state bureaucracy over the Protestant church of Prussia. And the largest Protestant church in the world, the United Evangelical Church of Prussia, maintained itself, although there were severe internal tensions.

Meanwhile, in strictly Lutheran areas such as Bavaria and Mecklenburg, a marked high-church tendency was apparent, akin in many ways to that of the Anglican Tractarians. Wilhelm Loehe of Neuendettelsau was a leading figure in the confessional and churchly revival of the 1830's. His *Three Books of the Church* (1843) outdid Newman or Pusey, and he was the chief agent in reviving ancient liturgical traditions, including private confession and unction for the sick. He also first introduced deaconesses into strictly Lutheran circles. He was active in the formation of the Missouri, Ohio, and Iowa synods in the United States. Kliefoth in Mecklenburg and Vilmar in

Hesse showed a related tendency toward clericalism and sacramentalism.

FEUDAL RELIGIOUS POLITICS. In the course of the Prussian church controversy political alliances had become clearer. In South Germany the pietist Awakening was generally unpolitical, or even disposed to constitutionalism, but in Prussia the active interest of court circles in religion polarized the political orientation of the churches. Already in the 1820's the brothers Gerlach, members of the Prussian aristocracy, were championing feudal politics and orthodox Lutheranism. Especially after the Revolution of 1830, the feudal party romanticized the Christian medieval Empire with its estates, guilds, manorial life, and its view of royal authority based on patrimonial private law. Until 1848 the nobility had a special status before the law in Prussia, and the guilds still functioned. With the accession of Friedrich Wilhelm IV in 1840 the feudal party had been strengthened, for the crown prince in the 30's had associated with the group headed by the Gerlachs. Until the controversy over mixed marriage in 1837 (see below, p. 208) there had been close co-operation from Roman Catholics; the formula "Restoration" came from the Roman Catholic convert, Haller, and one of the king's closest advisers was the Roman Catholic, Radowitz. Theological conservatives of all sorts gravitated to the feudal party.

The chief focus of this tendency within ecclesiastical circles was the *Evangelische Kirchenzeitung*, published from 1827 by Hengstenberg, Professor of Old Testament at Berlin. Hengstenberg unmercifully castigated constitutional government and democracy, along with all deviations from verbal inerrancy and the substitutionary atonement. Soon his influence was decisive in ecclesiastical appointments. The decade of the 1830's witnessed a purge in the universities of theological rationalists and liberals, and it became increasingly difficult to remain both a political liberal and an Evangelical. Hengstenberg was able to bring virtually all orthodox Protestant clergymen to the banner of throne and altar, and to keep them preaching against the constitutional movement, which was building up to the Revolution of 1848.

Friedrich Wilhelm IV had hopes of an international Christian solidarity against rationalism and infidelity, involving even the Roman Catholics. Toward this end the Anglican church seemed to him to occupy the strategic *via media* with her Protestant confession and "catholic" liturgy and hierarchy. He therefore cultivated the Church of England. In 1842 he visited Albert and Queen Victoria to become godfather to the Prince of Wales. Thus the two leading Protestant powers drew together. And ecclesiastically the King hoped to secure the Anglican "apostolic succession" through the institution of a joint Anglo-German episcopal see in Jerusalem. The see was to be filled alternately by English and Prussian nominees, but consecration would always be Anglican. The King even planned an episcopate for all Protestant Germany, with an archbishop of Magdeburg as primate, deriving "orders" from England and Sweden. He was convinced of this episcopal system chiefly by F. J. Stahl, a jurist from the center of Lutheran conservatism in Erlangen. The diplomat Bunsen also greatly admired the Anglican liturgy and episcopal hierarchy, although without conceding metaphysical necessity to the latter. The Prussian King apparently intended to hand over the normal administration of church affairs to his proposed German hierarchy when it should be instituted—retaining, to be sure, a royal right of intervention as in Anglicanism.

GENERAL SYNOD OF 1846. But nowhere outside court circles did there seem to be any enthusiasm for the proposed hierarchy. In 1846 the King summoned a Prussian General Synod to consider church government. The most generally admired proposal seemed to be that of the theologian Nitzsch, which would constitute presbyteries and synods by which the mind of the church might be articulated. The King dreaded nothing more, and prorogued the Synod. In these moves he resembled the Pope of the 1840's. Both toyed with reforms and awakened expectations they could never fulfill. And both, after the great explosion of 1848, were to subside into systematic reaction.

In one respect, however, the efforts of the court to actualize the "Christian state" met with partial success. What participation there was of the laity generally in the life of the church during this period was largely through what came to be called the "inner mission." This was the collective term for the multitude of philanthropic and evangelistic undertakings which had grown up with the Awakening, just as with the earlier pietism of Halle. And as with the earlier pietism, these activities appeared first in the more Reformed areas of South Germany and the lower Rhine, under Swiss, Dutch, and especially English stimulus. Most German cities had missionary societies by 1830. Basel had become the chief missionary center on the Continent, and at Beuggen in 1820 the parent house of a series of rescue homes was established by Zeller. The war and occupation had left a great number of orphans and uncared-for children for whom such homes were designed. On the lower Rhine, meanwhile, Fliedner built up a series of institutions around his tiny parish at Kaiserswerth. Chief among them were his hospital and his home for deaconesses. Influenced by the Dutch Mennonites and the Roman Catholic Sisters of Mercy, as well as by New Testament practice, Fliedner opened up a sphere of church work for women with his "deaconesses." In the great port of Hamburg at the same time, Amalie Sieveking developed the vocation of the professional nurse. Florence Nightingale was to study Fliedner's work, and by the 1850's there were deaconess houses in almost all large German cities.

WICHERN. The great co-ordinator and spokesman for such enterprises was J. H. Wichern of Hamburg. His patron, the syndic Sieveking, provided him with the "Rough House" in 1833 as a home for boys. But Wichern made more of his work than had Zeller or Fliedner. The "Rough House" became a training school for professional workers in such institutions. And from it Wichern sent out his *Fliegende Blätter* from 1844, and carried his message personally on scores of speaking tours. He was a born organizer as well as a marvelous pastor, and all kinds of related institutions, such as hostels for journeymen and city missions, sprang up under his stimulus. By 1848 some 1500 institutions were being gathered up in the network of Wichern's "inner mission."

By "inner mission" Wichern meant more than "home missions." He meant rather the total witness of the church at home, particularly as embodied in action. He aimed at the overcoming of the "alienation of the people from God" in all classes of society. Works of Christian love should make the parish a real living community and bind together noble and peasant, master and apprentice, in ties of Christian mutual responsibility. The priesthood of all believers should be actualized in practice, and thereby a genuine people's church might clothe with flesh the bones of the ecclesiastical bureaucracy. The Prussian court, perturbed by rising social unrest, supported Wichern's work and encouraged its rapid expansion. For although Wichern was one of the earliest to foresee the coming spiritual struggle with communism for the souls of the proletariat, and one of the first to recognize the tie between material circumstances and social environment and Christian nurture, nevertheless he never envisioned any possible political and social structure other than the traditional social hierarchy and dynastic absolutism. His "Christian socialism" was conceived in this feudal legitimist context.

The unrest of the 1840's, meanwhile, was expressing itself in republicanism and constitutionalism, as well as in the nationalist ambition for a united Germany. The theological orientation of this political liberalism was rationalist in the eighteenth-century tradition; or it was based on the idealism of Kant and Fichte; or, increasingly in the 1840's, it was influenced by left-wing Hegelianism. Hengstenberg had hounded nearly all the political liberals out of the church, although there were a few attempts to organize free churches among them. And, in general, the church program of the constitutionalist movement was separation of church and state. Separation would remove the legal barriers which for generations had kept "sects" from challenging the territorial churches.

KIRCHENTAG. In the face of this threat the territorial churches drew together. When the revolution actually broke out, some dreamed of one unified Protestant church as well as one national state. The Roman Catholic bishops met at Würzburg and a great Protestant *Kirchentag* convened at Wittenberg. Bethmann-Hollweg, who had presided at the General Synod of 1846, produced the unfinished agenda of that session as a working basis. The non-Prussian Lutherans, however, desired at most a confederation of German Protestant churches, and some wished to retain complete ecclesiastical autonomy. Wichern, who was put on the program by Bethmann-Hollweg, delivered a stirring address in which he urged that Protestant unity was to be found in co-operative Christian service, rather than by ecclesiastical reorganization or a fusion of confessions. And in fact the "Central Committee for the Inner Mission" was the most substantial ecumenical achievement of the *Kirchentag*. Within two or three years the program of the annual *Kirchentagen* was in the hands of that Central Committee.

Wichern had gladly accepted the patronage of the Prussian court party, and delighted in Bethmann-Hollweg and Stahl as the directors of the Central Committee. But the non-Prussian Lutherans were even colder to the Inner Mission, as they conceived it to be a stalking-horse for the Prussian crown and its united church. A countermeeting to the *Kirchentag* was held at Leipzig by the Lutherans of Bavaria, Hannover, Saxony, and Mecklenburg. The Lutherans of Erlangen, to be sure, supported the Inner Mission, and Loehe paid it the compliment of organizing a safely Lutheran imitation at Neuendettelsau. In general, however, the simon-pure Lutheran refused to countenance any voluntary Christian social action until the 1860's. On the one hand, it seemed demeaning to many Lutheran clergy to engage, like Fliedner, in aggressive pastoral calling. On the other, they were suspicious and jealous of any lay activity not immediately under their control, and the whole thing seemed to them to smell of Calvinism.

REVOLUTION OF 1848. Both in Prussia and in Germany generally, the net result of the Revolution of 1848 was for Protestantism comparable to that of the French Revolution for Roman Catholicism. German Protestantism was identified almost wholly with political absolutism and economic landlordism. The new social classes, on the other hand, and the new movements of liberalism and constitutionalism, as well as of socialism and communism, were forced into an antichurch position. The political parties of the emerging German state were shaped by this polarization, just as those of France had been defined by the French Revolution and those of England by the Puritan Revolution. Political liberalism in Prussia, in contrast to English Whiggery, grew out of rationalism and idealism and was largely antichurch. The conservative parties, on the other hand, were the "Christian" parties—some Roman Catholic and some Protestant, some oriented to Prussia and some to Austria.

In the face of these tensions, Wichern's dream of a people's church cooled into mere organized charities. German Protestantism had turned its back on the urban masses just as industrialism was setting in. Through the 1850's there was little popular political activity, but in the 1860's organized labor expanded prodigiously and adopted the anti-Christian world view of Lassalle, Bebel, and Liebknecht (see below, p. 242). German Protestantism was all the more dependent on the governing class, with its militarism and nationalism.

Chapter 13

PROTESTANT THOUGHT IN GERMANY

Although German Protestantism was generally uncreative in its corporate life and social ethics, it is quite another story in the intellectual sphere. Other Protestant traditions and Roman Catholicism generally maintained a traditional theology in a separate compartment from higher culture. German Protestantism alone embarked on a bold effort to achieve one coherent intellectual world for the modern Christian. The student must really go back to Leibnitz for the beginnings of this movement, but the achievement is that of the generation of thinkers and poets who emerged at the end of the eighteenth century and, with a bound, released German culture from imitation of the French. These artists and intellectuals established Germany in several respects, especially in philosophy and historical studies, as the teacher of all Western peoples. There were great risks in this synthesis of Christian faith and culture, and many fell foul of them, but it marked the boldest penetration of modern intellectual life attempted in any tradition. The Christian motifs and concerns expressed by representative figures varied. Strains of pietism, moralism, and mysticism emerged in strange new contexts, for in the nature of such a syncretism Christian strands had to be cut loose from corporate Christianity and doctrine. Historians and theologians have long attempted to disentangle the religious strands in German idealism and to cast the balance, but all of them have been forced to acknowledge the magnitude of the religious and intellectual undertaking.

The dominant philosophical orientation was idealism, and little of the European theology that followed can be fully understood save in the context of this tradition. In contrast to the tendency of Anglo-American philosophy to an empiricism oriented especially to the natural sciences, German philosophy began rather characteristically from the findings of introspection into the nature of human consciousness and was more influenced by the humanities. In the middle generation of the nineteenth century, when the German leaders had passed away, the same type of thought made itself felt in the influence of Coleridge and "transcendentalism" in the English-speaking world. The new historical criticism also reached Britain and America a generation or so after it had begun in Germany, in this case only in the last generation of the nineteenth century. Thus the course of religious thought in Germany in the years preceding the Empire prefigured much that was to happen to all Protestantism. Roman Catholicism and Orthodoxy also were to derive much from German Protestant philosophy and theology.

KANT. We should begin our study of this movement with an examination of philosophy. Here the starting point must be Kant, even though he belongs in his general intellectual orientation to the rationalistic moralism of the Enlightenment. Kant, however, treated the familiar themes of the Enlightenment with such vigor and profundity that a new intellectual start was necessary. On the one hand, Kant continued and deepened the philosophical scepticism of Hume. According to Kant, not only is all our knowledge confined to phenomena, the way things appear to our apprehension, but the very structure of phenomena, as in space and time, is imposed by our act of apprehension. Things "in themselves" are forever beyond our intellectual grasp, as Kant showed, in the crucial case, by his brilliant critique of the traditional Thomist arguments for the existence of God.

But, on the other hand, Kant found a new way of affirming the fundamental tenets of Enlightenment natural theology, God, freedom, and immortality. However sceptical he might be of the metaphysical powers of "pure reason," Kant had direct and incontrovertible certainty as to what his duty was. He became the great philosopher of duty, the most rigorous kind of stoic, and in this lies perhaps his greatest influence in shaping the code of German public life, especially in the army. From this primary certainty of the "ought," Kant postulated human freedom, a God who could ensure the success of dutiful action, and indefinite life after death to permit continued growth toward moral perfection. Thus Kant approached by the back door the things behind phenomena, free agents human and divine. Very few of his successors were to remain satisfied with this account of our knowledge of God and man. They would often proceed rather from the laws of consciousness in apprehension as a key to the objective form of reality.

So far as religion went, Kant was wholly moralistic. He esteemed the church as a school of moral education, with Jesus as the concrete model. According to this view, prayer serves to focus our moral idealism, but the further one advances morally the less he needs these crutches. A really good man should be quite independent of them, living only by the law in his conscience.

The generation of idealists which followed Kant, as we have suggested, rejected much of his epistemological scepticism in the conviction that the categories he had discovered had objective correlates. Fichte, Schelling, Schleiermacher, and Hegel, for example, all constructed different systems, but they have a family resemblance. Most of them drew on Spinoza and, like him, formulated monistic idealist philosophies with a mystical flavor which were often attacked as pantheistic.

HEGEL. Of these new systems Hegel's was the most elaborate, consistent, and widely influential. It became virtually the official philosophy in the universities, and was regarded widely as the final philosophy. This last aspect corresponded to the highly historical self-consciousness of Hegel himself. One of the most striking features of his thought was that instead of representing some kind of Neo-Platonic ladder of Being in a timeless world, Hegel's ladder of ascent was temporal and embodied in the historical process in a scheme of evolutionary progress. No great metaphysician before him had ever treated concrete history with such seriousness. Out of the seething chaos of human history Hegel was able to isolate at least certain crucial events and stages which embodied a chain of meanings connected by metaphysical necessity. The pattern of this necessity, as with that of all creation in Hegel's thought, was the dynamics of ratiocination, the never-ending process of the definition, contrast, and synthesis of ideas. For Hegel the fundamental structure of all Being, historical or otherwise, was rational, however much it might be obscured by a flux of irrational contingencies. The end of the historical process of objective reason was its elevation to self-consciousness in humanity. This goal could be described as freedom, the freedom of the human mind which knows and accepts the necessities that determine its existence. These necessities Hegel saw very concretely in the Prussian church and state of his day. His philosophy of history which explained how all human endeavor had contributed by necessary stages to this climax must also itself be the final philosophy.

With this conviction that ultimate meanings are to be read from the ebb and flow of historical struggle, Hegel could approach closer to the historical individuality of Judaism and Christianity than could his rationalistic predecessors. And, by reading the significance of whole epochs in theological terms, Hegel stimulated awareness of the relation of religion to all aspects of culture and the common life, in contrast to the pietist tendency to compartmentalize religion. Such a conception also expressed a recovered sense of the corporate character of religious as well as political life. Although Hegel emphasized the great men who embodied the new turns of the historical process, it was only because of that embodiment and not for their significance as individuals apart from the destinies of historical humanity. The religious community, the Church, could by Hegelians be more highly estimated than by either pietists or rationalists.

Despite his new sense for the social and historical character of Christianity, however, Hegel remained incurably intellectualistic. For him, theology signified merely a primitive, undisciplined, mythological way of stating philosophical truths. Although necessary for those incapable of pure thought, theology was, in principle, obsolete once Hegel had isolated its intellectual content. And this he honestly thought he had done. He was defending the faith by restating the truth which had been veiled in poetic language. The Fall, for example, represented the consciousness of moral freedom in man. Jesus embodied the idea of the Incarnation of the Absolute in man, the Atonement that of their reconciliation. In this way theological doctrines were reduced to universal and necessary philosophical propositions, and theology was replaced by a philosophy of religion.

SCHLEIERMACHER. But whereas for Kant religion remained merely morality, and for Hegel it was intellectual, the young Schleiermacher introduced a new approach to an understanding of religion. Like Herder, he felt that the moralistic and the conceptual versions of religion missed its essence. Coming from the circle of romantic poets around Schlegel and the *Athenaeum*, Schleiermacher set forth an aesthetic and romantic understanding of religion as communion with the infinite in his *Speeches on Religion to its Cultured Despisers* (1799). So defined, religion is prior to theology or dogma; it is a primary experience of infinite variety. No one can say he has all of the possible revelations of the Absolute. Neither Christianity nor any other religion is absolute. Religion is a psychological capacity which may be articulated in an indefinite number of specific religions. In conformity with this very individualist conception, fluid and ephemeral associations of like-minded spirits would be the most appropriate social organization. The state church system could only be a deadening incubus.

Two decades of war and peace, of major responsibilities in church and state and academic theology, however, tempered Schleiermacher's romanticism. In 1821 he published the *Christian Faith*, on which rests his reputation as the greatest systematic theologian since John Calvin. The work was written as a dogmatics for the new Prussian Union church and as a statement for Protestantism generally. Only occasional emphases, as on ecclesiastical self-government or election, indicate the Reformed background. Schleiermacher's own statement that he was a "Moravian of a higher order" is a better key to the religious experience which lies behind the *Christian Faith*.

The central thesis of Schleiermacher's early work is retained, that religion is not essentially doctrinal or ethical but rather piety. It is a quality or orientation of our consciousness, a

distinctive type of experience. The approach is thus psychological. Unlike the Reformers, one begins, not with the Gospel or with Christ, but with a general religiosity in all men.
When one presses for the content of this experience, it is described as the awareness of our absolute dependence. Such a
conception reduces the relation of God to man to one of mere
causality, after the fashion of Spinoza's *natura naturans*. As
has been observed, this doctrine was illustrated by Christianity
less effectively than by Islam. Hegel found it best exhibited in
the dog. A diffused mystical consciousness is not the same
thing as redemption from guilt and sin and reconciliation with
absolute holiness and love.

On the other hand, Schleiermacher was determined to be
Christocentric. He had learned much in the intervening years
of the social character of religion, and he now defined Christianity as the species of the genus of religion, in which the sense
of dependence is defined by faith in Jesus Christ as Savior.
What is salvation? It is the recovery not from rebellion, but
from immersion in sense-consciousness, which obscures our
awareness of God. Jesus knew no such distractions but lived
completely and perfectly in the consciousness of God. Here
Schleiermacher drew on John's gospel in which Jesus does not
seem to know moral struggle or intellectual uncertainty. This
is thus a theory of atonement by moral influence. The Holy
Spirit, again, is no third person of the Trinity, but simply the
spirit of the Christian community insofar as this is a heightened
God-consciousness. In this last respect Schleiermacher showed
his deepened sense of the Church as a fellowship of believers,
each ministering to his neighbor, a living community rather
than merely an institution. Consequently, both with regard to
Christ and the Church, Schleiermacher was to be of influence
on succeeding theologians, even though these emphases were
in some tension with his definition of religion and his idea of
God. The twentieth century has been inclined to challenge
him especially for not taking seriously the claim of ultimate
and distinctive truth in Christ. But Karl Barth himself declares
that it is not certain that even in our protests we are not still
his disciples.

Many of the most important intellectual tendencies in the

second generation of the nineteenth century can be related to Hegel and Schleiermacher. Most of Schleiermacher's followers were inclined to be more traditional than the master. They treated orthodoxy with less boldness, but still utilized the new conception and method of organization. For this they were widely described as "mediating theologians." Ecclesiastically, also, most of them, like Schleiermacher, supported the Lutheran-Reformed merger. The Hegelians, on the contrary, divided sharply. There were those who tried to use Hegel in a conservative way, to furnish a new apologetics for the churches by rationalizing dogma. A radical wing, however, "turned Hegel upside down," in Marx's phrase, and evolved the most revolutionary theories in church and state.

FEUERBACH AND MARX. Marx himself is the best known of these left-wing Hegelians; however, he was largely dependent for his views on religion on Feuerbach. Feuerbach began teaching philosophy at Erlangen, but did most of his work as a private scholar. Originally a student of Hegel, he became convinced that the Hegelian Absolute Spirit was merely a hypostatization or personification of human nature in some aspects, that it had no separate and independent existence. The same should be said, moreover, of all religious conceptions. They are all projections, the images of our desires or aspirations. Religion is illusion, and Feuerbach campaigned against it, as did Marx after him, with something of the zeal of a Lucretius. Priests and theologians are parasites who trade in this opiate which distracts men's energies from their real tasks. Both Feuerbach and Marx sensed a betrayal in the state-church system of their day, where organized religion seemed to provide both a sanction for a social system badly in need of reform and a safety valve which let off harmlessly the energy which might have brought about that reform. Marx elaborated the theory of wish-projections into that of "ideology" by relating it to the interests of conflicting social classes. But the fundamental conception was that of Feuerbach and had made him "the classical sceptic in theology, as Hume is in philosophy." In Marx, however, the class theory was combined with the Christian drama of redemption to make a philosophy of history progressing from a state of original innocence and brotherhood into the

inner social conflict brought about by the sin of private property and exploitation, a conflict which would once again issue
into harmony and peace with the conquest of the proletariat
and the ending of class struggle.

SCHELLING. Another form of protest against official Hegelianism came from one who had originally contributed to Hegel's own development. Schelling was, like Hegel, a Swabian
and a product of Tübingen, and had begun as an idealist.
About 1806, however, Schelling reacted from Hegel's intellectualism. He was concerned to account for those aspects of
reality which are not logical or rational. He saw the universe
as a process of dynamic creativity in which personality, in particular, is the bearer of real freedom and irrationality. He
sought thus to take a more realistic view of finite existence, and
this later metaphysic of Schelling's has been described as an
"existential dialectic." In its specifically theological bearings,
Schelling's philosophy sought to account for the historical religions and revelation in concreteness, without reducing them
to manifestations of eternal ideal concepts. Here he built on
Herder's views of myth and saga as the articulation of the divine immanent in the folk mind. Of all the great metaphysicians of the generation, Schelling was probably the most useful
and accessible for theology, but his influence was limited by
his disinclination to publish and by the difficulty of his language. When he came to Berlin in 1841 to lecture, however,
at an age when many American professors are compulsorily
retired, he made a sensation and broke the monopoly of Hegelianism.

KIERKEGAARD. An even more radical attack on Hegelian
intellectualism and cultural syncretism was made by the brilliant and eccentric Danish writer Kierkegaard. Using as he
did the language of a small country, and taking a very uncon-
ventional line, Kierkegaard was hardly noticed outside Denmark for two generations. Then, in the twentieth century,
he was rediscovered by both philosophers and theologians as a
major prophet of "existentialism." From this viewpoint the
truths that matter are the ones which involve a man's whole
being by way of personal decision, and the world shaped by

such decisions is not a rational or harmonious cosmos, but an incalculable vortex of danger and opportunity. The religious life, in particular, means the life of faith, which is a leap beyond reason and security, a venture. In thus stressing the centrality of personal decision in religion Kierkegaard recovered an element almost ignored in idealism; he himself, however, virtually denied the meaning of the Church or God's work in history.

NEANDER. Many of the insights developed systematically by the great philosophers and theologians are also to be traced in the disciplines of church history and biblical study. In the romantic era at the turn of the century a young Jew was converted from such preoccupations by the influence of Plato and by Schleiermacher's *Speeches*. He took the name Neander and went to Halle to hear Schleiermacher. When Halle was closed and the students robbed by the French troops, Neander went on to Göttingen, then the chief center of church history. Here he studied under Planck, a representative of the rationalist and pragmatist view of history. In 1813 Neander's monograph on Julian the Apostate won him a call to Berlin, where he taught until his death in 1850 as the chief representative, after Schleiermacher, of the new theological romanticism. In addition to numerous monographs he wrote a general church history in ten volumes. His stress was on individual religious experience, which he interpreted with great sympathy and with little regard for theological orthodoxy or ecclesiastical conformity. Personally very eccentric and unworldly, Neander was one of the greatest religious influences in German academic circles in the nineteenth century. He spent himself unstintingly on his students, of whom he usually had several hundred in his lecture room. He was the most beloved and popular teacher on the Berlin faculty, the most distinguished of his day.

BAUR. Neander found himself often at odds, on the one hand with the doctrinaire orthodoxy of his younger colleague Hengstenberg, and on the other with the pantheistic tendencies of the philosophers of religion, especially the Hegelians. It was among the latter, however, that the great church historian of the century, F. C. Baur, was to appear. Baur was professor of historical theology at Tübingen from 1826 to 1860 and was the dominant influence in the theological world generally in the second quarter of that century. His long series of publications and his great gifts as a teacher gathered about him a group of scholars, the "Tübingen school," who effected a revolution in New Testament studies. Baur himself also produced a series of studies on the history of dogma, largely couched in Hegel's terminology. This scheme, however, he somewhat shook off in his last period, which he devoted to church history. In 1852 he wrote the first extended analysis of the history of church history and the problem of its proper definition. Then came his own five volumes on the history of the church, which were the first to adopt consistently the critical empiricism of modern historical science. In contrast to Neander, Baur had the ability to seize on the dominant ideas of a period and to follow the intrinsic logic of their explication down the generations.

STRAUSS. The treatment of Christian history in terms simply of human agency and as if subject to the same patterns of development as social life generally was far more startling when applied to biblical materials. In this area the "Tübingen school" achieved its fame (or notoriety) and became the classical embodiment of the "higher criticism." The program had been sketched at the end of the eighteenth century by Semler, Herder, Lessing, Eichhorn, and Gabler, but it was the Tübingen school which first measurably carried it out, at least for the New Testament. Their organ was the *Theologische Jahrbücher*, edited by Zeller. Public attention was caught first, not by the master, himself, but by publication of his pupils. In 1835 D. F. Strauss created a real panic in the churches by his *Life of Jesus* (translated by George Eliot). For the first time the historical reliability of the Gospels was radically challenged. They were interpreted as myth and legend embodying eternal truths of a Hegelian order. Most theologians were already in the habit of allegorizing or rationalizing away some of the most incredible aspects of the biblical account, but the assumption was still general that the Gospels were the work of eyewitnesses. Strauss had shown that the generally accepted method of interpretation was inconsistent and untenable and thus seemed to threaten the very basis of the faith. He was discharged at Tübingen, and a radical government at Zurich which tried to call him to a chair there itself fell over the resultant uprising. Strauss, like Loisy later, lost his Christianity in bitterness over his treatment by the churches.

Strauss had driven home forcibly that the New Testament contained a substantial amount of historically unreliable material. To evaluate these elements it was now necessary to study the several writings and the circumstances of their composition. In this task it was again Baur who pioneered with the new method. Instead of plunging into the complicated historical problem of the Gospels, he began with the clearest body of literature, the letters of Paul, and sought to learn from them the character of the Christian community out of which the Gospels were written. He decided that the "pastoral letters" were not Pauline, but rather reflected the struggle of the church against gnosticism in the second century. Paul's work, on the other hand, was dominated by his struggle with the Jewish particularism represented by Peter. The Book of Acts was impugned by Baur as a late effort to smooth over and minimize this great internal struggle. With regard to John, the favorite Gospel of the theologians of the day, Baur opened a new era. He saw that the Gospel of John was of a different character from the three synoptic Gospels, a form of Christian gnosis, and of a later date. It also represented a very different world of thought from that of the Apocalypse, traditionally attributed to John. Baur was less successful with the three synoptic Gospels, being most suspicious of the reliability of Mark.

This whole reconception of the rise of Christianity was first set forth by Schwegler in exaggerated form, and then by Baur himself in his *History of the Christian Church of the First Three Centuries* (1853). Although various theses were qualified by adherents or opponents, Baur had revolutionized biblical scholarship by the methods of source criticism previously worked out by Niebuhr, Wolf, and Ranke in general history and classical philology. This transfer of methods, however, made the nature of revelation and inspiration more problematic than ever before. Nothing comparable took place in Old

Testament studies during that generation. The beginnings of such criticism were overwhelmed by the authority of the militant Hengstenberg, who represented a literalist rabbinical type of scholarship. Not until nearly the 1870's was work comparable to that of Baur applied to the Old Testament.

Apart from discussion over the new methods of critical history, the middle generation of the century was chiefly preoccupied with political, ecclesiastical, and social issues in the decades before and after the Revolution of 1848. The conventional classification of the theologians of this period is ecclesiastical rather than theological. There were three such groups: the liberals, the confessional theologians, and a so-called "mediating" group.

LIBERALISM. The liberals were widespread, since the old rationalistic moralism of the Enlightenment was still strong among pastors and the middle classes, even though it was nearly extinct in the theological faculties. Politically these old liberals became widely identified in the 1840's with the movement for a constitution. They were in part organized in the "Protestant Association," which defended toleration and the rights of congregations and the laity, within the framework of the Union of Reformed and Lutheran churches. The Association never really stood for religious liberty, however, but for the territorial system of state control of churches. Even the deeply religious Richard Rothe anticipated the withering away of the church into the ethical state. Thus even the liberals looked primarily to the state to further their cause, and were involved in the maneuvers of party cliques to capture the ministries of worship and education.

AUTHORITARIANISM. In such intrigues the liberals were foredoomed to defeat. The fundamentalist pietists of the Awakening had early persuaded the Courts of an intrinsic affinity of religious and political authoritarianism. Since the 1820's the Lutheran Veuillot (see below, p. 208), Hengstenberg, had been throwing journalistic vitriol at liberalism, both political and theological. The reaction after 1848 left even Hengstenberg behind in its ecclesiastical authoritarianism. In many court circles pietist fundamentalism was replaced by a confessional and clerical authoritarianism comparable to the Tractarian movement within Anglicanism.

F. J. Stahl, a kind of Prussian de Maistre, was the leader of the clerico-feudal party in the Prussian upper house (see below, p. 204), championing the divine right of kings, the privileges of the Junker class, and urging episcopacy in the church. Kliefoth led the reaction in Mecklenburg, and Vilmar in Hesse, each holding to an essentially Roman Catholic view of institutional authority, and asserting the primacy of *ex opere operato* sacraments over the Word, the divine right of the clergy, and absolute obedience to every jot and tittle of the confessions. Although this group of High Clerical Lutherans represented an extreme, there was a general tendency on the part of ministries of worship to fill chairs of theology and pulpits with orthodox spokesmen and put pressure on licentiates in this direction.

ERLANGEN. Such political intervention was not likely to produce significant results in theological scholarship. There was a party of respectable theologians, however, who took their stand on the confessions, especially in the strongly Lutheran areas. The Bavarian faculty at Erlangen in particular maintained a tradition through the century. They had learned from Schleiermacher at least the goal of conceiving and stating their position as a coherent and organic whole rather than according to the old method of a catalogue of *loci*. And they yielded enough ground to the results of the new biblical criticism to experiment widely with the theory of "Kenosis" in Christology. This theory of the "self-emptying" of the eternal Christ at the moment of the Incarnation made it possible to take more seriously the biblical account of Jesus' humanity than did the ancient creeds. Hofmann and Thomasius were outstanding representatives of the Erlangen confessionalism in the mid-century. Their very traditionalism made them in some respects more institutionalist and "Catholic" than the Reformation and the New Testament they claimed to champion. Within Anglicanism, again, one found a similar tendency to that of the Erlangen school in the work of such men as Westcott, Gore, and Hort. Although they occupied an essentially traditionalist position and fought against biblical criticism, they likewise experimented with "Kenosis" Christology.

"MEDIATING SCHOOL." The third school was closer to the confessional Lutherans than to the Hegelians. It tended to find its ecclesiastical base rather in the Union Churches, especially of Prussia, and for that reason had a less rigid confessional basis than the Lutherans. The chief point of debate between the two was in the area of sacramental theology, especially the doctrine of the Lord's Supper. This "mediating school" was also more aware of the apologetic problem and made more concessions to the liberals. In doing so, however, the mediating theologians appealed to Schleiermacher and Neander rather than to Hegel. The leader of the party in Rhenish Prussia was Nitzsch of Bonn, who moved to Berlin just before the Revolution of 1848 and there defended the Union against Lutheran efforts to break it up. Dorner, who joined him in Berlin, had formed a friendship with Bishop Martensen of Denmark while at Kiel, and the latter also may be classified under this head. Tholuck and Julius Müller of Halle were also widely-known teachers. And the most original and attractive, though not the most typical, representative of the group was Richard Rothe of Heidelberg. The name "mediating theologians" came from a program in a journal edited by Ullmann, *Theologische Studien und Kritiken* (1828), which was their chief organ. This whole party, however, remained rather academic in character. The governments were interested in a sharper definition of authority and were impatient with concessions to biblical scholarship or to philosophic thought. The laity were familiar only with catechetical materials or a rationalistic moralism. The Union itself was attacked and defended largely for political reasons, with little general understanding of the religious or theological issues at stake.

Chapter 14

ANGLICANISM AND THE ENGLISH
FREE CHURCHES

Roman Catholic France was the dominant force in European politics and culture in the seventeenth and eighteenth centuries. Her hegemony passed in many ways, after the defeat of Napoleon, to her traditional and bitterest enemy, Protestant Great Britain. The century 1815-1914 was in many respects the century of the *pax Britannica*. The Industrial Revolution had already begun to transform the social structure as well as the productivity of Britain in the eighteenth century, and had proceeded apace during the Napoleonic Wars. British leadership rested primarily on the fact that she was the workshop and the banker of the world.

EFFECT OF FRENCH REVOLUTION. In the history of the English-speaking world the crisis of the French Revolution has had no such significance as in Continental countries. Here it meant no long-gestated internal transformation, but only a terrifying threat from outside, an intrusion which passed with little enduring effect. Apart from the stimulus to trade and manufacture, indeed, the effect of the French Revolution was rather to delay than to accelerate social and political change. Social and constitutional reform which seemed to be within sight of achievement in the 1780's was postponed for a whole generation by the hysterical reaction against anything which could be labeled Jacobin. *Habeas corpus* was suspended and the Combination Acts of 1800 outlawed trade unions. In the postwar unemployment and demobilization came the "Peterloo massacre" by triggerhappy police at a protest meeting, and the Six Acts against freedom of speech. Even the "Calvinist" free churches which had stood up for the Americans in their revo-

177

lution, now swung toward the conservatism of Wesley and the Anglicans. So many of the upper classes entered the clergy of the state church as perceptibly to raise its social level. Only in the 1820's did Great Britain recover the freedom to continue her own natural development. And the great crisis of transformation of British life which radically modified the system built on 1689 took place in the reform years 1828-1836.

The ecclesiastical structure defined by the Act of Toleration had become somewhat modified by the early nineteenth century. It had become exceptional for the penalties of the Conventicle Act or the Test or Corporation Acts to be enforced in their full severity. But the Church of England held its position as the church of the governing classes and the state by social custom. The ecclesiastical lines were sociological rather than theological. The Anglicans were the town and rural folk and the gentry who held a monopoly on public office and the professions through their control of the universities. The Presbyterians took their color from the merchants and bankers, the Independents from the lower-middle class, and the Baptists from the poor artisans and clerks. The Presbyterians felt especially keenly their ostracism from the main currents of secular life which would otherwise have been open to them. They declined from about two-thirds of all dissenters to almost nothing at the end of the eighteenth century. But whereas the Baptists and Congregationalists were less exposed to this sort of temptation, in general a family tended to change denominations with change of occupation and status. In varying degrees all denominations were affected by rationalism and, after, by the Evangelical Awakening. Their common theological and ethical tradition gave them mutual accessibility religiously, if not socially and culturally, so that on both sides of the Atlantic a family of half a dozen denominations formed an ecclesiastical constellation quite distinct from that of Lutheran, Roman Catholic, or Orthodox societies.

POLITICAL EFFECTS OF DENOMINATIONAL SYSTEM. This ecclesiastical fragmentation in Britain had significant political consequences. The two-party system was based on the two-church system of state church and nonconformity, both Christian. There was thus room for changes of policy and administration without changes of ultimate principle, and free discussion was always possible within the common presuppositions. The decentralized, yet remarkably stable and conservative society which resulted was to prove uniquely able throughout the English-speaking world to maintain political democracy, even through crises which in Lutheran or Roman Catholic or Orthodox societies produced revolution and dictatorship. The superimposition of the Evangelical Awakening on Puritan and Whig political traditions produced the liberal democracy of the nineteenth century. As the historian Halevy wrote of this revival "We shall explain by this movement . . . what we may truly term the miracle of modern England; anarchist but orderly, practical and business-like, but religious and even pietist."

GROWTH OF POPULATION AND OF NONCONFORMITY. The Evangelical Awakening (cf. above, p. 92) was the most important single influence in British Christianity in this period. Whereas its chief leaders had seen the revival primarily as a means for rejuvenating the Church of England, in fact it contributed even more to nonconformity. Part of the reason was that the state church could not readily adapt itself to the new social frontier. It took nothing less than an Act of Parliament to create a new parish, and various vested interests were usually able to block it. The new industrial areas, consequently, were left with the same church facilities they had possessed as sleepy hamlets. Church of England parishes in Liverpool, for example, had now a seating capacity of twenty-one thousand in a community of ninety-four thousand. In Manchester the seating capacity was eleven thousand out of a population of eighty thousand; in London, one hundred fifty thousand out of more than a million people. There simply were no state church buildings for three-fourths of the new manufacturing population, and no prospect of getting any. A revival preacher who won a following might organize them as a Baptist or Independent congregation, or a Methodist type of Anglican mission. But pastors and people resented being merely tolerated as "missions," and if the Methodists had not broken with the state church they would surely have lost even greater numbers to dissent. By the end of the Napoleonic

Wars nonconformists probably numbered half of the Protestant churchgoers of England. In 1811 it had been prophesied in the House of Lords that a day was coming when dissent would constitute a majority of British Christians. Thus, as in America, the challenge of a new social frontier stimulated the growth of free and voluntary churches.

EVANGELICALS IN STATE CHURCH. Within the state church, meanwhile, Evangelical pietism gained steadily among the laity, more slowly among the clergy, and most slowly of all in the hierarchy. Until the 1830's and 1840's, however, there was no real religious alternative, and the opposition came from those who wished to treat religion merely as a social convention. The clergy sought to commend themselves to the sources of preferment, the gentry, and resisted Evangelical enthusiasm. There was widespread resentment to the appointment in 1815 of the first Evangelical to the episcopate. He was generally known as "the religious bishop." Yet by 1850 Evangelicalism had become the dominant current in Anglicanism as in all the major nonconformist denominations, a situation similar to that of the United States. As in the latter country, there was in England a great difference in the temper of Evangelical piety on the several cultural levels. In the proprietary chapels of the Evangelical gentry, revivalism was always held within the bounds of decent order, whereas among the unchurched poor "Primitive Methodism" grew out of camp-meeting revivals.

Another result of Evangelicalism was to bring nonconformity and the state church closer together. Before the Revival, as we have seen, latitudinarian views on the nature of the Church had weakened the theological grounds of difference. The Revival increased the tendency to individualize religion and to relativize institutions. Whitefield, for example, had preached in Presbyterian Scotland or Congregational New England as readily as in his own communion. Many wealthy Anglican laymen contributed to the support of Independent chapels and even to an Independent theological school to do the work of the Revival where their own church could not.

EVANGELICAL SOCIETIES. A characteristic manifestation of the Revival in all denominations was the creation of voluntary extraecclesiastical societies and associations for various evangelistic and philanthropic purposes. Thus the great new missionary societies began with Carey and the Baptists, then the London Missionary Society (1796), and then the "Church" Missionary Society (1799) (see below, p. 308). The Religious Tract Society was founded in 1799, and in 1804 the British and Foreign Tract Society was established. A relatively small group of wealthy and devout bankers and merchants, the so-called "Clapham Sect," played a major role in many of the societies. Thornton, for example, gave away six-sevenths of his income for such charities. Wilberforce was their parliamentary spokesman for a long generation. In the United States the Tappans were to play a somewhat similar role.

Sabbatarianism was a characteristic mark of the Revival. In 1787, at Evangelical urging, the King issued a proclamation against Sabbath-breaking, blasphemy, drunkenness, obscene literature, and immoral amusements. A society to enforce this program was inaugurated, and was reorganized in 1802 as the "Society for the Suppression of Vice." Similarly, there were societies for the prevention of cruelty to animals in cockfighting and bull- and bear-baiting; others to prevent the abuse of children as chimney sweeps or as factory hands; others for orphans, for the education of the poor, for the reform of prisons. "In our free society," Wilberforce wrote, "it is peculiarly needful to obtain these ends by the agency of some voluntary association; for thus only can those moral principles be guarded which of old were under the immediate protection of the Government. It is to us, like the ancient censorship, the guardian of the religion and morals of the people." And by this free moral suasion, in place of the old direct control by the police power, the Evangelicals effected a startling transformation in British humanity and morals by 1830.

One highly significant aspect of the movement was its interest in education. Robert Raikes is usually accounted the pioneer of Sunday schools, from 1780. Originally these schools were designed to teach reading, with the Bible as text, and sometimes arithmetic. Tory clergymen who feared to educate the lower classes above their station often opposed them. Nonconformists pushed the movement more than did Anglicans. Their British and Foreign School Society of 1807 was matched by the National Society of the Anglicans in 1811. Soon the two groups were clearly aligned behind two rival programs, the nonconformists demanding a national nonconfessional school system, the Anglicans insisting on control of education by the state church. This Anglican opposition delayed a public school system in Britain long after comparable countries had them. Not until the Forster Law of 1870 was a national system instituted, and then the Anglican schools were included on the public budget (see below, p. 258).

ABOLITION OF SLAVERY. The greatest triumph of social reform by means of Evangelical voluntary societies was the outlawry of the slave trade and, finally, of slavery itself. Here the great figure was William Wilberforce, a gay aristocrat, who was converted in 1784 (to his friends' dismay), and who devoted a long career in Parliament chiefly to this crusade. As in the United States, the Quakers had begun the antislavery agitation, and had been increasingly supported by Old Dissent, both rationalist and orthodox. Political agitation against slavery, as well as for religious liberty for nonconformists and Roman Catholics, would probably have been successful in the 1790's had it not been for the excesses of the French Revolution. Bills to abolish the slave trade were voted down no less than eleven times in these years. In 1805, however, Pitt forbade importation of slaves into England's new colonies, and in 1806 began the acts which led to total abolition in 1807. As the wars went on, each time a French colony was lost to the British, the slave trade lost ground; when the peace conference met, the House of Commons unanimously enjoined the Cabinet to solicit from all the sovereigns of Europe the immediate and universal abolition of the slave trade. The lukewarm statesmen were startled. After this the abolition of slavery itself was certain in time, and came in 1833-1834 with Buxton carrying on the work of Wilberforce. The Evangelicals, Anglican and nonconformist, had not been solely responsible, but without them it would not have been done. And the elimination of this system a generation before Britain acquired the largest share of Africa and the colonial world in general prevented evils defying imagination.

EVANGELICAL ALLIANCE. Still another significant type of Evangelical voluntary society was the "Evangelical Alliance" with its ecumenical interests. The nineteenth-century Awakening had a strong consciousness of its international and inter-denominational links, and there were efforts in Germany, the United States, Scotland, and England to bring about an international convention or federation of Evangelicals. The preparatory conference was held in Liverpool in 1845, the founding conference in London in 1846, and the initiative came chiefly from Great Britain thereafter. The Alliance included Anglican Evangelicals and nonconformists of many varieties. It was more warmly received by Continental Reformed churchmen than by Lutherans, since its concern for religious liberty led it often to criticize state churches, Lutheran as well as Roman Catholic and Orthodox Catholic. However, the Alliance did not fulfill the desire of some of its founders that some union of churches should be effected, and it remained only a society of interested individuals. It lacked a central organization, staff, and definite program. But through its world-wide annual week of prayer, its various periodicals, and its occasional great conferences it was the most effective nineteenth-century organization in stimulating an ecumenical consciousness. The slavery issue prevented the organization of an American branch until after the Civil War, but the New York Conference of the Alliance in 1873 was the greatest ever held.

CONSTITUTIONAL REFORM. The place of the churches in the life of Great Britain was significantly changed by the great group of legal reforms which finally broke the constitutional log jam. First of all came the repeal (1828) of the Test Act which had made of the Lord's Supper a qualification for public office. Hooker's old Elizabethan ideal of the national church was thus acknowledged to be impossible. Most Anglicans, though not their leaders, opposed it, as they did the Act of the next year for Roman Catholic Emancipation, which was forced through under threat of revolution in Ireland (cf. below, p. 207). These laws made it possible for non-Anglicans to sit in Parliament, so that the anomaly of Parliament governing the Church of England became unmistakable. And in the 1850's and 1860's, Convocations began to meet again for church business. The bitterly fought enlargement of the franchise, which was finally effected in the Reform Bill of 1833, also gave more representation to the largely nonconformist industrial areas. The bishops all opposed this reform, as did the University of Oxford to the end, and in nearly every village, the "black recruiting sergeant" of the state church.

Part of the resistance of Anglicans to these reforms arose from their certainty that the state church itself was on the agenda of the reformers. The church was extremely unpopular for its reactionary attitude. Bishops were burned in effigy outside their own palace gates. The abuses of the established church were attacked in influential tracts such as the *Black Book*. The great inequalities of income in church benefices were such as to make "a system of prizes and blanks." Taxes for the state church were a great grievance to dissenters and those who felt that that church was precisely the greatest barrier to justice and public liberty. Over half the country clergy were habitually nonresident. Many informed observers agreed with Arnold that "the Church as it now stands no human power can save," although very few agreed with him that the best answer was a comprehensive reunion with the nonconformists on the base of a constitutional episcopate so as to form once again a genuinely national church.

An Ecclesiastical Commission functioned from 1831-1835 to study reform and reorganization and succeeded in making some headway with the church authorities with regard to the abuses of nonresidence and financial inequity. In fact, the state church rode out the storm, although its relation to the state was now conspicuously illogical, and a process of gradual disestablishment was under way. The nonconformists won their long battle against church taxes, for example, in 1868.

It was out of the controversies of the reform legislation that a new party was distilled in the Anglican church. Just as in Lutheran Saxony and Bavaria, or Calvinist Holland and Scotland, the Revival had rejuvenated old confessions and church forms, so in Anglicanism some of the fervor of Evangelicalism flowed in the 1830's and 1840's into High Church channels. And here, as in these other cases, the new confessionalism found itself in a struggle with the rationalistic tendencies of the state bureaucracy. Within Anglicanism the movement found its most eloquent spokesman in John Henry Newman, and the Anglo-Catholic movement was to have more influence in its own sphere and church than did its counterparts elsewhere in theirs.

TRACTARIAN MOVEMENT. Newman used to date the Oxford Movement from Keble's sermon of 1834 on "National Apostasy," which was how Keble interpreted the eminently sensible parliamentary reorganization of the Anglican church in Ireland. From Keble's point of view the crucial point was that the Parliament was "suppressing" bishoprics. He and Newman and their friends now came to the same revolutionary decision which had been made by Lamennais' circle across the channel half a decade earlier. They came to feel that church independence was more important than the values of an establishment—precisely the position the Anglican fathers had excoriated in the Puritans. In a series of *Tracts for the Times* these anti-Erastian Anglicans now set their case before the Anglican clergy. They rested it on strictly clerical grounds, the theory of church authority as confined to the supposed historical succession of ordaining bishops from the days of the Apostles. Only with such legitimation were sacraments "valid" or powers of church discipline lawful. The bishops, Oxford officials, and the church at large, however, received this admonition much as the French bishops had received that of Lamennais. A crisis was reached when in Tract Ninety Newman argued that the *Thirty-nine Articles* could be understood in a Roman Catholic sense. As church disciplines were extended over the "tractarians," he became convinced that his "Catholic" Anglicanism was only a paper theory. And when he persuaded himself in the writing of his *Essay on Development* that certain types of modification of the primitive pattern were legitimate, he had removed the greatest difficulties Romanism held for him. In 1845 he submitted to Rome, carrying some fifty followers in England and about five in America with him. Ever since there has been a small but significant seepage of High Anglicans to Rome, although the bulk of the party has remained within its own church and has succeeded in making it definitely more than a paper theory.

After Newman's defection Oxford reacted from theological controversy and a generation followed there which was more interested in the sciences and in the utilitarian philosophy of Mill. In the 1850's nonconformists were finally admitted to take degrees at the two universities. The Anglo-Catholics, meanwhile, redeemed themselves in practical and parish work. Sisterhoods were created in the Church of England to do much the sort of work done by Fleidner's "deaconesses" in Lutheranism. And a group of "slum priests" developed the "ritualist" phase of Anglo-Catholicism. Newman and Pusey had not been interested in vestments, lights, elongated chancels, and ceremony in general. But now appeared the "Eastward position," altar lights (often the Roman six), flowers, surpliced choirs and sung services, Roman vestments, incense, crucifixes, the cult of Gothic. Perhaps the most bitterly debated point was sacramental confession before communion. The slum priests, Fathers Lowder and Mackonochie, were the centers of endless controversy. There were disgraceful riots in church, as there have been at intervals ever since, and a large number of litigations were brought before the antiquated church courts. Public opinion generally was strongly opposed to the new ceremonies but, by and large, they gained among the clergy. And apart from the controverted points of "ritualism," the general tone of worship, the concept of the ministerial office, and respect for the sacraments were all well served by the Anglo-Catholic movement. As the Anglo-Catholic tendency gained on the dominant Evangelicalism, on the other hand, it tended to deepen the cleavage between the Church of England and the free churches.

In social and economic issues, meanwhile, the Tractarians and the Evangelicals alike had little leadership to offer. Pusey contributed privately to charity like a devoted Evangelical, but the whole Oxford group was in principle politically reactionary and socially tied to the gentry. The Evangelicals likewise were mostly Tory, and in neither England nor America have they supported any great social reform since the abolition of slavery. Lord Ashley, later Earl of Shaftesbury, did succeed Wilberforce as the representative Evangelical reformer. He campaigned in the 1830's and 1840's for the ten-hours bill, and did much for the protection of the insane, for chimney sweeps, and for public health. But he was opposed to trade-unions and public education. In any case he found few churchmen, even of his fellow Evangelicals, to support him in these legislative reforms. The almost universal assumption in social and political thought was that of a pre-established harmony, a machine which worked best when each pursued his own interests and ignored those of the whole. As Wilberforce had put it in his *Practical View*, with "each thus diligently discharging the duties of his own station . . . the whole machine of civil life would work without obstruction or disorder, and the course of its movements would be like the harmony of the spheres."

NONCONFORMITY AND UTILITARIANISM. Anglicans generally contributed less to industrial England and its problems than did nonconformists. Nonconformist Evangelicalism became intimately associated with modern natural science and capitalism on the one hand, and trade unionism on the other. "It is in Nonconformist England," wrote the historian Halevy, "the England excluded from the national universities, in industrial England with its new centers of population and civilization, that we must seek the institutions which gave birth to the utilitarian and scientific culture of the new era. . . . The emotional piety of Evangelical religion and the hunger for experimental knowledge developed at the same time, with the same intensity, and in the same social milieu." The dominant popular philosophy of the English-speaking world in the nineteenth century was to be utilitarianism, stemming from Jeremy Bentham and James Mill. And despite its frank irreligion, enlightened selfishness, and mechanistic view, this school of thought found a permanent if paradoxical alliance with nonconformity. "British individualism is a moderate individualism, a mixture whose constituents are often mingled beyond the possibility of analysis, a compound of Evangelicalism and Utilitarianism."

In two points Evangelicalism and utilitarianism were at one —they were both individualist and both reforming in spirit. Since the Benthamites viewed men individually and socially in mechanical fashion, their conclusion was that a proper rearrangement of the environment would produce a perfect man and state. Therefore they ardently advocated the Panopticon model prison, Lancaster's model school, Bentham's new legal code, Robert Owen's model factory. They regarded all these devices as moral inventions ingeniously contrived for the automatic production of virtue and happiness. And in many or most of the reform movements of these years one finds a curious mixture of Evangelicals believing in original sin and sanctification only by grace with secular utilitarians out to produce a perfect society by tinkering with social institutions. Perhaps this alliance is explainable by some dim subconscious realization that each had hold of a half-truth requiring the other to complete it. Bentham said he would have been a Methodist if he were not what he was, and Robert Owen, raised by hyperorthodox Methodist aunts, dedicated his first book to Wilberforce as a leader in changing society by legislation. All such changes, it should always be remembered, presupposed the "iron law of wages" of Malthus and Ricardo. And respect for the laws of the free market helped to line up hundreds of nonconformist ministers in the anti-Corn Law league of Cobden and Bright, which opposed the tariff on grain as a charge on the manufacturing and laboring classes to subsidize agriculture.

COLERIDGEAN CHURCHMANSHIP AND SOCIAL ETHICS. The one significant denial of the general assumption that competition was the law of the social mechanism came from the followers of Coleridge, especially the "Christian Socialists" Maurice, Ludlow, and Kingsley. From this direction came an understanding of the nature of community in both state and Church which corrected the mechanical individualism of the Evangelicals and the mechanical clericalism of the tractarians. The later Anglo-Catholics were to find as much ammunition in Maurice on the nature of the Church and sacraments as in the tractarians, and perhaps more. And other traditions than the Anglican were to find him a great teacher.

With regard to social ethics, meanwhile, the Christian Socialists opened a new epoch. Ludlow had been in Paris in the 1840's and was acquainted with the many communitarian schemes there being urged. The co-operative workshops of Louis Blanc became the practical device which the Anglican "socialists" found to express best their view of the nature of human society as they organized in the face of the working-class Chartist movement. The practical accomplishments of the Christian socialists in producers' co-operatives, adult education, public health, and similar fields were not extensive, but they laid the theoretical foundations on which the Church of England could find a new social ethic at the end of the nineteenth century.

One last significant development of the middle generation of the nineteenth century must be mentioned. In the 1840's famine drove half of the population of Roman Catholic Ireland into the industrial centers of England, Scotland, and the United States. This tremendous immigration of Roman Catholics into countries where they had hitherto constituted an insignificant minority led to a series of new problems. The immediate reaction in both Britain and the United States was a great increase in anti-Roman Catholic feeling, expressed sometimes in mob violence and attempts at legislative action. The violence soon passed, but the conflict of clericalist patterns with a free democratic society shaped by Protestant conceptions was to increase.

Chapter 15

THE CHURCHES OF THE AMERICAN IMMIGRANTS AND FRONTIER

The religious history of the young United States of America must be seen in the context of tremendous social expansion. In 1790 the population totaled about four millions, with only one in twenty west of the Appalachians. From that time until the Civil War, the totals doubled every two decades and the geographical center moved steadily westward. By the outbreak of the War the census was in the thirty millions, already larger than that of the United Kingdom, and was almost equally divided between the old seaboard settlements and the new settlements, chiefly in the great valley of the Mississippi and Ohio. This latter area had been purchased from Napoleon by Jefferson in 1803 as "Louisiana." To it had been added Florida, Texas, Oregon, the Mexican cession after the war of 1848, and the Gadsden Purchase—the original thirteen states had grown to thirty-three. So vast a continental empire could not have been held together by eighteenth-century communications, but just at this time came the railroads, the telegraph, the steamship, in addition to overland roads and canals. The native Indian population, always very scanty, now offered only insignificant resistance to the advance. The frontier, which had meant insecurity and danger throughout the Colonial period, now came to signify great resources and opportunity.

This occupation of an empty continent, peculiarly well-suited for European peoples, took place with a minimum of external interference. The United States was briefly involved in the Napoleonic Wars, to be sure, but shortly thereafter Great Britain herself supplied with her navy the real sanctions to the "Monroe Doctrine," in which the new nation warned European empire-builders away from the Western hemisphere. From 1814 Americans could turn their backs on Europe and concentrate on the organization of their society and the conquest of the continent.

Such anomalous freedom from external danger and such possibilities of social expansion encouraged an unprecedented political and economic individualism. The Americans already had a sense of mission with regard to the civil and political liberties won in the Revolution and established in the Constitution. Everything in society—economic, social, moral, religious—was assumed to promise most healthy and harmonious fulfillment when left to the spontaneous development of individuals and groups by a state which should act, even as umpire, only in case of necessity.

EVANGELICALISM IN THE CHIEF DENOMINATIONS. The dominant religious type in this situation was similarly the most individualistic form of Protestantism, pietistic Evangelicalism within the Puritan denominations. At the end of the Revolution the Congregationalists were the strongest American church, with some eight hundred congregations, concentrated in New England, with state support, wealth, and an American-trained ministry. Next strongest were the closely-related Presbyterians, with some five hundred congregations, chiefly in the Middle states and the South. Third largest were the Baptists, with something less than five hundred congregations in much the same territory as the Presbyterians. The Episcopalians were fourth, with about four hundred congregations, mostly again in the Middle and Southern states. The three largest bodies, and a substantial group of the fourth, thus stood in the heritage of the Puritan ethos and the theology represented by the Westminster Confession and Cambridge Platform. But they held this tradition as individualized by the Awakenings of the eighteenth century.

How did these churches meet the challenge of the eightfold expansion and westward movement of the population in the two long generations under consideration? Outside New England they had no state support, and in the religious ebbtide of the 1780's and 1790's it was by no means obvious that the churches could survive on a purely voluntary basis. Less than

10 per cent of the population were church members, and for a time even this ratio decreased. Chief Justice Marshall thought the church was beyond repair and Benjamin Franklin did not expect it to last much longer. Around 1790, however, all groups noted indications of a change. At the very time when French infidelity seemed to be subverting religion and society in Europe, a great new wave of revivals began in America, the "second Great Awakening." And for the next two generations these revivals were almost continuous, continually reaching out into the new settlements to convert individuals into the voluntary churches. Despite the tremendous population growth they were largely instrumental in doubling the ratio of church membership in this period, up to 15 per cent of the population. This great "home missions" movement might be taken as the salient feature of American Christianity in this period.

The Awakening was closely related to its British counterpart, and in the early years was largely dependent on it in many ways. The first American interdenominational missionary society was modeled on the London Missionary Society, and the early missionary magazines borrowed much of their material from the leading British missionary publications. L.M.S. missionaries often made their way to Asia and the South Seas by way of America, kindling great interest here and drawing financial support (see below, p. 309). As in Britain, "women's mite" and "cent" societies flourished. Letters from British missionaries to the home base were printed in American as well as British publications. The "Concert of Prayer" for missions crossed the Atlantic, and praying societies and weekly prayer meetings became the chief nurseries of revivals in American communities. A mood of apocalyptic expectation was widely influential in the new century. The tribulations of the Roman Church under the impact of the French Revolution were read in terms of the prophecies of Revelation about Babylon, and the conversion of the heathen and the Jew was prayed for as a sign of the hastening return of the Lord. Not only did orthodox stalwarts like Hopkins, Dwight, Beecher, and Morse read the signs of the times so, but also even a Unitarian like Priestley.

THE EDUCATIONAL VOCATION OF THE CHURCH. All over the East and especially in New England there sprang up local mis-

sionary societies. The Indians, and even more the frontiers-
men, were generally considered to be more of an immediate
responsibility than the foreign field. And the Congregational
and Presbyterian churches still maintained a sense of responsibility for Christian nurture and the Christian shaping of culture.
Mere "conversion" was not enough. Lyman Beecher's "Plea
for the West" and Horace Bushnell's "Barbarism the First
Danger" showed the cultural and indeed political dimensions
of their concern along with the more narrowly "religious."
The prospect of the raw new West holding the balance of political and cultural power aroused apprehension. Although, as
we shall see, the churches relinquished elementary education
in this period to the states, they were very active in founding
academies and colleges. Between 1780 and 1860 probably
some four hundred colleges were founded in the United States,
of which half survived. The overwhelming majority of these
were founded by churchmen. Only twenty-seven were state
or municipal foundations, whereas 154 were founded by six
denominations, a third of these by the Presbyterians, the denomination most active in education.

The most conspicuous single theological rationale of the
Awakening was the "consistent Calvinism" of Edwards and
Hopkins. This group controlled the Massachusetts and Connecticut missionary societies and was active among "new
school" Presbyterians. It gradually drew the "old Calvinists"
into the missionary concern, as illustrated by the foundation of
Andover Seminary, whence came a number of the pioneering
foreign missionaries—Mills, Richards, and Judson, for example.
It set so high the glory of God and the duty of service to his
creatures as to require absolutely disinterested obedience, irrespective of one's own salvation. Equally heroic devotion
amid hardship, however, was to be found with the Methodist
circuit riders, whose theology was at the other extreme of a
synergism tending to run to perfectionism.

THE POPULAR CHURCHES. These Methodists displayed the
most remarkable growth of all in this period, growing from
less than a thousand in 1771 to become the largest Protestant
denomination on the eve of the Civil War. Next largest by
that time were the Baptists. These gains had been made largely

in the South and the new West, where these denominations had proved much more successful than the Congregationalists, Presbyterians, and Episcopalians. That success, again, was determined chiefly by the technique of evangelism, and specifically the revival meeting. The Methodists, the Baptists, and the new frontier groups of "Disciples" and "Christians" became the popular churches of the West by their radical simplification of church work to winning souls. In organization they included the extremes of centralized control and of local autonomy, but they agreed on a relinquishment of the learned ministry and the task of Christian nurture in order to concentrate all energies simply on preaching the gospel of conversion. The autobiography of Peter Cartwright, the Methodist circuit rider of the upper Mississippi Valley, illustrates Western scorn for the Presbyterian and Congregationalist missionaries with their book learning and manuscript sermons. The western, popular, Methodist and Baptist type of revival, consequently, may be contrasted with the churchly awakening in eastern Congregationalism and Presbyterianism. The revivals in the West were spontaneous and uninhibited, and most European travelers of the period reported in fascinated horror their hysterical excesses. But the revivals reached thousands who would not have been reached at all otherwise.

In the second generation of the new century western sectional feeling became evident in the churches, closely associated with cultural and class resentments. The westerners objected to being missionarized from the East. They were largely supporters of the Jacksonian democracy of the common man as against the cultured aristocracy of the older settlements. The Disciples, for example, extended their objections to creeds and confessions to any theologizing which could not be extracted by an uneducated frontiersman from Scripture. Many American Protestants learned to ignore the long historical development of Christianity and sought to relate themselves by a leap directly to the world of the New Testament. The revivalism of Finney illustrates some of the same tensions.

FINNEY'S REVIVALS. Charles G. Finney was the most famous revivalist of the period; he was, in fact, the first of the line of great American professional revivalists. He was a self-taught schoolteacher and lawyer, who was himself converted in 1821 at the age of twenty-nine and sent as a Presbyterian missionary to the frontier of Upper New York State. His commanding carriage (six feet two), his piercing eyes, and his techniques drawn from the devices of a sensational trial lawyer won great success. The last were called "new measures" and included shouting at individuals in the congregation by name, loud prayers for them on the "anxious bench," and permitting women to contribute to the excitement. Finney was called to the larger towns—Utica, Rome, Rochester—and at last to the intellectual and financial centers. Lyman Beecher had threatened to oppose him all through New England, but ended by inviting him to Boston. Finney conquered New York City in his "backwoods invasion of civilization" about the time Jackson entered the White House, and the two developments betokened parallel cultural changes in church and state. Finney won the New York merchants, the Tappans, who turned their large fortunes to supporting high-powered revivals and numerous moral reforms.

THE CHURCH SYSTEM AND THE REVIVAL SYSTEM. Although Finney worked primarily within Presbyterianism and Congregationalism, he leaned to Methodist theology and to perfectionism. His work shows the disintegrating effect of sensational revivalism on church order, theology, and worship. The revivalists reduced theology to a vulgar caricature. The notion of the corporate Church with its means of grace as something historically given and used of God was still further weakened. Finney, for example, was capable of suggesting that the good people should get together and "elect Jesus Christ president of the universe"—an extreme form of the common tendency to view the church as a voluntary association of individuals. These dangers were pointed out by Horace Bushnell and John W. Nevin, the latter contrasting "the church system" with "the revival system." Bushnell again protested the virtual reduction of God's commerce with his people to the crisis experience of conversion. And the high church Episcopalians raised comparable objections. But these more churchly voices were a minority in the day of evangelistic urgency. Denominations, like the Presbyterians, which tried to restrain revivalism and maintain a trained ministry, were split by schisms, in this case the Cumberland and New Light divisions. On the other hand the first effective bond among the autonomous Baptist congregations was the Baptist missionary society, and in the revivals the Congregationalists again shook off the "half-way covenant" (see above, p. 71).

As in Great Britain and on the Continent, the Awakening made for interdenominational co-operation in its first phase. The typical expression of this co-operation was the voluntary undenominational society for evangelism or philanthropy, such as the American Board of Commissioners for Foreign Missions (1810-1812), the Education Society (1815), the American Sunday School Union (1824; the early Sunday schools were also undenominational), the American Home Missions Society (1826), and both the temperance society and the antislavery society (1828). The two strongest churches drew together for the home missions enterprise. The Congregationalists, first of Connecticut and then of Massachusetts, New Hampshire, and Vermont, entered on fraternal relations with the Presbyterian General Assembly. Jonathan Edwards, Jr., devised the "Plan of Union" (1801), which, with later implementation, provided for co-operation in the West. Many Congregationalists felt that they must move in any case toward a more synodical system in order to perform as a church body the functions carried out by the Congregationalist magistrates before disestablishment. In the 1830's and 1840's, however, a rising tide of denominationalism, as in Europe, pulled most of these co-operative or undenominational organizations apart.

PHILANTHROPY AND REFORM. As in Great Britain, again, the humanitarian and philanthropic societies exhibited the highly individualist character of the Evangelical ethic. The great majority of these were undertakings for the benefit of the blind, deaf, paupers, insane, orphans, and other helpless wards of society. The reform movements, again, were largely directed toward individuals—criminals, for example, or those involved in drink or sexual vice. The temperance movement took shape in this period, along with a variety of food fads. And the churches enforced discipline on their members in matters of sexual and family morality. There was much less sympathy, on the other hand, with proposals to reform the social structure, although the campaigns for world peace, women's rights, public education, and the abolition of slavery were all significant.

The method of pursuing these goals in America was new, as in England. Lyman Beecher, who faced the implications of disestablishment in Connecticut, argued that under such conditions the churches could only fulfill their responsibilities for the moral leadership of society by influencing public opinion. He himself participated in a long series of propaganda campaigns for specific social and moral reforms. Finney, similarly, faced with the problem as to what to do with his converts, turned their energies to reform movements. Both the emotional excitement and the techniques of revivalism were thus transferred to the field of social reform activities, particularly in the Congregational and Presbyterian churches, where the Puritan tradition of social responsibility was strongest.

All the reform movements began as propaganda societies, seeking to win converts. And they conducted meetings where emotional and sensational preaching was used to bring audiences to an immediate public decision for action on specific points. Weld, for example, conducted "antislavery revivals"; and the Washingtonians, an organization of ex-drunkards dedicated to the rescue of alcoholics, employed the same technique. As the propaganda societies came in sight of a political majority, however, they faced the question of whether the sword of the state should be employed in such causes against the dissident minority. This question led to splits within two of the more important reform crusades, the temperance and antislavery movements.

The temperance society began in 1826 with sixteen leaders. By 1834 there were auxiliaries in every state and over a million "pledges." This movement radically changed the older tradition with regard to alcohol. The Puritans had consumed prodigious quantities of rum and cider. The churches were accustomed to providing free drinks at ordinations and church weddings. But this nineteenth-century temperance crusade was so influential that most Protestant churches in America today use unfermented grape juice rather than wine even for the sacrament of the Lord's Supper. By 1836 the movement already possessed several journals. And in that year came the first split at a national convention over the question as to whether legislative enforcement of the cause should be sought. One of the first actual experiments in such legislative coercion was the temperance law in Maine in 1851.

ANTISLAVERY. With regard to the problem of slavery this same issue separated the "colonization society," started in 1816, from the abolitionists. The former group doubted the ethical and constitutional wisdom of abolition of slavery by law, and hoped instead to resettle the Negro in Africa as a philanthropic activity. They foresaw that the threat of legislative action would confuse the issue with the problem of the jurisdiction of the states as against that of the Federal Government. In fact, of course, the controversy over slavery came to dominate and absorb all the others and to divide the whole country. It also led to a series of sectional divisions in the American churches, some of which have not yet been reunited. This controversy broke up the Methodists and Baptists in 1844, the New School Presbyterians in 1857, and the Old School Presbyterians in 1861, and had much to do with the end of the Congregational-Presbyterian "plan of union" in 1837. In fact, the only large denominations which were not split by slavery were the Episcopalians and the Roman Catholics, and they evaded the moral issue.

In the antislavery crusade some of the most conspicuous leaders were secular idealists, like Garrison. But the great bulk of support for the movement came from the churches, especially the followers of preachers like Finney and Weld, while Byrne supplied Garrison with much or most of his ammunition. The secularists, for example, Robert Owen and Fanny Wright, supposed man to be perfectible by education and moral effort alone, or by control of his environment. The churchmen supposed that at least the regenerate and converted soul was capable of observable moral growth. In practice they would combine in social reform. The overwhelming mass of Americans believed in the doctrine of a higher law of nature to which the state and all positive law must conform, and that it was the duty of each private citizen to see to it that the state should conform to this moral law. All constitutional and political debate took place in the framework of this universal tradition of natural law theory inherited from Locke. The democratic faith and Protestant Christianity paralleled each other doctrine for doctrine in this period, and especially with regard to the responsibility of every individual for the realization of the fundamental law in his community.

We have already mentioned the apocalyptic mood and millennial expectations so widespread in the revival. Several specific movements expressed it. William Miller won a wide hearing in many denominations when he calculated the dates for the Second Coming, first for March 1843, and then for October 1844. There was great disappointment at these times, but the Millerites continued as a movement, still expecting the Second Coming soon. As "Seventh Day Adventists" they are today among the most actively missionary of all church groups, illustrating still the dynamic which was central in the missions of the Evangelical Awakening.

MODEL COMMUNITIES. Similar eschatological expectations lay behind certain Protestant community movements of these years, for example, the celibate colonies of the Shakers and the Rappites, or the polygamous Mormons. In their several ways they expected to be instrumental in the inauguration of Christ's thousand-year reign on earth. The art and craftwork of some of these colonies, especially those of the Shakers, are now much sought by collectors. The communities which experimented with the family as well as with private property were usually able to survive only on the frontier. Noyes' Oneida community, which grew out of perfectionist revivalism, had moved from Vermont; it was within a generation forced to return, as upper New York became settled, to the prevailing pattern of sexual relations. The Mormons, similarly, were constrained to move from New York to Illinois to Nebraska and then pilgrimaged across the desert to Salt Lake and Utah. Had they not had the refuge of the open frontier these communist colonies might have undergone the fate of Münster in the Reformation.

The West was the frontier of European Protestantism as well as that of the United States. Much of this religious utopianism, as well as the secular which succeeded it, came directly from Europe. This may be said of the colonies of George Rapp and Jansson, and of those of the Shakers and the Mormons in large part. The majority of the last-named, for example, traveled directly from Britain or Scandinavia to Utah.

The secular counterpart of millennialism was the utopianism of the 1830's and 1840's, which in its turn produced a spate of model communities. From the standpoint of a century later, the idealists of the 1840's seem romantic and a little crazy, but the mood at that time was very widespread. As Emerson said, every reading man had a draft of the new society in his pocket. In the 1840's alone, some forty American communities were founded to demonstrate the theories of European utopian socialists Fourier, Cabet, Owen, and Weitling. The failure of these enterprises and of those of the native transcendentalists was a commentary on their theology. "Hopelands" failed, its founder confessed, because of the inadequacy of "virtue and wisdom" in its members. Louisa May Alcott's *Transcendental Wild Oats* describes the melancholia of the defeated leader of "Fruitlands." The novelist Hawthorne later treated the movement devastatingly in his *Blithedale Romance*, yet even so confessed to a nostalgic feeling that in the "beautiful dream" there was "what ought to be a truth." It was rather those like the Mormons, who, with whatever vagaries of personal interpretation, faced life and man with biblical realism, who survived and made the desert bloom.

NEW IMMIGRATION. It was in the thirties and forties that the Puritan tradition first encountered serious rivals for its leadership in American culture and society. In these years there suddenly developed a great migration from Ireland and the Continent. Some 600,000 came in the 1830's, 1,700,000 in the 1840's, 2,600,000 in the 1850's—the last influenced especially by the great Irish famine and the failure of the revolutions of 1848. In 1860 there were 1,500,000 Irish-born people in America and 1,000,000 German born. As late as 1830 the United States was 97 per cent non-Roman Catholic. But by the Civil War the Roman Catholics were the largest American denomination, as they have been ever since. Lutherans increased less substantially by the new immigration; and un-

like the Roman Catholics who crowded into the cities like
Boston, New York, Philadelphia, Cincinnati, and Chicago,
the Lutherans moved to Middle Western farm lands, where
they remained separated from the society around them by linguistic as well as cultural and religious barriers. This new Lutheran wave rescued the older American Lutherans from
disappearing completely in the general revivalist pietism and
the rationalism of the dominant Evangelical stream.

THE PUBLIC SCHOOL MOVEMENT. It was significant that
this emergence of rival religious traditions in the United States
coincided with the period of formation of the public school
system. In the colonies the most developed school system had
been that of Congregationalist New England, whose schools
were publicly supported and had a religiously integrated curriculum, with worship and catechetical instruction supervised by
the ministry. The growth of American population and the
broadening of the franchise convinced a growing number in
the early nineteenth century that publicly supported education
was a social and political necessity in a democracy. And all
important educational leaders up to the Civil War were agreed
that Christianity must be central in the curriculum of public
schools.

But what Christianity? The state which pioneered a free
common school system was Massachusetts, precisely the state
where a Unitarian schism had carried off an important section,
especially around Boston, from the main stream of Puritan theology. Massachusetts was still almost wholly Protestant in
1827, when the first law providing for free public education was
passed. This statute intended that all instructors should teach
"piety," but the attempt was made to keep the theological controversy of the Unitarian schism out of the schools by forbidding the teaching of particular tenets. This program of
"nonsectarian" Protestant Christianity was still a plausible one
in the United States, since the leading denominations were subdivisions of the one Puritan tradition. The prevailing pattern
in the public schools in existence up to the Civil War followed
this program, with Bible reading, hymns, and prayers, and with
more or less of direct religious admonition. But the attacks on
Horace Mann's attempt to execute this program in Massachu-

setts showed its difficulty even in a solidly Protestant community.

In New York City, meanwhile, the great new Roman Catholic concentration encouraged Bishop Hughes to attack the nonsectarian, but obviously Protestant, common school. Hitherto the handful of Roman Catholics had supported the common schools. But Roman Catholic parochial schools in New York City requested in 1840 a share in the funds of the Public School Society. When this was refused they appealed to the legislature. The latter set up a city school board, which decided to allot no funds for any church schools. From the Roman Catholic viewpoint, however, reading the uncommented Bible was a sectarian act and they criticized the public school for *all* religious expressions in public schools. This Roman Catholic pressure to secularize the public schools was increasingly felt in most of the eastern centers. By 1848 half of Boston's elementary school children were immigrants' children, with a high proportion of them Roman Catholic. Something of the "Know-Nothing" anti-Roman Catholic protest of the 1850's was occasioned by the Catholic opposition to the Bible in the schools, as well as by the general political attitude of the Roman church (see below, p. 207f.).

Frustrated in the effort to achieve a religious integration in the new common schools, both Roman Catholics and Protestants experimented with parochial schools, which had been the prevailing pattern in the Middle colonies before the Revolution. The General Assembly of the Old School Presbyterians voted for such a system in 1847, and soon had about 250 schools in twenty-nine states, the most ambitious Protestant system. The vast majority of Presbyterians, however, still supported the public school program and were unconvinced of the necessity of a separate system. The Civil War finally killed the effort. The Roman Catholic schools had not succeeded impressively either, chiefly for lack of teachers, but the massive importations of European teaching orders after the Civil War were finally to give the Roman Catholic church schools an effective program. The effect of revivalism on the Protestant denominations, meanwhile, made the Protestant ministry increasingly incompetent to give educational leadership either in church schools

or in public schools. Anti-intellectual pietism increasingly abdicated the task of education just when the nation's school
system was being established.

In this period new state constitutions, amendments, and
statutes laid down a pattern of the relation of the church to
education which was to be less significant only than the church
and state provisions of the Federal Constitution. The barrier
against the use of public funds for church-controlled schools
was most general, and in many states one also found provisions
against "sectarian" teaching in public schools. The interpretation of "sectarian" by the courts was henceforth to prove a
crucial issue. Before the Civil War, however, neither the Federal Constitution nor those of the states were understood to bar
the teaching of Christianity in the public schools.

CIVIL WAR. Then came the Civil War. And although the
churches gained in influence through the war by a series of
revivals, and carried on important philanthropic activities, the
war itself presented an ethical problem to which the churches
did not measure up. This problem can be illustrated by the
case of Lincoln, who, although an intensely religious man, did
not feel at home in any of the churches. The individualistic
moralism which had come out of revivalism had nothing to say
to his problem of how man should live in a tragic situation
where every alternative is partly evil and wicked. Lincoln
read Theodore Parker and felt something here of the old Puritan responsibility for power. It was Lincoln's tragedy that in
order to win the war against the old slaveholding aristocracy,
one had to give power to a new financial and industrial plutocracy. The old agrarian society which had been the basis of
American democracy was now disappearing before industrial
capitalism. The individualist pietism of all the people's
churches, originally the ethic of a politically disinherited class,
now proved dangerously inadequate for the moral guidance of
a middle class in control of a continent.

Chapter 16

THE ULTRAMONTANE REACTION TO THE REVOLUTION

The French Revolution had crippled the theocratic control of the Roman Church, even in its Gallican forms, and had created a rival political faith—that of humanitarian liberalism, nationalism, and, in germ, socialism. Henceforth the place of the Roman Catholic Church in states and societies affected by the Revolution would no longer be a matter of course and general acceptance, but would rest on legal contracts calculated for political expediency on the part of the state. Napoleon had set the pattern with his Concordat, and he had many imitators in the following years in many countries. How should the church comport itself in this uncertain position?

RESTORATION. The first reaction was the attempt to restore the system of the *ancien régime* as if the Revolution and Napoleon had been a bad dream. Every French improvement in the Papal States, from street lights and vaccination to the use of laymen in civil administration, was eliminated and the Jesuits were restored. Similarly, in France thirty new legitimist bishops were consecrated, the religious orders were expanded phenomenally, and revivalist missions were held all over France. Lamennais, De Maistre and De Bonald, the "prophets of the past," supplied the rationale of "traditionalism" which dominated French Catholicism for twenty years. It was an inversion of Rousseau, wholly sceptical of man's reason and virtue, seeing hope only in blind unquestioning submission to authority in theology and in politics alike.

"Restoration" was the watchword of the long generation from the end of the Napoleonic Wars (1815) to the wave of revolutions in 1848. Diplomatically it was dominated by Metternich, the Austrian minister, who sought to realize again as far as possible the role of the former Holy Roman Empire. "Legitimacy" was the political slogan and the Roman Church was particularly cultivated as a spiritual police against all liberal or democratic tendencies.

But this cultivation of the church rested, not on sincere conviction of Christian truth, but on calculation of its political utility. And the old independence of the church, in France, for example, was not restored. The clergy were no longer the First Estate of the realm, with a constitutional position of their own. And they were now on state salaries, no longer independent masters of vast land holdings and receivers of feudal dues. The civil code had cut into their judicial prerogative; the state now controlled the school system, even though it was staffed with clergy. In countless ways the Roman Catholic clergy found themselves limited and regulated by a greatly magnified state apparatus. The significance of their changed situation struck home only gradually and was only generally appreciated a generation after the Peace of Vienna, in the 1830's and 1840's, but then the consequences were drawn.

ULTRAMONTANISM. The result of the continuing Revolution on the inner life of the Roman Catholic Church was the death of Gallicanism, Febronianism, Josephism, and the triumph of ultramontanism, of papal centralization. Bishops no longer had the economic and political footing to take an independent line against the papacy. The increased power and the decreased religious conviction of the civil rulers rather pushed the bishops back on Rome for support. And as the Roman court found its political influence diminished, it sought to compensate by tightening central discipline within the ecclesiastical organization. The story of the two generations after Napoleon, consequently, can be written as the story of the ultramontane conquest of Roman Catholicism.

"LIBERAL CATHOLICISM." The character of ultramontanism also changed, however, in the post-Revolutionary situation. In Spain, Piedmont, and the two Sicilies, as in the Papal States, papalist theocratic rule could be restored in the old style through the princes. But something quite new had to be de-

vised for France when the restored Bourbons proved insuffi-
ciently amenable to clerical control. Lamennais proved to be
the prophet in proposing an alliance of ultramontanism with the
Revolution against the monarchy. He thus became the father
of "liberal Catholicism," which came on the scene internation-
ally during the revolutions of 1830. In most cases the appeal of
the Roman Catholics to liberal and national ideas against legitimate monarchs came where the monarchs were not Roman
Catholic. Thus the Roman Catholic Poles agitated against the
schismatic Tsar, the Roman Catholic Belgians against the Dutch
Calvinist king of the Low Countries, the Roman Catholic Irish
against the Protestant crown in Great Britain. In a sense Lamennais was assimilating the French situation to these, arguing
that in post-Revolutionary France the Roman Catholic church
must adopt the strategy of a party *within* the state. For the first
time in a nominally Roman Catholic country a Roman Catholic
leader urged separation of church and state, renouncing the
subsidies of the Concordat, and supported constitutional and
liberal ideas. *L'Avenir*, which Lamennais published with his
friends Lacordaire and Montalembert, advocated freedom of
religion, press, association, education, as well as universal suffrage and national self-determination for Poles, Belgians, and
Irish.

This "liberal Catholicism," however, was ultramontane in
purpose and liberal only in tactics. The intention was to organize and manipulate the genuinely Roman Catholic section
of the population as a disciplined party. As Lamennais saw,
the authority of the priest in pulpit and confessional makes it
possible for the Roman Catholic Church to operate on its native
authoritarian basis *within* a liberal mechanism. He felt that
such an organized Roman Catholic electorate in France would
enable the clergy to control the French state more effectively
than they could through their traditional connections with the
monarchy and aristocracy. And in any case this ultramontane
program would free the church from the golden chains of an
only nominally Roman Catholic state.

CONDEMNATION OF LIBERAL CATHOLICISM. The bulk of the
French episcopate, however, were still Gallican, and they believed that the safety of the church rested on the protection of

princes. The Pope, likewise, terrified by the specter of liberal and nationalist revolution in his own domain, insisted on submission to kings, even for the Poles. In *mirari vos* (1832) Gregory XVI repudiated "liberal Catholicism." Civil, political, and religious liberty was condemned. When Lamennais rebelled against the decree with an incendiary attack on monarchy, *singulari vos* (1834) condemned him by name and ruled that no Roman Catholic could support political liberalism.

The Roman court, and most Roman Catholics elsewhere, considered that direct papal control of territory in Italy was the only feasible basis for the independent papal government of the international church. Government by priests was inefficient, obscurantist, and despotic in this territory, often scandalously so. In 1831 the five Great Powers sent an unprecedented memorandum to the Papal Court, protesting against conditions there. But most Roman Catholics considered this misgovernment the necessary price for the greater good of the church at large. And in order to preserve this papal monarchy the popes felt that they must maintain solidarity with other monarchs against all liberal, constitutional, and nationalist reforming movements. In particular, the papacy depended on military support from Austria to maintain its regime, and hitched its international policy to that of Metternich. As long as the Papal States lasted (until 1870) these considerations governed papal policy.

ROMAN CATHOLIC MINORITY STRATEGY. The new ultramontanism thus made its way into the Roman Catholic Church from the periphery, from the countries where Roman Catholics were in a minority, and in apparent contradiction to papal policy. The Revolution of 1830 was successful in Belgium, where the Roman Catholic bloc allied with the liberals and won independence from the Dutch King William. The new nation then proceeded to draw up the most liberal constitution on the Continent; it was the first Roman Catholic country voluntarily to accept liberalism. Similarly in Ireland, O'Connell's threat of civil war won Roman Catholic emancipation without the state controls which had been attached to earlier proposals.

The papal condemnations of political liberalism were very embarrassing to some of these minority Roman Catholic populations, for whom Lamennais' program made more sense. Some Belgian Roman Catholic statesmen retired to private life after *mirari vos*. In the United States a "nativist" movement pointed out that Roman Catholics could not be loyal citizens under a free constitution. In these countries the episcopate was forced to compromise and permit adhesion to constitutional liberties.

FRANCE. In France also, under the constitutional monarchy of Louis Philippe, the friends of Lamennais, Lacordaire, and Montalembert proceeded to organize a Roman Catholic political party. The chief issue was the demand of the church to run its own schools. A Roman Catholic press came into existence and through it the ultramontane journalist Veuillot wielded such power as to become the lay pope of France for a generation. The Roman Catholic electorate was mobilized and Roman Catholic parliamentary leaders developed. And when at last this new party had proved its power, even the bishops abandoned their reserve and learned to utilize it.

In Roman Catholic Germany, meanwhile, a comparable organization of the Roman Catholic party was effected. Here the focal controversy concerned legislation about mixed marriages. In the eighteenth century, church canons had been widely disregarded in this connection, and the German states had become accustomed to determining such questions. After the Napoleonic Wars Prussia tried to regulate mixed marriages to favor Protestantism. A protracted controversy ensued. The climax came when the government arrested Archbishop Droste-Vischering in 1837. This became a *cause célèbre* with the agitation carried on by the publicist Goerres, and a new consciousness of the church as a separate body crystallized around this symbol. When the Revolution of 1848 broke out, the Roman Catholics of Prussia and Holland virtually adopted the program of Lamennais and the example of Belgium. The Prussian Constitution of 1850 gave the Roman Catholic Church the advantages of a public subsidy together with the independence of a free church. By this time the whole German episcopate was making liberal demands in the interest of ultramontanism.

In France the Revolution of 1848 was also supported widely

by priests and bishops, in contrast to their all but unanimous hostility to the Revolution of 1830. Well over two hundred Roman Catholic deputies were elected to the Assembly of the short-lived Republic of 1848. This government, however, was terrified by the socialist demands and demonstrations of the Paris workingmen. The Roman Catholic party became overnight the conservative party and supported the counterrevolutionary *coup* of Louis Napoleon. When he established his dictatorship he was warmly congratulated by Roman Catholics from the pope on down to Montalembert, and his regime was praised as a model of the traditional Roman Catholic principles of authoritarianism and hierarchy. The middle classes had returned to the church, just as in the first revolution the fear of constitutionalism had brought the aristocracy back to the church. And the proletariat now saw the church as the façade of exploitation. In the Latin countries Karl Marx was less the representative spokesman than Proudhon, but the hostility to the church was the same. "If ever democracy gets another inning, and I count for something" promised Proudhon, "it will be all up with Catholicism in France." The de-Christianization of twentieth-century France was thus foretold.

THE "LIBERAL POPE." In Italy, as in France, the initial phases of the Revolution of 1848 found Roman Catholics in sympathy. The Pope elected in 1846 as "Pius IX" encouraged many to think he himself would lead in a liberal nationalist reorganization of the peninsula. And when the risings came in 1848, he yielded to the demand for a constitution, following the example of the French, and of the Italian states of Piedmont, Tuscany, and Naples. He even yielded to nationalist pressure, and allowed the papal troops to be used in the attempt to drive the Austrians out of Italy. Then when he tried to withdraw from the war his government collapsed before the overwhelming nationalist tide. Pius had to flee Rome in disguise, leaving the city to the revolutionaries. From this situation he was rescued only by the intervention of the troops of Louis Napoleon, who recaptured the Papal States for him and supplied him with a garrison. But Sardinia-Piedmont declined to give up her constitution, and under the leadership of Cavour, continued through the Crimean and Austrian wars of the 1850's and 1860's to maneuver for a unified Italy at the expense of the Papal States.

Cavour hoped to solve the church-state problem in Italy on the "liberal Catholic" basis, and popularized Montalembert's formula, "a free church in a free state." But the papacy was horrified at the thought. The strategy of the minority could not be adopted in a "Catholic country." As Veuillot put it, "Where we Catholics are in the minority, we demand freedom in the name of your principles, where we are in the majority, we deny it in the name of our principles." The two types of strategy, however, were both aimed at closer clerical control of the church and, through the church, of society. Both were ultramontane in contrast to the dominant Gallicanism of the pre-Revolutionary centuries and they converged in support of further papal centralization.

The reaction of Pius IX from his liberal experiment of 1846-1848 was so sharp that the Italians referred to the rest of his reign as that of "Pio Nono Secondo." In exile in 1849 he assembled that coterie of advisers, chiefly the Jesuits of the *Civilta Cattolica*, who mapped out a strategy including what were to be the three chief ecclesiastical acts of his reign: the proclamation of the Immaculate Conception of the Virgin as an article of faith, the formulation of a list of sociopolitical heresies, and the definition of the infallibility of the pope separately from that of the church. The desperate situation of papal absolutism in the Papal States, surrounded as it was by Italian nationalism and constitutionalism, required a state of martial law in the church in which loyal Roman Catholics would not protest against extreme papal claims, and which was used to carry through an ultramontane revolution in the constitution of Roman Catholicism.

THE IMMACULATE CONCEPTION. The Immaculate Conception of Mary was a "pious opinion" which had been extended with the popular cult of the Virgin. There was no biblical basis for it and the weight of tradition, including not only all the fathers but also such medieval doctors as Bernard, Aquinas, and Innocent III, was overwhelmingly against it. But a theological commission assured the Pope that "the general agreement of the Church at any given period" was adequate for the definition of a dogma necessary to salvation, apart from Scripture or historical tradition. On this basis the Pope alone, without any council of the bishops, for the first time in history, propounded a new dogma of the faith in the bull *Ineffabilis* (1854). This action established two precedents of basic importance. The formulation of essential dogma in the Roman *1.* Catholic church might now rest on current opinion in the church, irrespective of either Scripture or tradition. And the power of the pope to define dogma separately from the church *2.* was become a *fait accompli* even before it was justified by the dogma of papal infallibility. Modern Roman Catholicism had moved well beyond even Trent.

CIRCUMSTANCES OF THE SYLLABUS. The list of modern errors and heresies, published ten years later as the *Syllabus of Errors*, can best be understood in the light of three events immediately preceding its promulgation. In 1863 two Roman Catholic conferences challenged the Jesuitical party. A conference of scholars met at Munich, the intellectual capital of Roman Catholicism, and spoke up for academic freedom and for modern historical scholarship as against scholasticism in Christian apologetics. At Malines, meanwhile, another congress heard Montalembert defend political liberalism as a program for Roman Catholics. He dared to criticize the Inquisition and demanded that Roman Catholics support universal suffrage, civil equality, liberty of press, education, association, and even of conscience.

Political liberalism and intellectual liberalism were thus being claimed for Roman Catholics at the very moment when liberalism incarnate in the new Kingdom of Italy was threatening the very existence of the papal government in Italy. For the French-Austrian-Italian War of 1859-1860 had enlarged the little Kingdom of Sardinia-Piedmont to form the Kingdom of Italy. Part of the Papal States had been incorporated, and a majority of the Pope's subjects desired annexation of the rest of the Papal States by "Italy." Papal sovereignty in Rome was maintained against the will of the Pope's subjects only by the presence of a garrison of French troops. To the beleaguered papal court "liberalism" signified first of all the program of its archenemy, the constitutional and national Kingdom of Italy.

THE SYLLABUS. Against all these various expressions of liberalism, in constitutionalism and in scholarship, was launched the *Syllabus* of 1864. The *Syllabus* was a sort of index of previous papal condemnations, the systematic summary of what Pius thought he had learned about church and state. The Pope selected a series of propositions and put them forth for the Roman Catholic world as the outline in error of the true Roman Catholic view of the political functions of the church. Feeling his ship of state shuddering under him, he nailed his colors to the mast. He worked to identify Roman Catholicism inseparably with the political system of the Restoration, the old regime of social hierarchy, monarchical absolutism, and ecclesiastical monopoly and intolerance, while insisting also on ultramontanism within the church.

As Pius stated in his introductory letter, the one great comprehensive error, of which most of those condemned in the *Syllabus* were specifications, was the rejection by modern society of the authority of the hierarchy to regulate public affairs. Governments and states should properly be subordinated to clerical theocratic control. In contrast to caesaropapism, on the one side, or co-ordinate jurisdiction of church and state on the other, the Roman Catholic position is clerical supremacy in and over the state. Separation of church and state, which was one program urged by those who opposed clericalism, was specifically condemned. Religious liberty, which would follow from separation, was not only condemned in principle, but the Pope also declared that it was not expedient in traditionally Roman Catholic countries to permit other forms of worship. The other nonclerical program, that of state regulation of the church in its appointments and actions by such devices as *placet* and *exequatur*, was also condemned.

Among the concrete issues in which the church might well differ from the state would be the control of education, marriage, property, and the civil law as relating to the church and clergy. In all these matters the clericalist position was defended by the *Syllabus*. Catholics could not approve of public school systems unless they were controlled by the clergy. Civil legislation on marriage and divorce was not valid unless it conformed to canon law. The state had no right to limit the acquisition of property by the church by restrictions such as *mort-main* or eminent domain. Nor could it properly try Roman clerics in its courts in civil or criminal cases, or require them to serve in its armed forces. On the contrary, the church had to have its own law courts with final jurisdiction, and it had a right of direct or indirect police power to enforce its decisions. To nail down this last point Pius initiated proceedings to canonize two judges of the Inquisition as Roman Catholic saints.

By denying that the popes had ever exceeded their powers or erred in the definition of morals, the Pope justified all the acts instigated or approved by his predecessors, including, as Lord Acton observed, the tortures of the Inquisition, the massacres of Protestants and heretics, the deposition of princes. Standing pat on this record he condemned the suggestion that "the Roman pontiff can and ought to reconcile himself to, and agree with, progress, liberalism, and civilization as latterly introduced." Roman Catholicism had effected a synthesis of Christianity with an earlier type of society and culture and could not be asked to do its work all over again.

But whatever the Roman court thought about constitutions and civil liberties, not only the English-speaking countries, but now also Prussia, Holland, Belgium, and even France and Italy had them and intended to keep them. To be sure, conscientious Roman Catholics were worried. The *Civilta Cattolica* found it necessary to quiet Belgian apprehensions and assure Belgian Roman Catholics that they were still permitted to exercise their civil rights and duties under a free and therefore "un-Catholic" constitution. The French government for a time prohibited the publication of the encyclical and *Syllabus* as contrary to the French Constitution. Leading Roman Catholics in more liberal countries embarked on efforts to qualify, minimize, or explain away the plain sense of the *Syllabus*. Newman in England and Ketteler in Germany argued that each of the condemnations must be understood in all the special circumstances of its original formulation, circumstances known only to rare experts, and that they could not be generalized as universal maxims, as the procedure in publishing the list would lead one to suppose was the intention. The most famous "interpretation" of all was that of the French Bishop Dupanloup.

His chief device was a distinction between absolute truth (the "thesis") and contingent necessities (the "hypothesis"). So long as the Church never compromised the former, he argued, she could afford to be accommodating in the latter.

It was reliably reported that the Pope did not care for this or other minimizing interpretations of what he had "really meant." He had meant what he said. And apparently one of Pius' chief concerns in working for the definition of infallibility for the next half-dozen years was to bind his *Syllabus* on Roman Catholic consciences forever as an infallible utterance. In this he did not entirely succeed, since doubt may be entertained as to whether the *Syllabus* comes within the terms of papal infallibility as finally defined; but, infallible or not, the *Syllabus* is binding on all Roman Catholics and requires their internal assent.

VATICAN COUNCIL. The Vatican Council of 1869–1870, the culminating event of Pius' reign, was designed in the minds of its manipulators to provide an occasion at which the Roman Catholic episcopate, already helpless before the central authority at Rome, should vote away the last remnants of its episcopal independence and make its abdication a dogma of the faith. These two articles, the direct authority of the pope in every diocese, and the doctrine of the papal infallibility, completed together the conversion of the Roman Catholic church into an absolute monarchy without constitutional restraints or responsibility. The Vatican Council was never concluded, but was only adjourned. But there is no particular reason to summon it again, since the whole bearing of its decrees was that councils of bishops neither have, nor ever had, any constitutional share in the government of the Church. In a literal sense the Vatican Council was a council to end all councils. Its decrees were a parliamentary plebescite acknowledging unlimited power in an ecclesiastical dictator.

The council was neither representative of the Roman Catholic Church nor was it free in its discussions. The representation from the more educated Roman Catholic populations in Germany and France was ridiculously disproportionate to the swarm of obscurantist Italian, Spanish, and Latin American clergy. The minority had far more learning on their side and established a superiority in debate from the beginning. But they were kept from being on the crucial committees; their meetings were limited by decree; they could not write to theologians at home for advice; they were not permitted to publish their views in Rome. The Pope personally intervened to insult anti-infallibilists and encourage infallibilists.

The ultramontanes, moreover, had been at work for more than a generation to capture the seminaries and rewrite the textbooks to present the Jesuit version of church history. The breviary had been interpolated, catechisms altered, even official synodical records tampered with in the interests of the doctrine of infallibility. Most of the bishops were not scholars and knew no more about the matter than they had learned from their seminary textbooks. They had come as loyal, not-too-learned churchmen to make a great demonstration of devotion to the persecuted Pope. They burned with indignation against the disaster hanging over the Pope's temporal sovereignty.

The theory of the majority was the same as in the case of the Immaculate Conception. The infallibilists could not be reached by appeal to the Bible or tradition. It might be proved, for example, (as it was) that a pope (Honorius) had been anathematized as a heretic by three ecumenical councils and at least fifty-five popes and that this anathema had been read once a year in the breviary by every priest in the Latin Church for centuries. The answer to this was that the present mind of the church overrules history and tradition. When Cardinal Guidi objected that even the idea of a separate infallibility of the pope was unknown to tradition prior to the fourteenth century, Pius dismissed his argument: "I am tradition." The church does not have the obligation of proof.

Lord Acton, a chief organizer of the opposition, was more troubled about the claim to moral infallibility than the claim to doctrinal inerrancy. Acton honored the papacy, but as a historian he knew it had often degenerated to appalling crime in its role as moral teacher. This practical aspect of the doctrine also interested Pius more than the doctrinal. He wanted to insure the authority of his *Syllabus*. More than once he told bishops that he would settle for an official declaration in favor of intolerance.

The vote was taken in the nick of time. The outbreak of the Franco-Prussian War led to the adjournment of the Council, the recall of the French garrison, and the consequent collapse of papal rule in Rome. From 1870 to 1929 there was no Papal State and the pope sulked in the Vatican, refusing the settlements offered by the Italian State. With regard to the new doctrine, however, the pope triumphed. One by one the minority bishops capitulated in the months after the Council. The "Old Catholic" group which refused to accept the decrees had a large number of distinguished scholars, but not one bishop from the minority had the courage of his convictions.

Part III

1870 TO WORLD WAR I

Chapter 17

THE INTERNATIONAL *KULTURKAMPF*

In the period after the Vatican Council, the Roman Church engaged in bitter struggle with several of the leading European states. The church's claim to the right to rule over the civil state, as expressed in the *Syllabus* and strengthened by the decrees of the Vatican Council, conflicted with the increasingly absolute claims of the modern state. This conflict became a "struggle for the character of civilization," to use the term arising from the controversy in Germany. In the areas of English-speaking Protestantism (with some qualifications for Anglicanism), a genuine system of co-ordinate jurisdiction and mutual autonomy of church and state had been achieved. Here was found neither a persistent drive for clerical control of government nor a strong insistence on the omnicompetence of the civil state. Consequently, in these countries there were no major violent conflicts of church and state such as were widely experienced by Roman Catholic peoples. We may review the *Kulturkampf* in Italy, Germany, and France.

UNIFICATION OF ITALY AND THE PAPAL STATES. Relations between the Roman Catholic Church and the Kingdom of Italy were dominated, until the decade before World War I, by the controversy over the former Papal States, the "Roman question." For centuries the papacy had opposed the unification of Italy, fearing that its own freedom would be restricted by a powerful neighbor. The nationalism of the nineteenth century, however, had not only brought the Italians together but also had led the overwhelming majority of the Pope's civil subjects to cast off his rule and to annex themselves and the territories they lived in to the new Italian state. Since 1849 the papal maladministration had been kept in power over the restive

219

people only with foreign military aid. The war with Austria in 1859 and Garibaldi's rising in the south produced the new "Kingdom of Italy" in 1861, reducing the Pope's dominions by two thirds and his subjects from three millions to seven hundred thousands. Nationalist agitation for the recovery for "Italy" of Venice and Rome continued and increased thereafter. In 1866 Venice was acquired in the Austrian defeat, and the Franco-Prussian War of 1870 recalled from Rome the French troops which had hitherto prevented that city's consolidation with the kingdom. In September 1870 the token resistance of the papal army ceased, and the troops of the Italian kingdom occupied the ancient city of Rome. A plebescite gave a clear popular mandate, and the pope's Rome became the capital of the new Kingdom of Italy. Assurances that the independence of the pope would be respected were sent to the chief Powers.

Attempts to negotiate a settlement with the papacy, however, failed completely. The suggestion of some sort of international guarantee of the independence of the church was rejected by the Pope himself, who maintained there could be no substitute for territorial sovereignty, and by the Roman Catholic powers, which refused to recognize the *fait accompli* as a basis for negotiation. Since the Pope also refused to negotiate directly on any basis other than restoration of the *status quo ante*, the Italian parliament perforce legislated a settlement unilaterally, the so-called "Law of Guarantees" (1871). This law defined the position of the Roman Court in Italy for the next two generations. Pius IX, however, promptly condemned the law and, as a gesture of protest, immured himself as "prisoner of the Vatican," a vantage point from which he and his successors poured forth a stream of fulminations against the Italian state which had despoiled the church.

The Law of Guarantees was largely framed in the spirit of Cavour, who in opposition to the clericals, on the one side, and the radical anticlericals on the other, attempted to realize for Italy Montalembert's liberal Catholic concept of a "free church in a free state." In return for its lost territories the Papal Court was allotted financial compensations, which were, however, spurned as "Judas money." The pope was assigned the permanent and inviolable and untaxed use of the Vatican and certain other properties, within which he was to have rights of extra-territoriality, while his person in general was inviolable as that of the king. He was to have active and passive rights of embassy, and the conclaves were to be guaranteed complete freedom of action. These provisions, again, were unacceptable to the Pope, because he was given only the use and not full possession of the properties concerned, and because the whole arrangement was juridically a legislative measure which could be revoked and changed by the unilateral action of the Italian state. Certain regalist powers of *placet* and *exequatur* were retained, pending a legal reorganization of ecclesiastical property administration. These pleased the anticlericals, who resented all the qualifications on the full sovereignty of the state which were conceded elsewhere in the law.

Anti-Italian "Crusades" and the *Non Expedit*. The anticlericals were strengthened by the intransigency of the clericals. Pius IX issued appeals to foreign Roman Catholics to come to his aid, and the Roman Catholic parties of Austria, Germany, and France talked so belligerently of "crusades" that the Italian government several times in the 1870's considered war a serious likelihood. This sympathy for the Pope was taken advantage of financially by the revival of "Peter's Pence," which soon came to exceed the revenue from the former Papal States. Straws from the "dungeon bed" of the "prisoner of the Vatican" and red flannel for the new "crusade" were distributed to the faithful. From the Vatican, meanwhile, the Pope denied to Italian Roman Catholics the right to participate in the political life of his despoiler, the Kingdom of Italy, either by voting or running for office. By such a "sit-down strike" of Italian Roman Catholics he hoped to force the government to meet his terms. This *non expedit* gave Italian Roman Catholics a choice between ecclesiastical obedience and patriotism. The latter alternative was not the loser. Leo XIII maintained the *non expedit* into the twentieth century, but it had long been apparent that the chief effect of this policy was to strengthen radical and socialist influences in the government.

The Italian left supported Bismarck in 1875 when he put pressure on the Italian government to modify the Law of

Guarantees. The Pope had issued an encyclical against the German May Laws (see below, p. 225) and the Chancellor attempted to hold the Italian government responsible for such hostile acts emanating from Italian soil. The Law of Guarantees survived this pressure, but the next year the Italian left came to power, with the program of joining the *Kulturkampf* against political Roman Catholicism. The occasion of most excitement was the proposed "Clerical Abuses Bill," which sought to penalize clergy who used spiritual pressures to attack the Italian state. French Roman Catholic threats of intervention in 1877 went so far that Italy took military measures for defense. More significant in the long run, however, was the Coppino education law of the same year. The secular state was concerned for the illiterate masses which the church had preferred not to educate and required three years of elementary education for them. Religious education in the state schools was to be made available at the request of parents; in fact, however, requests were in a minority, and priests often refused to provide such instruction. The net effect was a secularization of Italian education. On the university level Roman Catholic theological faculties were closed and the higher culture of the nation and the methods and conclusions of Roman Catholic theology became two unrelated worlds.

DIPLOMACY OF LEO XIII. In 1878 Leo XIII succeeded to the papal throne. For a quarter of a century he schemed tirelessly, but vainly, to recover the formal Papal States, seeking the assistance against Italy of Bismarck, Franz Josef, and even the Third Republic of France. Leo protested formally some sixty times against the spoliation of the church and retained in force into the twentieth century the *non expedit*. Leo's diplomatic maneuvers against Italy were a major factor in leading that state to join in the Triple Alliance (1882) in order to gain international support. The antagonism reached its bitterest peak in 1889 when a commemorative statue to the Renaissance philosopher, Giordano Bruno, victim of the Holy Office, was erected in Rome, and when a new penal code setting various restrictions on the political activity of the clergy was promulgated. A decade later the Italian government succeeded in barring Leo from the Hague Peace Conference, and in World

War I, similarly, Italy blackballed the papacy from the Versailles conference.

Although his cultivation of other states was completely unsuccessful in its chief aim, Leo did win a new moral influence for the Roman See. His encyclical letters on social and political issues won for the stateless papacy an influence which the pope-kings of central Italy, with their private political interests, had not enjoyed for centuries. By the time of Leo's death (1903) the "Roman Question" had really ceased to be a matter of passionate concern and was less significant in the relation of the church to the Italian government than the universal church-state problems, such as education, marriage legislation, freedom of speech and press, and property issues.

Kulturkampf IN THE GERMAN EMPIRE. The German *Kulturkampf* was less protracted than the Italian; *détente* was perceptible from the accession of Leo XIII in 1878. The same political motive, however, dominated the conflict in Germany, namely, the threat of Roman Catholic interests to a newly achieved and still uncertain national unity. In Italy the "Roman Question" imperiled the territorial integrity of the nation. In Germany the new Prussian-centered Hohenzollern Empire of 1870 feared disintegration as a result of Roman Catholic "states' rights" policies in German Poland, Alsace-Lorraine, and South Germany. Bismarck's chief foreign foes, Austria, France, and Poland, were also Roman Catholic. He feared Vatican diplomacy without as well as Roman Catholic centrifugal pressure within against the new Protestant Empire which had replaced the former Holy Roman Empire of the Germanies. And since his strongest internal support for German unity came from the "Liberal" party, he found it expedient to adopt some of the strenuous anticlericalism of this party, even though his own sympathies were closer to the Lutheran conservatives. It was the spectacle of the parliamentary force of clericalism in the Center Party in the first Diet which determined Bismarck on open hostilities. Here, under the leadership of Windhorst, the "uncrowned king of Roman Catholic Germany," was a consolidation of all the decentralist forces Bismarck most feared, and here, in the appeal of the Center for German intervention in Italy on the Pope's behalf, was evidence of the Roman Catholic preference for sectarian over national interests.

THE "OLD CATHOLICS." The German struggle was complicated by the schism of the "Old Catholics," that group, chiefly German and Swiss, which refused to accept the decrees of the Vatican Council. Before and during the Vatican Council the German and Austrian episcopate had tried to prevent the definition of papal infallibility. German Catholicism was the most intelligent in the church, and the overwhelming evidence of history against papal infallibility was more widely understood in that country. In the face of the *fait accompli*, however, all the bishops at last offered up the *sacrifizio dell'intelletto*. A large number of professors, however, headed by the ablest Roman Catholic church historian of the century, Döllinger, declined to subscribe to a known falsehood. The rebels were excommunicated, but they drew up a program, elected Reinkens as bishop, secured episcopal consecration for him from the Jansenist Church in Amsterdam (see above, p. 35), and organized themselves as a church in 1873 at a Congress in Constance. The Old Catholic church was formally recognized by the governments of Prussia, Bavaria, Austria, Baden, and Hesse and was given a share of church buildings and property. The Swiss government likewise granted it recognition. All the Roman Catholic churches in the canton of Geneva became Old Catholic, as did many in other parts of Switzerland. Vaticanist clergy were expelled. Herzog was consecrated bishop in Switzerland. When the papacy attacked the government in an encyclical (1873), the Swiss broke off relations. But although the Old Catholics had a large number of distinguished men, their popular appeal was small and they had great difficulty in securing clergy. In Bavaria there were fifteen churches to one priest. Their maximum strength, about 1878, was only some fifty thousand, and thereafter they suffered losses. They entered into relations with Eastern Orthodoxy and Anglicanism at the Bonn Conference of 1874-1879.

This schism raised problems in the state-supported Roman Catholic schools of Germany. Where teachers refused to acknowledge the Vatican decrees, the bishops suspended or excommunicated them. The government, however, protected the teachers by insisting that their appointment and removal lay in the hands of the state and not the hierarchy. Another controversy over education was centered in German Poland over the question of the German *vs.* the Polish language. Archbishop Ledochowski defied the government regulation that religion classes must be conducted in German, and when he set up private Polish-speaking schools he was arrested.

Feeling ran very high over these several issues, and the Prussian government embarked recklessly on a course of exceptional legislation to crush the Roman Catholic resistance. A Pulpit Law (December 1871) laid penalties on clergy for preaching against the constitution. When the Vatican rejected Cardinal von Hohenlohe as ambassador, a law was passed suppressing the Jesuit order (July 1872) and some associated orders from the Empire. This popular cure-all, however, only solidified the Roman Catholic front, and produced further evidence of Roman Catholic hostility to the Empire as such. The *Civilta Cattolica* looked forward to the end of the Empire, and the Munich *Vaterland* affirmed: "We do not value this German Empire of yours; we have never acknowledged it."

THE MAY LAWS. Bismarck and Falk, his Minister of Education and Religion, now pushed the attack to the point of actually amending the Prussian Constitution (paragraphs 15, 18) to permit interference with the internal life of the church. The "Falk" or "May Laws" of 1873 regulated the training and placement of the clergy. Clergy were required to be *Gymnasium* graduates with three years of theological study at a university. Church seminaries were to be controlled by state inspectors. All candidates must pass a state *Kulturexamen*. All ecclesiastical appointments and transfers, moreover, had to be submitted in advance for the approval of the provincial governors. The church was to be confined to purely spiritual disciplines, and appeal from ecclesiastical discipline could be made to a supreme ecclesiastical court of the state. The effect of this legislation may be indicated by a comment from the *New York Tribune:* "Imagine a law in America which should compel every Presbyterian clergyman to receive a certain specified education under state supervision, to pass a state examination therein, to accept a "call" only when the state approved, and to submit any troubles in which he, in his clerical capacity, might become involved, to the decision of a Special State Court, the majority of the members of which belonged to denominations bitterly opposed to his own."

The May Laws were widely disobeyed by the Roman clergy, and the imprisonment or exile of recalcitrant priests soon posed new problems. Arrangements had to be made for lay administration of vacant dioceses and for the election of priests. Doubt over the legality of marriages performed by refractory clergy pushed the government to the requirement of civil marriage, against the desires of many Lutherans. To put further pressure on the Roman Catholic Church the clerical exemption from military service was abolished and the German embassy at the Vatican was withdrawn. Bismarck attempted to get the Italian and French governments to support him against the Vatican. A Roman Catholic failed in an attempt to assassinate the Chancellor.

In 1875 Pius IX took the occasion of the arrest of three bishops to issue *Quod numquam*, declaring the May Laws "invalid." This was received as a denial of the sovereignty of Prussia, and its publication was banned. All religious orders save those for nurses were now excluded. The "bread-basket law" cancelled clerical salaries pending a formal declaration of obedience. The Roman Catholics were thus driven to organize a system of independent financing. Similar battles were taking place at the same time in Baden, Hesse, and Saxony.

DÉTENTE. At the accession of Leo XIII in 1878, after seven years of such warfare, there were nine vacant bishoprics, and over half a million Roman Catholics were deprived of pastoral care. Two thousand priests had been fined. Church revenues were cut off. Civil marriage had been made obligatory. Schools, colleges, and religious orders had been suppressed. General disrespect for religion had spread, meanwhile, and the Marxists seemed to be the chief beneficiaries. This last result concerned Bismarck especially. He had been ready for negotiations with the church from 1874 and, in 1878, he put out diplomatic feelers toward Rome. Leo's encyclical *Humanum genus* was interpreted by many as a similar overture, calling attention to the opposition of the Roman Catholic Church to socialism. In fact, the laws were not repealed outright, but in 1880 Bismarck received the power to use his discretion in enforcing them. Most of them were taken off the books altogether seven years later. Bismarck and Leo had discovered a community or convergence of interests on several points. And the struggle had consolidated German Roman Catholicism into possibly the most highly organized and politically effective Roman Catholic bloc in the world. The Center Party often held the balance of power in Germany in the quarter-century before World War I.

ROMAN CATHOLICISM AND FRENCH MONARCHISM. Like the new German Reich, the Third French Republic was born out of the Franco-Prussian War of 1870. And until World War I, at least, the most fundamental cleavage in French politics was the question of the Roman Church. Here the choice was between being a Republican and being a Roman Catholic. The hierarchy and the leading laity took it for granted that Roman Catholicism meant royalism. And had not four or five rival monarchist parties existed in the 1880's, France might not have had a Third Republic. The Republican form was adopted simply as a provisional regime, the government which would "divide Frenchmen least." Not until 1879 was the government actually controlled by convinced Republicans, that is to say, by anticlericals. In the interval the nation had turned against the Roman Catholic Royalist party because of its reckless willingness to launch France into another hopeless war with Germany in response to the Pope's repeated summons to intervention in Italy. The parliament at the beginning of the decade was more proclerical than any French government in forty years. It raised the church budget, encouraged a new expansion of regular clergy, gave the church control over charities, returned the administration of state education to clerical control, and permitted the church to establish universities. Despite these institutional gains, however, religious vitality was low, as could be seen from the absence of men in public worship, the low recruitment rate for the clergy, and the conquest of traditional French piety by the superstitious Italian style of popular devotions. The government of the clerical Royalists, however, so alienated the voters that after the coup of 1877 Gambetta won the elections for his Republicans with the slogan "Le cléricalisme, voilà l'ennemi!" Laymen were leaving the church as a center of conspiracy against the government and the national interest.

SECULAR MONOPOLY IN EDUCATION. The year after Leo's accession to the papal throne, the Republicans captured the French Senate as well as the Chamber, and the French *Kulturkampf* was launched. The crucial years were from 1879 to 1889. During this period, the anticlericals, led by the Freemasons, focused their efforts against the religious orders with their influence on education, charities, and the press. They sought to build up a secular public school system. Rigorous enforcement of the provisions of the Concordat regarding religious orders led to the forcible expulsion of regular clergy all over France, while the nation in general remained indifferent to their fate. With regard to education the five Roman Catholic theological faculties in the universities were suppressed and the church-controlled higher schools were denied the title "university" or the right to grant degrees. State normal schools and girls' secondary schools were established. Episcopal control of the administration of public education was broken. And most important of all, a series of laws made elementary education free (1881), compulsory (1882), and laicized the teaching staff (1886). Released time was provided for religious instruction. The whole program was fought by the Roman Church step by step, although not, as in Belgium, to the edge of virtual civil war. In both countries the last resort of the church was a huge building program of private confessional schools to rival the state system.

With the French, as with the German *Kulturkampf*, which he had likewise inherited from Pius IX, Leo XIII sought to make peace. His nuncio Czacki cultivated the Republican leaders and tactfully tried to wean French Roman Catholicism from the monarchist cause. However, Père Didon, the greatest preacher of his generation, was silenced from 1886 to 1892 for following the Pope's lead too boldly, and every conspiracy against the Republic, such as that of General Boulanger, found ready Roman Catholic support. Leo's hints in *Immortale dei* (1885) and *Libertas praestantissimam* (1868) as to how Roman

Catholics might co-operate practically with liberal and non-monarchical regimes evoked few echoes in France. At the beginning of the 1890's Leo took stronger measures, instigating Cardinal Lavigerie's famous "Algiers toast" to the Republic, a gesture which cost Lavigerie most of his financial support. And finally, with *Au milieu des sollicitudes* (1892), Leo came out with the official papal line of a "united front," of acceptance of the Republic for practical purposes. Many French Roman Catholics now began to pray for the conversion of the Pope, but at least Leo had broken the complete identification of French Roman Catholicism with hostility to the Republic. Vatican policy had taken a new turn when Rampolla was made Secretary of State in 1887. The earlier orientation toward the Central Powers was now laid aside for a pro-French policy in the campaign for recovery of the Papal States from Italy. But for any success here the feud of the French Roman Catholics with the state must be reconciled.

THE DREYFUS AFFAIR. Rampolla's years of quiet preparation, however, were brought to naught by the explosion, in the second half of the 1890's, of the Dreyfus affair. All neutral observers became convinced of the necessity for a retrial of Dreyfus, who had been convicted of communicating military secrets, as a result of later developments. Henry, the chief witness against Dreyfus, confessed to having forged his evidence and then committed suicide, and Esterhazy, the man whom the defenders of Dreyfus denounced as the real criminal, fled the country, despite the fact that the War Office had whitewashed him in court-martial. However, the War Office, the army, the professional patriots, the anti-Semites, the monarchists, and the Roman Catholics generally worked together in the attempt to prevent a retrial and to keep Dreyfus on Devil's Island. The Assumptionist fathers, who conducted the Roman Catholic newspaper, *La Croix*, carried on a violent campaign against Dreyfus, Jews, and Republicans in general. The Jesuit *Civilta Cattolica* informed the Roman Catholic world that "the Jew has been created by God to serve as a spy," and demanded the withdrawal of civil rights from all French Jews. The "Catholic democrats," inspired by Leo's *Rerum novarum*, made anti-Semitism their chief stock-in-trade, rivaling the propaganda of

Drumont's *Libre Parole* in preaching hatred and violence. *La Croix* and *Libre Parole* helped to raise a fund for the forger-suicide "martyr" Henry, and a "League of the French Nation" was organized by Maurras as the immediate ancestor of the atheistic but clerical fascism of *Action française*. And while in these ways the Roman Catholic Church (especially the religious orders) contributed to the atmosphere of hatred, passion, and prejudice, it abandoned to a handful of secular Republicans, such as the novelist Zola, the heroic role of being witnesses to truth and justice.

LAW OF ASSOCIATIONS.   This betrayal of Christianity by Roman Catholic fanaticism in the Dreyfus affair gave the fanatics of anticlericalism their chance.   National revulsion swept anti-clerical governments into power and the second chapter of the French *Kulturkampf* was now enacted.   The first move was an attack on the religious orders, who were made, and not without some justification, scapegoats for the nation's shame.   The "Associations Law" of 1901 was the most decisively anticlerical legislation since 1870.   The law gave greater freedom for incorporation in general, but in the case of associations of those living in common, or of mixed French and foreign nationalities, or holding corporate property—the Roman Catholic monastic orders, in short—a specific legislative act of authorization was required.   All orders beyond the five legally authorized were required to seek such authorization, and members of unauthorized congregations were denied the right to teach or direct schools.   The 1902 elections returned an even more anti-clerical Chamber, and Combes, a former ultramontane, now an equally doctrinaire anticlerical, headed a cabinet of Masons. Combes proceeded to enforce the Associations Law far more rigidly than its authors intended.   He closed thousands of schools conducted by unauthorized orders.   Only a handful of orders, moreover, received authorization from the parliament. Many of the rest declared they would yield only to force, which the government cheerfully used.   In the spring of 1903 nearly all the communities were dispersed.   Efforts of the church to arouse popular indignation met with little response; the orders had won little affection from the nation as a whole.

LAW OF SEPARATION. The next year the new pope, Pius X, described President Loubet's visit to the King of Italy in Rome as "an offense to the Holy See," and in the resultant scandal diplomatic relations between France and the papacy were broken off. Pius X, like Combes, was an intransigent doctrinaire, brought up on the conviction of the satanic character of the French Republic. The result of this head-on collision of "integral" Romanism and dogmatic secularism was the Law of Separation of 1905, which finally ended Napoleon's Concordat. Although sponsored by the anticlericals, the bill had become a rather statesmanlike measure in the course of parliamentary debate under the leadership of Briand, and the large majority of the French episcopate voted to accept it (May 1906). The substance of the law was that the church lost its public subsidies and legal privileges in return for the freedom of choosing bishops and holding assemblies without governmental controls. Boards of trustees were to be organized to take over ecclesiastical properties, and to raise and administer funds for religious purposes.

But the Pope would have none of it. He overruled the French episcopate and a series of encyclicals condemned the whole idea of separation and the free church in the free state. In particular he objected that the vesting in trustees of legal title to property denied the canonical hierarchical structure of the church. The state tried to meet this objection in a series of concessions (1907, 1908), but Pius refused all compromises and the Roman Catholic Church was not to have a legal basis in France until the 1920's. The Pope launched the church in a battle with the state which cost it heavy financial losses and lowered the intellectual and social level of the clergy, but enabled him to perfect ultramontane control. The majority of the French nation, meanwhile, had given up all relations and sympathies with Roman Catholicism. And indeed, by the outbreak of World War I the political and diplomatic influence of the Vatican had sunk so low generally that only a corporal's guard of diplomats remained in residence there.

Chapter 18

"CATHOLIC ACTION"

The international *Kulturkampf* of Roman Catholicism was intimately related to the inability of that church to adjust itself to the new political democracy and the self-disciplined cultural and economic initiative which now dominated Western Civilization. Anglo-American Evangelicalism had become intimately related to political democracy and to capitalistic individualism. It had provided both of them with a degree of ethical discipline and responsibility which, as a rule, they lacked in Roman Catholic and Lutheran societies. These latter Christian traditions remained wedded to economic traditionalism and political authoritarianism. In the societies which they dominated, democracy and the economy of the free market made their way without benefit of clergy, and, indeed, in their despite, because the churches opposed them in the name of monarchist, feudal, and preindustrial patterns. Let us first consider the attitude of the Roman Church to political liberalism and democracy, and then turn to its social and economic policy. In the first case, France and the United States posed issues; in the second, Germany and Central Europe.

The peculiarity of France in the Roman Catholic world in this period was that she had become a republic. In the other dominantly Roman Catholic countries of Europe, political loyalties still supported legitimate monarchs. In France, likewise, the overwhelming majority of Roman Catholics, lay and clerical, identified political royalism with their religious faith, and into the twentieth century every conspiracy and every attempted coup against the Third Republic—and there were several—found ready support among the Roman Catholics. It was a presupposition of French politics, at least into the 1890's, that if one were a republican or democrat he must be anticlerical. And since, for political reasons, the majority of the nation supported the Republic, the Roman Church suffered seriously from this orientation to political reaction.

The United States presented a similar case. Here the republican constitutional structure and democratic political pattern of life had been established under Puritan Protestant influences before substantial Roman Catholic immigration had begun in the 1830's. The nineteenth-century Roman Catholic immigration, however, was immense, and by the time of World War I American Roman Catholics were more numerous than French Roman Catholics, although less influential, to be sure, in the church at large. In any case, here was a second large contingent of Roman Catholics forced to live within a democratic political system created by non-Roman Catholics. Unlike the French, however, the American Roman Catholic by and large supported the republic and even the constitutional guarantees of civil and religious liberty and of separation of church and state.

POLICY OF LEO XIII. In his search for foreign aid against the Kingdom of Italy, Leo XIII was ready to make more concessions than his predecessors. And when, from the late 1880's, he definitely pinned his hopes on France rather than the Central Powers, it became all the more essential to his program to reconcile French Roman Catholicism with political liberalism, republicanism, and democracy. Through the activities of his nuncio, through his episcopal appointments, and through a series of official pronouncements, Leo sought to promote a reconciliation of Roman Catholics to the Third Republic. This last group of encyclicals must be particularly noticed, since they were to provide the rationale of Roman Catholic adjustment to political democracy down to the middle of the twentieth century.

Leo's politics can be conveniently analyzed in terms of the distinctions between "thesis" and "hypothesis" which Dupanloup had made famous in his study of the political bearings of the *Syllabus*. The two lines of thought were relevant severally to the French and to the Americans. As against the democratically-tempted American Roman Catholics, the "thesis" must be kept clear that the Roman Church is opposed to political liberalism and democracy, to separation of church and state, and to civil and religious liberty. As Leo had said at the beginning of his reign, "I desire that modern society should end by reconciling itself sooner or later to the *Syllabus*, by understanding all its aims." As against the stupid obstinacy of the French Roman Catholic anti-Republicans, on the other hand, Leo urged the hypothesis of temporary compromise for the sake of the interests of the church. He gravely tried the faith of many devout French Roman Catholics by virtually ordering them at length to accept the satanic Republic as a *fait accompli*.

LEO ON POLITICAL DEMOCRACY AND CIVIL LIBERTY. Leo stated, against the prevailing opinion of French Roman Catholics, that the Roman Church was not committed to any one form of government—monarchic, aristocratic, or democratic—and that Roman Catholics might accept any of the three. His more detailed analysis, however, indicated that he found unacceptable the moral presuppositions which lay behind modern democracy. Modern liberal democracy had been born in the Puritan Revolution of the seventeenth century with the creation of a new political force, the "consciences of private men." Leo, however, still represented the Roman Catholic tradition that private men are not called to responsible political initiative but only to obey their superiors. According to this view, political authority cannot be derived from or be responsible to the people, but is assigned by God directly to ruling castes or dynasties (*Diuturnum illud*). And to turn the matter about, the right of revolution, which is the necessary defense of democratic practice, was declared by Leo to have become dormant if it ever existed. Nurtured in such political ethics as this, Roman Catholics might be able to accept the external forms of political democracy, but they would never contribute their share to the moral energies from which it lived.

The problem went even deeper. Liberal democracy determines policy by the free discussion and deliberation of the whole body of citizens. Free discussion presupposes free circulation of facts and ideas—the whole range, in short of freedoms: freedom of religion, of conscience, of speech, of the press, of assembly. But all these freedoms are opposed in principle to the Index and Inquisition, to censorship and propaganda. Here again Leo affirmed the positions of his predecessors in *mirari vos* and the *Syllabus*. Roman Catholicism, ideally and in principle, condemns civil and religious liberty. But while agreeing with the French Roman Catholics in principle, in practice Leo urged on them the position of the Americans, that the freedoms of the Bill of Rights "may be tolerated where there is just cause." Where Roman Catholics are in a large majority, of course, there would no longer be cause for toleration.

CLERICAL SUPREMACY. The same issues may be viewed from the perspective of church-state relations. Liberal democracy rests upon the rejection of clerical supremacy in politics. There can be no democracy if policy is determined by a clerical hierarchy. And, in fact, liberal democracy had always involved either outright separation of church and state, as in America, or an approximation to it, as in England. But this was precisely the fundamental heresy of political liberalism and democracy which the *Syllabus* had roundly anathematized. Thus Leo insisted that all states are by right obliged to give official privileged status to the Roman Church. In practice, however, he declared that the church would not condemn rulers who might tolerate heretical sects "for the sake of securing some great good, or of hindering some great evil." Outright separation, as in the American Constitution, did not even come under the dispensations of the "hypothesis." It posed an interesting situation, consequently, when the American liberal Roman Catholics, Archbishop Gibbons and Mgr. Ireland, boldly asserted that separation was preferable to official establishment. Gibbons stated such views in Rome itself and declared that, if he were able, he would not in any way alter the American Constitution. Despite his liking for Gibbons, the Pope could not let this Protestantizing heresy pass. He served notice that the constitutional separation in America, however beneficial at the moment, did not satisfy the Roman Church in principle and that the latter aspired to "the patronage of the public authority" (*Longingue oceani*).

In the light of this record the sudden conversion of a large group of French Roman Catholics to democracy at the Pope's orders (*Au Milieu des Sollicitudes*, 1892) was received with only moderate enthusiasm by French democrats. These altars draped with the national colors, where a week before the priest had preached against the Republic, smelled strongly of policy. The enforced change-over was itself more contemptuous of democracy than the earlier honest opposition to it.

DEFINITION OF "CATHOLIC DEMOCRACY." Leo's flirtation with French democracy was swept aside, as we have seen, by the hotter passions of the Dreyfus case. And with his last important encyclical (*Graves de communi*, 1901) Leo set definite limits to the democratic tendency he had seemed to encourage in *Rerum novarum* and *Au Milieu des Sollicitudes*. He redefined the word "democracy" to mean government of the people, for the people, by authoritarians. "If there is such a thing as a perfect democratic form," said the Pope, "this is undoubtedly to be found in the Church." "Catholic democracy" since 1901 has thus meant properly benevolent despotism. Roman Catholic "democracy" could not mean political democracy and was to have no intention of diminishing the spirit of obedience to legitimate princes. Socially, again, class hierarchy and paternalism were affirmed as against democratic fluidity and equality of opportunity. And most important of all, Leo insisted on clerical control of all Roman Catholic political enterprises, thus precluding democratic determination of policy.

There were at this time two notable democratic movements of Roman Catholics in Roman Catholic countries, that of the Italians led by Romolo Murri, and Marc Sangnier's *Sillon* in France. Vastly more influential in the hierarchy and among Catholic intellectuals, however, was Maurras' *Action française*, which from one point of view might be regarded as the first significant fascist movement of the new century. And in the great purge of all "modernism" under Pius X, the *Action française* was primarily influential through the Vatican in stamping out democracy among Roman Catholics as "political modernism." From this ruthless purge, extending over some years, we may cite the fullest authoritative statement, the papal encyclical condemning the *Sillon* in 1910.

CONDEMNATION OF THE "SILLON." The Pope repudiated systematically the idealistic democracy of the *Sillon*. Those in Sangnier's movement believed that God vests political authority in the people, who then delegate it to their chosen rulers. This belief, said Pius, is contrary to Roman Catholic truth, according to which power descends from the higher social spheres and does not rest on the consent of the governed. The moral presupposition of democracy, a large body of responsible self-determined individuals deciding in free discussion on policy, was also condemned. Free responsible personhood is contrary to the Roman Catholic ideal of obedience to superiors, as illustrated by priests or saints. Among such free persons, further, it is chimerical to appeal to brotherhood, for there is no true fraternity outside Christian charity. The co-operation of the *Sillon* with non-Roman Catholics had been a very dangerous form of promiscuity and had dissipated energies which should have been kept in exclusively ecclesiastical channels. Even worse, the *Sillon* had not in practice respected the prerogative of the clergy to determine policy, but had discussed with priests as comrades. The Pope did not mean to suggest that a Roman Catholic could not be a democrat, but a Roman Catholic democrat must not hold any of the errors of the *Sillon*. In fact, of course, no Roman Catholic movement has ever come nearer to liberal democracy than the *Sillon*.

SOCIAL POLICY IN CENTRAL EUROPE. Let us turn from these issues of the forms and dynamics of political life, as debated especially in France, to the related questions of social and economic policy. The very intensity of political controversy in France seems to have delayed extensive development there. In Italy, on the other hand, where politics were forbidden by the *non expedit*, and in Germany where the Roman Catholic minority sought every means of tightening its corporate life and discipline by way of defense, Roman Catholic social action produced most conspicuous achievements. It may also be significant that the Industrial Revolution was now just reaching these countries. Belgium and France were already industrialized and here the Roman Catholic population was predominantly capitalist and individualist as in the English-speaking world, but without its vestigial sense of religious vocation in business. In Central Europe, however, the old preindustrial economic and social order was still fighting the introduction of the machine. Much of Roman Catholic social action here, and the papal social encyclicals, can be read as economic primitivism, an attempt to maintain or to return to medieval guilds, manorial regulations, and the like, as a defense against large-scale industry. The counterpart of this attitude of Leo XIII may be found in the English-speaking world in the social protests and nostalgia for the Middle Ages of Carlyle and Ruskin early in the century. And in his own day Leo XIII stood much closer in his social policy to the paternalism of autocratic Lutherans such as Bismarck than to anything in the English-speaking world.

In Central Europe Lutherans and Roman Catholics alike were led by the land-owning aristocracy, who represented a mentality both antidemocratic and anticapitalist. From natural interest they opposed the new power of fluid capital and sought to maintain the older social hierarchy based on land and fixed by law and guild regulations into a static system. Familiar with a system constructed of legal privileges and monopolies, they had none of the inhibitions about state interference in business found in peoples who had passed into the capitalist stage. Thus Bishop Ketteler preferred the socialist scheme of Lassalle to economic individualism and freedom. It was Lutheran Germany which pioneered in state social insurance fifty years before the United States accepted the idea. Lutherans and Roman Catholics alike supported proposals for state sanction for guild regulations over production and wages. In Austria, similarly, the Roman Catholic feudal nobility sought to strengthen by law guild powers over prices, production, and the freedom of choosing an occupation. Here also the anti-free market program was combined with opposition to parliaments and democracy. A few French Roman Catholics led by De Mun also attempted to organize a movement to bring back the Bourbons and the medieval guilds and to actualize the *Syllabus*, but in France such a program was already hopelessly out of date. In all these countries the notion was entertained of building legislative bodies out of these guilds, rather than establishing them by general election—the general conception made familiar later in the form of Mussolini's "corporative state." Leo XIII followed closely this international movement among Roman Catholic conservatives in the 1880's and preferred these views to the capitalistic individualism dominant among French, Belgian, British, and American Roman Catholics. In particular, he was enthusiastic for the restoration of the guild system and a legislative body based on it in preference to representative democracy.

"RERUM NOVARUM." In 1891 the Pope definitely put the church on the side of the Central Europeans in the famous encyclical *Rerum novarum*. Leo set his discussion firmly on a conservative basis by taking the inviolability of private property and the class divisions of rich and poor as unalterable. Within these conditions he then commended a benevolent paternalism on the part of the state. Matters such as the regulation of hours and working conditions, however, he would prefer to see in the hands of an industrial guild than a state office. And he defended the right of association of workman and masters into such organizations as a "natural" right. In Western Europe and America many were startled to find the right of workmen to organize and the duty of the state to regulate industry being asserted from such a source as the Vatican. And on the Continent Leo's encyclical gave great stimulus to social action of all sorts among Roman Catholics.

ORGANIZATION OF "CATHOLIC ACTION." Roman Catholic social organization was already well under way in a great variety of situations. Peasants' unions with co-operatives and credit unions were flourishing under Roman Catholic auspices in south and west Germany and in Belgium. Roman Catholic labor unions were designed to save workmen from the Marxist propaganda of the socialist unions. Secretariats distributing information and literature on social questions were organized in Germany, Italy, and France. All these associations and many more were supervised and directed by clerics and—at least in Germany, Holland, and Belgium—mobilized into Roman Catholic political parties. In this way the whole Roman Catholic population was disciplined and manipulated by the episcopate so that even under democratic political forms a clerical theocracy still exerted great political power. Protestantism carried on substantially the same sort of social activities but with little or nothing of the effort at co-ordinated social control of an ultimately political character which distinguished "Catholic Action."

Even the quasi-military discipline of Roman "Catholic Action," however, was strained to the breaking point by controversies over social questions in the 1890's. Roman Catholic workers and some priests interpreted *Rerum novarum* as justifying at least a measure of industrial democracy, whereas the aristocrats and employers who generally dominated the Roman Catholic parties were scandalized at such insolence. In Italy and Belgium the general Roman Catholic organizations were torn apart and the Pope attempted reorganization on a new basis. In France the debate gathered additional heat, owing to political complications, since the champions of industrial and social democracy were also usually defenders of the Pope's attempted reconciliation with the Republic and were hated and attacked on this ground by the monarchists as well as by social and economic conservatives. *Graves de communi* was an attempt to resolve this controversy and, as we have seen, repudiated all suggestions of political democracy in the Roman Catholic social program. *Rerum novarum* was to be read in the spirit of paternalist philanthropy, not economic democracy.

REACTION UNDER PIUS X. Pius X was to press the reaction even farther, in this sphere as in all others. In his purge ended this third notable upsurge of liberal Roman Catholicism of the nineteenth century. After World War I conservative Roman Catholic social theory was to take on new vigor in the form of clerical fascism.

Chapter 19

CONTINENTAL PROTESTANTISM

The strength of Continental Protestantism in the forty-five years before World War I was most conspicuous in its theological scholarship, which we will treat in a separate chapter. Church life, by contrast, was less creative and vigorous on the Continent than in Great Britain or the United States. Consequently, we will attempt to survey the more conspicuous aspects of both Lutheranism and the Reformed churches in a single chapter.

GERMAN LUTHERANISM. We begin with German Lutheranism, both because it is the largest single body of Protestants on the Continent, and also because it was most conspicuously related to the new social and political forces of the period. The churches of Lutheran Scandinavia might be preferred as being in some ways more "normal" or healthy, but their normality consisted in considerable measure in the fact that they were not yet confronted with dynamic capitalism, socialism, and militaristic imperialism. The German Hohenzollern Empire which emerged victorious from the Franco-Prussian War of 1870 was the most powerful state on the Continent politically and economically; this empire was the scene, consequently, of the struggle of Lutheranism to relate itself to these new forces.

The two most conspicuous representatives of the social and political witness of Lutheranism in the first quarter-century of our period were Chancellor Bismarck and the Prussian court preacher Adolf Stoecker. Both men derived from the pietist orthodoxy and political reaction of Restoration Lutheranism. Their natural assumption was that of traditional Lutheran social thought—of a feudal social order, based on the landed gentry and the king, ruling with benevolent despotism over the lower orders. The use of force by the prince within and without was taken for granted in a world of sin. The Christian element in the system was the benevolence and personal loyalty in the ties between lord and subject, master and servant, father and children. A static agrarian society was presupposed.

This was the traditional ethic within which German Lutherans now sought to cope with the social effects of industrialism. In 1850 Germany was still more rural and feudal than England had been in 1750. Peasants were still often little better than serfs, and workmen were still in considerable measure regulated by the medieval guilds. But the railroad had been introduced and coal, iron, and steel production expanded phenomenally, with their social consequences in the factory system. By 1860, out of a population of about thirty-five million, perhaps one in seven belonged to a new proletarian class. At the other end of the scale, the masters of finance and industry increasingly challenged the traditional squirearchy for influence in, or control of, the state.

The new proletarians brought from their peasant backgrounds no hopes or expectations of political power; they were used to submission. But in the mass concentrations of the factory all the personal patriarchal concern and the personal loyalty were gone. There remained only impersonal abstract relations between employer and employed, relations which could readily be interpreted as characterized by injustice and exploitation. In the one short decade of the 1860's the new German proletariat became convinced that this interpretation was the right one. Lassalle's demagoguery began the convincing, popularizing Ricardo's "iron law of wages" and Marx's theory of "surplus value." In 1864 Marx captured the International Workmen's Association and sent Liebknecht to evangelize Germany the next year. Liebknecht won over the twenty-five-year old Bebel, who was soon to become the most famous protagonist of Marxist socialism in Germany. The demand for universal suffrage was granted in 1867 and confirmed for the Empire in 1871, although it was qualified by a class system which in effect gave plural votes to the upper classes. By the time of the founding of the Hohenzollern Empire the whole German labor movement was oriented to the capture of political power, and was convinced that the existing state and the existing Protestant church were tools of their oppressors. The Lutheran attempts to justify this social system as the divinely sanctioned "orders" of society seemed to them ideology in its technical sense of class rationalization. The presence of this completely disaffected bloc within German society was to be the chief internal problem of the Hohenzollern Empire. By the time of World War I Germany was to have the largest Marxist party in the world, a phenomenon closely related, as we have seen, to the church-state structure, social ethic, and class relations of German Lutheranism.

MARXISM AS JUDAEO-CHRISTIAN HERESY. It was not then recognized generally, as it was to be in the twentieth century, that Marxism was in a real sense a Judaeo-Christian heresy. The earlier writings of the young Marx were chiefly theological in the current of left-wing Hegelianism. And the appeal of Marxism lay in its affirmation of certain prophetic emphases of the biblical tradition, especially the demand for justice and brotherhood. The "dialectic" of history which, Marx prophesied, would bring them to birth was merely a Hegelian disguise for the Lord of History. And the pattern of a primitive Eden, corrupted by the intrusion of private property and succeeded by long weary generations of toil and conflict until the messianic servant, the proletariat, should bring in the New Jerusalem of the classless society and peace and brotherhood—all this was inconceivable save in a Christian culture. It was in the name of these biblical convictions that the Marxists fought the churches. They adopted for public purposes the liberal slogan, "Religion is a private affair," but this did not represent their real conviction. No Marxist who wished to maintain a positive relation to institutional Christianity could hope to hold office for the party.

NATIONALISM AND VITALISM. A second development of these years which put unexpected strains on the Lutheran social ethic was the dynamism of nationalism, heightened by the Industrial Revolution. The older Lutheran ethic had been largely a *social* ethic, seeking to perpetuate a medieval social structure, but not oriented to state power as such. But Bis-

marck adapted himself to the new forces of history, and with
a ruthless devotion to state power, rode roughshod over principles of legitimacy, international justice, and loyalty to
persons. The traditional Lutheran defense of the sword, wheel,
and gallows as necessary to the maintenance of social order
took on new dimensions when it was applied to the dynamic
imperialism of the industrialized nation-state. In foreign, as
well as social policy Lutheran patriarchalism seemed to supply sanctions for injustice, exploitation, and aggression. What
had been devised as a pessimistic concession to the inescapable
evils of the common life now became increasingly a positive
affirmation of powers and tendencies which had very little to
do with Christianity. It was chiefly when proposals of social
reform were made that Lutheranism retreated into its pessimistic and quietist attitude.

In this situation Bismarck became the model for the most
widespread Lutheran adjustment to the situation. He carried
still further the Lutheran separation of the two realms of grace
and nature with their two types of ethics. In private life the
Christian should take as his standard the Sermon on the Mount,
but in public affairs he must perform the duties of his station.
There was no possibility of harmonizing the two and within the
ethics of public office a Christian could thus conscientiously
adopt the code of social Darwinism. In a somewhat different
way the Lutheran theologians of Erlangen insisted on the same
double ethic. They did not affirm activity in the world with
the vigor of a Bismarck, teaching rather a quietism and an
eschatological expectancy. But they would offer no resistance
to a policy of "blood and iron" and had no use for the tradition
of natural law, popular sovereignty, and social contract, as
maintained in the Reformed and Puritan countries and even, to
some extent, by the Roman Catholics.

Apart from the solidly anti-Christian socialist bloc, there
was also a very widespread revulsion from institutional Christianity among educated people. Perhaps the deepest antagonism to Christianity in these years was expressed by Frederick
Nietzsche. To some degree he viewed Christianity as did the
Marxists, as an instrument for achieving social docility and
conformity, an "ethic for slaves." He would brush aside these

artificial inhibitions and strive for new levels of human life on the basis of atheistic vitalism. Although Nietzsche himself was contemptuous of nationalism, imperialism, and anti-Semitism, his aristocratic code of self-expression and creativity was increasingly vulgarized to serve these programs. Some elements of this general outlook were to become a widespread pseudo religion in the twentieth century in the form of Freudianism.

A somewhat less radical manifestation of the reaction against industrial urbanization and middle-class and ecclesiastical conventionality was the German youth movement, which was active from about the turn of the century. Here, along with nature mysticism and vitalism, was a cult of folk-culture, songs, dances, and life near the soil. Walking tours among the *Wandervögel*, and work camps helped to break down class barriers and build group intimacy. Only small groups were involved in the years before World War I, but they were a symptom of the fact that the great body of German youth found no vision or vocation in the bourgeois society and its churches.

Also approaching the character of a religious movement was the cult of national culture, national spirit, national imperialism. Richard Wagner contributed substantially to this movement with his operas based on ancient Germanic myths and designed to interpret and develop the national soul. The racist theories of Count Gobineau and Houston Stewart Chamberlain attracted more of a following in this kind of atmosphere than was true of similar views in other Western countries. Here, then, was a widespread basis of nationalist and racist romanticism, among people whose connection with Christianity was purely nominal, on which National Socialism later could build.

The state churches of Germany thus held their position in society on a rather tenuous basis, being oriented so definitely to the interests and perspective of one class and the political machine. Nominal Christianity was a part of general etiquette. Over 95 per cent of the Germans received Christian baptism and marriage. There was a social stigma attached to withdrawal from the church, and the Marxist campaign for such withdrawal was able to persuade only about three to twenty thousand a year from 1900 until the great postwar revulsion from the church. The demand for disestablishment evoked little response from either government or clergy, both of which found establishment useful. But, as has been said, the Christianity of the great majority was purely nominal, as could be illustrated from figures of church attendance. It was symptomatic, for example, that in Berlin in 1880 there were church sittings for one in thirty of the city's population. And wherever the people were really moved by religion they seemed to move toward formations outside the established churches, as with the "community movements" from 1890 on, or the various gnostic, theosophical, mystical, and nationalist cults.

The monopoly of the state church, in contrast to conditions in England or the United States, left no *Christian* alternatives. Christian free churches in Germany claimed about 1 per cent of the population. In German life there was no equivalent to the "nonconformist conscience."

ORGANIZATION OF GERMAN CHURCHES. Let us glance briefly at the constitutional structure of this established Protestantism. The political unification of most of the Germans in 1871 had not entailed their ecclesiastical consolidation. The territorial churches of the several states, with the exception of Prussia, retained their separate administrations. Prussia dominated the structure of the Protestant church as she did the constitution of the new Empire. The enlarged Prussian state acquired a unified administration for its Protestant church, a church which thus constituted about half of all German Protestants and was, on paper, the largest Protestant church in the world. The sense of community among German Protestants generally was chiefly embodied in the network of voluntary societies—Inner Mission, Foreign Missions, Gustav Adolf Verein, and the like—which bound them together, at least as individuals, around specific projects. The territorial churches as such were also represented at the Eisenach Conferences from 1852, which were purely advisory in character. From 1903 they acquired a standing commission and carried on more effectively co-operative efforts in such matters of common concern as the chaplaincy, new translations of the Bible, religious education, and church architecture.

UNION CHURCH OF PRUSSIA. Among the score and more of German Protestant churches, we may consider particularly the Evangelical Union Church of Prussia as by far the most important and largest. The constitution of this church, like that of the Prussian state since 1850, was characterized by a display of machinery for self-government which was still largely window dressing for monarchical absolutism. Attempts were made to develop congregational organization and life, as well as synods, even to the extent of imposing them where they were not wanted. In 1869 provincial synods were called, and in 1873 a new church constitution was promulgated with these arrangements. Congregations were given more scope in the choice of elders and pastors than before. In 1911 this church contained about ten thousand parishes in nine provinces, further subdivided into districts of six hundred superintendents and twenty-four general superintendents. Over all, however, ruled the Supreme Evangelical Church Council, which was directly responsible to the Pontifex Maximus, the Kaiser. The Emperors, moreover, took their ecclesiastical responsibilities seriously. Kaiser Wilhelm II intervened in theological debates, modified church policy several times in public issues (as we shall see), and actually conducted services personally.

STOECKER. The public policy of this church in its first decades may be illustrated in the persons of the Kaiser, the Chancellor, and Adolf Stoecker. Adolf Stoecker was called to Berlin as court preacher in 1874. He represented the views of Restoration Lutheranism, sharing the Junker outlook and despising liberal parliamentarism as degenerate, and capitalism as mammonistic and Jewish. He was deeply concerned over the effects of urbanism and industrialism on the poor and spent much of his life in Inner Mission work. He reorganized the Berlin City Mission and tried to rouse the church to the danger of spreading revolutionary socialism. To win back workmen from Marxist seductions, he organized in 1878 a "Christian Social Labor Party" to rival the Social Democratic Party. He also urged protective labor legislation and social insurance. His campaign speeches before hissing, booing socialist crowds were often ended by the police and his party attracted only the upper classes, the lower middle classes, and that group from the ranks of labor in the provinces whose outlook was still traditional. And he soon found that the only really popular plank in his platform was his attack on the Jewish capitalists and plutocrats.

BISMARCK'S "CHRISTIAN SOCIALISM." Bismarck agreed with Stoecker on the desirability of labor legislation and social insurance, for paternalistic Lutherans had no such inhibitions about government intervention in economic matters as did the British or Americans of the period. But Bismarck, and most Lutherans, wanted the Protestant Church to stay out of social and political questions. As Uhlhorn, the historian of Christian philanthropy, protested against Stoecker, the Lutheran Church is a fellowship only of worship; the laity are to be wholly passive and the clergy are to tend to the Word and Sacraments and leave all public matters to the constituted authorities. And although Bismarck was ready to try to buy off the proletarians with social insurance, he had no intention of really giving them a share in political power. All policy was to come from the Christian Hohenzollerns and their Chancellor, and this policy he called "Christian socialism." There was to be no political organization or activity of Protestants as such. In 1879 the Supreme Church Council ordered all pastors to retire from political activity.

The rise of Marxist socialism was, as we have already seen, one of the chief reasons why Bismarck turned from the *Kulturkampf* with Rome. He now tried to suppress socialism with the same kind of exceptional legislation he had used against the Roman Catholics. And with the other hand he represented the advantages of Christian monarchism in the great scheme of social insurance of the 1880's. But the Socialists, like the Roman Catholics, thrived under repression. From 1887 to 1890 their popular vote doubled, and in 1890 the Imperial government announced that new efforts would be made to aid the workers, and the antisocialist laws were repealed.

EVANGELICAL SOCIAL CONGRESS. This turn of the wheel seemed again to provide an opening for Lutheran social politics, and Stoecker was one of the leaders in calling an "Evangelical Social Congress" in Berlin "to bring the educated people and the workmen together, and to prevent the latter from supposing that religion was only a tool to keep the workmen down." In fact the congresses, which became annual affairs, were highly academic, with a distinguished list of professors on the executive committee. Adolph Harnack, the great theologian and historian, for example, was president of its sessions for some years.

Stoecker, meanwhile, had been deprived of his post as court-preacher because of his political activity. When he began to extend his social concern to agricultural labor, the Conservative Party, representing the landlord interest, also cast him out. And within the Evangelical Social Congress the younger men seemed more drawn to a program different from his, that of the left wing, led by Friedrich Naumann. In 1896 the supreme bishop, William II, made public his condemnation:

"Stoecker has finished as I predicted some years ago! Political pastors—an absurdity. . . . 'Social Christianity' is nonsense. . . . Pastors ought to attend to the souls of the faithful and cultivate charity, but let politics alone, for it does not concern them."

NAUMANN. Friedrich Naumann succeeded Bismarck and Stoecker as the most striking exponent of Prussian Lutheran social ethics in the latter half of our period. Naumann had come from conservative Lutheranism, had worked on the staff of Wichern's "Rough House" in the 1880's, and then was led by his experience in an industrial parish past the Inner Mission viewpoint to Stoecker's political concerns. Unlike Stoecker, however, Naumann was not concerned primarily to proselytize for church and monarchy. He no longer oriented himself to the Prussian Junker class, but rather to the new powers of the machine age, and adopted the position of political liberalism. Bismarck, himself, although he sprang from the Junker class, had made extensive concessions to the liberal party, led by the industrialists and financiers of the new society and based on the educated middle class.

To orient Lutheran political ethics to liberalism, however, was less natural than to orient it to agrarian conservatism. The Christian roots of liberalism were Reformed and left wing, and when liberalism entered Germany it was in secular form. In

contrast to conservatism, which was "Christian" by definition,
liberalism stood for the secular state and for treating religion as
a "private matter," the idiosyncrasy of certain individuals. Similarly, culture, education, and economic life were to be secular
and autonomous. One could not really make a *Christian* political ethic of liberalism. One could at best consider that Christian love to one's neighbor might best be actualized by liberal
politics, but the connection never seemed intrinsic or necessary,
as the connection of Christianity with conservative politics did
seem to most Lutherans.

To bring together liberal nationalism and social concern
seemed equally difficult. Naumann had a rare gift for penetrating the psyche of the worker and interpreting it with elo-
quence to the educated classes. His *What Does Social Christianity Mean?* (1894) argued that the only basis for "social
Christianity" lay in the consciousness and suffering of the
worker—specifically mass poverty—and that to meet Marxist
socialism, Christians must face this problem *with* the disinherited and from their standpoint. From such a standpoint individual charity was hopelessly inadequate and only political
action was practicable. Even in industrial society, personality
was the ideal. His colleague Paul Goehre, general secretary of
the Evangelical Social Congress, had revealed an unknown
world to churchmen with his *Three Months as a Factory La-
borer and Apprentice Workman* (1891). In 1895 the Supreme
Church Council issued another warning against churchmen in
politics, and Naumann, like Stoecker, resigned from the ministry to continue political and social work. Naumann and
Goehre formed a "National Social Union." Their following,
however, proved to be chiefly intellectuals without political
weight. To give national liberals a social concern seemed to
be like combining sour herring with whipped cream. Goehre
decided to cross the Rubicon and in 1899 became a social
Democrat (Marxist). For this he was forbidden to use the
title "Pastor" or to administer the sacraments, and was boycot-
ted by churchmen. The great majority of pastors and active
laymen could not conceive how a real Lutheran could be a socialist or a democrat, and they were more severe in their reaction to social than to doctrinal heresy. Naumann moved

rather to the National Liberals, whom he represented in the Reichstag from 1907 to 1918.

Naumann's later development illustrates an aggravation of the paradoxical Lutheran tension of faith and culture. Under the influence of Rudolf Sohm he became increasingly convinced that the church was a purely spiritual society. A visit to Palestine in 1898 impressed him with the radical contrast between the conditions of Jesus' day and those of modern industrial society. The sociologist Max Weber helped to persuade him of the irrelevance of the New Testament to twentieth-century problems. Jesus had presented a saintly and eschatologically oriented ethic in a preindustrial culture. But we live in a world of great national states, where "Militarism is the foundation of all political order and civil prosperity in Europe." Social improvement is possible only in a national state in industrial expansion and with military power to hold its own or expand among other states. We Christians should live the life of the Sermon on the Mount "where we are free," but in most social relations we are bound by iron compulsions. Thus Naumann strenuously supported the Kaiser's naval policy, and at the defeat in 1918 urged passive resistance against the victors. Great numbers of German contemporaries could not see that Christianity was a very important ingredient in this outlook. It was clear enough that the twentieth-century Naumann was as fundamentally oriented to this-worldly culture as Luther himself had been to a transcendent Christ. His was a liberal Christian humanism, a *Kulturprotestantismus*, and that was the dominant tendency of his generation.

EFFECT OF WORLD WAR I. The nemesis of this Lutheran surrender of church leadership to the ever more dubiously "Christian" monarchical state came with the collapse of the German princes in 1919. During the period of the Weimar Republic, German Lutheranism was left a headless and boneless torso, yearning back to the Kaiser who alone could give it a voice and a policy. And at the same time with its characteristic weaknesses were revealed its characteristic strengths. For out of German academic theology came, in the hour of defeat, new guidance for Christendom. In 1917 Rudolf Otto published the *Idea of the Holy*, in 1918 Friedrich Heiler his

Prayer, and in 1919 Karl Barth his *Commentary on the Letter to the Romans*—works which were to change the mind of the next generation.

THE REFORMED CHURCHES. The Reformed Churches of the Continent were, on the whole, able to relate themselves more effectively and flexibly to industrialism and nationalism than were the Lutherans. To a considerable degree political and economic liberalism on the Continent, as in the English-speaking world, had been penetrated and shaped by these churches. In contrast to the almost monolithic Lutheran orientation to monarchism, aristocracy, and the duty of passive obedience, the Reformed Churches had wide, if not very active, relations with liberalism, individualism, and democracy, peace movements, social reform—even, sometimes, socialism. Their problems were thus rather different from those of the Lutherans. We must be content to notice a few of the more important developments in the Reformed Churches of France, Switzerland, and the Netherlands.

The Protestants of France were at last given their freedom as a by-product of the Separation of 1905, which was designed as an anti-Roman Catholic action. As free churches, however, the Reformed were not yet able to bring together their liberal and their confessionally oriented synods. French Switzerland followed the French example, and in 1907 Calvin's city of Geneva, which now had a Roman Catholic majority as a result of nineteenth-century immigration, abolished its budget for religion. The "National Protestant Church of Geneva" received its new constitution in 1908. Neufchatel had meanwhile rejected a similar proposal. But in 1911 Basel effected amicably a partial disestablishment. The pressures for disestablishment generally came from large sections of the population who, as Roman Catholics, socialists, or others, objected to public support of Protestant Christianity and to its influence in the common life.

RELIGIOUS SOCIALISM. In Württemberg and Switzerland there arose in these years a significant new current, gathering tributaries from several directions, that of "religious socialism." Out of Swabian pietism came Christoph Blumhardt, son of the

Möttlingen pastor who had discovered such remarkable gifts of healing and exorcism in the mid-nineteenth century. At his sanatorium of Bad Boll the senior Blumhardt had been the center of a movement which seemed to represent the Christian life once again not merely as ideology, but as a transforming power in the world. His son, similarly, reacted from pietism to a faith in God's Reign on earth and in society, in the power of the Resurrection life. He continued the pastoral care, healings, and preaching and about 1900 also entered political action with the Marxist socialists, despite (or because of) his faith in God in Christ. He wrote little, but had a tremendous personal influence, especially on Ragaz and Kutter.

Ragaz came from Swiss Protestant liberalism and deepened it with his sense of the living God in history, as in such movements as socialism. Kutter, an ex-pietist, published *They Must!* (1905) as a theological interpretation of socialism. The next year Ragaz sent out his manifesto, *The Gospel and the Present Social Struggle*, and the religious socialists began to organize. Disagreements arose as to how far to support socialist politics. Blumhardt served for years in the Württemberg *Landtag*. Ragaz was active in Swiss politics. Kutter, however, disassociated himself from Ragaz at the time of the Zurich strike in 1912. He held to the church, in contrast to the others, who like Rauschenbusch in America, opposed the "Kingdom of God" to the church. Ragaz championed cooperatives, folk schools, settlements, and pacifism, the last especially during World War I, when for a time the religious socialists had the full confidence of the Swiss workers. Kutter's more quietist and eschatologically oriented wing produced, under the impact of the War, a new prophet in a young Swiss minister named Karl Barth.

DUTCH NEO-CALVINISM. In the Netherlands there were some manifestations similar to the religious socialist movement of Switzerland. But the most striking developments came out of Calvinist confessionalism. In 1870 Abraham Kuyper, an ex-modernist minister, moved to Amsterdam and inherited the mantle of Groen van Prinsterer as leader of the neo-Calvinist "Antirevolutionaries." Their hope was to return to the organic society of the old regime, and especially to its federalist, decentralized character. In contrast to the unitary modern state standing over against a mass of individuals, they believed that the state should properly be but an association of independent smaller social groups—families, villages, municipalities, churches, guilds, universities, provinces, within which men were knit together in personal relations. In the "liberal" society relations in state and economic life were become impersonal and dehumanizing, encouraging ruthless competition and class war. In this sense state socialism would be the logical consequence of liberalism, and dictatorship the end of all. Kuyper agreed with socialists on the necessity for labor legislation and social insurance, but instead of looking to nationalization he hoped for a revival of guilds. Most of his program of social legislation had been realized by his retirement in 1913. He had made the Christian Democrats or the Antirevolutionary Party a mass party, which in coalition with the Roman Catholics has controlled the state most of the time since. He was Prime Minister from 1901-1905 and, in all, perhaps the most influential figure in Dutch politics in the last century.

Apart from social issues, the chief concern of Kuyper's policy was religion in education. The Antirevolutionaries had fought for public funds for confessional schools and in the 1870's they effected a "monstrous unity" with the Roman Catholics on this platform. This coalition defeated the liberals and won subsidies for their schools in 1887. Out of similar controversy was organized on the higher level the Calvinist Free University of Amsterdam. The result of this whole development has been to make the Netherlands the extreme example of a confessionally fragmented educational system.

Controversy over the Free University and other matters brought Kuyper to lead another secession from the state church, which produced the "Mourning Church" in 1885-1886. Within the next few years this group coalesced with the seceders of the Restoration period to form the "Reformed Churches of the Netherlands" (1892), of a third to half a million members. The orthodox tendency also remained strong within the State Reformed Church.

Chapter 20

BRITISH CHRISTIANITY

The later portion of the Victorian epoch exhibited the continuation of earlier religious movements and, alongside them, great social and cultural changes which contributed to the beginnings of a major realignment in the Edwardian Age.

EVANGELICALS. In 1870 the predominant type of British religion, among Anglicans and Free Churchmen alike, was still "Evangelicalism," the Anglo-American form of individualistic pietism. The "Second Great Evangelical Awakening" had begun in Ulster in 1859 and spread over Britain in the 1860's. In 1873-1875 Dwight L. Moody campaigned for conversions in Britain with as great success as in the United States. The greatest popular preacher of the period was the Baptist Spurgeon, who regarded himself as standing in the tradition of Whitefield, and for years filled the great Metropolitan Tabernacle in London, with its capacity of six thousand.

We must consider elsewhere the marvelous foreign missionary outreach of this movement. Here it is enough to recall the predominance of Evangelicals, especially Free-Church Evangelicals, among the great names. There was a similar vigor among home-missions enterprises. The Y.M.C.A. was in this period a genuinely Evangelical mission to urban young men. City "missions" flourished. William Booth's *In Darkest England* (1890) exploited the parallel of the home-mission enterprise to that in "darkest Africa." And like many foreign missionaries in this period, Booth had become convinced that oral communication of the gospel was inadequate in some social situations, such as the modern slum. Unable to persuade the Wesleyan bureaucracy of his thesis, he had launched his "Salvation Army" in 1877. With its rescue homes, labor exchanges, and similar enterprises, the Salvation Army displayed a most effective passion for the outcasts and sinners, the "submerged tenth" of the modern city.

ANGLO-CATHOLICS. Besides the Evangelicals, their sworn opponents, the Anglo-Catholics, were also increasingly diffused, and slowly gained ground through this period. This divergence of views not only led to continual guerrilla warfare within the Church of England, but also rendered increasingly difficult the ready co-operation of Anglicans and Free Churchmen which had been characteristic of the first generation of the century. *Punch* expressed the widespread distaste for Anglo-Catholic "ritualism," and Queen Victoria lost few opportunities to show her dislike of such "un-English" manifestations. The Archbishop of Canterbury even warned against the growing practice of confession. But numerous lawsuits and episcopal regulations only exacerbated the Anglo-Catholic urge to martyrdom, and by sheer importunity the ritualist priests gradually accustomed parishes all over England to long-forgotten practices. The "slum priests" also demonstrated the evangelistic effectiveness of ceremonialism, at least for the type of situation in which they performed their devoted service. And as we shall see, the Anglo-Catholics took the initiative from the Evangelicals from this period on in the leadership of the social ethics of English Christianity. In this, as in evangelistic and liturgical work, the new religious orders, especially the Community of the Resurrection and the Society of the Sacred Mission, played an increasingly important role. Toward the end of our period the Anglo-Catholic party claimed the adherence of about one-sixth of the clergy and about one-twentieth of the laymen of the Church of England.

FREE CHURCH WORSHIP AND CHURCHMANSHIP. This divergence of Evangelical and Anglo-Catholic parties increased the tensions between Anglicans and Free Churchmen. When, under the leadership of Hughes of the "Young Methodists," and the Congregationalist Berry, the National Free Church Council was formed in 1892, one common concern was the growing danger of "sacerdotalism." At the same time the Council itself was a manifestation in the Free Churches of some of the same forces which produced Anglo-Catholicism. The Council was able to produce an "Evangelical Free Church Catechism," which manifested a high regard for the "visible Catholic church." Also in these years there was a revival of concern for public worship in the free churches. The movement dated back to the "Catholic Apostolic Church" in the first half of the century and was much strengthened from the Church of Scotland, where solid scholarly work was done in Protestant liturgics. Although the early stages often manifested a romantic eclecticism, the result was an increasing recognition that Protestant worship was not properly "free" in the sense of being formless, but embodied a very definite structure and an unrivaled tradition of corporate praise. The movement began to produce directories and liturgies in England as well as in Scotland.

STRUGGLE FOR RELIGIOUS EQUALITY. It was particularly the old political struggle for liberties and social and civil equality for Free Churchmen that occasioned the difficulties between them and the Anglicans. The Free Churches were gaining in numbers, in large part as a result of the Evangelical Awakenings; indeed, to judge from the statistics of church sittings, their collective active adherents were more numerous than those of the state church at the beginning of the twentieth century. With the progressive democratizing of the British constitution, their numbers also gave them increasing political power. At the beginning of the period now being considered there still remained indirect disabilities of various sorts on Free Churchmen and a social ostracism which cut them off from many of the main currents of national life. Their "Liberation Society," led by such men as Miall and Dale, had fought a long and bitter battle to be free of taxation for the establishment, to win access to the ancient universities and the professions and status for which these were the nurseries, and to receive equal treatment with regard to marriage, burial, and the registration of births. Their ultimate goals were the disestablishment of the Church of England and complete religious liberty.

The extension of the franchise in 1867 strengthened the position of the Free Churchmen, who became a mainstay of the

Liberal Party. They were freed of church rates in 1868. In 1871 the privileges of the two old universities were opened to them, with the exception of staff appointments, and even these followed a decade later, save in divinity. In 1869 Free Churchmen supported Gladstone's bill for the disestablishment and disendowment of the Anglicans in Ireland, who claimed, at most, one-eighth of the population of that overwhelmingly Roman Catholic island. Similar demands were made for Wales, where four out of five were Free Churchmen, but Anglican resistance held off disestablishment there until World War I.

FORSTER EDUCATION ACT. The major battle during this period, however, was over the place of religious teaching in public education. In contrast to the situation on the Continent, and even in the United States, public education came very late to Great Britain. Until the last third of the century education had been a matter of private enterprise, largely associated with the churches, and (after 1833) with some grants-in-aid from Parliament. The bulk of these schools were Anglican, and Free Churchmen led in the campaign for a public nonsectarian system. They were influential, for example, in the creation of the University of London and the other municipal nonsectarian universities. On the elementary level, the franchise extension of 1867 persuaded the nation that general education must be provided on a scale which was beyond the resources of the churches. The Forster Education Act of 1870, consequently, established a system of local school authorities with powers to tax and the responsibility to provide school facilities as needed. This system of "Board" schools was to supplement rather than replace or incorporate the existing voluntary, and chiefly Anglican, schools. Thus a dual educational system was established, and when (in 1880) elementary education was made compulsory, parents could choose which type of school they desired, save in "single-school areas," which were chiefly rural. In 1895 there were four scholars in the church schools to every three in the Board schools.

There was no intention that the Board schools should be secular, but their religious instruction was limited by law to "undenominational" matter, a pattern peculiar to the countries dominated by the Anglo-American group of denominations. Prayer, hymns, and Bible reading were universal. Often instruction included the Lord's Prayer, the Ten Commandments, and the Apostles' Creed. With this, Free Churchmen were generally satisfied. In Scotland, on the other hand, as in Continental countries, both Protestant and Catholic, religious instruction in schools was specifically confessional. But where one found the whole family of Anglo-American denominations, differing chiefly in polity and agreeing essentially in theology, as in the United States, Canada, Australia, and South Africa, the system of "undenominational" instruction became the prevailing pattern in this period. The English arrangement of granting public funds to church schools was adopted to some extent in Canada, but was prohibited in the United States and Australia. Churches and other groups in these countries were generally free, however, to establish their own schools with little or no state regulation, in sharp contrast to the educational monopoly maintained by the state in such Continental countries as France and Germany.

EDUCATION ACT OF 1902. Under the dual system the church schools—nine-tenths of them Anglican and about one-tenth Roman Catholic—found themselves at a certain financial disadvantage as against the Board schools. After a bitter controversy, these two groups succeeded in securing the passage of the Education Act of 1902, which gave church schools a substantial share in school taxes. According to this act, they were still to provide their buildings, and to control their teachers and religious instruction, but maintenance and instruction costs were to be carried by taxation. Free Churchmen, who had liberated themselves from Anglican tithes only a generation before, saw in this legislation a reinstatement of the hated injustices of the past. Anglicans gloated publicly over the partisan advantage they had gained along with the Roman Catholics, and exasperated Free Churchmen, led by John Clifford, went to the extreme of conscientious refusal to pay school taxes. Thousands of summonses were issued, hundreds of sales of furniture of those in arrears took place, and scores went to prison rather than be taxed for instruction in Anglican or Roman tenets. The net result of the controversy was to decrease greatly the sympathy of the public and, especially, of educators for *any* religious education. Church schools lost pupils in great numbers, whereas in Board schools there was a movement to whittle down or even eliminate religious instruction.

EVOLUTION AND SOCIAL DARWINISM. This weakening of the place of Christian teaching in education as a result of partisan controversy was assisted by other factors in the social and cultural situation. The great controversy over evolution was at its peak at the opening of this period. Lyell, Darwin, Spencer, and Huxley had popularized the theory, which was widely understood as a social and ethical, and even metaphysical, view. As such it was not easily compatible with Christian conceptions. The evolutionist found it difficult to pay deference to traditions or revelations from less advanced stages of society. What truth there was in the concept of sin would, they felt, be taken care of by the natural improvement of the race. And although some stressed the role of co-operation and the social virtues in the evolutionary process, the prevailing understanding of "survival of the fittest" was that it justified ruthless competition from the viewpoint that might makes right. Reflective men, such as Tennyson, were not wholly reassured by this vision of "nature red in tooth and claw," and a whole generation of "agnostics" among literary figures could no longer either credit or forget Christian teaching.

As late as the 1880's religion had been the most popular category in publishers' lists, but by the end of the century many other types of books were finding more readers. "Science," in particular, became in the popular mind a way of life and of salvation; science would create the good life. A secular utopianism came increasingly to dominate the nation, often generously humanitarian in its sympathies, confident of progress through the moral effort and scientific skill of the natural man. The education which was expanding so rapidly was preoccupied with technology. Reflection on the ends of life, especially from the Christian perspective, received an ever smaller amount of attention.

BIBLICAL CRITICISM. In addition to the general temper of self-sufficiency and optimism, one specific application of scientific thought had a very damaging effect on the position of Christianity. German historical criticism of the Bible made its popular impact in this period, especially through the mediation of Free Church and Scottish scholars. All the major churches were rent by debate, and one result was to undermine the minister's and layman's confidence in the Bible. The layman ceased to read his Bible and no longer was concerned to teach it to his children. The scholarly preacher, uncertain that he had the latest critical opinion, tended to turn to social and moral topics. As a result, the first generation of the twentieth century was probably less influenced by the Bible than any preceding generation since the Reformation. And all problems within the church became more difficult of solution, for there no longer seemed to be any generally recognized point of authority and appeal. This was especially true of the Evangelicals, who found it ever harder to hold the allegiance of the more cultivated and intelligent.

The first two decades of the twentieth century saw many liberal and "modernist" attempts to reconcile Christian faith with the new critical and scientific views. The prevailing tendency was to stress the immanence of God in his creation, to assimilate him to the evolutionary principle. Stress on the moral capacities of all men led to a merely moralistic, rather than redemptive, understanding of Jesus Christ, and the "religion of Jesus" was opposed to the "religion about Jesus," or Jesus to Paul. Representative of the more extreme modernism of the early century was R. J. Campbell of the London City Temple. In his progressive view of things Jesus could figure only as a model social reformer and philanthropist. To explain the Atonement he pointed to Keir Hardie campaigning for justice for the workers in the House of Commons. The Roman Catholic modernists, Tyrrell and Von Hügel, who were influential among Protestants, made more place for the transcendent, and for concrete historical revelation, as did the Free Churchmen Forsyth and Oman. But the generation was one of great theological controversy and uncertainty, perhaps best typified by the appeal of Bishop Weston for a formal trial for heresy of two of his fellow bishops in 1913. This "Kikuyu controversy" involved both the confessionalist-modernist issue and the Protestant-Catholic divergence on the doctrine of the Church in Anglicanism. By temporizing and compromise the Archbishop managed to avoid the threatened rupture, but the episode illustrates the explosive situation.

Social and political developments, meanwhile, were posing new questions to the British churches. At the beginning of our period Anglicanism was equated with the landed gentry and their supporters, and was conservative in politics. The professional, mercantile, and industrial classes, on the other hand, were generally Free Churchmen if they were religious, and were liberal in politics. This latter phenomenon distinguished Britain from the Continent, for comparable groups there tended to anticlerical liberalism or atheistic socialism. In the United States, on the other hand, the former group was lacking. The presence of both traditions in Britain gave great flexibility to the churches. Democracy, liberalism, and socialism were all penetrated by Christianity in Great Britain as thoroughly as were aristocracy, monarchism, and paternalism. Schism among the churches, moreover, seemed to be a significant retarding factor in this situation against secularization.

EVANGELICAL ETHIC. In this period it was largely the Free Churches which gave a sense of social obligation to the men who administered the "workshop of the world." The political and economic theory through which this "nonconformist conscience" was expressed was the utilitarian individualism which went back to Locke and Adam Smith and which was to be still recognizable two generations later in America in Herbert Hoover. The ideal was the free responsible individual in politics and business, and Evangelical Protestantism helped to produce a society with an unprecedented number of such individuals, a society of great initiative and flexibility. In this view the functions of the state were to be held at a minimum to leave the fullest opportunity for private initiative. One might well feel an obligation to help his neighbor in need, but would prefer to do so by private rather than public agencies. And one would help his neighbor in order that he might as soon as possible help himself.

The activities which grew out of this Evangelical social ethic were all calculated to preserve or foster individual self-discipline, integrity, and responsibility. The term "nonconformist conscience" arose over the protest of the Methodist Hughes against the toleration in public men, in this case Parnell, of marital infidelity. Similarly "temperance"—or, more accurately, total abstinence—movements, had been characteristic of Evangelicalism ever since Wesley's attack on the curse of gin in the eighteenth century. Many organizations expressed this concern in the late nineteenth century, and most Free Church congregations and virtually all Methodists were sympathetic. Gambling and Sabbath-breaking were similarly capital vices in the Evangelical ethic.

SETTLEMENTS, INSTITUTIONAL CHURCHES, AND DENOMINATIONAL AGENCIES. Various forms of philanthropy were especially characteristic of the Evangelicals. Orphanages and similar institutions were supported widely by them. Beside the city rescue mission there developed in this period the "settlement" as a center for a more varied Christian work in the slum. The settlement was a colony of reformers, often connected with universities, who would learn of the life of the disinherited by daily contact over some time. The work of Samuel Barnett at Toynbee Hall from 1884 was widely emulated, and the movement gained in both Britain and America up to World War I. On the eve of that conflict Siegmund-Schulze even transplanted the institution to Germany, where sharper class lines made such undertakings more difficult. The so-called "institutional church" was a related phenomenon of this period of urban decay. A church in a declining area would become "institutional" by attempting to meet the needs of its community with an extensive educational, recreational, and social welfare program.

Free Church leaders in such Evangelical social action included Hughes, active in city mission work and the first president of the National Free Church Council; Dale of Birmingham, scholar and founder of Mansfield College and a national figure in education and social service; and the Unitarian Chamberlain. In specifically political activity such men as these were generally more useful in municipal government, where their personal integrity was at a premium, than in national policy, where individualism was ever less helpful. Early in the twentieth century the Free Churches entered officially into the field of "social service," beginning with the Wesleyans, led by Scott Lidgett in 1905. John Clifford and Silvester Horne similarly served the Baptists and Congregationalists. In 1911 these several denominational bodies were organized under Gore's presidency into the Interdenominational Conference of Social Service Unions (I.C.S.S.U.). One of the most successful functions of the I.C.S.S.U. was the "Collegium," a research seminar enlisting very able leadership. The Anglican William Temple was its chairman, the Quaker Lucy Gardner secretary, and the great Conference on Christian Economics, Politics and Citizenship of Birmingham in 1924 was largely built on I.C.S.S.U. preparations (see below, p. 396). Local councils had also been created, in which Anglicans and Free Churchmen could work together.

In the early 1870's Britain was in the full tide of Victorian prosperity, a prosperity that had been felt even by the workers. But the long depression from the middle seventies to nearly the end of the eighties persuaded many that the individualism of Evangelicalism and utilitarianism was inadequate to the crises of an industrial society. An enlarged conception of the proper function of government in such matters made ground rapidly, if not among Free Church businessmen, at least among the landed class with their paternalist tradition. The most clear cut of the new social programs was that of the Fabian Socialists: nationalization of the chief means of production through democratic procedures. Such views now found a readier hearing among Anglicans than among Free Churchmen, hitherto the leaders in progressive politics.

CHURCH SOCIAL UNION. The (Anglican) Church Social Union, (C.S.U.), became in the 1890's the most important church agency for social education and action. Scott Holland was its organizer, and Gore and Wescott related its program of Christian Fabianism to the social implications Maurice had discovered in Church and sacraments in the preceding generation. The chief effect of this propaganda was not on business or labor, with which Anglicanism had few contacts, but on the clergy of the Church of England, and particularly its bishops,

those traditional pillars of immovable conservatism. The
Lambeth Conference of Bishops first touched on social issues
in 1888, and then only hesitantly; but the next conference of
1897 accepted moral responsibility for the economic and social
order, and suggested that social service agencies be formed in
every diocese. In 1908 Lambeth declared that a "living wage"
should be the "first charge" on any industry. By the time of
World War I fourteen of the bishops were C.S.U. members.
The "Fifth Report" of the Archbishop's Committee on Christianity and Industrial Problems, published in 1918, represented
a full thirty years' tradition of C.S.U. study and was probably
the most mature and competent analysis and program of any
church body in the world on such issues at that time. Such was
one side of the revolutionary realignment of the English
churches on public issues effected during this period.

The other side of the realignment was the changing relation
of the Free Churches to labor. In the nineteenth century it
had been the Free Churches, especially the Primitive Methodists, that had most served the working population. In the seventies a majority of trade-union leaders came from such a background—Thomas Burt, the miner's M.P., and Joseph Arch, the
founder of the Agricultural Workers' Union, for example.
And men such as Keir Hardie and Arthur Henderson carried
into the ethos of the twentieth-century Labor Party an idealism
derived from their Free Church backgrounds. The liberal humanitarian aspect of British socialism, which contrasts so
sharply with the militant Marxism of the Continent, is traceable
in large part to these sources.

But in the early years of the twentieth century came a shift.
The old pattern was apparent in the Liberal-Labor government
of 1905-1910 which marks the high point of Free Church
power in politics. But the alliance was already crumbling.
The chief Free Church groups had by now largely won their
battle for equality. They were primarily a respectable middle-
class constituency, and few of their leaders showed any sympathy for the new Labor Party or its program. They were still
commending "temperance" and Sabbath observance. It was
rather the Anglican clergy who now began to play an active
role in labor politics. The (Anglican) Church Socialist

League (C.S.L.), led by the ebullient Father Noel, affirmed "Christianity is the religion of which socialism is the practice." The pan-Anglican Congress of 1908 hotly discussed this relation of Christianity and socialism.

In 1909 the C.S.L. was active in a great demonstration of the unemployed in London. In 1912, George Lansbury, then chairman, led a procession over Westminster Bridge to protest against the bishops' hesitation to take the miners' side in the lockout. The movement was internally divided, however, among Fabian, Marxist, and guild socialists, and Anglo-Catholic gains split them theologically. After the war the C.S.L. broke into three chief fragments. Nothing comparable, however, was to be found in Free Church circles. The initiative in social politics had passed to the Anglicans.

The Roman Catholic cause in the British Isles, meanwhile, rested in the hands of the Irish. In Ireland itself the agrarian problem embittered relations with England and both were complicated by religious differences. Political Roman Catholicism grew steadily more effective. The "Catholic Association," founded in 1903, sought to drive Protestants from Ireland by boycott and economic pressure. Such activities only further convinced the Protestants of the "six counties" of northeast Ireland that Irish Home Rule would mean ruin for them. By 1914 North and South Ireland had rival armies facing each other, and the Irish Free State was founded in 1921 only after bloody struggle.

ROMAN CATHOLICS AND SOCIAL ETHICS. Millions of Irishmen had emigrated, meanwhile, into the slums of England, Scotland, and the United States, forming the dominant bloc of Roman Catholics of each of these countries. Manning, who became Archbishop in England in 1865, thus became commander-in-chief of this Irish invasion. In his first years he was most active in the preparations for the Vatican Council, where he was the chief manipulator of the infallibilist party. Thereafter he concerned himself chiefly with public issues, campaigning for temperance, labor legislation, and philanthropies, like the leading Evangelicals of his day. His hold over the Irish workmen enabled him to win the "Cardinal's peace" out of the great Dock Strike of 1889, a token of things to come in the twentieth century when Roman Catholicism would realize its political power through this immigrant labor. Before World War I, however, British Roman Catholics were generally apathetic on political and social questions, although the Catholic Social Guild, founded in 1909, took its place beside the other denominational social service unions.

Newman was succeeded as the intellectual and spiritual leader of British Roman Catholicism by Tyrrell and Von Hügel, who will be discussed later. Several literary men—Francis Thompson, Coventry Patmore, G. M. Hopkins—were winning new respect for Roman Catholicism in England. In the twentieth century Chesterton and Belloc carried on this role on a more popular level. In public questions they championed a romantic program of return to medieval agrarianism and the "bold peasant," together with guilds, but at least on the negative side they contributed solid criticism of large-scale capitalism and of socialism, as in Belloc's famous *Servile State*. By 1914 Roman Catholicism had so far overcome its alien complexion in Britain that a nominal Roman Catholicism had become a possibility.

Certain Anglo-Catholics, meanwhile, had been disappointed by the firm decision of Leo XIII in 1896 that "ordinations performed according to the Anglican rite are utterly invalid and altogether void," and that the Anglican Church possessed no true bishops or priests.

THE UNITED FREE CHURCH AND THE CIVIL COURTS. One last development in Scotland must be noted, the process of reunion among Scottish churches and the resultant church and state controversy. In 1902 the Free Church (dating from the Disruption of 1843) united with the United Presbyterians. A recalcitrant minority, the "Wee Frees," sued in the civil courts for the property of the Free Church. The court of last resort, the British House of Lords, nearly provoked a civil war in Scotland by awarding all the property to the handful of diehards. The Lords had followed the tendency not uncommon in British courts to deny to churches the right of self-determination. They refused to consider the churches as living bodies capable of developing and defining their own doctrine and practice in obedience to their living Head. Rather, they treated the church as a trust and held it mechanically to its subordinate standards of a past day. In the process, to be sure, they also put themselves in the position of deciding such issues as what were and what were not legitimate developments of the Westminster Confession. Thus the whole issue of the Disruption was opened again, as the British judiciary once again denied that the churches in Scotland had inherent rights and intrinsic powers. This particular controversy was at length decided by legislation providing for a more equitable settlement, but the deeper issue of the rights of churches was also clarified in the Church of Scotland Act of 1921. That Act recognized that the Church of Scotland "as part of the Universal Church ... receives from ... its divine King and Head, and from Him alone, the right and power subject to no civil authority, to legislate and to adjudicate finally, in all matters of doctrine, worship, government, and discipline in the Church." Negotiations for reunion of the United Free Church with the Church of Scotland were begun in 1909, and were to be concluded successfully after World War I.

Chapter 21

THE AMERICAN SOCIAL GOSPEL AND THEOLOGICAL LIBERALISM

The Civil War really provided no dividing line in the history of American religion, nor, for that matter, did World War I. There was an essential continuity in the religious history of nineteenth-century America from the Evangelical Awakening at the opening of the century until about 1890. And the problems and issues which were redefined at that time endured until about 1930. Both this chapter and that on American religion between World Wars, consequently, take their structure from the fact that a major watershed is found at just about the middle of the time-span covered in each case. It should also be observed that the United States is so large and so various in its regions that a periodization based on events in the Northeast will probably be quite inappropriate to the South or the Far West.

DECLINE OF CALVINISM. The dominant religious pattern in America after the Civil War as before was Evangelical Protestantism as found in the four or five denominations affiliated with British nonconformity. The several denominational peculiarities had become somewhat blurred in the revivalist emotionalism of the eighteenth and nineteenth centuries and there was a certain assimilation to a common type. One might perhaps identify this common type generically as Methodist, and characterize a great part of the theological history of American Protestantism between the Civil War and World War I as the progressive retreat of "Calvinism" before "Arminianism" and universalism. At the end of the Civil War the great body of Presbyterians, Congregationalists, and Baptists, together with a substantial group of Episcopalians, stood solidly on the "covenant theology" of the Westminster catechisms. By the 1890's the bulk of Presbyterians, to say nothing of Congregationalists, were no longer satisfied with the Westminster standards. In these churches one rarely heard from the pulpit of election, or *a fortiori* of reprobation. The issues involved were so far from central to the churches that the Presbyterians could reunite with the antipredestinarian Cumberland Synod in 1906, and the Northern Baptists could merge with the Free-Will Baptists in 1909. Most striking of all is the theological distance between the Congregationalists' "Burial Hill Declaration" (1865) and their "Kansas City Creed" (1913). Some time about 1890 there had taken place a radical break in continuity in the theological leadership of the chief denominations which effectively dismissed the theological traditions central, up to that time, in American Protestantism. The movement, in fact, went, in many of its manifestations, beyond Wesley in a Pelagian direction.

AND OF REVIVALISM. But whereas much of this tendency to a more anthropocentric religion might be traced to the effects of revivalism, revivalism itself rather lost ground in this period. Dwight L. Moody, to be sure, was probably the best-known religious figure of the English-speaking world in the last quarter of the nineteenth century, but most of his successors gave the impression of calculated artifice. The respectable urban churchmen of the end of the century (and respectability was quite important) would probably have picked Phillips Brooks as their model minister. Following Bushnell's *Christian Nurture* the Congregationalists had, in effect, relinquished their doctrine of the gathered church for that of the right-wing of the Reformation, although the substance of the "new theology" was far enough from any Reformation views. The prevailing tendency was to deprecate exaggerated views of human sin and the need of redemption and conversion. Like Finney before him, Moody himself turned increasingly to education in his later years as he discovered that conversion still left some problems. But religious nurture itself proved more and more difficult. Revivalism had largely washed out of the churches theological education, ordered worship, and sacramental practice, and the new theology and ethics drew to a marked degree on sources extraneous to the faith, especially on popular science.

EVOLUTION. Darwin's *Origin of Species,* published in 1859, was widely discussed in America only after the Civil War, especially in the 1870's and 1880's. The first reaction by both churchmen and scientists was vehement rejection. In the 1870's hostility was still strong, although not so violent. "Darwinism" seemed to contravene the biblical doctrine of a creating God, to rob man of his unique religious and moral character and, by implication, to deny biblical inspiration and revelation in principle. The resultant view of man seemed to replace moral responsibility with amoral habits and "adjustments."

Attempts at harmonizing, however, were soon made. In 1876 John Fiske's *Cosmic Philosophy* argued that "evolution is God's way of doing things." It was significant as to what was happening in the minds of the better-educated laymen in the cities of the Northeast that Henry Ward Beecher, "the great weather vane," accepted evolution in the 1880's; he was the first prominent Evangelical minister to do so. In the nineties the educated leadership of the Protestant ministry ceased to oppose evolution. Lyman Abbott, Beecher's successor at Plymouth Church and editor of the *Outlook,* the most influential religious journal of the end of the century, laid down in his *Theology of an Evolutionist* (1897) the classic American statement of Christian idealistic evolutionism. As "God's way of doing things," evolution could be combined with the idea of Providence, and greatly strengthened the prevailing faith in "Progress." Sin became for some "our brute inheritance," and men were enjoined to "let the ape and tiger die." The course of empirical history was read as the gradual redemption and sanctification of the race.

This whole theological development meant the breaking down of the compartmentalized pietist-rationalist outlook which had characterized Anglo-American Protestantism since the seventeenth century. From about 1890 German idealism became the dominant intellectual structure in place of the older Lockean empiricism joined to revealed theology. And, following Schleiermacher and Coleridge, the attempt was now made to achieve one unified and coherent system of Christian thought. One began with the investigation of religious experience, rather than with God as revealed, and in this study of religious consciousness, following Bushnell, the symbolic and "poetic" character of religious affirmation was often stressed. Biblical imagery and the conceptions of evolutionary cosmology could be treated as alternative metaphors for the same religious insights.

HIGHER CRITICISM. Most of these ideas reached few outside of the intellectuals, at least before World War I, but an issue of great popular concern was raised by the "higher" criticism of the Bible. Revelation, it now appeared, was also evolutionary, or "progressive." The Old Testament seemed to lose much of its authority when it was claimed that Moses had not written the Pentateuch, and that there were at least two Isaiahs. Fierce controversy followed and heresy trials were held of the sort experienced in the preceding thirty years in Britain. New England Congregationalism went through the struggle first, for example, at Andover Seminary and with Munger and Gordon. Then, in the 1890's, came the Presbyterian trials of the biblical scholars Charles Briggs and Henry Preserved Smith, and of the historian A. C. McGiffert. Early in the twentieth century the Methodists dealt with Bowne and Mitchell and the Episcopalians with Crapsey. Baptists and Disciples generally entered the fray after World War I. The chronology roughly indicates the relative sensitivity of the denominations to theological scholarship generally, although the variety of types of denominational machinery for enforcing orthodoxy is also significant. Virtually none of the "heretics" recanted; several shifted denominations. The seminaries under such pressure often tended to try to free themselves from direct ecclesiastical control, a development made possible by the substantial endowments many received at this time. Union Seminary, for example, broke its official connections with the Presbyterian Church. Distrust of the seminaries among the conservative popular churches increased in the same proportion.

FUNDAMENTALISM. As the number of liberal Evangelicals multiplied in the seminaries and leading pulpits, the distressed conservatives organized in reaction. Among them were the orthodox in the strict sense, who still oriented themselves to the Reformation confessions, such as the Missouri Synod among the Lutherans and some of the Dutch and Scots among the Reformed. More widespread, however, among many denominations, were the pietist and revivalist premillennialists, who found a characteristic expression in a system of regional "Bible conferences" which developed from the late 1870's. Such a Bible Conference at Niagara in 1895 drew up a platform of "fundamentals" of Evangelical pietism. There were five fundamentals: the inerrancy of the Scriptures, the deity of Jesus Christ, the Virgin Birth, the substitutionary theory of the Atonement, and the bodily Resurrection and imminent bodily Second Coming of the Lord. Bible conferences, revivals, periodicals, tracts, and pamphlets preached these fundamentals all over Protestant America. The climax was the publication of twelve well-written volumes on *The Fundamentals* (1909-1915). Two wealthy Los Angeles oilmen named Stewart financed the distribution of three million copies of the *Fundamentals*, presenting free copies to every minister, "Y worker," and denominational official in the nation. The fundamentalist ministers, with important exceptions, were less well trained than the liberals and usually had to content themselves with the less sophisticated and, on the whole, less wealthy congregations. But they remained close to the people and reigned unchallenged over vast rural areas, especially in the South, Middle West, and on the Pacific Coast. By the time of World War I the liberal-conservative split was the most fundamental polarity in Evangelical Protestantism. Inherited differences among the denominations were relatively insignificant in comparison to this cleavage which cut right across most of them. There would almost certainly have been a major explosion then if the war had not intervened and postponed it until the 1920's.

SOCIAL CHANGES. While American Protestantism was thus confused and distracted by the theological difficulties occasioned by science—typically in the theory of evolution—vast social and economic changes likewise posed new questions to the Evangelical ethic. American Protestantism, attuned to an agrarian democracy, found itself suddenly yoked more or less uncomprehendingly to an industrialized, urbanized plutocracy.

Social changes proceeded so rapidly that great sections of the nation remained unaware of what had happened and what these changes meant. As Wilson told the veterans of the G.A.R. "the nation in which you live is not the nation for which you fought." Population increased, for example, from thirty-one million in 1860 to fifty million in 1880, and seventy-six million in 1900. In a period of less than two generations, then, the population was nearly tripled. Many of the new people took up farm land. The first transcontinental railroad was completed in 1869. In the decade of the seventies an area as large as Great Britain and Sweden combined was opened to agriculture. In 1900 there were more people on farms alone than had inhabited the whole country in 1860. And, virtually unrestrained by external controls or inner compunctions, "rugged individuals" exploited the natural resources of the continent for their own ends. The remaining "frontier" was swept aside with impatience—witness the treatment of the Indian and the buffalo. The waste of at least half of the lumber of Wisconsin was typical of this pillage of the "robber barons." And in the midst of this movement most of the churches west of the Mississippi were established.

This agricultural expansion on the frontier, however, was no such radical innovation in American life as the concurrent growth of the cities, which increasingly controlled agriculture. The victory of the North in the Civil War had released forces long checked by the agricultural South and West. Financial and industrial capitalism captured government as well as society. In 1890, one-third of the population lived in cities of 4,000 or more. By 1900, this proportion had increased to 40 per cent of the total population, and by 1910, to 45 per cent. This increase in concentration continued until about 1910, when city folk began to be diffused again to the suburbs. But a new type of civilization, the metropolitan, had appeared in history. The urban mind has increasingly come to dominate the whole culture. The farmer has become in the popular mind a butt, a "local yokel," whereas in fact he has changed his attitude toward the soil and life on it by becoming a rural businessman.

ROMAN CATHOLIC IMMIGRATION. Cultural and religious patterns were also radically affected by immigration from Europe; this immigration accounts for a major part of the great population increase. The new immigrants came mostly from southern and eastern Europe, rather than as formerly from northern and western Europe. This shift meant that there was a great intrusion into an Anglo-American Protestant society of a solid bloc of chiefly Roman Catholic non-English-speaking peoples. The result was the establishment of the American Roman Catholic Church as, at least potentially, the one significant religious rival to Evangelical Protestantism. At the time of the Second Plenary Council, called at Baltimore in 1866 to face the problems of Reconstruction, the Roman Catholic population had grown in one man's lifetime from one in a hundred Americans to one in ten. By 1920 some twelve to nineteen million Roman Catholic immigrants had swelled the total to eighteen million, about one in six Americans, a ratio which has held static since the ending of mass immigration.

In the intervening period the Roman Catholic Church was pre-eminently the church of the cultural alien. Its history was almost entirely an internal struggle to assimilate, unify, and organize this mass invasion of peoples of various tongues and traditions. The two dominant problems were, first, the construction of ecclesiastical unity, and especially one close-knit hierarchy out of French, Germans, Irish, Italians, Poles, and others; and, second, the provision of a safely Roman Catholic education in the face of a rapidly expanding school system of a dominantly Protestant tone. Throughout the period the bulk of Roman Catholics felt themselves to be "foreigners"; indeed, half of them were still in foreign-language churches at the time of World War I. Only in 1908 did the United States cease officially to be a Roman Catholic mission field and become organized independently of Propaganda. The Roman Catholic Church, preoccupied with late nineteenth-century immigration, was thus involved with a very different set of problems from those of the older American Protestant churches. Only the Lutherans among the Protestant churches experienced some of the same difficulties.

The immigrants were chiefly uneducated peasants, and they became the laborers in the new factories. By 1900, for example, nearly nine-tenths of New England mill workers and Pennsylvania miners were either foreign born or children of foreign born. American Roman Catholicism thus became the church of urban industrial labor, while the older Protestant stock had relatively little direct experience of the meaning of the mill, the mining town, or the slum from the receiving end. The class divisions of industrialism were thus deepened by religious, linguistic, and cultural differences, and the responses of the various churches to the social problems varied accordingly. The largely rural Protestant churches, such as Baptists, Disciples, and Lutherans, hardly realized the problems of industrial society in this period. The churches of the urban upper classes—the Congregationalists, Episcopalians and Presbyterians—provided the most intelligent and progressive reformers. The church of the immigrants themselves, the Roman Catholic Church, seemed very conservative on social questions, being still defensive toward the surrounding society.

"GOSPEL OF WEALTH." The mood in the years immediately after the Civil War was one of complacency. American experience, with its unprecedented economic opportunities, its frontier, its social fluidity, seemed to bear out the view that unregulated individual initiative would provide the most rapid economic development and rewards roughly proportionate to ability and energy. In the generation before the Civil War such an economic theory had been generally associated by Protestant economists with the doctrine of Providence.

Out of this background Andrew Carnegie, writing for his generation of Protestant businessmen in 1889, elaborated the "Gospel of Wealth." According to this theory, the gifts of management would, in a free competition for property, inevitably accumulate great rewards. And although a certain social price would be paid in this competition, it would assure the survival of the fittest in every department of life. Bishop Lawrence of Massachusetts even believed that the gifts of management were so associated with moral habits that "in the long run it is only to the man of morality that wealth comes." The conclusion to this theory of a natural aristocracy is that the man of wealth is responsible to God for his stewardship of property, but not to the less fit of his brethren. "God," said Rockefeller, "gave me my money." G. F. Baer of the Philadelphia and Reading Railroad put this most crudely in 1902: "The rights and interests of the laboring man will be protected and cared for, not by the labor agitators, but by the Christian men, to whom God, in his infinite wisdom, has given control of the property interests of this country." By 1902, to be sure, the religious press was ready to handle "divine-right Baer" roughly.

While churchmen and theologians urged charity, they were careful also to warn any businessman who might be tempted that charity should not adulterate the competition for property or the determination of the wage level. So Bushnell expressed himself. The *Presbyterian Quarterly* considered that since poverty was generally the consequence of vice, it should be treated as a crime. Henry Ward Beecher was confident of the general truth that no man suffered from poverty in the United States except as a result of his sin. It is true that workmen did not subscribe wholeheartedly to such middle-class Christian economics. As early as 1866 the *Methodist Christian Advocate* noted with more complacency than alarm that Methodists had become removed from that level of society whence most of them had arisen. As time went on, however, church leaders became increasingly concerned over the loss of religion among the "less fit." Rescue missions, the Salvation Army, and the Volunteers of America expressed this concern.

A series of violent social upheavals, however, convinced at least a few more thoughtful Protestants that they were no longer living in an open agrarian society where such views made sense. The Knights of Labor had been organized in 1869, and in 1877 came the railroad strikes, "the first serious explosion of labor dynamite in America," involving pitched battles with police, militia, and troops in many cities. In 1886 the bomb thrown into the protest meeting in Haymarket Square in Chicago led to a famous trial of "anarchists." The Homestead steel strike of 1892 witnessed a battle resulting in ten deaths and sixty wounded and the summoning of eight thou-

sand state militia. Similarly, in 1894 President Cleveland sent
two thousand troops to "guard the mails" during the Pullman
strike in Chicago. Industrial strife in America seemed more
bloody than in almost any other Western country, partly, perhaps, just because of the relative lack of class consciousness in
that country. The first reaction, even of the most thoughtful
Protestants, was generally panic and a call for the militia. Big
business and its government made no concessions. The courts
supplied injunctions against labor unions; the Congress hiked
the tariff even higher in 1894 to subsidize "the interests"; the
Supreme Court threw out the income tax bill as unconstitutional in 1895. And the Chicago World's Fair of 1893 celebrated the triumph of the ideology of the acquisitive society.
Yet the year 1890 is as good as any to mark the turning of the
tide, and the emergence of a new school of social ethics to challenge the compartmentalization of Evangelical Protestantism
with its rationalistic natural-law ethics in state and society.

HOME MISSIONS AND SOCIAL WORK. The traditional response to social need was charity. One expression of this response, shaped also by the changing pattern of the cities'
growth, was the "institutional church." Muhlenberg in New
York and T. R. Beecher in Elmira were pioneers of this effort
to make a social welfare, recreational, and educational center
out of the local church. The most impressive instance early
in the twentieth century was St. George's (New York), which
had for vestryman one of the noted Protestant laymen in the
country, J. P. Morgan. Rainsford built the membership from
seventy-five to four thousand and led a full-time staff of thirteen in 1906. Russell Conwell's Baptist Temple in Philadelphia
was similar. But although the institutional church created a
great furor in its day and led to a great building of "parish
houses" across the land, in the long run most churches found it
wiser to leave such functions to other agencies such as the
Y.M.C.A., neighborhood houses, and settlements.

The settlement movement which came from England was
similar, seeking to bring together university students and the
disadvantaged. And whereas Great Britain developed fifty
settlements, the United States acquired four hundred, many of
which are still functioning. The Y.M.C.A. also had a greater

expansion in the United States than in its homeland, Great Britain, as did the Salvation Army, which was brought to America in 1880.

The efforts of the Protestant American churches to meet the needs of the new immigrants in the cities came to a not insignificant total. The characteristic agencies were "settlements," "institutional churches," and "neighborhood houses." All three of these forms of institutions carried on much the same range of educational, recreational, social welfare activities. Their leadership and personnel as well as their funds were overwhelmingly from the older Protestant churches. And since the great bulk of immigrants they served were Roman Catholic and (in New York) Jewish, the contributions to their orientation were made largely without ecclesiastical self-interest and with only an occasional minor effort at proselyting. It was estimated in 1933 that probably one hundred million dollars had been expended by Protestants in this work, to say nothing of the lives devoted to this service. The religious ministry for these people would have to come from Judaism and the Roman Catholic Church, but Protestants had at least made a significant contribution to their social and educational orientation. The whole enterprise tapered off rapidly with the end of immigration in the 1920's and with the assumption of many of the same services by the government in the 1930's.

THE SOCIAL GOSPEL. The "social gospel," however, went beyond the charity of settlements and institutional churches to raise questions about the justice and viability of the structure of society and the system of *laissez faire*. Here, again, as in theological exploration, the Congregationalists supplied the largest number of pioneers. Washington Gladden, perhaps the most influential of the early "social gospel" ministers, was moderate in his proposals. He would have regulated the struggle for property to the extent of giving labor the "belligerent rights" of organization, and some share in production through co-operatives and profit-sharing systems. He also advocated nationalization or public control of such natural monopolies as railroads, utilities, water power, and mining. George Herron, the most sensational prophet of the 1890's, rode rather on the agrarian Populist protest of those years. His base of operations was a professorship at Grinnell, and his greatest response in the upper Middle West. F. G. Peabody and R. T. Ely, also proponents of the "social gospel," were college teachers, and Walter Rauschenbusch became professor of church history in the Rochester Divinity School. The leaders of the movement were all clergymen, and although they created tremendous propaganda in books, speeches, articles, periodicals, and resolutions, only very gradually did they make headway among their fellow ministers, to say nothing of laymen. The years before 1900, as Rauschenbusch recalled later, were years of lonesomeness and of shouting in the wilderness. And yet this "social gospel" may have been the most important single contribution to the idealistic reforming enthusiasm of the "progressive" era of Teddy Roosevelt and Woodrow Wilson.

To a considerable degree the "social gospel" was a movement looking for a theology, as is indicated by the title of Rauschenbusch's work, *A Theology for the Social Gospel* (1917). It arose on the one hand from the recognition of very concrete human needs and wrongs, and from a noble moral enthusiasm. And just at the moment that this need made itself felt, the challenges of evolution and biblical criticism were also affecting theology. To some extent the preoccupation of many ministers with social problems may have been an escape from theological perplexities. Whatever they ought to believe, this much was surely required of them. The result was a very general, although not complete, identification of theological liberalism with the "social gospel." Most of the leaders came out of individualistic Evangelicalism, and in their new social concern they remained unchurchly, pinning their faith to progress. The appeal was now to the "social teachings" of Jesus and the prophets with little or no reference to the sources of renewal in forgiveness or their nurture in the communion of the faithful or the means of grace. There was almost nothing in America of the High Church social radicalism then leading the field in British social ethics. The other side of the coin was that conservative pietism and orthodoxy in the United States still remained generally attached to *laissez faire* and the unregulated struggle for economic survival. The liberals came to terms with evolution in theology; the conservatives swallowed "social Darwinism" tail and hooves.

In the first decade and a half of the twentieth century the "social gospel" established itself in the official structure of the Protestant churches. In 1901 the Congregationalists and Episcopalians each took steps toward official social service programs. The Presbyterians were the first to acquire a full-time official social service secretary, Charles Stelzle, who was also to be loaned to the Federal Council to pioneer in the same function there. The "Social Creed" of the Methodists (1908) was to supply the basis for the Federal Council "Creed" of 1912. By that date all the major denominations had acquired some sort of official program. Rauschenbusch noted that a new type of minister was emerging, that many were coming to feel that social reconstruction was the very purpose of the denominations, and that even the old men and the timid were falling into line. The criterion for the vitality of a congregation was now no longer the prayer meeting (by that criterion vitality was running low), but the social activity of the people. There was in that movement a glow and enthusiasm which the orthodox would only match in a revival, and which is very hard for those of a later period, who have seen the reduction of most of these hopes to problematical prose, to recapture. But whatever has happened to the hopes, it was the "social gospellers" who convinced most American Protestants of the scope of their responsibilities.

INTERDENOMINATIONAL CO-OPERATION. The "closing of the frontier" and the shift from rural to urban problems about 1890 had far-reaching implications for Protestant institutions. The complete localism and sectarianism of the nineteenth-century rural pattern were no longer feasible. In 1872 the International Sunday School Lesson Committee had initiated the "uniform" curriculum. The foreign missionary agencies of the denominations began to meet together annually from 1893. Similarly, the home missions enterprises, discovering what a chaotic and overchurched inheritance they had come into, began to draw together. In 1908 the Home Missions Council was organized, together with its associated Women's Council. And since the various denominations were now acquiring religious education departments alongside their new "social service" committees, a Sunday School Council of Evangelical Denominations seemed a wise step in 1910. In part to coordinate the denominational social service activities, the Federal Council of Churches was created in 1908. For its first half-dozen years the Federal Council was a small and insignificant undertaking, running on a shoestring. American Protestantism was still so local, provincial, and sectarian in its attitudes as to admit only grudgingly that these co-operative enterprises were either possible or useful. Only the experience of the churches in World War I convinced the denominations sufficiently of the need for common action so as to establish the Federal Council as the organ of co-operative Protestantism.

Chapter 22

EUROPEAN PROTESTANT THEOLOGY

A survey of Protestant theology in the last three generations must be largely a survey of German theology, with an occasional reference to other countries. The score or more of Protestant German university faculties probably contained a larger company of competent scholars devoted to theological inquiry than was to be found in all the rest of the world together. These men had also more academic freedom, in relation to the churches, than was elsewhere the case. The system was highly competitive, and scholars reviewed each others' publications with ferocious thoroughness. The results were sometimes disconcerting or dangerous for the faith of the layman and did not always provide the best atmosphere for the training of pastors. But these faculties did constitute the world's greatest arena for the systematic exploration of all possible viewpoints in all their implications. As a result of the activities of these faculties, the period under consideration was the golden age of theological scholarship in modern church history.

The word is "scholarship," to be sure, rather than creative originality. In the age of Bismarck there were no successors to the great thinkers—Kant, Hegel, Schleiermacher, Schelling. Industrialism and power politics accompanied loss of faith in speculative construction. Practical realism was the mood of the age, and the most pervasive outlook was the "scientific." The culture of the nation was no longer dominated by either Christianity or idealism. Philosophy and theology were just departments among others, as the world of thought was parceled out into specialities. Monographs or editions of sources were more admired than "systems," and "facts" more than

speculations. The great encyclopedias of theological scholarship, the Hauck-Herzog *Realenzyklopaedie* and the twentieth-century *Religion in Geschichte und Gegenwart* are fit
symbols of the age.

RITSCHL. The three theological "schools" of the 1860's
(see above, p. 174f.) gave an impression of exhaustion and
stagnation. When a vigorous new orientation was set forth by
a former student of Baur, who had now turned from New
Testament studies and early church history to systematic theology, it won a ready response among young scholars. Albrecht
Ritschl became the most influential theologian of the seventies
and eighties, provoking new questions in church history, biblical exegesis, and practical theology, as well as dogmatics.
Ritschl drew students to Göttingen, and won more by his
writings, chief among them his *Christian Doctrine of Justification and Reconciliation* (1870-1874). The *Christian World*
provided a vehicle for the full range of interests of the new
group. Harnack, the historian, and Herrmann, the theologian,
were to become Ritschl's most famous followers.

The Ritschlian program was in part a reaction against the
influence of philosophy of religion, especially that of Hegel,
over theology. The new interest was practical, confining itself to matters directly of moment for the Christian life. Christian theology, according to this program, should study subjects
to which the believer attaches value. Much of inherited dogma
and speculative philosophy of religion falls outside this limita-
tion. In method, similarly, Ritschl wanted to begin not with
God the Absolute, but with God as revealed in concrete historical fact. In this recommendation he made his great appeal
to a realistic fact-minded generation, and he gave his theological support to the tremendous expansion of biblical scholarship.
The historical understanding of the Bible established itself, in
fact, in the same decades as the Ritschlian method and in close
association with it. Agnosticism in metaphysics and confidence in historical scholarship were characteristic of the generation.

As the title of his chief work would indicate, Ritschl made
forgiveness central, which required a more transcendent and
personal God than had been the case with Schleiermacher.

He also did more justice to the Church, the community of believers, as the medium of salvation. He consciously attached himself to the Bible and to Luther. Thereby he took much of the wind from the sails of the mediationist school and the right wing; the mediationists, in fact, largely abdicated to him.

There was a marked one-sidedness, however, in Ritschl's presentation of salvation. He denied the doctrine of original sin and held, rather, that men have a tendency to good. Their cultural achievements, consequently, he esteemed optimistically, in terms of progress. God, similarly, is simply love. The biblical and Reformation attributes of holiness and wrath receded. There was here no sense of judgment on man and his culture. The work of Jesus Christ, in bringing the believer to God, meant bringing him into a Kingdom of moral ends. This Kingdom seemed little more than a stage in the moral progress and unification of the race. Ritschl conceived that there is a real possibility of perfection in moral life; that there is no fundamental difference between us and Jesus Christ on this point. Ritschlianism became thus the theological framework for much of the liberal social gospel, as a program for the mastery of life for which God's support was available. Ritschl had no feeling for the inner corruption of modern civilization, as preached in his day in different ways by the Marxists, and in theology, by his own colleague Lagarde, or by Nietzsche's friend, Overbeck, the "unbelieving theologian."

HARNACK. The Ritschlian conception of Christianity was brilliantly illustrated historically by Adolf Harnack's great *History of Dogma* (1886-1889). With verve and great gifts of sympathetic presentation, even where he did not agree with his subjects, Harnack employed his vast learning to show how the supposedly simple spiritual and ethical religion of Jesus of Nazareth had been elaborated and obscured by the growth of dogma in the ancient church. Just in the years when the historical approach to the Bible was becoming finally established, Harnack similarly set the classical creeds in the context of Hellenistic philosophy, depriving them of their unconditional authority. In contrast to the view of Christian history as a necessary rational development, as set forth by Hegelians like Baur, Harnack found instead a degeneration and obscuring of the primitive gospel by Hellenism. He brought home to many, even to those who did not share his position, the need for restating the Christian faith in terms not bound by the ancient philosophical categories of the creeds.

Even more than Ritschl, Harnack represented the identification of a moralized Christianity with the higher culture of his day. At the end of the nineteenth century he was not merely the representative theologian of his day in the university world, but, as such, was recognized as the finest representative of the world of scholarship generally. Active at the court and in the educational system, libraries, Evangelical Social Congress, and churches (so far as they would let him), Harnack was a kind of universal scholar. Through him, especially, the history of doctrine held the center of theological discussion as never before, although only a Harnack could have kept to second place his more consciously Lutheran rival, Reinhold Seeberg, whose researches into medieval and modern theology complemented Harnack's studies of the ancient church. Harnack's student, F. Loofs, also added to the achievements of historical theology.

WELLHAUSEN. The results of historical scholarship in this generation, however, were perhaps even more influential in biblical studies, especially studies of the Old Testament, than in the history of dogma. Julius Wellhausen became the representative figure here, as Baur had been a generation earlier in New Testament studies. Count Graf, his teacher Reuss, and the Dutchman Kuenen had all pioneered the method, but Wellhausen formulated the results so as to present a new and comprehensive understanding of the Old Testament as a whole (*The History of Israel*, 1878). As Baur had done, Wellhausen worked backward from the earliest period which provided firsthand sources for historical analysis, in this case the eighth century. From the conditions prevailing in that period he sought to interpret the documents about the earlier development. The whole conception of Hebrew history was revolutionized as a result. Wellhausen argued that, in place of the order of events as hitherto supposed, the prophetic works came before the law, and the psalms last of all. Moses' achievement then appeared in a different light, and most of the pre-Mosaic tradition was assigned to legend altogether. The prophets gained in religious meaning in this reinterpretation, and the gains were exhibited by Duhm, and, in the English-speaking world, by George Adam Smith. The development of Jahvistic religion from Moses on became psychologically intelligible for the first time. There was bitter resistance, however, just for this reason, in the 1880's and 1890's from those who had conceived of biblical revelation as a group of oracles unrelated to historical development. In Scotland Robertson Smith was tried for heresy for propounding Wellhausen's concept of Hebrew history, as was Briggs in America. Yet by 1890 the older view could find almost no defenders among the rising generation of scholars in Germany. New theological problems arose, however, as to the implications of "progressive revelation" and the new view of biblical inspiration.

In New Testament studies, meanwhile, there were at this period no comparable great reinterpretations. The Tübingen school had already made the first efforts with the historical method. In this generation the preference for the synoptics over John as historical sources, and the "two-source hypothesis" for the synoptics won over most of their opponents. The Cambridge scholars Westcott and Hort produced their text of the New Testament in 1881. A pervasive tendency in interpretation, meanwhile, was indicated by the series of "lives of Jesus" which began in the 1860's with the works of Renan, Strauss, and J. R. Seeley. The tendency was obviously parallel to that of Ritschl in its unconcern for dogmatic formulations and its stress on the concrete historical humanity of Jesus of Nazareth. Many hoped to get behind the Christ of the creeds to the "Jesus of history."

ESCHATOLOGY. Just on this point, however, the advance of scholarship raised radical difficulties in the 1890's. It was a main concern of Overbeck to demonstrate the contrast of the other-worldly spirit of early Christianity with the modernized optimistic version of such men as Ritschl and Harnack. In his view they were seeking to maintain merely the illusion of Christianity. It had apparently never occurred to Ritschl to doubt that Jesus intended to found an enduring community, but Johannes Weiss' pamphlet *Jesus' Preaching of the Kingdom of God* (1892) took the eschatological element in the Gospels seriously, producing a figure which looked quite different from the "historical Jesus" of the liberals. Albert Schweitzer summarized this line of inquiry in 1906 in his study called, in English, *The Quest of the Historical Jesus*. His radical view made Jesus virtually inaccessible for his own religious purposes, since he could not accept the eschatology which he considered central to the thought of Jesus.

This discovery of apparently alien elements in the mind of Jesus heightened a general problem which began to trouble the younger Ritschlians in the nineties. In the endeavor to escape from speculation they had appealed to the "Jesus of history." Harnack tried to isolate Jesus' teaching from the testimonies about him. But an increasing number of scholars came to doubt whether the "Jesus of history" could ever be distilled from the biblical Christ. And further, supposing that it could be done, would this historical figure automatically evoke the "value judgment," "My Lord and my God!"? Could history ever uncover more than a religious genius and prophet? And could it ever achieve certainty, more than a moral certainty or a high probability? Was it on such bases that the Christian faith rested? What was the relation of the Christ of the believer's faith to the Jesus of history?

THE "HISTORY OF RELIGIONS" SCHOOL. From another side, also, the views of Ritschl and Harnack were challenged in the 1890's. If the idea of historical development were to be used as a key to the understanding of biblical religion, why not extend it to a universal perspective, and place the religion of the Bible in its continuity with the other religions of the ancient Near East? The Ritschlians were accused of arrogant provincialism. By way of correction the influences of, for example, Egypt, Assyria, and Persia were traced in the Old Testament, and the religion of Jesus and Paul was distributed among various sources—mystery religions and Oriental and Jewish cults. Christianity was described as the "syncretistic religion" and both its distinctive character and the authority of the biblical canon seemed in process of dissolution. The movement centered at Göttingen, with Ritschl's colleague Lagarde, from whom it derived a certain missionary zeal. Lagarde was a sort of religious prophet as well as learned Orientalist. He considered that the forms of religion of his day, especially Protestantism, were exhausted and sterile, and wished to summon up a new and Germanic concretion of the "universal gospel." There was a deliberate intention here to break down the authority of the Bible and of tradition in the church. Books were presented in popular form to spread the views of the "history of religions" school. Gunkel and Bousset were its leaders.

TROELTSCH. This approach to biblical religion and Christianity in relation to other religions was akin to another phenomenon of the nineties, the revival of interest in natural religion, or religion in general. The philosophy and psychology of religion which Ritschl had sought to render superfluous again drew attention, and Schleiermacher, especially, returned as an influence. Perhaps the fullest heir to Schleiermacher's legacy, and certainly the chief systematic thinker of the "history of religions" school was Ernst Troeltsch. Schleiermacher's view of "religion" as a universal capacity in men which finds an indefinite variety of social manifestations was now reasserted, reinforced by a century of extraordinarily varied historical research. Christianity is but one among many religions, all relative to their time and circumstances, and none absolute or final for all time. To be sure Troeltsch retained something of the Hegelian sense of teleological development, within which he saw Christianity as the decisive turn to a religion of personality, and he could not conceive how a higher religion might be formed. Troeltsch died before bringing his wealth of views and knowledge into coherent system, and his work remained a torso. He had served as a major personal and intellectual force in the first two decades of the twentieth century. He brought more to fruition as historian than as philosopher of religion and theologian, especially with his brilliant *Modern Protestant Christianity and Churches* (1909) and the *Social Teachings of the Christian Churches* (1912), works which have been corrected in detail by further study but which have not yet been replaced. His last work, *Historism and Its Problems* (1922), shows the last stage of his thought but remained uncompleted.

HERRMANN. At the other pole from Troeltsch in the early twentieth century was Wilhelm Herrmann, the most distinguished theologian among Ritschl's disciples. In contrast to Troeltsch with his extraordinary range of interests, Herrmann concentrated on the exploration of the meaning of reconciliation in Christ. Like Ritschl, he wished to free religion from the metaphysicians and found his objective ground in the person of Jesus Christ. For him, however, Christ was not merely the historical founder of the Kingdom, but directly the object of worship, God incarnate. The *Communion of the Christian with God* (1886) sets forth a present personal relationship with the Risen Lord as the basis of Christian faith. The Ritschlians of the English-speaking world, such as the Scots Denney and H. R. Mackintosh, or the Englishman Forsyth, were especially drawn to Herrmann. Karl Barth also honors him as his teacher.

The church historian Karl Holl was stimulated by Ritschl to studies of Luther and concentrated on the religious meaning of justification until he made his historical studies a religious force closely akin to that of Herrmann. He sharply attacked Troeltsch's effort to relegate Luther to the Middle Ages and thus leave him largely irrelevant to modern life.

EFFECT OF WORLD WAR I. A new temper appeared in European Protestant thought with the shattering experiences of World War I, the consequent deflation and economic distress, and the effect of the Bolshevik Revolution. Spengler's *Decline of the West* was only one manifestation of a widespread sense of general collapse of the foundations of culture. This collapse necessarily was felt in theology, as involved in this culture. There was a sharp reaction against "culture-Protestantism," liberalism, modernism, and all currents which had confused Christian faith with or closely related it to social, political, philosophical, and ethical programs. Eschatology became a central theme of theological discussion. The catastrophe was interpreted by some as judgment by God, and the theological movement turned inward, searching for the grounds of specifically Christian faith in God's revelation to sinful humanity. The cue was given by Karl Barth's *Commentary on Romans* (1919). If the prewar theological situation were to be defined in terms of the polarity represented by Troeltsch and Herrmann, the change might be expressed as a violent reaction from the tendency of the former to that of the latter. One might even say that the pendulum swung over beyond Herrmann to the biblical and confessional theologians who had eschewed the apologetic task.

Herrmann and Troeltsch both died shortly after the war, but other figures who had made their mark beforehand, such as Rudolf Otto, Karl Heim, Reinhold Seeberg, and Karl Holl, only now reached their full powers. Ritschlians like Harnack and Kattenbusch were also still active. For a decade these men still dominated the field academically, for those most decisively shaped by the crisis did not at once set forth their views systematically and at length. But there was a marked tendency —among the young, especially—to discredit the older theology generally and to lose continuity with it. And from the other side, a Harnack could observe with sad amazement that he had no organ for understanding the Barthians.

Some of the most successful movements in theology, however, such as "form-criticism" in biblical studies, and the "Luther renaissance," were in direct continuity with prewar developments. In them, as in theological work generally, however, there was a perceptible shift in emphasis from relatively disinterested historical study to a more consciously theological perspective, even in historical studies.

HISTORICAL STUDIES. Least influenced by the new turn were church history and historical theology. No great scholars arose to replace Harnack, Seeberg, and Loofs; but, on the other hand, these disciplines were pushed from the center of interest to the periphery and attracted fewer students. Although Lietzmann wrote his notable history of the early church toward the end of the period, the characteristic interests of the generation were rather the Reformation and the nineteenth century, both explored for theological clarification. The Luther renaissance emphasized especially the young Luther and his struggle with ideas of God and justification. Karl Holl, Reinhold Seeberg, Loofs, Kattenbusch, and Boehmer were among the leaders. Other reformers were similarly studied and Calvin, for example, drew more attention in Germany than ever before. Within the nineteenth century the foci of

historical interest were Schleiermacher and the great idealists, who were being challenged as the corrupters of theology by the "crisis theologians." The meaning of church
history itself was also now explored as never before, in relation to the general discussion of philosophy of history. Little
energy was devoted to the study of non-Christian religions, as
one might expect from the general current, and what was done
in that area was chiefly by scholars of non-German countries,
such as the Scandinavians Söderblom and Lehmann and the
Dutchman Van der Leeuw.

In biblical studies, on the other hand, the generation after
World War I was rich and productive. The reaction against
disinterested "presuppositionless" scholarship sharpened theological self-consciousness generally and led to a revival of
biblical theology with men like Eichrodt and Koehler in Old
Testament studies, and Dibelius, K. L. Schmidt and Bultmann
in New Testament studies. In some extreme cases, as with
Vischer, one even found an attempt to revive the old dogmatic-
allegorical method of biblical interpretation.

DOGMATIC THEOLOGY. In the systematic disciplines the
striking development was the great resurgence of dogmatic
theology and the subsidence of philosophy of religion. Speculative philosophy of religion still found significant champions,
to be sure, Rudolf Otto, Paul Tillich, and Richard Kroner developing respectively the Kantian, Schellingian, and Hegelian
legacies, while Karl Heim related theology to the new currents
in the natural sciences. Rudolf Otto's *The Idea of the Holy*
(1917) proved to be the most widely read theological book of
the period. But the characteristic tendency which won the
widest influence was the essentially dogmatic enterprise of the
"dialectical theology" of Karl Barth, Thurneysen, Brunner,
and Gogarten. Here the desire was to take God's sovereignty
in complete seriousness, to think theologically from His revelation in the Word, rather than from man's ideals or religious
feelings. Now at last Kierkegaard came into his own, along
with the Blumhardts and Dostoievsky. *Between the Times*
was the organ of this group from 1923, but the members were
pulled in various directions. The Lutheran-Reformed tension,
together with German nationalism, separated Gogarten and

Barth, while Brunner and Barth debated over the question of whether there is any place for a natural theology not derived from revelation in Christ. The dialectical theologians as a group formed the core of the intellectual resistance to the Nazi "German Christians" as led by E. Hirsch. A distinctively Lutheran school maintained itself, meanwhile, against the strong Reformed flavor of the Barthians, being represented by Elert and Althaus, in connection with the Scandinavians Nygren and Aulen. On the popular level, a tendency to repristinate the confessions and to strengthen biblical literalism expressed the general trend of the generation.

Chapter 23

ROMAN CATHOLIC THEOLOGICAL LIBERALISM

The thirty years before World War I witnessed a remarkable theological development within the Roman Catholic Church. The third quarter of the nineteenth century had been so preoccupied with political and ecclesiastical controversy over the temporal power and papal infallibility that little else was heard of. The promising beginnings of Roman Catholic scholarship in the first half of the century, mostly in Germany, had been nipped in the bud by Pius IX. In the Latin countries, theological education and scholarship were in a deplorable situation. Probably the majority of seminaries taught no Bible or church history courses, and the philosophy and theology consisted of inconsequential textbooks, largely eclectic or Cartesian in flavor. Apart from censorship Roman Catholicism had no defenses against such writers as Comte and Renan. The controversies over education had removed Roman Catholic theological faculties from the universities, so that there was little theological scholarship beyond the elementary level. When such scholarship was again encouraged in the pontificate of Leo XIII (1878-1903), consequently, the full impact of nearly a century of Protestant biblical and historical study was suddenly felt. American Protestantism, similarly, received very late the matured results of the historical method in theology, and the American Protestant heresy trials occurred in the same years as the controversies over Roman Catholic "modernism." Not that the new Roman Catholic theological scholarship acknowledged its dependence either on Protestant or on ill-fated earlier Roman Catholic efforts, but indirectly and only half-consciously it built on both.

The Pope himself was chiefly responsible for "modernism."

Leo was more or less aware of the intellectual poverty of the Roman Catholic Church and endeavored to repair it. He opened to historians the Vatican archives—up to a date safely remote from the present. He gave his blessing to the struggling neo-Thomists as against the rival Cartesian, Scotist, and Platonist schools of theology and philosophy. He encouraged biblical scholarship. In all this he displayed his own theological naïveté, supposing that general theological inquiry would automatically arrive at the conclusions he had been taught in his own carefully insulated education.

THOMIST REVIVAL. The encyclical *Aeterni Patris* (1879) made the study of Thomism all but compulsory in the seminaries and colleges. Significant groups of Roman Catholic scholars remained unconvinced that the "prince and master" of the medieval doctors had defined the ideal of Christian philosophy once and for all, but the Pope pushed through the policy in practice. Universities received subsidies for the support of Thomist teaching; periodicals were established in its interest; textbooks were rewritten, and professors were made to understand that while promotion might lag for those of other persuasions, there might even be a red hat to be found in the pages of Thomas' *Summa*. Partly as a result of these devices, much of the opposition was forced to define itself as one or another school of interpretation of Thomas, and the use of a common terminology by a large group of thinkers made Thomism a significant force in the cultural world at large. The weight of emphasis in Thomas' own thought, moreover, provided a useful counterweight to the prevailing drift, on the one hand, to a historical approach to religion, and on the other, to the psychological and epistemological approach.

Among the centers of Roman Catholic scholarship France now played again a major role, authorizing five institutes for higher studies in 1875. The French scholars were largely dependent on German methods and conceptions, but in this period Roman Catholic Germany scarcely rivaled France in biblical studies.

ROMAN CATHOLIC INSTITUTE OF PARIS. The chief center of the new scholarship in its early stages was the new Roman

Catholic Institute of Paris, opened in 1878 with four professors. Louis Duchesne, the church historian, had been an ardent ultramontane and infallibilist but was cured of this by his study of church history in the 1870's. He aided his protégé, Alfred Loisy, in securing appointment in 1881 as professor of Hebrew. The two collaborated closely until the end of the 1880's. Duchesne was suspended for a year (1885-1886), but was then reinstated. Loisy, meanwhile, attended the lectures of Renan at the College to learn how to refute him. Renan was the French popularizer of radical German Protestant biblical criticism, such as that of Strauss and Baur. By the early 1890's Duchesne and Loisy had had a perceptible influence on the leading French clergy and the teachers of the diocesan seminaries and the provincial Catholic Institutes, both through their teaching and through their *Bulletin critique*.

The application of historical criticism to the Bible, of course, raised difficulties with regard to the doctrine of inspiration and inerrancy. Was it possible to question the accuracy of some historical or scientific propositions in the Bible? Some of the biblical scholars, such as Loisy, thought so. The first crisis came in 1892-1893. In that year the superior of the seminary of Saint Sulpice forbade his students to attend Loisy's lectures because of his radical exegesis of Genesis. The rector of the Catholic Institute, Mgr. d'Hulst, attempted to defend Loisy in an article, "The Biblical Question." The defense, however, proved even more disturbing to the traditionalists, and, in any case, Loisy declined to accept his rector's distinction of matters of scientific fact from matters of religion and morals in Scripture as a solution. Such a distinction, thought Loisy, made the Bible a "mosaic of divine truths and human errors." The result of the furor was that Loisy was dismissed and retired to a girls' school as chaplain for the next five years. And the Pope reasserted the fundamentalist doctrine of biblical inerrancy as defined at Trent in *Providentissimus Deus* (1893).

DEVELOPMENT IN DOGMA. Comparable difficulties were arising in the same years in the fields of church history and historical theology. The Pope might encourage historical study, but what if sifted historical evidence should point to unorthodox conclusions over the large areas of factual assertion familiar in church tradition? Were there not extensive passages of historical life on which the Roman Catholic scholar must simply accept the church's teaching, evidence or no evidence? Duchesne scandalized many by his criticism of the legends about the origin of the church in France. His studies of the theological views of the anti-Nicene fathers cut even deeper. Was it not the case, as Boussuet had maintained against Jurieu, that the Roman Church has kept the faith static and unchanged from the beginning? Could the idea of change or development in doctrine, dogma, or sacrament be admitted? Various conceptions of development were proposed: the more cautious, like Franzelin, admitted only a logical explication of the original deposit of doctrine; the followers of Newman proposed a more flexible dialectical development; and at the other extreme, Le Roy and Tyrrell contended that the unchanging elements lay in the personal relations of God and man, which might be expressed in various dogmatic or theological definitions.

PHILOSOPHY AND THEOLOGY. In such a radical position, of course, there were philosophical and theological implications quite different from those of scholasticism. And there were new currents of this sort in the 1890's. The rationalistic positivism which had dominated Latin culture for two or three decades was challenged about 1890 by a new voluntarist, intuitionist, "pragmatist" tendency. Bergson, Poincaré, and Boutroux were influential. The "bankruptcy" of positivistic science was declared, and a new reconciliation of Christian theology and philosophy made possible. Such a reconciliation, however, must also be at the expense of dogmatic scholasticism. Ollé-Laprune, professor of philosophy at the *école normale,* was the center of a group pursuing the Platonizing tendency of Bautain and Gratry. One of his students, Blondel, created a sensation in 1893 with his thesis on the "philosophy of action." Blondel's major work was very obscure, but he wrote some provocative brief essays, and Laberthonnière popularized his thought. It was argued that revelation, inspiration, and faith must be understood in terms of personal confrontation, and could not be adequately expressed in static Aristotelian categories. The intellectual element in faith is only one element in a relationship which engages the whole personality. Religion is a life rather than merely a doctrine, and both biblical and church tradition are to be understood as articulations of that life rather than final and closed revelation. The *Philosophy of Religion* of Auguste Sabatier, dean of the Protestant theological faculty at Paris, was congenial to many Roman Catholic liberals and helped to spread such ideas. In Germany at the same time Schell was setting forth a rather similar Augustinian dynamism and protesting against clerical authoritarianism.

Most of these new currents found expression in the five international Roman Catholic scientific congresses which were held between 1888 and 1900. Scholars of various countries met and conferred with great enthusiasm and many provincial boundaries were broken down. The authorities, however, were very uneasy at the hearing given there to men like Loisy and von Hügel, and in Munich in 1900 the congresses came to the same fate that had befallen the conference of 1863 in the same city (see above, p. 211).

VON HÜGEL. At the Fribourg Congress in 1897 Baron von Hügel challenged the obvious sense of *Providentissimus* by his scholarly paper on the multiple sources of the Hexateuch. Von Hügel, with his international connections and range of theological interests, was the chief personal link among the representatives of the new currents in the 1890's. Settled in London since 1871 and married to a converted English peeress, the Baron devoted himself to studies which made him the greatest Roman Catholic lay theologian of all times. Everywhere he sought out Roman Catholic scholars of promise. He visited d'Hulst, Loisy, and Duchesne at the Paris Institute, and Mgr. Mignot, the chief scholar of the French hierarchy, on the Riviera. "Modernism" in Rome itself may well be dated from von Hügel's winters there at the beginning of the nineties, when biblical criticism and mystical theology were eagerly discussed. At Rome, von Hügel worked to save Blondel's *L'Action* from the Index in 1894. He was associated with Schell and other German Catholic liberals and was mainly responsible for bringing George Tyrrell, the Irish Jesuit, into the main current of "modernist" thought. Paul Sabatier, a romantic liberal Protestant, played a similar episcopal role among the Roman Catholic progressives, championing their cause and making them acquainted with each other.

The new intellectual currents, historical and theological, were involved in complicated fashion with the political and social movements of the same years. Leo's policy of *ralliement* and of cultivating industrial labor had encouraged the "Catholic democrats" and embittered the Catholic monarchists. The democrats, especially, being often in the position of addressing large audiences with many nonbelievers, were attracted by the new biblical criticism which enabled them to escape heckling about Jonah and the whale, the Flood, and the serpent and Eve. The Christian democrats tended to be hospitable to the new ideas, although they were by no means universally so. There were also many among the extreme political reactionaries who in their own thinking were very sceptical in theology, but these "atheist Catholics" tended publicly to defend the *Syllabus* and to attack as heretical liberal Catholics whose politics they opposed.

DISCIPLINARY ACTIONS. A second set of warnings came from the Roman court in 1899. Professor Schell in Würzburg was put on the Index for raising questions about the eternity of hellfire. The same year saw Leo's condemnation of "Americanism," the "phantom heresy." It was perhaps more French than American, since the occasion was the controversy excited in France by the programmatic preface to the French translation of Elliott's life of Hecker. The book aroused the fury of the French reactionaries, since it was used by the Catholic democrats. But even in America the bishops of the Milwaukee province, bitter opponents of Cardinal Gibbons and his liberal supporters, declared that they felt the Pope's intervention had been needed. Even more important was Leo's letter to the French hierarchy, which censured all the chief "modernist" tendencies. For the biblical critics the warning of *Providentissimus Deus* was repeated. The philosophers and theologians were advised against subjectivism and metaphysical agnosticism of "Protestant origin," and referred to the Aristotelian directives of *Aeterni Patris*. The "Catholic democrats," finally, were enjoined to greater moderation and discipline.

The liberals were not silenced by the repressions of 1899 and the first general manifesto was yet to come from the leading biblical critic, Loisy. With the aid of Newman, whom von Hügel had commended to him, Loisy had been improving his time by writing a large apologetic treatise directed especially against the Protestant liberals Harnack and Auguste Sabatier. One of his pseudonymous articles, however, was denounced, and Mgr. Mignot and von Hügel, Loisy's closest friends, intervened to prevent his condemnation by the Index. Puzzled by the complications of the "biblical question," Leo set up a Biblical Commission (1902) of three cardinals and a dozen consultors (several of whom were liberal) to decide on these cases. Just at this time Houtin had published his sardonic *Question Biblique* in which the tortured devices of the clergy to interpret the Deluge, the Creation story, and the like in some relation to modern science were mercilessly exposed.

THE GOSPEL AND THE CHURCH. With the encouragement of von Hügel and Mgr. Mignot, Loisy now decided to publish a popular summary of his unpublished apologetic treatise. They thought it might assist his candidature for the episcopacy, to which he had been invited to offer himself. Thus appeared *The Gospel and The Church* (1903), as a refutation of Harnack's *What is Christianity?*. Against the liberal Protestant tendency to reduce Christianity to optimistic humanitarianism by interpreting the "Kingdom of God" as essentially private and internal, Loisy took New Testament eschatology seriously. Jesus, he said, was not just preaching the "fatherhood of God," but the coming of an objective, future Messianic Kingdom. When that Kingdom did not at once materialize, consequently, the institutional church was organized and dogma defined as a necessary vehicle for preserving the Gospel in the interim Around this argument the new theologians gathered with enthusiasm.

Although Bishop Mignot had approved the book, the *Univers* attacked it and eight French bishops forbade it to their dioceses. The Congregation of the Index voted to ban it, but Leo refused to sign the decree. Loisy now sought to clarify his position with *Autour d'un petit livre*. Just at this time, however, the aged Pope died, and his successor exhibited none of his uncertainty. At the end of 1903 the Biblical Commission was reorganized in a strongly conservative direction and five of Loisy's books were put on the Index. Similarly a *motu proprio* on social and political "Catholic Action" severely restrained "social modernism." Pius X had no patience with either theological or political novelties. For the next three years, however, he was so occupied with the political controversy with the Third Republic of France, with the resultant Law of Separation of 1905, that the theological purge indicated in 1903 was postponed until 1906 and 1907.

FOGAZZARO AND TYRRELL. It was in this interval that the term "modernism" came into general use in Italy, replacing the older term "liberalism" for the same type of theological and political phenomena. In this interval, also, new personalities came to the fore. Loisy and Tyrrell were both in retirement, from whence the latter was writing under pseudonyms. A distinguished Italian layman, Senator Fogazzaro, now published a novel, *The Saint*. In one chapter the novel's hero consults privately with the pope about four vices of the church—falsehood, clericalism, avarice, and immobility—vices which recall the "wounds" of Fogazzaro's master Rosmini. This chapter became a program document for many modernists. Fogazzaro was also instrumental in launching a modernist review, *Il Rinnovamento*, about a year and a half after the liberal *Demain* had appeared at Lyons. Fogazzaro also translated into Italian an anonymous English *Letter to a Professor of Anthropology*, which urged Roman Catholic doubters to remain in the Church despite the problems raised by modern science.

The *Letter* was traced to Tyrrell, and he was expelled from the Society of Jesus early in 1906, the first in a new series of disciplinary actions. Fogazzaro's *Saint* and books by Laberthonnière were put on the Index in the following months. The Biblical Commission, meanwhile, was releasing a series of decisions. It was to be maintained by Roman Catholics, for example, that the inspiration of the Apocrypha was plenary and inerrant, that Second Maccabbees was no whit inferior to the fourth Gospel. The bulk of the Pentateuch was written by Moses, and the creation story was to be taken as literal historical truth. The "beloved disciple," John, similarly, was the author of the fourth Gospel, and the long speeches of this Gospel were to be taken as authentic historical records. We may here anticipate chronology and note that in 1911-1912 the Commission rejected the "two-document hypothesis" of the synoptic Gospels, asserting that the first three Gospels were all written before A.D. 70 in the order Matthew, Mark, Luke. Similarly, Hebrews was placed among the letters of Paul in 1914, and in 1915 it was announced that the Lord's Return was not conceived as imminent by the Disciples, to say nothing of Jesus himself.

LAMENTABILI. In 1905 and 1906 Pius had also released his series of attacks on the Italian Catholic democrats, and early in 1907 Murri was suspended *a divinis*. The pragmatism of Professor Le Roy's *Dogma et Critique* was banned in May 1907. And in the summer came the new syllabus of errors, *Lamentabili sane exitu*. Some sixty-five propositions were condemned in this encyclical, over fifty of them apparently drawn from Loisy, and others involving Mignot, Tyrrell, Le Roy, Houtin and (inadvertently) Cardinal Newman. It was not clear whether these propositions were formally heretical, or merely inopportune or in bad taste. And nearly all of them were so garbled in statement as to caricature the positions they were apparently intended to state.

PASCENDI. The full definition and condemnation of the "modernist" heresy, however, were presented the next month in the encyclical *Pascendi*. This long encyclical, apparently drafted chiefly by the Jesuit Billot and the ex-modernist Benigni, presented modernism in the guise of a conspiracy propagating a heretical system in the church. The "philosophy" of the system was set forth as underlying its historical and biblical studies. Heroic disciplinary measures were decreed to stamp it out, culminating in a system of espionage with "councils of vigilance" in every diocese. As a result, nearly every diocese produced its "case," if only to demonstrate the orthodoxy of the ordinary. The consequent corrosion of the church with delation and spying is illustrated by the anecdote that when Pius' successor took over administration seven years later, he found on the papal desk charges against his own orthodoxy.

The most conspicuous replies to *Pascendi* came from Tyrrell and (anonymously) from Buonaiuti. The latter was the author of *The Program of Modernism*, which showed without difficulty that there never had been a modernist conspiracy or a modernist philosophy. There was, in fact, a great variety of views among "modernists" and many or most of them could in good faith deny that the encyclical was properly sent to their address. *The Program* further announced an international society of religious scholarship. Tyrrell, meanwhile, had attacked the encyclical violently in two long letters to the *London Times*, prophesying that a large group would submit to excommunication but would continue to share, insofar as possible, in the life of the Catholic Church in passive resistance to its despotic and obscurantist rulers.

In fact, however, only a handful were able to maintain the heroic course championed by Tyrrell. Denunciation led to purges all over the Roman Catholic world, and under attack most modernists either submitted or left Rome to become Protestants or socialists or secularists. Loisy, Murri, and Minocchi all left Rome. In Germany, to be sure, where there were still Roman Catholic faculties in the universities and the church had to keep up the appearance of intellectual integrity, the chief journals avoided publishing *Pascendi* and Cardinal Kopp wrote the Pope that it could not be applied without great danger. Councils of vigilance were not set up in that country, and professors such as Schnitzer who accepted such ideas as the expectation of an imminent Second Coming in the synoptics, and the allegorical character of much of John, were not disciplined. Elsewhere the purge ran freely. In the United States Driscoll of the diocesan seminary of New York at Dunwoodie, and editor of the *New York Review*, was discharged, and the bishops even had to fight to save the *Catholic Encyclopedia*. Father William Sullivan of the Paulists was the best-known American modernist; he became a Unitarian. When Tyrrell died in June 1909, the soul of the resistance was gone and nearly all the remaining modernists went underground.

THE ANTI-MODERNIST OATH. To smoke out this underground remainder of "modernism," Pius imposed in 1910 the famous anti-modernist oath. All clergy and teachers were required to take it or be discharged. The terms of the oath committed those who took it to the whole range of condemnations of *Lamentabili* and *Pascendi*. In addition, all clerics must affirm the cogency of the cosmological argument for God's existence, and commit themselves to the opinion that the best arguments for the divine origin of Christianity, even in our time, are the external arguments from miracles and prophecy. They must reject all interpretations in church history or Bible which rest simply on evidence, apart from the views currently received in the church, and in particular, they must reject the heretical notion of the evolution of dogma. All over the world bishops called in their priests and teachers to take the oath.

This oath faced hundreds of Roman Catholics with a terrible trial of conscience. Some took it and wrote anonymous letters to the newspapers stating that they did so only as an act of obedience and without conviction. As was said in 1911 of the Italian clergy, "of a hundred clerics from forty years of age onwards, no less than sixty keep most jealously in their private desks the best products of the modernist literature." A few refused to take the oath and accepted the bleak destiny of the excommunicated Roman priest, a destiny which in some cases ended in literal starvation.

The alternatives posed to the Roman Catholic conscience by the oath may be illustrated by the case of Maude Petre, who was summoned to subscribe to these documents when she announced that she was preparing a life of Father Tyrrell. Miss Petre, a member of one of the most distinguished Roman Catholic families of England, replied by distinguishing three ways in which she might affirm such an adhesion. First of all, she said, one might claim that he could make such an affirmation simply as an act of obedience to superiors without reference to his own personal convictions. Some regarded this as legitimate, and it was certainly the only way out of the impasse without pain and scandal. The case of Fénelon seemed to serve as precedent here. Miss Petre, however, could not in conscience take such a course.

The second alternative was that of the casuist, who by distinctions and interpretations twists documents from their intended meaning. Thus Newman, for example, that "glorious sophist," as Lord Acton called him, had operated on the Thirty-nine Articles when he was an Anglican, and on the *Syllabus of Errors* and Vatican Decrees when he was a Romanist. Miss Petre, however, declined this course also. The decree and encyclical should either be accepted in their clear intended sense, or not at all. If she should subscribe these documents she would do so for the spirit as well as the letter, from the first line to the last. Before making such a solemn decision she desired to know from her bishop whether each and every proposition involved was a matter *de fide* and would always be *de fide*, for which she should risk life itself, as for the faith of the Apostles' Creed. To this inquiry the Bishop did not care to reply, but instead gave secret orders to withhold the sacraments from Miss Petre. Such a case was rare; as Loisy observed, the Roman Catholic Church does not ordinarily train consciences to such a pitch of integrity.

Why did modernism collapse so quickly? There never had been more than a few hundred modernists. Although they included some of the most profoundly religious spirits of their generation, such as Tyrrell, Von Hügel, and Buonaiuti, there were also among them some who were at heart mere rationalists or humanists or democrats without deep Christian convictions. But most important of all, there was not enough theological comprehension among the Roman Catholics in the Latin countries to appreciate what was at stake. Jansenism, which had lasted for generations under severe pressure in a more religiously minded generation, might well have collapsed as rapidly as modernism in the conditions of the early twentieth-century church. But then, whereas Jansenism reached to the heart of the issues of salvation, most modernist controversy was over the less central problem of apologetics. Viewed from the wider perspective of general church history, it may be that the chief modernists, such as von Hügel, were less influential in their own communion than in Protestantism, especially Anglicanism.

Chapter 24

PROTESTANT MISSIONS, 1796-1914

In the sixteenth and seventeenth centuries Protestantism had needed all its strength to establish its right to live at all. There had been no Protestant missionary activity in any way comparable to the great missions campaign of the Counter Reformation, led by Spain and Portugal. In the Reformation itself the Anabaptists realized most intensely the missionary obligation. This concern was inherited in the eighteenth century primarily by Continental pietists, especially the Halle Lutherans and the Moravians. The British, of course, were transplanting Christianity to their colonies, especially in North America, but they contributed less to missions among non-European peoples than did the Germans. Up to the end of the eighteenth century, it seemed that Protestantism was the religion merely of northwestern Europe, with only a few million Protestants sprinkled about elsewhere in Europe and outside Europe. As late as 1836, in fact, Cardinal Wiseman used as an argument against the Protestant claim to be part of the Body of Christ that it was so geographically and culturally provincial.

BRITISH AND AMERICAN EVANGELICAL MISSIONS. Wiseman was a full generation behind the movement of events in his estimate of the situation. For during the French Revolution had begun the great missionary campaign of English-speaking Evangelicalism, an expansion which was to dominate all Christian missions up to World War I and provide what was, until the war, the most spectacular diffusion any body of ideas had experienced in world history. This movement which centered in Great Britain in the nineteenth century was closely emulated by the new United States and stimulated new activity in Protestant churches of the Continent. All through the nineteenth century Great Britain was to lead this effort both in terms of personnel and financial support, and only in the decade immediately before World War I was the United States to edge into the lead in Protestant missions. Of a total of 13,600 Protestant missionaries in 1900, for example, 5,900 were British, and 4,100 American. The English-speaking peoples thus provided about three-fourths of the total Protestant effort, and as a result the Christianity which was so widely disseminated in that century was predominantly the Evangelical type of Protestantism dominant then in the English-speaking world. One of the striking results of this movement was the consolidation in the twentieth century of a genuinely ecumenical world community of Protestant Christians, a possibility scarcely conceived of before the nineteenth century.

The characteristics peculiar to Evangelicalism in general marked the methods and character of this new missionary campaign. These missionaries sat freer to the state than any comparable group in history. Great Britain, to be sure, was the largest colonial power and the greatest commercial center of the period, and the missionary movement was not unrelated to political and economic imperialism. The British government gave less direct support, however, than did the governments related to Eastern Orthodox or Roman Catholic missions, and British missionaries were often at odds with the policies of colonial administrations and traders. The great bulk of the American missionaries worked in areas where their government had no political interests, and a large number of them where there were no important commercial relations. The missionary impetus was sometimes aided and sometimes hindered by Western imperialism, but its central motive was the passion for souls for whom Christ had died, wherever they could be reached.

Anglo-American Evangelicalism also sat freer to ecclesiastical institutions and doctrine than any comparable missionary movement. Continental Protestantism was much stricter on confessional orthodoxy and High Anglicanism on ecclesiastical order than were the Evangelicals. Many of the Evangelical societies were interdenominational; the London Missionary Society from 1795 and the American Board of Foreign Missions from 1810 enlisted Episcopalians, Methodists, Congregationalists, Presbyterians, and Baptists. Not that they lacked convictions—they were individualistic Bible Christians, seeking a wholehearted personal commitment and conversion to Christ and only as much of doctrine or church order as seemed indispensable for this message of salvation. So far as the converts were concerned, the demands of personal conviction and moral standards were higher than had been the case with any earlier missionary expansion. From William Carey down to John R. Mott this movement took quite literally the whole of humanity as its responsibility and was disposed to co-operate with all Christians who shared its central concern. The slogan of the Student Volunteer Movement epitomized the purpose held throughout: "the evangelization of the world in our generation." No one can take the measure of nineteenth-century Anglo-American Evangelical Protestantism without reference to these thousands of men and women who for four generations poured out to the ends of the earth to die among strange peoples of alien tongue in order to tell them the good news of what God had done in Christ. Whatever one thinks of their theology, their social ethics, their churchmanship, there is something to learn here of religious seriousness and power.

BRITISH BEGINNINGS. Carey, perhaps the chief pioneer of Evangelical missions, derived part of his inspiration from reading of the work done among the Indians in Colonial America by John Eliot and David Brainerd (above, p. 75). This reading, and his reading of the *Voyages of Captain Cook* combined to inspire his dream of a mission to all humanity. A society of British Baptists was organized in 1792 to support Carey's venture. In 1795 the London Missionary Society (L.M.S.) was formed, largely as a result of his inspiration, by Evangelicals of various churches, chiefly the Congregationalists. Four years later Anglican Evangelicals, especially the Clapham group of Wilberforce, Grant, and Thornton, (see above, p. 181) established the Church Missionary Society. The same men were active in organizing the British and Foreign Bible Society in 1804. In the meantime, an interdenominational Religious Tract Society came into being in 1799. In Scotland, likewise, the new current produced the Scottish Missionary

Society and the Glasgow Missionary Society before the eighteenth century had ended. The typical pattern thus was a voluntary association more or less independent of the established ecclesiastical machinery.

UNITED STATES.   Across the Atlantic a comparable current was under way, expressed in a multitude of local missionary societies designed to gather funds and pray for the conversion of the heathen.   The first American societies asked to become auxiliaries of the British, but this plan did not prove practicable. In 1810 the American Board was organized, chiefly by Congregationalists and Presbyterians.   They sent Judson to India in 1812, and when he turned Baptist, the Baptists set up an American Baptist Missionary Convention (1814) to support his work.   In 1816 there appeared an American Bible Society and, the next year, an American Colonization Society modeled on the project of the English Evangelicals in Sierra Leone in 1787.   Soon the several denominations created official boards for missions.   Together with these larger groups, there were more than a hundred local and state Bible societies and missionary societies.

CONTINENTAL PROTESTANTS.   Even before the larger American societies had appeared, the impulse of the London Missionary Society had produced new developments on the Continent.   The Netherlands Missionary Society, founded in 1797, was almost an auxiliary of the L.M.S.   In Berlin the new Evangelical movement made contact with the older Moravian and Halle missionary tradition, as Jänicke, pastor of the Bohemian church there, opened a training school for missionaries (1800) with some financial support from England.   Most of his first graduates went out under the auspices of the London Missionary Society, the Church Missionary Society, or the Netherlands Missionary Society.   Another famous training school opened in Basel in 1815 and, as with Jänicke's graduates, the early missionaries from Basel went out to the missions of the British societies.   In the second quarter of the century, however, a number of German missionary societies were organized and the Basel school also developed its own mission fields.

The religious revival whose spread we are recording by this

crude measure made itself felt also in the Restoration period in Protestant France and Scandinavia. In 1818 appeared a Paris Bible Society and ten years later a Paris Evangelical Missionary Society. The Danish Missionary Society was organized in 1821, and in the 1840's and 1850's appeared similar organizations among the Lutherans of Norway, Sweden, and Finland. Various German societies, as we have said, were organized at that time: the Rhenish or Barmen Society in 1828, the Hermannsburg Society in 1849, the Dresden (later, Leipzig) Missionary Society in 1836. The American Ohio Lutheran Synod worked through Hermannsburg and the Missouri Synod worked through the Leipzig Society.

This is a very sketchy sampling of the thousands of Protestant societies which enlisted hundreds of thousands of laymen in Europe and America in the missionary cause. Let us turn from consideration of what this vast activity signified of religious life in the West, to an examination of the fields to which the emissaries of the Gospel went. In general the first two generations of the century may be described as the period of foundations. Stations were established, languages mastered, Bibles translated, and contacts (but few converts) made. This was also the period when the names of individual pioneers became inspirations to followers. William Carey and Henry Martyn in India, Robert Morrison in China, Robert Moffatt and David Livingstone in Africa, John Williams in the Pacific (the last four all L.M.S. missionaries)—these were names known in most religious homes of Britain and America. Oceania, in particular, furnished many martyrs in the first generation.

The last third of the century at last began to see substantial results from the small beginnings. A notable increase of missionary personnel, funds, and societies coincided with great new opportunities rising from political changes. About 1860 the effect of the Sepoy Mutiny led to a new regime in India. New treaties opened China to missionary activity. Perry persuaded the Japanese to break their walls of isolation. The hitherto unknown interior of Africa was opened by missionaries and explorers. For all these reasons the tempo of missionary activity increased markedly from the 1860's to World

War I. Toward the end of this period American Protestants took over the leadership with new methods of recruiting personnel, raising funds, and consolidating an overhead organization of the world-wide Protestant missionary enterprise.

INDIA. Let us begin, with India, a swift survey of the chief Protestant mission fields. In India the missions of Lutheran pietism, supported also by the S.P.C.K. (see above, p. 87), had first begun their work at the beginning of the eighteenth century, and here the Evangelical Awakening sent its famous pioneer, the Baptist cobbler William Carey, during the French Revolution. Under the British East India Company in the decades before the Sepoy Mutiny (1857) nearly all the larger societies—the S.P.C.K., the London Missionary Society, the Church Missionary Society, the American Board, the Church of Scotland Mission, the Basel Society, the Leipzig Missionary Society, the American Baptists and Presbyterians—established themselves. The total of missionaries, however, was less than five hundred at the time of the Mutiny, and the Indian Protestant community numbered then only about one hundred thousand, chiefly in the Madras area. Apart from strictly evangelistic work, to which the American Board deliberately confined itself, the chief activity was educational. The Church of Scotland mission specialized in higher education, and Alexander Duff, one of Chalmers' former pupils, was very influential in founding an educational system built on English literature and English political and moral ideals which was to prove a mighty ferment in India's national life in the twentieth century.

After the Mutiny and the direct assumption of government by the British Crown, missionary activity expanded rapidly. The government now aided medical, educational, and philanthropic work, most of which had been introduced by missions. Medical work by women for women proved to be a particular need of Indian society; on the other hand, there was little call for orphanages. The majority of converts came from outcast groups or from animists, a circumstance which made it difficult to develop strong native leadership and prolonged Western paternalism in the church. Upper-class Hindus, however, showed the Christian influence in various reform movements like the Brahma Samaj and the Rama Krishna Mission which turned against such Hindu abuses as caste, child marriage, and idolatry. Also, the new interest in charity and reform bore witness to a change in attitude toward this life, contrasting with the hopelessness and fatalism general in India. Improved agricultural methods also were of crucial importance in a land 90 per cent agrarian and desperately poor.

Throughout the century the Protestant community was growing much more rapidly than the Roman Catholic and numbered about one million in 1914. Four-fifths of this Protestant membership were said to have come in by groups. The great organizational diversity of Protestantism was also in process of consolidation, first by comity agreements, then by mergers within the same denominational families, and finally into such integrations as the South India United Church, formed in 1908 of bodies connected chiefly with Scottish Presbyterians, American Reformed, and English and American Congregationalists. More inclusive projects were under way which were to result, after 1914, in the National Christian Council. Indian leadership, following on the earlier generation of Azariah, Goreh, Chatterjee and K. T. Paul, was rapidly emerging. A rising tide of nationalism in twentieth-century India made this process of devolution imperative.

INDONESIA. East of India Protestant churches were similarly organized in every land save French Indochina and, by 1914, had equaled in influence the earlier Roman communities in China, Japan, and Korea; in the latter two countries Protestants had also overtaken the Roman Catholics in numbers. The greatest concentration of Protestants in the Far East, however, was in Netherlands India. We may discuss Indonesia first, since here alone nineteenth-century missions were both building upon and were handicapped by, foundations from the seventeenth and eighteenth centuries. Indonesia or the Malay Archipelago geologically includes the Philippines, and whereas the Roman Catholic Spaniards had pre-empted the Philippines, the more southern islands—chief among them Java, Borneo, Sumatra, the Celebes, and New Guinea—had fallen to the share of Protestant imperial powers, chiefly the Dutch. The chief language and most of the population were Malayan, and in many islands there were various animistic tribes.

Densely populated Java held three-fourths of the total population and was Moslem in religion. In many parts of Southeast Asia, as in Africa, there was a race between Islam and Christianity to win the animistic peoples.

The earlier mass baptisms of the seventeenth and eighteenth centuries left Indonesia with a community of nominal Protestants numbering perhaps one hundred thousand at the end of the Napoleonic Wars, when the Dutch government took over control from the Dutch East India Company. For the first half of the nineteenth century, however, the government exploited the natives and hindered missionary work. State paternalism enervated the church as it did in the Spanish colonies of Latin America and the Philippines. Following the example of the Prussian Union of 1817, the King of Holland united Lutherans and Reformed in Indonesia into one state church under the governor. The church was dependent on Dutch leadership and displayed a lack of vitality until after 1914.

The new missionary interest in Europe, however, sent numbers of new workers, chiefly Dutch and German, to labor among the unchurched islanders. The Netherlands Missionary Society sent out graduates from Basel and Jänicke's school, as well as its own Dutchmen. In the second half of the century theological controversy in Holland led to sharp divisions and soon no less than eight societies, mostly one or another variety of Dutch Calvinism, were at work. The Dutch government also reformed its colonial policy, especially under the Kuyper ministry. The German Rhenish Society, led by Nommensen and, later, Johannes Warneck, penetrated the interior of Sumatra. By 1914 this group had transformed the Bataks and had called into being a Batak Church of 160,000. Similar sensational successes were achieved in the Celebes, especially in Minahassa and among the Alifars and Toradjas. On Java, meanwhile, there was no such penetration of the Moslems by the Christians. Islam, to this day is perhaps gaining more from Christianity than it loses to it. More converts were made, however, from Javanese Moslems than from all the rest of the world's Moslems in this period. The Javanese puppet plays and Javanese music were used to present Christianity, and by 1914 a community of ten to twelve thousand was created. The total of Indonesian Protestants must have been somewhere about one third to one half a million in 1914. As elsewhere, literacy, medicine, scientific agriculture, and improvement in the status of women had been introduced, and head-hunting, cannibalism, sorcery, and werewolves had been suppressed. In 1918 Indonesia was to become a "commonwealth," and Christianity was to continue rapid gains after the war.

THE PHILIPPINES AND LATIN AMERICA. In the Philippines to the north, meanwhile, Protestantism was growing rapidly. In 1898 Protestantism was not permitted in the island. Fifteen years later it counted 204 missionaries and a community of between fifty and one hundred thousand. This Protestantism came almost entirely from the United States. Although it was variegated denominationally, it was co-operatively organized almost from the beginning, and pointed toward the future Evangelical Church of the Philippines.

From the Philippines we may look across the Pacific to the similar situation of Spanish and Portuguese America. Protestants had been more rigidly excluded from Latin America in the Colonial period than had Roman Catholics in the English colonies of North America. But in the nineteenth century Roman Catholics moved into the Protestant United States, and a generation or two later, Protestants entered Latin America. There were, first of all, Protestant merchants, especially from Germany, and some ex-Confederate sympathizers from the United States. In addition, there were millions of Indians still untouched by any form of Christianity. And lastly, there were lapsed and nominal Roman Catholics, including almost all the upper classes and the new working classes. Among this last group, American missionaries were more conspicuous than the British, for the Anglicans, with a delicacy which was not reciprocated, scrupulously refused to treat countries with a strong Roman Catholic Church as mission fields. They blocked the inclusion of Latin America at the Edinburgh Missionary Conference of 1910 on these grounds.

In general the Protestant communities were formed chiefly among Indians, half-breeds, and the lower class, and in many areas they pioneered in education for these groups. Protestant schools were the basis of the later public school systems in some cases. In Peru, Ecuador, and Colombia Protestants found gaining a foothold difficult. Over half the Protestants on the West Coast were in Chile, where Pentecostals were especially vigorous among workers. Argentina had a still larger community, especially in Buenos Aires, where there were seven self-supporting Anglican congregations alone in 1905, and the Methodists, the largest group, had a theological seminary. But the strongest Latin American Protestant community was in Brazil, where the largest number of Protestant immigrants had also come. By 1914 there was a rapidly growing Latin American Evangelical community of about 120,000 and a Committee on Co-operation in Latin America was organized to prepare unification.

THE FAR EAST. By 1914 Americans were also dominant among the Protestant missionaries in Japan, Korea, and China. In Japan Protestants had no earlier communities and affections to build on, as did the Roman Catholics, yet they quickly overtook the latter. They found an audience chiefly among the middle class and the intellectuals of the new cities and made no significant impression on the feudal and rural mentality. In the generation and a half before World War I, however, Protestantism exerted a significant influence in social reorganization, through co-operatives, hospitals, social work, new conceptions of women's status, and schools at all levels. Because of the greater stability of Japanese culture, however, Protestant influence there was less than that in China. By 1914 the Protestant community numbered over one hundred thousand, half again as large as the Roman Catholic Church in Japan. Three-fourths of the Protestants were grouped in four churches deriving respectively from Episcopalian, Presbyterian and Reformed, Congregationalist, and Methodist missions.

In Korea, similarly, Protestant work was only undertaken from the 1880's, but was more extensive by 1914 than the older enterprise of the Roman Catholic Church, owing partly, perhaps, to its more extensive use of education and of medical and public health work. By 1914 the Protestant community of nearly one hundred thousand was roughly three-fourths Presbyterian and one-fourth Methodist. This community had been rather critical of the Japanese administration since the annexation of 1910 and suffered accordingly from efforts to make its adherents conform to Japanese nationalism.

China, last of all, witnessed a remarkable development from 1807 when Robert Morrison, the first Protestant missionary, landed. At that time there were already two hundred thousand Roman Catholics in the Empire. When Morrison died in 1834, he had seen ten Chinese baptized, and looked forward to the possibility of one thousand by 1934. There were not yet one hundred converts at the outbreak of the tragic Tai Ping Rebellion in 1850. But after Chinese Gordon had put down the Rebellion and the Anglo-Chinese War of 1858-1860 had opened the interior, expansion was rapid. In 1877, already, thirteen thousand converts were counted. Great numbers of missionaries and scores of societies came from all countries. Colleges, middle schools, hospitals, and medical schools were opened. One hundred years after Morrison had landed, an International Conference of Missions was held in Shanghai. There were then in China 3,445 Protestant missionaries from 63 societies, with nearly 10,000 Chinese pastors and teachers serving a very rapidly growing community of about 330,000. The Roman Catholic community was at least three times as large, but it was less influential in the culture and public life of the nation. "It is Protestantism rather than Roman Catholicism which has created the new medical and nursing professions, pioneered in the public health program, led in introducing secondary and higher education of an occidental type, and inspired general movements for moral reform such as the New Life Movement," wrote the historian Latourette.

Chinese Protestantism was more diversified denominationally and theologically than other branches of Asian evangelical Christianity. The cultural influence mentioned stemmed from the philosophy represented especially by Timothy Richards and the theological liberalism and humanitarianism of the American social gospel. Other Protestants in China stressed a highly individualistic and "next-worldly" religion. These two emphases fitted certain predispositions of Chinese Confucianism and Buddhism, respectively.

The largest and most widely distributed society of missionaries in China was the China Inland Mission. This mission was a type of the "faith missions" of Protestant Evangelicalism. The mission had no stated ecclesiastical backing but drew on Evangelical Christians of all denominations, both for personnel and for funds. The workers had no stated salary but set off to their posts with faith in the watchword, "the Lord will provide." Many more single women were used than ever before. The emissaries of the China Inland Mission concentrated on evangelistic preaching, not even stopping to form churches. Many of them dressed and lived as Chinese and they penetrated hitherto untouched districts. The mission was the creation of Hudson Taylor, who died in 1905 in Changsha, capital of Hunan, the most resistant of all provinces to Protestant missions. And although the foreign staff of the China Inland Mission suffered more than any other Protestant society in the Boxer uprisings, they refused to accept compensation even when it was offered. In 1895 they constituted 40 per cent of the total missionary staff, a proportion which decreased thereafter. By 1914 the Presbyterians had more Chinese members, and nearly as many missionaries. Also, by 1914 the process of consolidation which was to result in the Chinese National Christian Council was well under way and had produced over a dozen provincial councils.

NORTH AFRICA AND THE NEAR AND MIDDLE EAST. Looking westward from India one encounters a belt of predominantly Moslem peoples stretching from the Persian Gulf to the Mediterranean and across North Africa to the Straits of Gibraltar. The political core of this region in the nineteenth century was the Ottoman Empire, and its rule extended up the Balkans into Europe. The chief states were Turkey, Persia, Egypt, and Arabia. There were a variety of small Christian minorities scattered through the area totaling perhaps a million, the largest being the Nestorians, the Copts, the Greek Orthodox, the Armenians, and the Maronites. They represented vestiges of pre-Moslem communities, and they had become defensive, extremely conservative, and enervated. Since under Moslem rule no Christian evangelistic work was permitted, the Westtern missions—Protestant and Roman Catholic—were confined largely to educational, medical, and philanthropic work; what gains were registered were largely at the expense of the older

Christian groups. On the whole, there may even have been a net Christian loss among these peoples in the century, as a result of emigration and massacre.

In the Near East the Protestant effort was led by American missionaries, especially the American Board, and after 1870, the Presbyterians who left that Board. They introduced modern medicine to the area and conducted many schools in Turkey and Syria. In the 1860's were founded the two colleges which were the capstone of the educational work, Robert College in Constantinople, and the Syrian Protestant College (now the American University) of Beirut. The Church Missionary Society, with a predominantly German staff, was also active at Malta, Smyrna, Cairo, and in Palestine. The Anglicans had inherited the joint Anglo-Prussian episcopate at Jerusalem which had caused such scandal to the Oxford Tractarians (see above, p. 158). The hospital at Jerusalem and the one at Beirut connected with the Syrian Protestant College were both conducted by Kaiserswerth deaconesses (see above, p. 159). Eastward the Church Missionary Society and the American Board (after 1870 the Presbyterians) worked among the Nestorians, the Armenians, and the Jews of Persia. And to the south, Protestant work in Egypt was carried on almost entirely by Anglicans (especially the Church Missionary Society), and by the American United Presbyterians. The latter were chiefly effective among the Copts. In all this area Protestant strategy in the first half of the century was not to emulate the Roman Catholics by proselyting from the older Christian churches, but to strengthen and invigorate them. In most cases, however, the Eastern churches resisted and excommunicated those members influenced by new ideas, so that separate Evangelical communities were organized in the second half of the century. Their identification with despised minorities, moreover, rendered the Western missionaries even less effective with the Moslems. World War I, of course, was to bring to its climax the political disintegration of the Turkish Empire in the Near East.

AFRICA. The last major area of missions remains—Africa south of the Sahara. The vast equatorial basin and the southern pastoral plateau of the interior were largely unknown to geographers in the first half of the nineteenth century. Exploration of "darkest Africa" caught the imagination of the West in the middle of the century, and the millions of primitive tribes in this area succeeded Oceania as the most romantic field of Christian expansion. Then, after 1870, the European powers became converted to imperialism, and in a little over two decades almost all of Africa was parceled out into European colonies or protectorates. Great Britain and France took the lion's share, and among Protestant missionaries the British were dominant, as were the French among the Roman Catholics.

Of this vast and diverse area we may single out South Africa, in which were to be found over half of all the Christians in Africa south of the Sahara. Here, of course, were the chief European populations of the area, the Boers and the British. But the whites are outnumbered six to one, and two-fifths of all the colored Christians of Africa below the Sahara are also below the Zambesi. Among both black and white Christians, Protestants are overwhelmingly predominant. Malayan, Indian, and Chinese immigrants contribute to perhaps the most tense racial conflict in the world. The question of missions to natives and the status of natives, in general, have been part of the main grounds of antagonism between Boers and Britons. Boers once burned down David Livingstone's station. It was in this situation that Gandhi first tried his tactics of nonresistance before World War I and won much British Christian support.

Modern missions in South Africa were begun by the Netherlands Missionary Society. Robert Moffat and David Livingstone were L.M.S. missionaries. Scottish societies were also active from the beginning and founded the industrial and agricultural training center at Lovedale which has helped to shape South Africa. Livingstonia is a daughter institution on Lake Nyasa. The two undertake a program not unlike that of Tuskegee in America. In general, the Protestant missions cultivated a more self-reliant, the Roman Catholic a more docile type of character. In the second generation, however, the Anglicans, and particularly the S.P.G., built up what came to be the best organized work. Anglo-Catholicism was strong and much of the staff was composed of Anglican monks, and sisters or deaconesses. In addition, enterprises were undertaken by the Paris Evangelical Missionary Society, the Basel Mission, the Rhenish Society, the Leipzig Society and most of the other leading Continental societies. When the French took over Madagascar in 1896 the British turned over their work there to the Paris Evangelical Mission. South Africa was one of the few major areas where American missionaries were in a decided minority. Africa south of the Sahara, as a whole, proved one of the most successful Protestant mission fields, with a rapidly growing community of perhaps one and one half million in 1914.

GENERAL CHARACTERIZATION. Throughout the world Protestantism had made more significant contributions to social reform, education, medicine and the like, and ministered more to cultures in transition than had Roman Catholic missions. It had not confined its energies to building an ecclesiastical community. But in the same measure Protestantism had given more hostages to fortune, for much of this cultural influence depended on a continual influx of missionary forces to sustain it until strong indigenous churches should be founded. Protestant missions were to prove more vulnerable in war or revolution than more modest and self-contained Roman Catholic communities.

The obvious necessity of co-ordinating and unifying the variegated Protestant efforts led to a series of conferences both in the countries sending and in those receiving missionaries. These conferences began in the 1850's and produced in 1893 the Foreign Missions Conference of North America, a similar Conference in Britain and Ireland in 1912, and the so-called "Ecumenical Missionary Conference" of 1900 in New York. This movement reached its climax in the Edinburgh Conference of 1910, at which missionary history passes into the history of the ecumenical movement. From the continuation committee of this conference was to crystallize the permanent International Missionary Council, the Protestant counterpart to the Congregation of the Propaganda and the first institutional section of the ecumenical movement.

Chapter 25

ROMAN CATHOLIC MISSIONS, 1814-1914

In the Restoration Period began a revival of Roman Catholic missions, comparable to that of Protestantism but less spectacular and about a generation later. It centered to a high degree in France, the chief Roman Catholic colonial power, which was the source of over half the total Roman Catholic missionary effort in the century before World War I. Two-thirds to three-fourths of the Roman missionary priests and four-fifths of the nuns and the teaching brothers were from France. Of 119 priests killed in the nineteenth century on the mission field 95 were French.

The rest of the enterprise was carried by Italians, Germans, Belgians, and Dutch. English-speaking Roman Catholics did little in this period for missions, although the Irish emigration into Great Britain, the United States, Canada, and Australia was preparing a startling growth in these countries of Roman Catholic strength. Spain and Portugal exhibited little religious vitality.

The body of Roman Catholic missionaries, as for centuries, was made up of celibate monks or clergy of a great variety of orders, congregations, and societies. The once-dissolved Jesuits played a major role, followed by the Oblates, Holy Spirit Fathers, Lazarists, Marists, Dominicans, Franciscans, Capuchins, White Fathers, and dozens of others. The seminary of the *Société des Missions Etrangères* of Paris was conspicuous among the schools specializing in training secular clergy for foreign missions. A new characteristic of this century, however, was the greatly increased role of women missionaries, chiefly nuns, who provided over half the total by the time of

321

World War I. Scores of different communities were also involved here. In the late 1870's women from some sixty congregations numbered about thirty-five thousand of the total of
sixty thousand Roman Catholic missionaries. About 1900
there were fifty-three thousand women of a total of seventy
thousand Roman Catholic missionaries.

POPULAR SUPPORT. The growing separation of the Roman
Church from the states of even "Catholic" Europe which had
been perceptible from the days of Lamennais (see above, p.
206) affected also the character of the missionary enterprise.
Three or four aspects of this may be mentioned. For one, as
the Roman Catholic movement in the second quarter of the
nineteenth century developed, the missionary concern became
a popular lay interest as it had never been before. This
is evident in the new societies for support of missions, of
which the most important was the Society for the Propagation
of the Faith, founded in Lyons in 1822. Lay folk in humble
circumstances were solicited to pray daily for missions and to
contribute at least a penny a week on the pattern of many Protestant societies. The Association of the Holy Infancy, also
French, and two German societies, the Leopoldine Association and Ludwig Missionsverein, were of similar character.
Before 1914 nearly two hundred such organizations had been
founded, drawing on the subscriptions of millions of people,
largely those of moderate means. Again, the largest share of
these subscriptions, and perhaps over half the total, came from
the workmen and peasants of France. Such a financial basis
for missions was very different from the gifts of a few aristocrats or princes, which had been the earlier pattern.

The governments of nineteenth-century Europe, on the
other hand, having generally declared ecclesiastical neutrality,
were on the whole less able to use missions as instruments of
foreign policy. In the Counter Reformation, Spanish, Portuguese, and French Roman Catholic missions had been subsidized
and controlled by their respective monarchs for imperialist
goals. For the frequently anticlerical governments of the
French Third Republic and the Kingdom of Italy, such a relation was impossible. The French, to be sure, were often willing to subsidize in the colonies the same congregations they

were restricting at home, and Roman Catholic missions were in general much more closely tied to political imperialism in this period than were the Protestant missions, particularly those of the English-speaking countries. The contrast with the earlier pattern, however, was conspicuous.

PAPAL CONTROL. The tendency of nineteenth-century Roman Catholicism to go ultramontane as it lost its position in the state expressed itself also in missions. Earlier Roman Catholic missionaries had been emissaries of this or that Roman Catholic king more than of the pope, but since the French Revolution missions have been more and more centralized at Rome. The Propaganda, which had been discontinued under Napoleon, was re-established during the Restoration. Thereafter it co-ordinated and supervised the world-wide missionary enterprise to an increasing degree, seeking to carry the work through the four stages of mission stations, apostolic prefectures, apostolic vicariates, and, finally, the full development of an indigenous hierarchy. Several dominantly Protestant countries, such as Great Britain, the United States, Canada, and Holland remained technically mission fields under the supervision of Propaganda until 1908, but in this chapter we will be concerned only with non-Western cultures. There was something of a struggle at the end of the nineteenth century to free Roman Catholic missions from French foreign policy. Propaganda won its victory and in the twentieth century the religious orders around the world are generally the militia of the Papal Court under centralized control.

NEW METHODS. A fourth aspect of the new popular and ultramontane character of post-French Revolution Roman Catholicism was a new emphasis on religious maturity on the mission fields. There was little of the old mass conversion at the point of the sword. Converts were brought in by individuals or families—with some exceptions, to be sure, as in India and Africa—and were generally expected to know something of the meaning of Roman Catholicism before undergoing baptism. Here again, this was less true of Roman Catholicism than of Protestantism, but the contrast with Counter Reformation missionary practice was still marked.

LATIN AMERICA. The area of the greatest successes of that earlier practice in the sixteenth, seventeenth, and eighteenth centuries had been Latin America. It is notable that Latin America was the area of the least success in the nineteenth-century expansion, and it may even have represented a net decline. Certainly Roman Catholicism suffered more loss than gain in Latin America in the first half of the nineteenth century, and what recovery then followed was due to further Roman Catholic and Protestant missionary activity from Europe and the United States. Indigenous Latin American Roman Catholicism remained anemic and unable to maintain itself without constant infusions from overseas.

The chief trouble seems to have been the heritage of the conquest. State patronage and European paternalism had produced a passive enervated community, which treated the Christian Indians, however benevolently, as serfs. Roman Catholicism in Spain, Portugal, and Italy was the most degenerate in Europe, blighted by the Inquisition and corrupted by wealth and political power. All these weaknesses appeared in heightened degree in Latin America. The clergy were avaricious, sensual, and obscurantist, the laity ignorant and superstitious to a degree unknown elsewhere in Western Christendom since the Reformation. The contrast with the religious vitality of the North American Protestants was startling.

During the Napoleonic Wars, when the home countries of the Latin American churches were conquered by the Corsican, the movement for independence began (see above, p. 133). Simon Bolivar was the most conspicuous leader in the struggles of the early Restoration Period. Argentina, New Granada, Chile, Mexico, Peru, Ecuador, and Bolivia all claimed self-government within ten or fifteen years. Great Britain and the United States protected them from the efforts at reconquest of the Restoration powers, and the Latin American church henceforth was to deal with a score of distinct governments in very diverse circumstances.

For the first generation or so there was great difficulty regarding higher ecclesiastical appointments. Up to the eve of independence nearly all the Latin American prelates were European, and in the struggle for independence they were usually against it, in contrast to the lower clergy. Many then returned to Europe. By the end of the 1820's only five of the nearly forty Latin American bishoprics were being actively administered. For a generation or two more the kings of Spain and Portugal sought to retain their former rights of ecclesiastical patronage in Latin America against the new claims of the succession governments. The papacy was slow to recognize these governments at all, and even slower to concede them rights of nomination to benefices.

In the second half of the nineteenth century, church and state conflicts became endemic. The central issues were usually economic, the church with its great holdings striking a natural alliance with the great landlords against agrarian reform and the attempts to eliminate tithes. Economic and educational movements for the betterment of the impoverished Indians were usually opposed by the hierarchy and usually sponsored by anticlericals such as Juarez or the new Protestant groups. Demands increased for religious liberty and for separation of church and state, and both were secured in several Latin American states against the bitter resistance of the Roman Catholic Church. The old pattern was strongest on the west coast. In Peru, especially, private non-Roman Catholic worship was felonious until 1839, and religious liberty for Protestants was not legal until 1915.

A significant immigration took place especially after 1880, chiefly from Italy, Spain, and Portugal, but also from Germany and even Japan. There were thus over two million Italian nationals in Brazil in 1915. On the whole these new immigrants were not well served religiously, although dozens of religious orders—Italian, Spanish, and German—undertook work in Latin America in this period. The educated classes in Latin America generally were alienated from the church, and at the end of our period perhaps three million Indians were still pagan animists. Of a total population of more than one hundred million about one-fifth were Indian, another fifth "Caucasian," and the rest mixed. In the twentieth century some new vitality in evangelistic, educational, and social work was exhibited here and there by Roman Catholics, partly under the stimulus of Protestant rivalry. But despite the generations of Christian work, the area was still a mission field, unable to supply its own ecclesiastical needs either in personnel or in finances.

PHILIPPINES. The work of the Spanish Counter Reformation missionaries had proved more successful in the Philippines than in Latin America. By the nineteenth century the large majority of the population were at least nominal Christians. And only with the Spanish-American War of 1898 did tensions comparable to those of nineteenth-century Latin America begin to appear. Resentment against the great landed wealth of Spanish friars and their monopoly of higher ecclesiastical office then flared up in the nationalist Aglipayan schism. Protestantism from the United States was also introduced, and these two rivals prodded a rather somnolent Roman Catholic Church to new activity. Reinforcement came from Germany and the Low Countries and by 1914 Christianity in general, and Roman Catholicism in particular, were stronger than ever in the Philippines. The Filipinos were the only dominantly Christian Asiatic people and they equaled in numbers all other Asiatic Christians.

After Latin America the non-European areas where Roman Catholicism entered the nineteenth century with the greatest initial advantage were in Asia. Of the considerable Christian communities built up in the Counter Reformation missionary campaign there still remained at the beginning of the nineteenth century 330,000 to 500,000 in India, 250,000 in China, and some thousands, more or less clandestine, in Japan. They were all suffering from international decay, however, and outward difficulties. The suppression of the Jesuits was a serious blow, (see above, p. 39), and the wars of the revolutionary period cut off supplies of both personnel and funds. In India, which we may consider first, Roman Catholicism seemed to be dying until nearly the middle of the nineteenth century.

INDIA. The most conspicuous problem in the middle of the century was the same issue which was distracting Latin American Roman Catholicism at that time—controversy over the rights of political protectorate and ecclesiastical patronage. The Portuguese Crown insisted on its traditional *padroado* over all Roman Catholics in India, although its political control had passed long since to the British East India Company and it could not furnish clergy to supply vacant benefices. In the 1830's Propaganda attempted to suppress Portuguese patronage in British and French spheres, and set up four vicariates apostolic. The Portuguese hierarchy and clergy in India thereupon revolted, and all over the Roman Catholic sections of India were two competing sets of Roman clergy. The controversy was most bitter in the 1840's and 1850's, and yet in this period general recovery began, especially in the non-Portuguese territories. The Jesuits came back in several areas; Oblates, Salesians, Holy Cross Fathers, and dozens of other orders opened missions. About the time of the Vatican Council the Roman Catholic community numbered over a million, shepherded by twenty-one bishops and nine hundred priests, half of them French. Leo struck a compromise with Portugal in 1886 which eased tension, but the difficulty was not wholly solved at the time of World War I, when the great majority of Indian Roman Catholics were from among marginal groups— primitive tribes, such as the Telugus, or Hindu outcasts hoping for improvement in status or drawn by relief at time of drought or famine. And, in general, Roman Catholic missionaries were too preoccupied with their own nominal adherents into the twentieth century to devote much energy to conversions. Most of the Roman Catholic increase was by births.

Within the church, meanwhile, there was the problem of caste. Great divergence among the dioceses was discovered at the time of the Vatican Council, some grouping all the Christians together as one caste, analogous to that of the Moslems, others accepting caste divisions within the communities of Roman Catholics. The acceptance of caste by the Catholics was more general than it was among the Protestants. Propaganda insisted from 1849 that no caste lines be drawn in the schools, which were extensively developed with the aid of British grants-in-aid. Some congregations, however, were split over caste, and the priesthood was generally closed to members of the lower castes. A determined effort was made to build a native priesthood. There were nearly fifty schools for ecclesiastics in 1910, headed by the pontifical seminary at Kandy. Hospitals, orphanages, asylums, and centers for distributing literature were developed as on most mission fields. The economic problems of converts led also to the organization of Christian villages on new tracts of lands and the development of credit unions, co-operative stores and buying agencies, and the like.

By the time of World War I the Roman Catholic community of India had regained its nominal strength for the end of the seventeenth century, about 2,250,000. There were approximately a thousand each of Indian and European priests. The chief concentration lay in the south—on the west coast from Goa down, on the east south from Pondicherry—but the rate of growth was faster in the north. This community was more than twice the size of Indian Protestantism, then about one million. Protestantism, to be sure, had entered much later and was growing more rapidly. The two branches of the faith together made up about 1 per cent of the poverty-ridden three hundred million people living in the jungle of Indian religions and superstitions.

INDOCHINA. In Indochina, China, Korea, and Japan the expansion of Roman Catholic Christianity was borne primarily by French missionaries and was closely related to the political imperialism of France. In Indochina, for example, where the century opened with about three hundred thousand Roman Catholics under the tutelage of Spanish Dominicans and the French Society of Foreign Missions, Roman Catholicism gained in close correlation with the French political conquest during the period from 1860 to the 1880's. The preceding generation had known intermittent persecution and hundreds of martyrs, both of native and European Christians. In 1858 the attack of the Western Powers on China was widened to Indochina. By the end of the war there, in 1862, some five thousand Christians had been killed. The period of consequent missionary advance was interrupted in the 1880's when the French attacked again. In an effort to complete the conquest the French committed the native Christians to their cause, pressing them into service as guides and interpreters to the troops and as sources of military intelligence. The effort was made by the native forces, consequently, to exterminate the Christians in the bloody "Annamite Vespers" of 1884-1886. Some twenty missionaries and fifty thousand Christians were massacred before peace was restored. Yet the church continued to grow, whole villages coming over at one time. By World War I there were nearly a million Roman Catholics in Indochina, about 5 per cent of the population. There was an unusually large number of indigenous clergy, yet the identification of Roman Catholicism with the cause of French imperialism was very close. Western medicine, social welfare, agricultural methods, and education had also been introduced.

THE FAR EAST. In China, Japan, and Korea, meanwhile, a scattered Roman Catholic community of about the same size as that of Indochina experienced a similar development. A population of about four hundred million, one-third of the human race, here disdained the culture and religion of the Western barbarians and resisted religious and commercial penetration. There was a Christian residue from the seventeenth-century missions here, but until deep into the nineteenth century it seemed to be dying out, as Christianity had perished twice before in China. In Japan the Christians lived a clandestine existence without clergy, and it was a touching experience for the French missionaries entering in the 1860's to discover survivors of the Christian communities in the Nagasaki area. Korean Christianity, similarly, barely survived intermittent persecution especially in the climactic periods of 1800, 1839, and 1866-1868, in which thousands were killed. Here toleration really existed only from the 1880's. In the case of both Korea and Japan the Roman Catholic community numbered 65,000 to 75,000 by World War I.

In China proper the Christians were stronger, about a quarter of a million at the beginning of the nineteenth century, with a few dozen missionaries and a few score Chinese priests. Until the Opium Wars, however, they lived by the indulgence of officialdom and at the mercy of popular feeling. The British attacked the Manchu Empire in 1839, primarily to force greater trade concessions for Indian opium—a commerce which the Chinese government was, wisely enough, attempting to prohibit. The Treaty of Nanking (1842) ceded Hongkong to Britain and opened the five "treaty ports" for the residence and religious liberty of foreigners. The French won a share in these benefits, which gave new opportunities for missions, by the treaty of Whampoa (1849). Discontent continued on both sides, however, and flared up again in new Western aggression in the Anglo-Chinese War of 1856-1860, in which the French joined. The treaties of Tientsin (1858) and Peking (1860) wrung still further concessions from the sullen Chinese. More ports were opened to foreign trade, travel in the interior was permitted, and Christianity was tolerated and even granted protection, the French being commissioned to guard these rights for all Roman Catholics.

The French minister and consuls, even of anticlerical governments, exercised this protectorate punctiliously into the twentieth century, esteeming it a more efficacious means of French imperial penetration than commerce. The assistance of missionaries in litigation before magistrates became one of the chief attractions of the Roman Catholic Church to the Chinese in this period, and the exercise of civil jurisdiction by the Roman clergy was an important grievance preparing the Boxer Rebellion. In the imperialist rivalries of the 1880's and 1890's the Italians and Germans sought the right of protectorate over missionaries of their own nationality, but missionaries of neither were numerous, and the Italians were ineffective and often discouraged. The French protectorate over non-French Roman Catholics lapsed with the separation of church and state in France in 1905.

The vast population of the Empire was allotted to various societies. The Lazarists, who had carried the main burden in the early part of the century, were assigned to the north, including Peking and Tientsin. On the eve of World War I their 193 European and 170 Chinese priests were ministering to more Christians than was any other society in China, Protestant or Roman Catholic. The Jesuits concentrated on the lower Yangtze, where Zikawei, their headquarters on the outskirts of Shanghai, became the chief center of Christian institutions in China. At Zikawei they had a press, orphanage, school, college, novitiate, scholasticate, museum of natural history, and an observatory. In 1912 their staff numbered 129 European and 66 Chinese priests.

An even larger total of Franciscans of various nationalities also worked in the central provinces. The Scheutvelders labored in the interior, in Mongolia. The largest area of all, chiefly in the south, fell to the Paris fathers, of the Society of Foreign Missions. They were responsible for Szechwan, Yunnan, Kweichow, Kwantung, and Kwangsi, as well as Tibet, Manchuria, Korea, and most of Japan. In 1912 they had at work in this vast expanse 400 European priests and 197 Chinese clergy. These clergy were supplemented by some 2,000 sisters, the majority of them Chinese, who were, among other things, chiefly responsible for the hundreds of orphanages. The Chinese workers were used in various capacities as "catechists," of whom there were seven thousand by World War I. At that time there were only some 700 Chinese priests, although there were 54 seminaries with 1,600 students. There was considerable resistance among the European clergy, some of whom despised Chinese culture, to giving Chinese clergy responsibility. No empire-wide organization nor Chinese episcopate existed until after World War I.

Unlike their earlier Counter Reformation missions, or the contemporary Protestant missions, the Roman Catholic missions and communities exhibited little intellectual activity. Their constituency was composed almost entirely of peasants, fishermen, and the like, with none of the intellectuals. They used the press and education much less than the Protestants. Despite their greater numbers, consequently, they had less effect on Chinese society as a whole than did the Protestants. As in the homelands, the Roman Catholic Church was more inclined to defensiveness and isolation than to penetrating and informing culture and society.

The smoldering resentment of the Chinese against the "foreign devils" was exasperated by further aggressions in the 1880's and 1890's. The French attacked and seized Tongking in 1884. The Japanese defeated China in 1894-1895 and moved into Korea, Formosa, and Port Arthur. The murder of two Bavarian Jesuits gave the German Emperor an excuse to seize Kiaochau in 1898, and the British took Weihaiwei as "compensation." The Russians were acting as though they owned Manchuria. China seemed to be dissolving into leaseholds and spheres of influence for the well-armed barbarians. The revolt broke in various provinces as the Boxer Rebellion of 1900. Westerners were struck by the dramatic siege of the Peking cathedral and the Western legations. After harrowing delay, the siege was lifted. But the heaviest blows fell on the Chinese Christians, the "secondary foreign devils," of whom perhaps sixteen thousand perished.

The effects of the Boxer Rebellion and its suppression, however, were to convince the Chinese of the necessity of Westernization (already begun by Japan) and, incidentally, to open new opportunities for Christianity. Mission schools, chiefly those of Protestants, were now crowded, and a government system of education was begun on their foundation. The social pattern of family life, the status of women, and the very Manchu Empire itself were radically changed in a great revolution. The Chinese republic was born of the crises of 1911–1912. The Christian churches were growing apace and by the time of World War I the Roman Catholic community numbered well over a million, three or four times larger than the more influential Protestants. The numerical total was less than 1 per cent of the population, but the impact of Christianity far exceeded the size of its constituency in importance.

NORTH AFRICA AND THE NEAR EAST. Back on the Mediterranean, North Africa and Western Asia, the original base of Christianity, now constituted the homeland of Islam. Half of the world's Moslems, to be sure, lived under British rule in India and eastward, but in the Near East were to be found the shrines of Arabia, the intellectual center in Cairo, and the one remaining Moslem political power, the Ottoman Empire. The "sick man of Europe" maintained himself from the time of the Crimean War chiefly by playing the several Western powers off against one another and had become a shadow of his erstwhile terrible self. To the scattered enclaves of surviving Christian communities—Armenians, Maronites, Nestorians, Copts, Jacobites, Greek Orthodox, and Latins—the surrounding Moslems still offered the threat of persecution and massacre into the twentieth century. The Armenian pogroms of 1895 and during World War I were the worst examples of Moslem persecution. In this area Roman Catholicism gained during this period by European immigration into North Africa and by

proselyting from the older Christian churches of the Near East
From Islam no significant number of conversions were made.

French, Spanish, Italians, and Maltese had migrated in large
numbers to Morocco, Algiers, and Tunis after the French conquest of the Algiers pirates in the Restoration. The provincial
administrators, however, prevented Christian missions among
the natives for a generation, fearing to excite Moslem fanaticism. In the last third of the century Archbishop Lavigerie was
at last permitted aggressive missionary work. He built a
church over the death place of St. Louis and attempted to restore Carthage to its former splendor as capital of Christian
Africa. His ambitions, which reached over the whole Continent, were as much French as Christian. He was instrumental
in winning Tunis for France, although there were a dozen times
as many Italians as French in the area. As the Italian minister
Crispi ruefully observed, "His presence there is worth an army
to France." And his extraordinary administrative gifts rapidly
developed churches, schools, hospitals, and orders to possess the
new conquest. His "White Fathers," so named for their Arab
dress, were to win impressive results south of the Sahara after
losing many members in the attempt to penetrate the desert itself. By the time of World War I there were perhaps 750,000
Roman Catholics in Algeria and Tunis.

Leo XIII developed a vigorous program of proselyting
among the various old Christian churches of the Levant and
Asia Minor. Instead of denationalizing converts by making
them use Latin and the Roman liturgy, he commended the
Uniate system, using several seminaries in Rome to train clergy
for the various Eastern liturgies. The largest group of such
Uniates were the Maronites of the Lebanon, who suffered terrible massacres from the Druses in 1860. There were about
half as many Uniates of the Greek rite, mostly in Syria, and a
few thousands each of the Chaldaic (Nestorian), Syriac (Jacobite), Coptic (Monophysite), and Latin rites. These prose-
lytes were gathered especially by Franciscans, Jesuits, Lazarists,
Capuchins, Assumptionists, Dominicans, the Daughters of
Charity, and the Brothers of the Christian Schools. Some influence was exerted on Moslem attitudes with regard to personal dignity, the role of women, and philanthropy. The ideas

of the Young Turk revolutionists, meanwhile, were clearly affected by the nationalism and liberalism of the French revolutionary tradition. France benefited perhaps more from these missions than did Christianity, proudly exercising her protectorate over Christians. In Turkey, Persia, and Lebanon Roman Catholics were called "Franks."

AFRICA. The greatest gains of the Roman Catholic Church in Africa were made (again, chiefly by French missionaries) south of the Sahara. Everywhere primitive animistic tribes proved readier to adopt Christianity than did peoples of highly developed religions such as Buddhism, Islam, or Hinduism, and central Africa constituted the world's chief concentration of such tribes. Protestant missions dominated the region south of the Zambesi, but Roman Catholic missions had great success in the Congo basin and in German and British East Africa and Uganda. Livingstone and Stanley had exposed the appalling slave trade of this area, and Lavigerie became a chief crusader against it. Nearly half a million slaves were sold yearly in Africa, and for every one sold, probably ten were murdered. Lavigerie's White Fathers carried the burden in Equatorial Africa and Uganda and were rewarded, especially in the latter, with mass conversions. Across the continent in the French Congo and Angola the Holy Spirit Fathers were predominant, whereas in the Belgian Congo more orders were at work than anywhere else. By 1914 there were over a million Roman Catholics in this central belt across Africa, to which number should be added a half-million more from the offshore islands, Madagascar and Mauritius especially. The European missionary generally exercised a benevolent despotism, but he was cushioning the shock of adjustment to Western culture and substituting agricultural training and medicine for the abuses of the slave trade, polygamy, fetishism, and witchcraft.

Chapter 26

EASTERN ORTHODOXY IN THE NINETEENTH CENTURY

The course of Orthodox history which we traced in an early chapter had resulted by the nineteenth century in the overwhelming numerical predominance of the Russians. The ancient patriarchates of Jerusalem, Antioch, Alexandria, and Constantinople lived a miserable existence as tolerated aliens within the Ottoman Empire. The total number involved in Asia Minor and Egypt was insignificant. These communities were fossils, and symbols of the past. And the more numerous Orthodox Greeks, Serbs, Bulgars, and Rumanians of the Balkans had to endure the same Turkish oppression. Only the Russian Orthodox were free, and they numbered about four-fifths of all Orthodox Christians.

EMANCIPATION OF ORTHODOXY IN THE BALKANS. Before turning to the history of Russian Orthodoxy in the nineteenth century, however, we should take notice of the religious effects of the slow contraction of the Ottoman Empire. In the course of the century between Napoleon and World War I every Orthodox people of the Balkans won its independence from the Turks. The Greeks launched their War of Independence in the 1820's and the Turks took their revenge on the innocent Patriarch of Constantinople. They hanged him in his vestments on Easter outside the door of the patriarchal church. When the Greeks had secured their liberty, they set up a synod like that of the Russians so that their church would not be ruled by the subject of the Sultan. A generation later the Bulgarians likewise broke away from the Patriarchate of Constantinople (1870), even before political independence was in sight. Serbia had had a quasi-independent metropolitan since 1830, and in 1879 the Serbian Orthodox Church became autocephalous. Rumania won her independence in 1881, and four years later the Rumanian Orthodox Church became autocephalous. The jurisdiction of the Patriarchate of Constantinople was by these several steps reduced to a mere remnant, and Orthodoxy in Greece and the Balkans entered upon a new epoch. The habits of generations of oppression had to be unlearned and the churches would have to redefine their relations to the states, to the nations, and to the cultures emerging into the light. Similarly, relations with the churches of the West—Roman Catholicism and the Protestant communions—could now be free and uninhibited. After World War I, indeed, Orthodox churches were to play a surprising role in the ecumenical movement.

RUSSIAN ORTHODOXY. As we turn to Russian Orthodoxy for a closer analysis, we confront a double problem of interpretation. On the one hand, the Russian Church was the least articulate intellectually of all the chief divisions of Christendom. The Russian people were overwhelmingly illiterate and their church sought to reach them primarily through the imagination—through religious painting and architecture, magnificent choral music, and liturgical splendor. Nowhere else was common worship developed to such a degree. But in contrast to Western Christianity, that of the East made very little attempt at systematic moral discipline or intellectual formulation. Russian Christianity has been compared to Judaism for its slight theological interest as contrasted to its great stress on the elaborate traditional ritual of daily life, family, and corporate worship. This round of saints' days, feasts, blessings of seedtime and harvest, and icons in every room and shop permeated the whole common life.

From the seventeenth century, to be sure, there was theological instruction in Russian seminaries. But it had been imported from the Western Jesuits through the Kiev Academy, and Aristotelian scholasticism appeared alien to the Russians and unsuitable for an interpretation of Christianity as they knew it. For lack of a Christian intelligentsia Russia was not to produce an indigenous theology until well into the nineteenth century, and then it rose first from the laity rather than the clergy.

This brings us to the second reason for the silence of Russian Christianity. The whole ecclesiastical structure was gagged and bound to the chariot of the Romanov Empire. Under the system inaugurated by Peter the Great the church had no organs with which to express itself and no powers of self-government on the national, the diocesan, or the parish level. Civil bureaucrats determined all matters of policy and finances, and all publications and even sermons were censored. The church was in a Babylonian Captivity for two centuries before the Bolsheviks, even though it enjoyed the prestige and perquisites of establishment.

Under the system of serfdom in the early nineteenth century some one hundred thousand families owned the soil of Russia, to which four out of five Russians were attached as serfs. Until the middle generation of the nineteenth century the higher culture of Russia was carried by this leisured class of landed aristocrats. It was the peculiar fate of this cultured class to be directed toward Western Europe after the reforms of Peter the Great just at the moment when the dominant influence in the West was the French Enlightenment with its hostility to religion. The Russian gentry employed French tutors for their children and sent their sons to France and Italy to study, thus forming a mentality which would make them still less able to come to terms with the religion of the great Russian masses.

ORTHODOX RENAISSANCE. The long war against Napoleon, however, and especially the burning of Moscow, consolidated a national reaction against French ideas. In the Restoration Period Russian thought was rather dominated by the counter-revolutionary romantic currents of Germany. Hegel and Schelling, in particular, set the categories of most Russian philosophizing in the 1830's and 1840's and, of course, opened many points of contact with Christianity. The renaissance of Orthodox theology which began in that generation has been deeply influenced ever since by philosophical idealism, especially of Schelling's variety.

A second tributary stream to this renaissance was the revival of patristic studies. The statement that the patristic period lasted into the nineteenth century in Russia is true both with reference to general religious mentality, and also with regard to the specific influence of the Fathers. In the late eighteenth century Abbot Paisi Velichovski developed a new study of Greek patristic devotional literature, translating it into Slavonic. His manuscripts were inherited in the nineteenth century by the monks of Optino, who continued the work of editing, collating, and translating not merely into Slavonic, but also into Russian. Later in the century Bishop Feofan of Visha also edited a new five-volume version of the *Philokalia*. These writings, together with the Russian Bible, which was widely distributed through the efforts of Metropolitan Philaret and Prince Golitsyn, provided the literate Russians with a substantial literature. The idealist neo-Platonic character of the Greek Fathers proved readily congruous with the German idealism.

These theological currents were given authority among some nineteenth-century Russian intellectuals through their contact with deep devotional life in the monasteries. Despite the confiscations of Catherine in the eighteenth century, a revival of religious life began in the monasteries and continued to the Bolshevik Revolution. The characteristic phenomena of this revival were the *startsi*, or "elders," and the pastoral function they performed for the tens of thousands of pilgrims who sought them out. The Russian *staretz* did not hold a specific ecclesiastical office, although he was usually a monk, but he was recognized and sought out for his charismatic powers. Pilgrims came to confess sins and crimes, to be healed of diseases, and to ask advice on practical decisions. They came in great numbers to some of the more famous *startsi*, so that the holy man would sometimes interview thousands in a day. Serafim of Sarov was one of the most famous of the *startsi* in the early years of Nicholas I. Philaret of Moscow was a contemporary who was spiritual director to the Kirievsky brothers, lay intellectuals who were to be founders of the new Russian theology. On his death Philaret passed the Kirievskys on to Macarius of the famous monastery of Optina Pustyn, and they co-operated in the translation of the Fathers being carried on there. Dostoevsky the novelist, and Soloviev the philosopher made a joint pilgrimage to Optina Pustyn in 1879. The whole institution of the *startsi* is probably most familiar to Western Christians from the portrayal of Father Zossima in Dostoevsky's *Brothers Karamazov*. Dostoevsky apparently derived his conception of Zossima from the famous *staretz* Tychon. Father John of the naval base at Kronstadt is an example of a parish priest who was a *staretz*. Bishop Feofan's religious correspondence reached all over Russia in the 1870's and 1880's, and the seven volumes of letters published after his death were very influential up to 1917. Father Alexi of the Zossima monastery was a member of the Sobor of 1917 and thereafter continued pastoral work in secret under the Bolshevik persecution.

The intellectual expression of this Russian Orthodox spirituality first came to birth in the Restoration Period. The reign of Nicholas I, from 1825 to 1855, under its rigid censorship and reaction nourished the most brilliant generation of writers and thinkers Russia had yet seen. The writers are particularly important, for since the censorship of Romanov Russia prevented direct discussions of social, political, and religious issues, fiction became the most authentic voice of Russia in the nineteenth century. As nowhere else in Western Europe at that time, novels, stories, and poetry were written and read in dead earnest as interpretation of life's meaning.

HUMANITARIANISM IN LITERATURE. The dominant interest among these writers was probably humanitarian social reform. The French utopian socialist and idealist democrats, like Fourier or Lamennais, were much read and discussed, although one could be sent to Siberia (as was Dostoevsky) if he were caught doing so. Dickens was popular for his sentimental humanitarian appeal and the implication that changes in social and political environment were the chief desideratum. Dostoevsky's first novel, *Poor Folk*, was written in this genre and won instant recognition with Nekrassov, the poet of the sorrows of Russia, whose portrayals of the oppressed Russian serf were to have tremendous influence on the next generation. Alexander Herzen and the critic Belinski were perhaps the most influential in the reformist movement stemming from this generation.

The focus of all reform was, of course, the great mass of illiterate, poverty-stricken serfs of Russia. How should they be redeemed? And how could the great gulf between the en-

lightened intellectuals and the religious peasants be bridged?
What was meant by social salvation? Here the philosophy of
history also came into play. There were those who held that
Russia was simply a backward nation without history, to be
made over as soon as possible by Western standards. Others
argued that Russia had a peculiar tradition of her own, namely
her Orthodox faith, which was more valuable than all the
most useful Western acquisitions. Thus the deepest cleavage
between the so-called Westernizers and the Slavophiles concerned their attitude to the church.

The Westernizing humanitarians were inclined to feel that
democracy or socialism embodied everything of value in Christianity—its emphases on peace, brotherhood, and justice.
These men were haunted night and day by a sense of the condition of the peasantry. Belinski, for example, asked himself,
"Has a man after all this, any right to forget himself in art, in
knowledge?"

In the sixties came the great reforms of Alexander I (1855-
1881), the emancipation of the serfs, the new judicial procedures. And from the circle of ideas we have indicated grew
up the so-called "populist" movement, especially in the universities. Hundreds of students deserted the universities to
"go among the people," to live with the peasants. Aristocratic
girls who knew nothing of housework plunged into heavy
physical labor fifteen hours a day, ate coarse and revolting
food, and slept among vermin, out of a deep sense of guilt for
their privileges.

The young educated idealists, however, found that they
were misunderstood by the peasants. And, like all Russian reformers, they found themselves baffled by the persistent religion of the peasants. Herzen had found it impossible to avoid
religious discussion as his socialistic secular *Weltanschauung*
confronted the theological view of the world. Belinski would
not take this religion seriously and savagely attacked Gogol for
doing so: "The Orthodox Church has always been the supporter of despotism and the whip; but why did you bring Christ
into all this? . . . He was the first to proclaim to men the
teaching of freedom, equality and brotherhood, and in His
martyrdom He sealed the truth of His doctrines."

SLAVOPHILES. In this way the Westernizers set up Jesus the social reformer against the Orthodox Church, the supporter of despotism and the whip. The so-called Slavophiles, on the other hand, although they mourned the reactionary manipulation of the Orthodox Church, were convinced that concealed within it still lay the redeeming power of God. When men like the Kirievskys and Khomiakov talked of the peasant masses, consequently, they spoke as men who shared the religion of the peasants and agreed with the peasants that no reforms promised much which did not rest on that religion. "We must learn from the people to become intellectually humble; we must realize that in the peasants' conception of the world there is more truth than in ours," said Leontiev. Several of these intellectuals, like Dostoevsky, became reconverted to Orthodoxy from their contact with the naïve faith of the peasants. The hope of the Russian people, and indeed of the world, was to be found not in science from the West, but in something already present among the serfs of Russia. The poet Tyutchev set forth the Slavophile conviction in the famous poem "Those Poor Villages."

> Laden with the burden of the cross
> All through thee, my native land,
> In the form of a servant, the King of heaven
> Walks about, bestowing his blessing.

KIRIEVSKY. In the salons of the Moscow homes of Khomiakov, the Aksakovs, and similar families, all these social, philosophical, and religious ideas were brilliantly discussed. Most of the Slavophiles, however, found getting books past the censor as difficult as did the Westernizers, and their full influence was not felt until the twentieth century. Kirievsky, and especially Khomiakov, were the most important thinkers of the first generation. The chief interest of Kirievsky lay in the justification of intuition as against the analytical and discursive intellect. To know truth is to appropriate it, to become like it. Thus religious knowledge, in contrast to knowledge about religion, is necessarily sanctification. Here Kirievsky supported himself with such Fathers as Isaac the Syrian against the scholastic syllogistic method of Latin theology. Somewhat arbitrarily he contrasted the mystical organic East with the rationalistic, critical, and sterile West.

KHOMIAKOV. Kirievsky's friend Khomiakov, a retired officer of the Horse Guards, completed his interpretation of the nature of religious knowledge with a discussion of the nature of the religious community within which such knowledge is possible. Khomiakov's thought focused on the Church. Here, also, he supported himself with the Fathers against ecclesiology of the papal or protestant Latin Church. The Church, he held, could not be defined institutionally or doctrinally if one took seriously its character as the Body of Christ, the organism of grace and love, the first fruits of the new eon. It was constituted by *sobornost*, a brotherhood or togetherness of men involving integration of each. No one can be saved alone; to be saved is to be saved into *sobornost*. Such community, however, must be voluntary and free; it cannot be imposed either by the state or some coercive clericalism, as with Rome. The great heresy of Rome, Khomiakov felt, was this clericalism which sinned against Christian brotherhood. The papacy was the first significant expression of individualistic arrogance against the Church, and Protestantism had simply universalized the error. Thus Rome had unity without freedom, and Protestantism freedom without unity. He denied the ruling authority of the hierarchy, especially the Romanist distinction of the church *discens* from the church *docens*. Here he could support himself by the Encyclical of the Eastern Patriarchs of 1848 against the infallibilist claims of Pius IX. The infallibility of the Church, the Patriarchs had said, far from being localized in one separate office, the papacy, "resides solely in the ecumenical fellowship of the Church, united together by mutual love, so that the guardianship of dogmas and the purity of rites is entrusted, not to the hierarchy alone, but to all members of the Church, who are the Body of Christ."

This exalted conception of the nature of the Church was far removed from the realities of Orthodox Russia. And although apparently Metropolitan Philaret of Moscow was friendly to Khomiakov, the bureaucrats who ran the state church viewed him as a dangerous free thinker. He was as critical of the reactionaries as of the Westernizers with their admiration for a secular disintegrating individualism. He wished religious liberty in Russia. And with regard to social problems he believed that the mission of Orthodoxy was to realize *sobornost* in economic and political reality. In the village communities of the Russian peasants he saw the seeds of a new social order, with its parallels in the communal outlook of the *arteli* of the workmen. Here was the vision of Christian brotherhood which it was Russia's mission to develop.

It is interesting also that this father of modern Russian theology was perhaps the first Orthodox theologian who had the deep sense of the sin of division which lies behind the later ecumenical movement. In many of his judgments, to be sure, Khomiakov was unfair and arbitrary. Yet his vision of the Church was deeper than his attempts to define its concrete limits. And at least in the case of Anglicanism, for which he felt much sympathy, he contributed to actual conversations. Thus was foreshadowed in the days of the Oxford Movement and the Russian Orthodox renaissance that non-Roman but "Catholic" bloc which now occupies such a significant role in the ecumenical movement. Even under Pobedonostsev (see below, p.346) at the end of the century, such ecumenical conversations (chiefly with laymen, to be sure) were permitted.

DOSTOEVSKY. The novelist Dostoevsky has perhaps done more than any other single writer to bring to Western Christendom the depth and power of Russian Orthodox religion. He had begun as a humanitarian writer in the 1840's and for being associated with a radical group was sent to Siberia in 1849 after the shocking experience of a mock execution, called off at the last moment. In Siberia he lived four years in a convict camp, learning to know the Russian people. In his suffering he learned much about the potentialities of human nature for evil and for good and he recovered faith in Christ. When he returned to Russia and sought to rehabilitate his career as a writer he moved from the Westernizers to the Slavophiles. Through the latter half of the 1860's he lived and wrote abroad to avoid imprisonment for debt, for he had many dependents and his personal management was very disorderly. In the 1870's he returned to Russia, having achieved a certain domestic stability and a recognized status as a writer. In this decade his religious ideas were still further clarified by acquaintance with the young philosopher Soloviev, who is considered to have inspired the figure of Ivan Karamazov, and with the writing of Feodorov. In *Crime and Punishment* and *The Possessed* Dostoevsky probed the psychology of the radical intelligentsia, relating the varieties of socialist or anarchist views to concealed religious attitudes. The incompleted *Brothers Karamazov* exhibited both the range of his scepticism and the depth of his faith in redemption. Here are all the characteristic notes of Orthodox spirituality—the insistence on human freedom; the yearning for the transformation of nature and the cosmos; the strong apocalyptic strain, and the centrality of faith in the resurrection; the emphasis on redemption through humiliation, suffering, self-sacrifice. Thus Dostoevsky continued the "Christian socialism" of Khomiakov.

SOLOVIEV. The younger philosopher Soloviev had a similar vision of the universality of the Church and the duties of that Church in social action. He grew up in the heyday of the Darwinians and burned his icons at the age of fourteen. He matriculated at the University of Moscow in natural science in 1870. After two years of this variety of dogmatism he transferred to philosophy and even created a sensation by entering the intellectual ghetto of the Moscow Theological Academy to hear lectures on theology. He traveled abroad, studying spiritualism and occultism, and returned to Russia as the most popular lecturer on philosophy, yet without hope of academic appointment. In 1881 when the Tsar was murdered, Soloviev finally ended his public career by appealing to his successor for mercy on the assassins.

For the following twenty years Soloviev labored for the reunion of the churches, and the reconciliation of Christians and Jews, while writing a series of works in the philosophy of religion. He disapproved of the repressive policy of Pobedonostsev toward the Jews, which was driving so many of them to emigrate. As to reunion, he worked with Bishop Strossmayer of Croatia for reconciliation of the Pope and the Tsar. The Roman Catholics, however, interpreted this simply as his return and submission to the true Church, and Soloviev lost hope in organized Christianity. In 1896 he did receive the sacrament from a Uniate priest in Moscow to demonstrate the real unity of the Church. This was no "conversion," however; he was no "Russian Newman," and received the Orthodox sacraments when he died. His great practical concern had been to realize the unity of Christendom and thereby to end the warfare of classes and nations and the conflicts of society with its rebels and criminals. All this was set in a metaphysical context of organismic thought. His last and most important work, *Three Conversations*, set forth a vision of a coming anti-Christian totalitarianism akin to Dostoevsky's prophecies.

In the second half of the century the Westernizers and Slavophiles had drifted further apart. The former tended in the direction of materialism and positivistic science, whereas the second generation of Slavophiles became more chauvinistic. There was a great variety of initiatives, however, and freedom to find a natural equilibrium was impossible. After the murder of Alexander II in 1881, Pobedonostsev, the lay Procurator of the Holy Synod, ruled church and state with an iron hand for a quarter of a century, and only in the twentieth century, and especially in the crisis created by the Russo-Japanese War of 1904-1905, was there again free discussion.

The dominant polarity now lay between Marxist materialism and the new philosophy of religion. The latter was represented by the Princes Trubetzkoi who developed the more Christian side of Soloviev and by some ex-Marxists, like the economist Bulgakov and Berdaiev, his collaborator on the review *The New Way*. Prince Eugene Trubetzkoi was to be vice-president of the Sobor of 1917 and died in 1920. He had contributed to the new interest in icons with his "incarnational aesthetics." Gregory Trubetzkoi, also a member of the Sobor, was to be Under-Secretary of Foreign Affairs in Wrangel's short-lived government, and later a center of the Russian emigration in Paris. Bulgakov was ordained priest in 1917 and also served in the Sobor. His book *The Orthodox Church* (1935) is probably still the best presentation of Orthodox theology in English. The poets Blok and Bely were also influenced by this current. The majority of the intellectuals of Russia, however, were ignorant of Christianity and indifferent to it when the crisis came in 1917.

TOLSTOI. Leo Tolstoi was a religious force of significance, although perhaps as much outside Russia in Western Protestantism as in his native land. Late in life he had a religious conversion and turned his back on the privileges and amusements of an aristocrat and landholder who had established himself as one of the great novelists. In the era of Pobedonostsev, he attempted to conform his whole life radically to the teachings of the Sermon on the Mount, especially the injunctions to nonresistance. This entailed a rejection of war, the state, the judicial system. He engaged in a polemic against the Orthodox Church, not only in its civil prerogatives, but also in its dogma and ritual. His works were suppressed and he was excommunicated. His religious attitude was closer to that of some of the Russian sects than to Orthodoxy, with elements of mystical pantheism, transmigration, and vegetarianism. However eccentric his grasp of the Gospel, Tolstoi's power lay in his search for integrity of life and faith, with the rejection of all attempts to domesticate the faith in modern culture.

POBEDONOSTSEV. In certain external respects the rule of Pobedonostsev (1881-1905) aided the Orthodox Church. Pobedonostsev was a devout Orthodox who hated parliaments, general education, a free press, and trial by jury. He aided the parishes economically and especially contributed to a great expansion of the hitherto moribund parochial schools of very low quality. From 1885 to 1900 church schools multiplied nearly tenfold, from 4,500 to 42,000. Similarly, Pobedonostsev's policy of forced Russification and Orthodoxy on Russia's borders, although it led to deplorable effects among the Jews and in Finland and the Baltic countries, contributed elsewhere to commendable missionary expansion. Earlier in the century the work of Veniaminov, the apostle of Alaska, had led to his elevation to the Metropolitan See of Moscow. Makari, similarly, had pioneered in Eastern Siberia. The Theological Academy of Kazan became a great center for missionary work among Tartars, Kalmucks, and other tribes of Central Asia. Here Ilminski, in particular, translated Christian materials into numerous languages. Even so, the Moslem agencies were even more numerous at the end of the century. In Japan, lastly, Nicholas Kosatkin built up an indigenous Japanese Orthodox

Church, with which he identified himself to the extent of praying for Japanese arms in the war of 1904-1905 against Russia. On the other side Pobedonostsev used the church for his terroristic methods. Anti-Semitism was apparently deliberately fostered to distract the peasants from economic grievances. Clergy were used as secret government agents. Bishops and monks commended the murderous reactionary secret societies, such as the "Union of Russian People," and were responsible for massacres. Only a few, to be sure, engaged in such activities, but they had a free press, whereas nothing was heard from the others to dissociate the church from such outrages.

The situation in the parochial high schools, the so-called seminaries, illuminates vividly what a Religio-Philosophical Conference of these years described as "the nightmare of the Christian State." These parochial high schools were virtually reserved to the sons of the clergy, who received free tuition there. The one obsession of the students was to transfer to secular schools and escape the fate of their fathers. The schools were run like prisons, with constant abuse, and the students rioted regularly, often over the food (a cockroach in the borscht or a mouse tail in the soup). The rector at Smolensk was whipped; the rector at Kharkov had acid thrown in his face; the rector at Odessa was beaten before his faculty. Bombs were set off at Voronezh, Moscow, and Nishni Novgorod. In the autumn of 1905, forty-eight of the fifty-eight seminaries had strikes. The students at Tobolsk declared "We do not know of one graduate of our seminary who has entered the priesthood out of sincere conviction." The students in these schools were far better grounded in Kautsky and Bebel than in theology.

REFORM PROPOSALS. The defeat by Japan in 1905 led to such self-examination in Russia that momentarily the veil was drawn aside from the real desires of the church. Members of the St. Petersburg Theological Academy produced a memorandum asking for reforms of the church, and in particular a national council or Sobor. Count Witte wrote in favor of the memorandum and Pobedonostsev, of course, opposed it. In the crisis, however, Pobedonostsev was at last ousted and the

Tsar promised a Sobor to the metropolitans. A decree of religious liberty led to mass withdrawal from Orthodoxy to other communions. A commission was set to work in 1906 and compiled criticisms and proposals with regard to the parochial system, the financial support of the clergy, the episcopate, and clerical education. A flood of uncensored articles revealed the almost universal desire for extensive reform. Even the peasants were losing faith in the church. Probably half of the nominal Orthodox really belonged either to the Old Believers or the sects. And, to judge by peasant congresses in 1905, the mass of peasants wished complete religious liberty, state control of all schools, and the nationalization of all the land, including that of the church. It was significant that of the sixty-three bishops appointed by Pobedonostsev, largely on the basis of their subservience, sixty-one were for the Sobor and independence of the church from the hated Synod. The second Duma opposed, four to one, the privileges of the Orthodox Church in education, religious liberty, and property. In 1907, however, the Sobor was indefinitely postponed and silence was soon imposed again. The Romanov Empire was to keep Russian Orthodoxy captive till its own demise in World War I, which it had mishandled so appallingly. In the confusions of 1917 the Provisional Government pushed through the arrangements for the long-desired Sobor on the very eve of the Bolshevik dictatorship.

Part IV

FROM WORLD WAR I TO
THE MID-CENTURY

Chapter 27

ORTHODOXY AND THE U.S.S.R.

During World War I the real power in the Russian Empire was Rasputin, the "holy devil" who dominated the neurotic Empress Alexandra. So outspokenly did the Duma criticize the ministers he had appointed and their policies that it was prorogued in 1916. When it reassembled in February 1917, Rasputin had been murdered and Russia was in general revolt. Even the generals were demanding the abdication of the Tsar. Thus the liberals of the Duma found power and responsibility thrust upon them; they could resume the effort of 1905 to reorganize Russia as a liberal constitutional monarchy. The Marxists, to be sure, refused to support the coalition of liberals and began organizing their Soviets. In opposition to the liberals, they demanded abandonment of universal suffrage and withdrawal from the war. But the machinery of government was in the hands of the Provisional Government of Prince Lvov and, later, Kerensky. The government sought to shore up the crumbling armies of Russia through the summer while the Western Allies (nursing their secret treaties) stalled and postponed the proposal of a conference to effect a general peace.

The church policy of the Provisional Government was essentially the policy of reform so generally urged in 1905—religious liberty for Orthodoxy and for the other churches, including restoration of the patriarchate, and state rather than church control of the schools. In line with this policy the convocation of the long-hoped-for Sobor was proclaimed in the spring. The government retained the structure of the Synod pending a reorganization by the Sobor, but it replaced the High Procurator by a "Ministry of Confessions" which could be as-

sociated with a number of churches. In July full religious liberty was granted for the first time in Russia, permitting
transference from one communion to another, or even to none,
without civil disabilities. In June all state-supported schools
had been placed under the control of the Ministry of Education, a change which was demanded by the teachers of the
church schools. The government financed the Sobor and left
the Orthodox Church free to draw up its new constitution.

The reaction of Orthodoxy to these actions was mixed. On
the general political issues the majority of the parish clergy
supported the Provisional Government enthusiastically. The
liberal clergy of 1905 were once more heard from. There was
even an "All-Russian Society of the Democratic Orthodox
Clergy and Laymen," headed by Popov and Father Vvedensky
in Petrograd, which advocated agrarian reform and industrial
democracy, the equality of women, and abolition of the nobility, as well as church reforms. However, the majority
looked askance at such radicalism. A convention of clergy and
laymen in Moscow in June seemed friendly to the Provisional
Government but anxious about the tendency to equalize religious privileges and to separate Orthodoxy from the state.
They protested against the transfer of church schools to the
Ministry of Education. The hierarchy, meanwhile, having
been selected in the first place for loyalty to monarchical absolutism, displayed slight sympathy for the Provisional Government. The pre-Sobor committee contained several bishops
who had been affiliated with the Black Hundreds, like Archbishop Agathangel, or who shared its spirit of fanatical reaction.
In July the pre-Sobor committee issued a pronouncement
claiming from the state full financial support, state validation of
all church actions, compulsory religious education, and at the
same time complete freedom of the church from state control.
The hierarchy was beginning to talk about the "anti-Christian"
government. The elections to the Sobor, which was convoked
in August, were largely swung by the conservatives, and at the
Sobor the reactionaries were strongly entrenched.

SOBOR OF 1917. The Sobor consisted of 564 delegates—the
bishop, and two clergy from each diocese, together with three
elected laymen. Each university had a delegate, and the four

theological academies sent four representatives each. The conference met in two houses. The episcopal section, largely dominated by the conservatives led by Metropolitan Antony of Kharkov, was given the right of veto over all decisions, despite bitter opposition. The moderates, headed by vice-president Prince Eugen Trubetzkoi and Father Bulgakov, had most of their strength among the laymen. There was also a very small leftist party. The government turned the Sobor loose with the announcement that as soon as new organs of church administration were approved, the powers of the state through the High Procurator would be withdrawn.

In the sessions of the Sobor a widespread resentment against the confessional policy of the government was voiced. A secret session discussed Kornilov's mutiny, and undoubtedly there were many who hoped for a monarchist restoration to overthrow the Provisional Government. A delegation waited on the government to protest its educational policy. The government refused to reconsider its action with regard to the control of the state-supported parochial schools, but it was willing to discuss the restrictions which had been imposed on religious education in the state schools. Argument on the proposal for restoring the patriarchate was interrupted by the thunder of guns of the Bolshevik Revolution in October. There were suggestions of adjournment, but in the fear that the Sobor could not meet again a vote was pushed through. The number of members had so dwindled that the vote for the patriarchate passed with a total of only 141, just one-fourth of the qualified voters.

NEW CHURCH CONSTITUTION. The office thus restored was not to be the autocratic patriarchate of the past. The new patriarch was to be subject to the Sobor, assembling periodically, and was to act in the interims as the executive head of the Holy Synod for internal affairs and of the Supreme Ecclesiastical Council for legal and financial administration. The patriarch would be elected for life but could be impeached by the Sobor and deposed by a two-thirds vote, with other Eastern patriarchs present, if possible.

A similar reorganization was legislated also for the dioceses and parishes. The number of bishops was greatly increased, so that every large city would now have one. Clergy and laymen together would elect the bishops from nominations made by the diocese and by the other bishops. The diocesan government would be administered by the "Diocesan Assembly" and the "Diocesan Council" with functions analogous to those of the national Synod and the Supreme Ecclesiastical Council. In this way the hated control of the government bureaucrat at every level of church administration was eliminated and the church would become master in its own house with a blend of episcopal and presbyterian polity.

The Sobor proceeded to the election of its patriarch. Three archbishops were selected as candidates: Metropolitan Tikhon of Moscow (formerly head of the Russian Church in North America, 1898-1907); Archbishop Arsenius of Novgorod; and the violent reactionary Metropolitan Antony of Kharkov. Tikhon was chosen by the drawing of lots. On November 21, 1917 he was solemnly enthroned in the patriarchal Cathedral of the Assumption with elaborate robing and liturgy and a procession around the Kremlin. The Orthodox Church of Russia had emerged at last from two and one half centuries of captivity to the state and was in a position to redeem itself before the Russian people. Or, rather, it would have been in such a position if the Provisional Government had survived. But to the surprise of the government (and indeed to the surprise of the revolutionists themselves), political power in Russia had fallen into the hands of the most fanatical revolutionary wing, the Bolsheviks.

BOLSHEVIK RELIGIOUS POLICY. The Bolsheviks did not have general support for their antireligious policy. They had said little or nothing about religion. They had undermined the Provisional Government by campaigning for Russian withdrawal from the war and by urging agrarian reform. The Russian masses were utterly war-weary and were disillusioned with a criminally incompetent military leadership. They responded to the slogan "Land-peace-bread," without ratifying or even understanding the general Bolshevik program. In the general collapse and anarchy a closely disciplined group, even a small minority, could control the situation. And gradually, over the following months, the Bolsheviks disclosed their intention of systematically extirpating Christianity whether the Russian people liked it or not.

The Bolsheviks had not interfered with the Sobor, but in the following December and January a series of decrees were issued which fundamentally altered the status of the church. All the lands and buildings of the church were confiscated outright and without compensation, and the church was denied the right to acquire more. The buildings might still be used by the church, but the conditions for securing such use were to become increasingly difficult. And at the same time all state salaries for the clergy were discontinued and the church was given one month to organize a system of voluntary support in a time of general economic collapse and bankruptcy. Its whole economic base was thus removed.

A second set of Bolshevik decrees was calculated to secularize family life and education. Civil marriage and civil birth registration were made compulsory and civil divorce became possible. Religious instruction was forbidden in private as well as public schools. This prohibition of religious education was to remain the most damaging single inhibition on the Russian church. As defined in 1922, it was a criminal offense in Russia to teach religion to minors. How could a church survive which could not teach its own children and young people, especially when they were to be exposed to a steady pressure of atheistic indoctrination in the schools and youth groups? The censorship of all religious literature would also contribute to the goal of religious illiteracy.

ORTHODOX RESISTANCE. To these decrees the church replied with defiance. In his first pastoral letter Patriarch Tikhon declared war. A committee of the Sobor headed by Eugen Trubetzkoi reported that the law of January 23, 1918, later referred to as the law for "separation of the Church from the State and the School from the Church," was an attempt to destroy the church. The Sobor ratified the position taken by Tikhon and put all Orthodox under strict penalties neither to publish nor to obey this law. The Sobor denied the validity of civil marriage or divorce for Orthodox and ordered the clergy not to give up the books of registry. Stirring appeals to the masses were sent out, urging the organization of Orthodox "brotherhoods" in every parish to resist the confiscation of property. These "brotherhoods" became foci of former monarchist leaders. There were riots in almost every city of Russia, with excesses on both sides and with hundreds of casualties. The appointment of a substitute for the Patriarch was ordered in case of accidents and Tikhon was given a twelve-man bodyguard. The Sobor denied the jurisdiction of the Bolshevik dictatorship and planned for its schools, churches, printing establishments, and the like, as if nothing had happened. By the middle of 1918 the state had seized most of the bank credits, stocks, bonds, and lands of the church, and with the cancellation of salaries, little religious instruction was left. The church still held most of its buildings.

The Fifth Communist Party Congress was meanwhile devising the Constitution for the Russian Soviet Republic. The question of religious policy was one of the few issues debated in the Constitutional Committee. All were agreed on Lenin's fundamental proposition with regard to religion: "All contemporary religions and churches, all and every kind of religious organization, Marxism has always viewed as instruments of bourgeois reaction, serving as a defense of exploitation and the doping of the working class . . . there can be no good religion, or, perhaps, better religion is still more dangerous than poor religion." On this common conviction there was a disagreement among the Bolsheviks as to tactics. Some held that since religion was simply the ideological superstructure of bourgeois control, once the middle classes were ousted, the church separated from the state and its material basis removed, it would wither away automatically. If it were persecuted outright then it might well produce the sort of counterrevolutionary reaction which had occurred after the Terror in the French Revolution. The contrary opinion was that *unless* it were attacked directly the church would become a focus of counterrevolution. The former opinion prevailed at first, and resulted in the constitutional formula, "religion is a private affair of the citizen." Lenin was dissatisfied, however, and substituted the final formula of Article 13, "freedom of religion and of anti-religious propaganda is granted to all citizens." The implication was that religion meant worship only. For the next generation Bolshevik policy was to oscillate back and forth between the two tactical conceptions as to how to eliminate religion.

Article 65 of the Constitution also disfranchised the clergy along with the *bourgeoisie*. This provision was less significant as regards the right to vote than in its implications for ration cards, admission to trade unions and co-operative societies, opportunities for employment, rents and taxes, and the right to have children educated beyond the elementary school.

FOREIGN INTERVENTION. As with the French Revolution, in the Russian Revolution identification of the church with the prerevolutionary regime was greatly intensified when foreign intervention was organized to support the monarchists. From 1918-1920 Russia was torn by civil war. The French, Japanese, Americans, and Poles all sent troops or supplies to aid the White Russian troops, and the Bolsheviks fought in Siberia, the Crimea, on the Polish front, and on the White Sea. Lenin's victory was due in part to a nationalist spirit aroused by these interventions, especially the Franco-Polish attempt in 1920. It was this civil war which made Trotsky's Red Army a national Russian army. Both sides were utterly ruthless with civilians and executed hundreds of thousands of hostages. There was real famine in the cities in 1918, and educated bourgeois elements, particularly, were left to starve without bread cards or prospect of work. Industrial production in 1920 was down to 13 per cent of 1913 levels. A drought in the Volga area, with a population approximately equivalent to that of Italy, contributed to the general economic breakdown, and in the Great Famine of 1921-1922 some five million died outright—despite United States help, which was limited to feeding children.

KARLOVTSI SOBOR. In this desperate situation of 1921 Patriarch Tikhon appealed to foreign churches for aid. The church set up a committee to raise relief funds, but the jealous Bolsheviks demanded that the cash be handed over to the government. Then, when income dropped off, they let the church take over again. In December an emigré Sobor met at Karlovtsi in the Balkans, headed by the most reactionary leader, Metropolitan Antony, formerly of Kiev and Galicia. Nine archbishops attended, as did representatives of two of the

White generals. The Sobor resolved that the throne should be occupied by an Orthodox Romanov and frankly hoped the famine would break the government. The Soviets viewed this Sobor as the revolting French did the pope and Coblentz exiles, (see above, p. 117) and suspected the church at home of agreeing at heart with the emigrés. Tikhon's alleged collusion with the Karlovtsi Sobor was never proved, however, and is unlikely.

The suggestion was now made that the treasure of the church should be contributed. The Tsars had confiscated church plate and jewels in the past. It was noted, however, that the government did not touch the imperial jewels. Tikhon permitted all unconsecrated utensils (no great amount) to be taken, but declared that the canons forbade the use of others. Many Orthodox laymen and clergy disagreed with this opinion. In any case the government ordered the seizure of all objects not actually used in worship and many clergy obeyed the Patriarch's injunction. Some 1,400 bloody encounters took place, and clergy were arrested wholesale.

There followed the sensational trials of 1922–1923. The chief trials were in Petrograd, where eighty were indicted, including Metropolitan Benjamin, and in Moscow, where the Roman Catholic Archbishop Cepliak and the Vicar-General Budkevich stood in the dock with the Orthodox Archbishops Arsenius and Seraphim. Of some seven hundred tried in over two hundred trials, forty-four were sentenced. The shooting of Archbishop Benjamin and Vicar-General Budkevich especially aroused international protest. In all, the unorganized violence of these first six years of the Revolution had resulted in the killing of twenty-eight bishops and over one thousand priests.

SCHISM OF THE LIVING CHURCH. This crisis over the church plate and the Patriarch's inflexibility proved the occasion for the leftist minority of the Sobor to come to the front again. Twelve priests published a letter in *Izvestia*, and a proclamation was issued calling on the Sobor to discipline those making the church into a counterrevolutionary party and to establish normal relations with the government. A delegation visited Tikhon in detention and blamed him for the Moscow verdicts, citing his anathema and opposition to the decrees in 1918, his blessing on the Tsar at Ekaterinberg, and his ordaining of many monarchists. They demanded his resignation. Tikhon agreed to nominate a substitute. In the meantime the group won his agreement to let them conduct the chancery. Without permission they constituted themselves a Provisional Supreme Ecclesiastical Administration and moved into the patriarchal headquarters. They affirmed themselves canonical possessors of their office and constituted what became known as the "Living Church." Thus, as in the French Revolution, the church was split by a schism over its attitude to government policy. And as in the French Revolution the government supported the schismatic church against the conservatives, turning over church buildings to them.

In May 1922, the platform of the Living Church was set forth as theological modernism, socialism, liturgical reform, election of pastors, larger share by laity in administration, and eligibility of married clergy for the episcopate. In the course of further discussion, however, the socialist clergy split on this issue of married or unmarried bishops and soon there were, in addition to the "Living Church," a "Churchly Regeneration" group and an "Ancient Apostolic Church." Under threat of recall of the British mission, however, Patriarch Tikhon was released in June 1923, and most of the clergy submitted to him and were pardoned by him.

After 1923 the temper of the government's religious policy moderated down to the general relaxation of the New Economic Policy. At the end of the program in 1928, Russia had revived industrially almost to the 1913 level, although agricultural productivity was still below the pre-World War I level. As to religion, the pressure was steady but not extreme. Priests' sermons were submitted to the censor from the end of 1922. Heavy taxes and fire insurance premiums were laid on church buildings. Tikhon died in 1925 and the government would not allow the election of a new patriarch. Acting patriarchs were arrested.

In the meantime, under the constitutional liberty of anti-religious propaganda, the Communists organized a program. In 1922 the Atheist Publishing Company was established. That Christmas saw the first anti-Christmas carnival with mock processions in which the miracles, the Immaculate Conception, and shrines were caricatured, with the Young Communist League dancing around the floats. The Militant Atheists' League was launched in 1925, which organized these carnivals and put out great amounts of literature on the themes that religion was (1) disloyal, (2) superstitious, and (3) exploitation. The *Beshboshnik* was a periodical of about thirty pages with colored cartoons and pictures caricaturing the Bible and sacraments, somewhat after the fashion of Streicher's anti-Semitic *Stürmer* in Germany.

The churches worked out their own methods of survival. In this period the Free Churches, especially Baptists, apparently grew sensationally, running up to about four million. The churches also went in for various social activities, reading groups, libraries, excursions, mutual aid societies. A "Christomol" youth group actually won over the "Comsomol" in some districts.

RENEWED VIOLENCE IN FIRST FIVE-YEAR PLAN. The half-dozen years of the N.E.P., during which the split and disorganized church struggled to recover from the violent persecution and to maintain itself against the atheist propaganda and legal restrictions, ended in new violence. In 1928 the first Five-Year Plan was projected, with the particular goals of large-scale industrialization and enforced collectivization of agriculture. Associated with these goals was an intensified effort to wipe out what was left of Christianity, including now the Baptists and "Gospel Christians" also.

The most direct method was simply to eliminate the clergy, and especially to break the Apostolic Succession, which is essential for the Orthodox view of sacraments. Thousands of priests were exiled or executed, and at one time there were 150 bishops in prison. This is more than the number of dioceses, and it points to the desperate efforts of the church to consecrate new bishops as soon as the old were imprisoned. The bleak Solovetzsky monastery in the White Sea was the prison where most of these clergy were confined. Short of outright arrest, moreover, the clergy were driven out of the cities by the passport system. "Nonworkers" were not permitted in the big cities and were thus driven to isolation in the countryside.

Clergy not only could not vote, but also could not get food cards. Public worship was broken off by the device used during the French Revolution of changing the seven-day week. Instead of the French *decadi*, the Bolsheviks introduced a six-day week in 1929, and to enforce attendance, it was ruled in 1932 that one absence from work meant loss of one's job. In 1929 over a thousand churches were closed, often amid riots, very often by vote of groups being coerced into collective farms. Such difficulties were experienced in persuading the peasants into collective farms, however, that in 1930 the closing of churches was dissociated from this aspect of the program. Up to 1928 over 98 per cent of the peasants had declined to enter collective farms. Easter food and Christmas trees could not be sold after that year.

A second line of campaign was educational. With the Five-Year Plan, systematic antireligious education was introduced into the school system, especially with new texts in sociology. School children were taken on excursions to antireligious museums, often converted from churches or monasteries. No defense of religion in speech or writing could legally be made.

To prevent the new type of community influence which the church had sought under the N.E.P., a new decree was passed effectively cutting off all social, charitable, and recreational activities. No co-operatives, no charities, no mutual aid societies, no excursions, playgrounds, libraries, sanitariums, or asylums were permitted. Also no special prayer groups or Bible classes for women or young people or children would be legal. The church was to be isolated in every way from community life. On the negative side, moreover, Christians were penalized in other aspects of life. They could not expect promotions and often found no jobs at all. Some unions would not supply services to religious people or organizations.

RELAXATION OF PRESSURE. The program was to have been climaxed in the Second Five-Year Plan of 1933-1937. At its beginning Yaroslavsky was reported to have set the goal that there should be no church left in the Soviet Union by 1937. The church, however, apparently had Hitler to thank—and, perhaps, the pope and Canterbury, who made protests—for some easing of the pressure. Stalin was more discerning of the meaning of the Nazi victory in 1933 than were the Western democracies, and at once sought to strengthen his international position, even to the point of making concessions on the antireligious program.

In 1934 the easing of pressure began to appear. Many churches which had been closed in 1929-1930 now reopened. Antireligious rallies were reduced and the atheist mockeries at Christmas and Easter stopped. In 1935 the special Easter cakes and food were again sold, even in state stores; Christmas trees were lit again; and the state began selling wedding rings, implying state recognition of religious marriage. The Marxist indoctrination in grammar schools was dropped altogether and was limited in secondary schools, although it was still maintained in higher education. The children of the clergy were once more allowed in all grades of the schools in December 1935, and in the new Constitution of 1936 all the disabilities and disfranchisement of so-called "nonworkers" were removed.

PURGE OF 1937-1938. Despite the new Constitution of 1936, or perhaps partly because of it, a third outbreak of violent persecution flared up again, particularly of the clergy. At the end of 1937 large numbers of clergy were arrested along with the Old Communists in the great Trotskyite purge, on charges of espionage, sabotage, and arson. At Easter 1938, there were wholesale arrests, although there was no direct interference with public worship. In 1937-1938 ten thousand religious associations were taxed out of existence.

Yet it was in the midst of this third phase of direct and violent attack that the most impressive witness of the strength of Christianity was made. In the census of January 1937 a question was introduced with regard to religious convictions, apparently with the thought of disclosing how feeble was the handful who would still stand up to be counted. The results of this part of the census, however, were never published, and there is virtual certainty that the Party was deeply disappointed. And certain figures published thereafter, without documentation, seem to rest on the census returns. Yaroslavsky, head of the Militant Atheists' League, declared that in the towns two-thirds and in the villages one-third to one-half of the population over sixteen were atheists. The same figures were announced in 1940 in the *Monthly Journal* of the League. Turned about, they give the remarkable result that one-third of the townsmen and one-half to two-thirds of the villagers— that is, about 45 per cent of the population—were willing to declare themselves believers in God in the face of the known attitude of the Party and after twenty years of systematic, and at times bloody, oppression.

These believers in God were widely scattered, as Tertullian remarks of the Christians in the pagan Roman Empire. There were enough of them in the trades unions so that some unions held a position of neutrality on the religious issue. Yaroslav- sky complained that most members of the Communist Party and Young Communists League were neutral, many of them even keeping icons and performing religious rites. Believers in God were also to be found in the Red Army. Apparently the persecution, although it had been devastating, had fallen far short. This seems to say something about the nature of reli- gion, even in somnolent and secularized forms. As Luna- charsky said, "Religion is like a nail; the harder you hit, the deeper it sinks into the wood."

RELIGIOUS REVIVAL. Despite the Neronian violence of the counterrevolutionary purge of 1936-1938, there was a percep- tible religious revival under the Third Five-Year Plan. The seven-day week with Sunday rest was restored and labor laws were relaxed to permit the religious festivals. Religious sym- bols, icons, and wedding rings, were made and sold. Shrines were reopened. By the outbreak of World War II almost all church holidays were once again observed in the villages. Civil rights were restored to the clergy, and both Orthodox and Ro- man Catholic clergy served as chaplains in the Red Army. Collective farms were beginning to support churches.

Important changes in educational policy also affected reli- gion. School manuals and texts were revised to expurgate the scurrilous attacks on religion. Antireligious museums were closed and blasphemous plays and movies were no longer pro- duced after 1938; the great publishing enterprise of the God- less Union was suspended. Many official publishers refused to consider antireligious manuscripts and the Young Communists' League allowed its campaign to lapse. There was by 1939 only one institute for higher antireligious education left, and the antireligious clubs were often empty. In the majority of the provinces no antireligious propaganda organizations remained in 1939. The Militant Atheists' League disintegrated as the Communist Party and Young Communist League lost interest in it. Attendance at lectures on atheism was thin.

In addition to the attitude of a younger generation which cannot be persuaded that Christianity is any danger, there is a positive current toward religion in the nationalist cultural revival. Ivan the Terrible and Peter the Great are coming back into favor, as are Tchaikovsky and Rachmaninoff. There is a vogue of the historical novel and of national heroes, even if they were both Christian and Tsarist. The terrible losses of World War II, moreover, turned many to hunting for some steadying orientation deeper than politics, and the government, always realistic, accepted the contributions of religion to morale.

There is, lastly, the new ecclesiastical imperialism of the restored Moscow Patriarchate on which Stalin placed his blessing. Even a theological seminary was opened. Claims of jurisdiction over Baltic, Balkan, and even North American Orthodox have been pressed. During World War II, however, the Bolshevik Reign of Terror was applied to Christians in occupied countries—Esthonia, Latvia, Lithuania, Bessarabia, and Poland—despite the fact that there were millions of Christians in the Red Army. And none of the concessions to religion touched the great barrier against religious education of youth under eighteen.

Chapter 28

ROMAN CATHOLICISM AND THE TOTALITARIANS

There is a saying that World War I was won militarily by the French, economically by the United States, and ecclesiastically by the Roman Catholic Church. The truth of this last proposition, however, was not so apparent in the days of Benedict XV, who reigned from 1914 to 1922. For most of the war, the Vatican Secretariate of State apparently expected and desired the victory of the Central Powers. Benedict never would speak out in condemnation of the German violation of Belgian neutrality, and his peace overtures seemed to the French, for example, to be timed for the maximum advantage of the Central Powers. At the Allied victory the Pope was barred from the peace conference and watched with pique as Wilson and the League occupied the post of international arbiter. Benedict felt so isolated diplomatically that he declared that if France would but reach out to him her little finger, he would seize it with both hands. Yet the Vatican's recovery, particularly in diplomatic strength, was remarkably rapid. Pius XI (1922-1939) manipulated a steadily expanding diplomatic corps for a political influence no pope had exerted in generations. Political and diplomatic activity took an ever-increasing share of resources at the Vatican. Protestantism and Orthodox Catholicism seemed politically ineffective by comparison.

This new strength and initiative of the Roman Catholic Church were not due to a marked increase in numbers. In general, Protestantism probably was still gaining more from Rome in conversions and by intermarriage than the Roman Catholic Church won from Protestantism. The new strength was the strength of a disciplined quasipolitical international organization in a revolutionary situation. Protestantism, whatever its numbers, was not unified, had no strategy, and even in its divisions was not disciplined by church authority so as to be a comparable *political* force. The very leadership Protestantism had exerted in penetrating and moralizing the prewar political and social structure implicated Protestantism also in its collapse. The War for Democracy nearly ended democracy. After the war a series of authoritarian revolutions replaced liberalism and democracy over most of Europe. Individualistic economic and business practices were threatened by a new collectivism. Middle-class culture in general lost its hegemony. And with it all was proclaimed "the end of the Protestant era." The new dictators whose careers dominated the headlines of the next generation were almost to a man of Roman Catholic background: Mussolini, Hitler, Dollfuss, Schuschnigg, Tito, Franco, Salazar, Pétain, Peron. In many cases they won or retained power by Vatican support. And although some of the most startling Roman Catholic political gains were in democratic Britain and the United States, nevertheless the world policy which the Vatican under Pius XI pursued with the funds derived from a generally democratic constituency in America was pro-Fascist.

The new alignment of forces meant the virtual elimination of the middle-class anticlericalism which had opposed the Roman Catholic Church in nineteenth-century France and Italy. Socialism had now become such a political threat to privileged classes that a consolidation of all conservative parties seemed indicated. For different reasons Roman Catholicism and the new totalitarians combined in an attack on parliaments, civil liberties, and freedom of thought. The collapse of liberal culture mirrored intellectually, as well as politically, in the loss of confidence in reason, science, and the moral sense, and in a general turn to authority, which favored the more conservative forms of Christianity as well as various non-Christian political religions.

VATICAN POLITICAL POLICY. The pro-Fascist direction of Vatican policy was the deliberate choice of Pius XI. His predecessor was rather of the school of Leo XIII and had started off on another tack. Benedict had withdrawn the *non expedit* for

Italian Catholics on the eve of the 1919 elections as a kind of blessing on the new People's Party then being launched. Under such auspices this Roman Catholic democratic party at once became the second party in the nation. Similarly, in the Weimar Republic Benedict set his new nuncio, Pacelli, to cooperate with the democratic tendency led by Erzberger. But with the accession of Pius in 1922 all such ventures in Roman Catholic democracy were rejected. Pius had just come back from a mission in Poland, where he had seen the Red Army, and he retained throughout his reign an obsessive fear of Communism. Being contemptuous of democracy anyway, he developed a policy of supporting militarist authoritarian governments which could be counted on to fight Communism. And thus by an irony native to politics he helped create Communist dangers where there had been none and helped increase those which were there.

THE VATICAN AND ITALIAN FASCISM. Pius threw the considerable weight of Roman Catholicism against democracy first of all in Italy. On three or four critical occasions when Don Sturzo's People's Party offered serious resistance to the Fascist climb to power, the Pope deliberately sabotaged the *popolari*. He finally forced the resignation of Sturzo at the height of the conflict and forbade that alliance of the *popolari* with the moderate socialists which was the only practicable alternative to Fascism. And having thus paved the way for Mussolini's rise to power by breaking Catholic democracy, the Vatican proceeded from 1926 to 1929 to draft a series of agreements with the dictator. By the Lateran Pacts of 1929 the "Roman Question" was at last settled, as the church was given outright the miniature state of Vatican City, together with a series of assurances for its independence. In return for its lost territories the Vatican accepted a large sum in Fascist bonds, which made it one of the largest investors in the new political system. And, lastly, a treaty defined the relations of church and state in such a way as virtually to establish the Roman Church, but to place its control in the hands of the Fascist state. This control was exerted chiefly by means of a Fascist right of veto over church appointments and the management of church finances. The church was given certain rights on paper in the field of education and youth activities, but they were limited and were not honored by Mussolini. The Pope protested this breach of faith in the encyclical *Non abbiamo bisogno* of 1931, in which, however, he carefully avoided condemning the Fascist party and regime.

The degree to which the Roman Catholic Church was bound to Mussolini's chariot wheels became apparent to all at the time of the Abyssinian outrage in 1935. Not only did a major section of the Italian hierarchy applaud this cowardly assault as a "holy war"; not only did world Roman Catholicism generally (especially in England and America) follow the cue; but the Pope himself went out of his way to acclaim the victory of the Fascist government, which over fifty nations had branded as a lawbreaker, as a "contribution to world peace."

AUSTRIA. In Austria, meanwhile, Mussolini's example was much admired by the Roman Catholic party. Mgr. Seipel, the leader of this party, dreamed of the restoration of a Hapsburg *Mitteleuropa* by a revolution in the Danubian Valley. Hungary, Yugoslavia, and Czechoslovakia should all yield their predominantly Roman Catholic sections to form a new state which could dispense with liberal institutions. Seipel contributed to the formulation of the encyclical *Quadragesimo anno* of 1931, in which the program of a "corporative state" was outlined. In the guise of reaffirming the economic traditionalism of Leo XIII, the clerical Fascists were really shaping a system whereby feudal landlords and industrialists might rule autocratically without being inhibited by parliaments, parties, trade unions, or civil liberties. Since such a program could never be democratically voted in Austria, the Roman Catholic party built up an illegal private army, the *Heimwehr*, headed by Starhemberg, for a *putsch*. One effort failed in 1929 and Seipel died, to be replaced by Dollfuss. In 1930 Dollfuss began to rule by decree. The next year came the *Heimwehr* assault on Vienna, an outbreak marked by the barbarous slaughter of noncombatants in the working-class quarters of Vienna. The Austrian "Christian" corporative state, the first modeled on *Quadragesimo anno*, was founded in 1934 on this massacre and was maintained by martial law.

PORTUGAL AND SPAIN. The second state which waved the banner of *Quadragesimo anno* was Portugal. Here, too, a clerical Fascist rule had been installed from 1926, with the leadership of Salazar. The corporative state here, too, disposed of civil and political liberty. And Portugal became a refuge for the organizers of the Fascist assault on the Republic of Spain in 1936, which was to prove the opening skirmish of World War II in Europe. The war was launched by a section of the Spanish military, in conspiracy with Hitler and Mussolini, who used it as a proving ground for their expanding military establishments. The character of a brutal Fascist conquest, however, was qualified by the general support of the Vatican and Roman Catholic hierarchy in Spain. The church in Spain had become so identified with the old regime of Alfonso XIII and Primo de Rivera that the fall of the latter was celebrated by a wave of church burnings over Spain in 1931. The succeeding Spanish Republic was strongly anticlerical, but not predominantly Marxist. The Spanish church, however, was unwilling to undergo the purgation necessary to re-establish itself morally with the Spanish people. Its leaders conspired to win back power and privilege through violence. All but two of the bishops acclaimed the insurgents' invasion as a "crusade" in 1937, and they appealed to the episcopate all over the world for support. The protests of a few Catholics, such as the French writers Maritain, Mauriac, and Bernanos, against the "holiness" of this war, were drowned in the official clamor. The American hierarchy played a major role in cutting off American arms for Spain, and the support of the Republican government by the U.S.S.R. was inadequate to match the earlier and more extensive contributions of Hitler and Mussolini to the rebellion. Franco triumphed and erected another "corporative" state in 1939, in time to supply U-boat bases to Hitler in World War II. The Spanish-American priesthood, meanwhile, were among the chief agents in spreading the program of Fascism of Franco's type in the Western hemisphere.

FRANCE. While political Roman Catholicism thus launched civil wars in the name of unashamed reaction in the two ancient centers of the Counter Reformation, France and Germany displayed a more complicated development. War service had strengthened the prestige of the clergy and church in French society, and in 1921 diplomatic relations with the Vatican, broken since 1904 (see above, p. 231), were resumed. The church could make itself useful to France, for a consideration, in helping to discourage the autonomy sentiment in the new province of Alsace-Lorraine (now incorporated into France). France and the Vatican also had parallel interests in the cordon of succession states west of Russia, in the Levant, and in the Far East. Internally the legal status of church property was regularized in 1924 on terms substantially identical with those which Pius X had spurned as quite impossible in 1905. With the political swing to the left in 1924 there was a brief and unsuccessful attempt to revive the old middle-class anticlerical movement. Nothing has been heard of it since.

"ACTION FRANÇAISE" CONDEMNED. A great internal crisis was brought about in French Roman Catholicism by the condemnation of Maurras and the *Action française* in 1926. The isolationist, cynical, imperialist mentality of this French form of Fascism had prevailed in upper-class circles, especially among Roman Catholics, ever since World War I. At the instance of Cardinal Mercier of Belgium, however, the Vatican investigated the *Action française* and condemned it as heretical. In fact the Vatican announced that the draft of the condemnation had been in hand since the eve of World War I, but had been suppressed until a more opportune time. Its publication now rocked French Roman Catholicism to its roots and led to the resignation of a cardinal and a purge of irreconcilable clergy. The anti-Semitic, antidemocratic current remained strong, especially in the officers' corps, as was to be demonstrated by such collaborationists as Weygand and Pétain in World War II. But the condemnation was taken seriously by many, especially a small group of intellectuals such as Maritain, who henceforth provided in the Roman Catholic world the chief voice of criticism to the prevailing Fascist orientation. This little group spoke up against Mussolini's attack on Abyssinia, against the Axis outrage at Guernica in Spain, against the attempt at a Fascist coup in France. And they became identified with a vigorous home missions effort in France, which turned from political maneuver to a vital apostolate among industrial labor, the peasants, and the intellectuals. A careful sociological analysis of the hold of the church in France, broken down by classes and regions, gave the measure of the missionary task. New experiments were undertaken, both in reanimating parish life through the liturgical movement, and in new forms of extraparochial work, such as the worker-priests and the various youth movements, most conspicuously Cardijn's "Jocists." Among the intellectuals, Léon Bloy and Charles Péguy now replaced the more traditional Roman Catholic novelists with a prophetic critique of bourgeois society and religion.

GERMANY. Across the Rhine in Germany was to be found a comparable religious revival, together with such political gains that people spoke of a "Second Counter Reformation" under the Weimar Republic. In part this was due to the strength of Roman organization in a shattered society and to the capacity of the international Roman Catholic Church to throw men and funds into a fluid situation while Protestants were closing down one institution after another for lack of comparable assistance. In part it was due to the flight from freedom and the search for emotional security which strengthened Roman Catholicism, nationalism, and communism alike. The radical antihumanism of the dominant Protestant theology of the time offered no such points of contact with the interests of cultured people as did the Roman Catholic sacramental revival. This liturgical movement seemed more spontaneous and powerful than the officially inflated neo-Thomist revival. Under the Weimar Republic the number of monks doubled, and the contemplative orders, especially, gained.

LITURGICAL REVIVAL. The liturgical movement had begun just before World War I, in the Low Countries, in Germany, and in Austria. The Benedictine abbeys were the chief centers, and the movement first excited general interest in Belgium, where it was closely related to social action. In Holland chanting by the laity was more successful than elsewhere. In general, Roman Catholic congregations have found the combination of Latin texts with Gregorian settings just too much to compass, however desirable lay participation may be. The whole movement is embarrassed by the fact that the obvious solution to the problem of intelligent lay participation is unavailable because it was discovered by the Reformation—namely, the translation of the liturgy into the vernacular and the use of appropriate congregational hymns for the variable parts of the service. But a compromise is found in the use of missals as guides to the mass, rather than the rosary or other private devotions. And often the ancient (and Reformed) location of the altar in the midst of the congregation, with the celebrant in the basilican posture, is adopted. In this renewed emphasis on the sacrament as an act of the Church, rather than of just the clergy, social and ethical implications became visible.

The Benedictine Abbey of Maria Laach became the theological center of the revival, headed by Abbot Herwegen and with such scholars as Dom Odo Casel. Their peculiar contribution was to formulate a sacramental vocabulary and rationale based on the Greek fathers. In many respects the liturgical reformers have been drawn to Orthodox sacramental views and practices, and some of them actually left Romanism for Orthodoxy. In a lesser degree the movement approached Reformation conceptions of explicit faith, the doctrine of the Church, the priesthood of all believers, and a more biblical and Christocentric orientation. From still another perspective the liturgical revival meant a resurgence of some of the deeper religious impulses of the suppressed modernist movement. It was carried especially by the youth groups, which were also marked by a renewal of interest in the Bible, and a new missionary calling, as in France.

There was a vigorous counterattack, led especially by Jesuits. Private devotions, the rosary, the cult of the Virgin and of the Sacred Heart, and novenas of all sorts, although admittedly destructive of corporate worship, were defended as necessary for those of little religious depth. In the encyclical *Mediator dei* many of these practices, such as the adoration of the reserved sacrament, were to be specifically defended. The great argument against lay participation involving use of the vernacular is that it would certainly disintegrate the world-wide uniformity into infinite variations and centrifugal tendencies. In any case, the movement was effectively restricted in this generation to Germany and the Low Countries. It had no comparable success in the Mediterranean Latin countries or in the English-speaking world, where Roman Catholicism was primarily political and "activist."

THE CENTER AND THE NAZIS. In Germany also, of course, Roman Catholicism was highly political. The Roman Catholic Center Party held the balance of power in the Weimar Republic and shifted back and forth ten or a dozen times from the socialists to the nationalists in the hopes of gaining concessions for the church, especially in education. Eight of the fourteen chancellors up to 1933 were from the Center Party. In the process, however, party discipline grew weaker, and an ever larger proportion of Roman Catholics voted outside the Center. The Vatican apparently decided about 1928 that the Center was too weak a political instrument. The Roman Catholic Chancellor Brüning ruled by decree from 1930, scheming for a monarchist restoration with Nazi support. In the event, of course, the Nazis threw over both the Center and the nationalists, but they made their separate deal with the Vatican. The Nazi-Vatican Concordat negotiated by Von Papen in 1933 was similar in character to the Concordat with Mussolini of 1929 and for a time papered over the radical divergence of Nazism and Christianity. It has been suggested that of the three forms of totalitarianism, the Communists' outright hostility was less dangerous to Christianity than the half-concealed paganism of the Nazis, and that the latter was less dangerous than the Fascist campaign to maintain and use Roman Catholicism. This line of thought could be brought to a climax in the study of the spiritual anatomy of the Spanish and Latin American *falange*.

In 1933 and 1934 the Nazis were preoccupied with their attempt to capture the Protestant Church (see below, p. 386) and left German Roman Catholicism in relative peace. Individual Roman Catholics, however, gave strong support to the Protestants in the defense of the Old Testament. Then in 1935 and 1936 the Nazis turned their attention to the Roman Catholics. The Concordat was unscrupulously disregarded by the government. Some of the political pressure, as in the trials for "smuggling" or the great publicity given to alleged instances of monastic homosexuality, was probably a form of blackmail to gain Vatican support for foreign objectives, particularly the *Anschluss* with Austria. In 1937 the Pope expressed his disillusionment with the Nazis in *Mit brennender Sorge*, an even more vehement protest than the reproach to Mussolini in *Non abbiamo bisogno*. Here again, however, Pius avoided censure of political totalitarianism as such. He died a deeply disillusioned man in 1939. It was left to his Secretary of State Pacelli, who succeeded him, hastily to reorient his maneuvers of a decade toward the hitherto despised liberal democracy in World War II.

The strength of this democracy lay in the English-speaking world, and here the Roman Catholic Church had made a particular effort to fortify itself in the generation between wars. In Great Britain, Canada, the United States, and Australia the Roman Catholic Church had largely organized and unified the great immigration of the preceding two generations and was in a very strong political position as a closely organized bloc. Roman Catholicism, lacking the internal organs of self-criticism, was also most vigorous religiously and morally where it was not the dominant body.

THE UNITED STATES. The overwhelming bulk of financial support for the world Roman Catholic Church now came from the United States, and the American church now occupied a role of greater importance generally. In character it was not distinguished by devotional practice or theological scholarship; in these it was inferior to various Protestant churches. More than any Protestant denomination, on the other hand, it was characterized by political-mindedness and "American activism."

A new epoch in the life of American Roman Catholicism can be dated from the establishment of the National Catholic Welfare Conference (N.C.W.C.) as the co-ordinating administrative staff in 1919. Annual meetings of the hierarchy also date from that year. The N.C.W.C. department of social action, headed by John A. Ryan, also marked a new initiative in social policy, which promptly took the lead from the Protestant "social gospellers." American Roman Catholicism was 85 per cent urban and was more identified with industrial labor than any other denomination. Since the beginning it had claimed half of the American labor movement, and in the generation between wars it exercised political leadership in that movement and rode to power with it.

In the 1930's the Roman Catholic Church trained many priests in industrial problems, began to open labor schools, and developed a program of penetrating and manipulating the labor unions in rivalry to the Communist effort. By World War II organized labor was the single most important base of Roman Catholic political power in America.

General Roman Catholic political consciousness was first occasioned by the presidential campaign of 1928, in which the able and progressive Roman Catholic governor of New York State, Al Smith, was the Democratic candidate. During the campaign the chief issues between the liberal democratic tradition and that of the Roman Catholic Church were aired. Mr. Smith published a famous liberal Catholic manifesto which was subjected to a penetrating critique by the jurist C. C. Marshall.

A new impetus was given by *Quadragesimo anno* (1931) and American Roman Catholicism found an alliance with Roosevelt's New Deal through the big-city Democratic machines. The National Recovery Administration experimented briefly with a modernized guild system akin to that of the encyclical. The strength of the clerical position in politics was indicated at the time of the Spanish Civil War. Although polls indicated that most American Roman Catholics favored the Loyalists, the pro-Franco hierarchy and its press apparently convinced the President and Congress that they could deliver the "Catholic vote." The Spanish Republic was accordingly denied the means to defend itself. And the American press was bullied by the new device of censorship, the economic boycott, into the suppression of information and views damaging to the Franco cause.

In the field of education the drive to build the parochial school system profited by the financial gains of the 1920's, in which all the churches shared. Ninety-eight per cent of the private elementary schools of the country, and two-thirds of the private secondary schools were run by the Roman Catholic Church in the late 1920's. An attempt on the part of the Oregon legislature to require all children to attend the public schools was thrown out by the Supreme Court in 1925 as a denial of the right of freedom of education. On the other hand, the Roman Catholic lobby blocked federal aid to an increasingly desperate public school situation in the less wealthy states, while in many cities Roman Catholics were accused of using their political power on school boards to weaken the public schools. Efforts to gain direct or indirect tax subsidies or allocations for confessional schools remained the single point of greatest tension between Roman Catholics and Protestants. The effort to maintain the school system seemed to absorb virtually all Roman Catholic intellectual energies, and there was little to show of intellectual life or cultural leadership until the arrival of numerous refugees from the European dictators.

Chapter 29

CONTINENTAL PROTESTANTISM AND THE NAZIS

Although less hard hit than Eastern Orthodoxy by World War I and its revolutionary consequences, Continental Protestantism suffered greater damage than did Roman Catholicism. The nominal size of the European Protestant bloc, 108,000,000, shrinks radically if any criterion of serious religious concern is applied. The greatest concentration of these Protestants, moreover, was precisely in those countries which lost the war and suffered most from it. Protestants (predominantly Lutheran) in Germany were numbered at forty million and formed by far the most powerful and influential European section of Protestantism. The political, economic, cultural, and spiritual disaster which struck this nation as a result of the war bore heavily also on their religious life and institutions.

The conditions most desperate in the defeated Central Powers were scarcely confined to them. The postwar inflation was in some ways more catastrophic socially and morally than the war itself. The endowments of churches and church institutions of all sorts were wiped out, the basis of foreign and home missions withdrawn, and in many areas ministerial salaries cut to subsistence and lower. There were an appalling lack of Protestant clergy and desperately inadequate means to train recruits. Students could not find books, clothing, or housing, and died of tuberculosis and undernourishment all through the 1920's, even when they had conquered the weight of despair and hatred and fear which inhibited most from considering the ministry at all. As Adolf Keller of the Central Bureau of Evangelical Relief wrote a decade after the war, "In fourteen countries, due to an accumulation of calamities, the Protestant Church is fighting for its life."

377

There were some countries, such as Lutheran Scandinavia and Reformed Switzerland (and, to some degree, Reformed Holland) which largely escaped from the avalanche of disaster. Sweden and Switzerland strove manfully to fill the breach both in terms of financial aid and other relief, theological scholarship, and the institutional and spiritual program of the so-called ecumenical movement. Swiss dogmatic theology and Swedish historical theology have been influential all around the world in the last generation, with such names as Barth, Brunner, Aulen, Nygren, Brilioth, and Söderblom.

THE PROTESTANT DIASPORA. If we momentarily withhold consideration of Germany as the central bulk of Continental Protestantism, we may survey briefly conditions in southern and eastern Europe. Here the typical condition of Protestants is suggested by the term "the Protestant Diaspora." Protestants, that is, were generally minorities—often racial and linguistic, as well as religious—and were subject to more or less open oppression by Roman Catholic, Eastern Orthodox, and Marxist states. The treaties which reorganized Europe after World War I left some thirty million people as minorities within states whose political, cultural, and religious traditions were often uncongenial to them. In proportion as their new masters distrusted them and felt insecure behind the new frontiers, minorities were oppressed as potential enemies within the gates. The very principle of defining a political state on the basis of nationality, as President Wilson enunciated it, implies persecution, for a minority is by definition a group which cannot adhere to the principle on which the state is constituted. Thus minorities were the most inflammable and the bitterest issue of European relations between wars. Persecution was widespread, especially by Roman Catholic Poles, Orthodox Rumanians and Greeks, and Bolshevik Russians. And that the fears which inspired these persecutions in part were not groundless was demonstrated by events in the Saar and Danzig and Sudetenland in the late 1930's.

IN ROMAN CATHOLIC LANDS. To consider Protestantism in the various areas of the Diaspora in succession, there is first of all the Roman Catholic Latin cultural sphere: France, Belgium,

Italy, Spain, and Portugal. Only in France was there a substantial Protestant community, about one million. A considerable segment of these, however, were scattered over the country without pastors and were served only by colporteurs and itinerant evangelists. The Protestants of the other four states totaled only about 150,000 and suffered under a number of governmental and social pressures. Only in Belgium was there religious liberty, and this did not extend to the Belgian Congo, where persecution of Protestants was blatant and outrageous. The rise of the dictators in Italy, Spain, and Portugal meant in each case that the Protestants were offered to the tender mercies of the Vatican in part payment for Roman support for the new tyrants. As for centuries, Protestant history in the Latin countries was, with the exception of France, reduced to a desperate effort for mere survival. The French Protestant community, of course, has always had a highly disproportionate influence on French life because of the intellectual and moral leadership it has provided, especially in law, medicine, finance, and the social applications of Christianity.

ON THE BALTIC. Finland and the Baltic countries were part of a belt of territories which had suffered on the eve of the war under the oppressive Russification of the Orthodox Tsar. With the Russian Revolution and the intervention of the Western Powers in Russia, these border lands seized the opportunity to declare their independence. There were about three million Lutherans in Finland, and as many more in the newborn states of Esthonia, Latvia, and Lithuania, chiefly the so-called "Balts" of German origin. It was obvious to all, however, that the Bolsheviks did not look upon these losses as permanent and would seize an early opportunity to win free access again to the ports of the upper Baltic. This would also mean the application to the Baltic lands of the anti-Christian terror which was in force across their frontier to the east against uncounted millions of Russian Protestants as well as Orthodox Russians. The Damocles sword of Soviet anti-Christian expansion hung over the prospects of Protestants in these states.

In Lithuania, the southernmost of the new Baltic states, Protestants had to suffer from political persecution by a Roman Catholic government, just as was the case in the new state of

Poland. The Protestant Prussians were the hated former masters of the Roman Catholic Poles, and the million or so Protestants in the new Polish domain paid a heavy price. Here, as in Lithuania, Vatican diplomacy was active in securing privileges for the Roman Catholic Church by concordats, especially in education and marriage legislation. The Polish government delayed for years any legalization of Protestant ecclesiastical status, meanwhile interfering arbitrarily in Protestant affairs at Roman Catholic instigation. Property, even church buildings, was confiscated with the approval of the Ministry of Worship, and the life of Polish Protestant congregations resembled that of Huguenots in old-regime France. Protestants were not allowed to remedy their desperate shortage of clergy from Germany, the only available source. The regular meeting of the Lutheran synod of Lithuania was forbidden by police orders.

IN EASTERN EUROPE. As we move southward from Poland into the new states built up out of the former Austro-Hungarian Empire—Czechoslovakia and Yugoslavia—here again Protestants were in a minority position, about 1,000,000 out of the 13,000,000 in Czechoslovakia, and 250,000 each in Yugoslavia and in the new rump Austria. The block of Magyar Protestantism, the largest Reformed community on the Continent, and perhaps in the world, was split by the division of Hungary, 750,000 to the Rumanian share of Transylvania, and 250,000 to Czechoslovakia. Two-thirds of the territory of Hungary had been given away, and all her neighbors now controlled minorities of Hungarian Protestant tradition. Rumania was the most notorious oppressor of her minorities, both Roman Catholic and Protestant, crippling their schools and educational program in particular. In the rest of the Balkans—Bulgaria, Greece, and European Turkey—there were scattered thousands of Protestants, isolated, poor, without adequate leadership, and under constant social pressure when not outright persecution.

Perhaps education was the crucial problem for most of these millions of Protestants in the eastern and southern European Diaspora. Countries such as Poland, Yugoslavia, and Rumania attempted to stamp out alien traditions of their new minorities by placing restrictions on the use of the minority language. Often the confessional schools of the minority, where both the minority religion and language were taught, were closed down or taken over by a state school system, Roman Catholic in Poland, or Orthodox in Rumania. In addition, the agrarian laws and attempts to break up large estates often hit church endowments, which in Eastern Europe were normally in landholdings. There was thus a very widespread danger that the younger generation, deprived of both church and religious education, would grow up quite ignorant of their tradition. There were many parishes in Austria, Russia, and Czechoslovakia which had been looking for a pastor for years. A traveling preacher in Rumania reported he had found many groups of Protestants, from fifty to three hundred in number, who had not seen a pastor or attended a service of worship in fifteen years. Some of this lack was remedied in part by such Western European organizations as the British Tract Society and British and Foreign Bible Society and by the German Gustav-Adolf Verein. But without evangelical schools, in the long run the Protestant Diaspora was doomed to strangulation. Such activities of West European churches as home and foreign missions and social service enterprises were scarcely known at all in East European Protestantism, which lived simply by home, school, and church worship.

GERMANY. Let us now turn to Germany, the homeland of organized Protestantism, and the center on which the fate of all Continental Protestantism measurably depends. Here had arisen the greatest Protestant religious music and hymnody, the most highly developed philanthropic and social welfare program, and most famous of all, the greatest tradition of Protestant religious scholarship. Prewar Germany had possessed some eighteen theological faculties in state universities of an academic caliber equaled in the United States by not more than two or three faculties. In addition to these Germany had some thirty independent seminaries run by the churches. More than 60 per cent of all the Protestant theological students of the Continent studied in German theological faculties, to say nothing of the steady pilgrimage from Britain and overseas.

What had the war done to this German Protestantism? Church leaders and world-famous theologians had supported the war effort without qualification. German bayonets bore the legend "Gott mit uns" and ammunition belts "Für Gott und König." The first years of the war had seen an increase in interest in the churches and religion. As the blockade took effect and the casualty lists mounted, however, indifference to the churches set in. In those terrible four years in which Germany had virtually fought all Europe singlehanded she lost two million young men, the best of their generation, with thousands more crippled or blinded. She raised a generation of rachitic and undernourished children—in 1918 the death rate for children between four and fourteen had doubled. Wilson's Fourteen Points broke the German will to resist, but when the navy had mutinied and terms had to be sought, the Allies broke the Armistice agreement and starved the Germans until they signed a treaty which mocked nearly every one of Wilson's points. The Emperor, most of the generals, the kings, and the grand dukes fled in one mad rush and, to save Germany from complete disintegration, the Social Democrats undertook the thankless task of forming a government to negotiate a peace which was bound to be a terrible shock to the nation. The Social Democrats were harried by the Junker reactionaries on the one side and the Bolshevik Spartacists on the other; however, with the backing of most of the trade unions and the Roman Catholic Center Party, they beat off attempts at revolutionary violence and established the new constitutional rule of the Weimar Republic.

PARTIAL DISESTABLISHMENT. Under this Weimar Republic of socialists and Roman Catholics, the Protestant church of the Hohenzollern Empire could scarcely occupy the same position in the state. World War I had laid bare the fiction of the state church. Three-fourths or so of the nominal members of the state churches were really quite indifferent to Christianity. And now that the Christian kings were gone the churches could no longer represent the faith of the rulers either. All over Central Europe and the Danube Basin churches were disestablished in the years right after the war. So it was in Germany, Austria, Poland, Yugoslavia.

The general result, however, was only a partial disestablishment, for the clergy and congregations were unprepared for self-government and self-maintenance. In Germany the old

Landeskirchen, the territorial churches of Imperial days, lived on in their several traditions. They were still aided by the states, receiving subsidies for pastors' salaries and having the use of state machinery for the collection of church taxes. There were some thirty of them, and apart from their regional peculiarities of liturgy or administration, they fell into three classes confessionally speaking: the pure Lutherans, the Reformed, and the United churches. The United Evangelical Church of Prussia included just short of half of all German Protestants with its eighteen million. Then came two Lutheran churches, that of Saxony with 4,500,000 and that of Hanover with 2,500,000. Of the remainder only five numbered more than one million each—the churches of Württemberg, Thuringia, Bavaria, Schleswig-Holstein, and Hamburg.

On what basis were these churches now organized? Here was just the trouble. For generations the churches of Germany had been living in an emergency system, created in Luther's day to meet a crisis, but theologically indefensible. The Augsberg Confession, devised as a conciliatory statement, furnished no adequate grounds for a doctrine of the Church. And, in fact, Lutheranism had never developed an adequate doctrine of the Church. Church law in Germany was simply an administrative division of civil law, and it ascribed to the state ecclesiastical powers which were less and less justifiable in terms of the fading religious character of the state.

In the 1920's Lutheranism began again a discussion which had lapsed for centuries. What constitutes a true visible Church? How is it to be governed: by bishops, like the Swedes and Anglicans, or by representative bodies, like the Reformed? How much authority should be accorded to the state and its consistories, if it is to pay the bills? On what basis are such questions to be settled—mere administrative convenience, or are there religious principles at stake? In general, there was a perceptible increase in the vigor of congregational life or, rather, congregational life first began to be perceptible at all in this period. But there was such widespread antagonism to the churches as such, especially among the youth, that no substantial effort was made to reconstitute the churches on the basis of the religious life of a Christian community. Even under disestablishment, church law was still positivistic, seeking protection from the state rather than resting on its own God-given commission. Everyone born in a given area and baptized was to be accounted a church member unless he formally resigned. There was also, to be sure, a small number who belonged to Free Churches such as the Mennonites or Methodists, where membership represented something more. But on the whole, no such radical adjustment as the situation demanded took place in most of the churches.

For common representation to the Republic or to churches of the Ausland, the new peoples' churches combined in 1921–1922, a year after the Swiss churches had done the same, into a Federation. This Federation had an Assembly, a Council, and an Executive Committee with a central office to handle affairs. The President of the Federation was also the chief administrator of the Old Prussian Union, which, as we have seen, was four times the size of the next largest church.

SOCIALIST AND NATIONALIST OPPOSITION. In the nation at large the Protestant churches bore much of the onus for the defeat of the old Empire with which they had been so intimately connected. Two classes in particular turned in substantial numbers from Christianity to other (political) religions. Industrial labor was one. Before the war even Marxists had usually baptized their children and retained nominal church membership. In 1919, however, the Communists led a mass movement from the churches, especially in the large cities of Prussia and Saxony. By 1925, 1,330,000 were registered as having no church affiliations. The movement continued on through the 1920's as an indication of the hatred felt by workers toward a socially and politically reactionary church. Most of the clergy were monarchists and had slight sympathy for the Weimar Republic and less for socialism or democracy. The handful of "religious socialists" around Tillich and Mennicke could not bridge the gap between the clergy and the masses.

The German cultured class was the second considerable group in the community which, like industrial labor, was more sharply estranged from the churches than were the corresponding classes in the West. Whereas the proletarians nourished themselves on the vulgar materialism of the Marxists' *Erfurt*

Programme, the upper classes cultivated a romantic idealization of German tradition, aristocratic, heroic, antibourgeois, often pantheistic, in the tradition of Nietzsche and Richard Wagner. Among the variety of new organizations expressing these forms of tribal religion were the Tannenberg Bund, supported by former chief of staff Ludendorff, Hermann Wirth's Society, and Wilhelm Hauer's "German Faith Movement." An influential minority of the Nazi Party shared these religious aspirations and, after 1933, was able to win almost a monopoly of the religious education of young Germany. Their manifesto was to be read in Rosenberg's *Mythus des Zwanzigsten Jahrhunderts* (1930), where Christianity, purged of Judaism and the degrading notion of sin, was founded again on the myth of German blood and the German soul. All denominations should unite on this.

BARTHIANISM. Among the clergy, meanwhile, the diametrically opposed tendency of "dialectical theology," of the neo-Reformation movement, was spreading like wildfire through the 1920's, taking its cue from Karl Barth's *Commentary on Romans* (1919). The theologians of crisis radically attacked all attempts to identify Christian faith with cultural, social, or political programs. They sprang from Swiss Christian socialism, with its critique of domesticated bourgeois Christianity, but they were now also suspicious of Christian socialism itself. All such forms of "hyphenated Christianity" seemed to be tainted by humanism, by the notion that man could heal himself. The Barthians recovered the conviction of the Reformers that man stands naked and helpless before God, who alone can forgive and who is genuinely and unconditionally Sovereign. On these grounds they resisted the temptation to which many German theological liberals succumbed, of identifying Christianity with the renascent nationalist enthusiasm. Professor Hirsch, on the other hand, reproached Barth as having no historical sense and no capacity for passionate participation in the creative process by which a national community was being reborn.

"GERMAN CHRISTIANS." In these circumstances, with nearly all Protestant clergy nationalist and reactionary in politics, and with many Protestants identifying their religion closely with nationalism, the Nazis came to power in 1933. The year before, they had organized a church party, the "Evangelical Nazis," or as Hitler preferred, the "German Christians." With the Nazi revolution these "German Christians" set out to capture the Protestant Church. They would exploit the widespread impatience with the divisions among the churches and with the remoteness of the churches from the people. With the support of the triumphant Nazi Party they demanded a unification of all churches into one church for the Reich, a church which should be purged of half-Germans. Thus was launched in 1933 the great church struggle in Protestant Germany, a struggle which produced shameful betrayal as well as great heroism and many martyrdoms, and which tore German Protestantism into fragments even more irreconcilable than the earlier confessional and local differentiations.

THE NEW CHURCH CONSTITUTION. Under the German Christian pressure for ecclesiastical unification, the Federation of Churches appointed a committee to draw up a constitution for one national church with a governing synod and Reichsbishop. But when the German Christians tried to force their candidate Müller into that office, the Council of the Federation nominated the universally respected head of the Inner Mission, Pastor Bodelschwingh. Having failed of their coup, the German Christians then turned against the new administration and forced both Bodelschwingh and President Kapler of the Federation to resign. The government appointed a Commissar for church affairs, who dismissed pastors illegally right and left and made new appointments. Müller announced that he was assuming the presidency vacated by Kapler, and the Commissar Jaeger recognized him as the head of the Church of the Old Prussian Union. And when in the summer the Federation Assembly approved the new constitution and elections were called to acclaim the new Reichsbishop, all the machinery of terrorism and propaganda, including an appeal by Hitler himself on the eve of the election, were used to "elect" the German Christian candidate.

But although the Nazis had won this travesty of an election and had thrown church administration into chaos, the growing opposition had consolidated into a definite group which won a startling number of votes in the face of Party pressure. The group was called "Evangel und Kirche" (the Gestapo would not let them use the title "Evangelische Kirche") and its chief leaders were Barth (now professor of theology at Bonn) and Asmussen. Their opposition was not political, but religious. The church, they maintained, was not to be conformed to a state, a party, or a *Weltanschauung*, but only to Christ. They opposed the attempt to "Aryanize" it and called upon the German Christians to clear themselves of the heresy represented by the Tannenberg Bund, Hermann Wirth, and Bergmann.

In September the break was sharper at the meetings of the first national synod under the new constitution and of the synod of the Old Prussian Union. The "Evangel und Kirche" group walked out of the Prussian synod in protest when the German Christian majority voted to expel from church office all those with Jewish grandparents or with wives so tainted. The Pastors' Emergency League found 2,500 pastors to sign a pledge not to compromise the nature of the church as defined by the confessions by enforcing the Aryan paragraph. Two thousand sent a petition to the national synod. A memorial, signed among others by Niemöeller and Jakobi, protested against the Aryan paragraph, against arbitrary intervention in church government, and against the pressure to preach nationalism. Twelve New Testament professors cited biblical evidence to prove that Jews must be eligible to Christian sacraments and church office. The two parties were estimated at this time as of about equal strength, with 2,500 actively involved in each of the New Reformation and the German Christian parties. The great majority, about 15,000 pastors, were still uncommitted.

THE CONFESSING CHURCH. Hundreds and thousands of simple Christians who had not understood what was at stake were enlightened in November when one Dr. Krause addressed twenty thousand German Christians in the Sport Palast and let the cat out of the bag. Krause proposed that the New Testament be revised, in part to clarify the German ancestry of Jesus, and that the Old Testament be dropped altogether and a separate church be set up for Jewish Christians. The New Reformation Movement tripled to seven thousand, and even the cautious Lutheran bishops of Bavaria, Baden, Hannover, Hesse, and Württemberg came to their support. There was no more possibility that the German Christians could unite the church. A considerable section of German Protestantism was convinced that the very essence of the Christian faith was at stake and that no compromise was permissible. Believing that the machinery of church government held by the Nazis was no longer Christian, they organized as a church in opposition, the so-called "Confessing Church." In May 1934 this church held a synod at Barmen, and in opposition to the German Christian program drew up in six points their manifesto, the Barmen Confession. In the fall a Provisional Church Administration was organized and was recognized as the legitimate government by those Lutheran *Landeskirchen* which had not yet been taken over by Müller's administration.

From the end of 1933, however, the Confessing Church found itself in the position of Christianity in Russia in the unequal struggle against modern totalitarianism. All the means of mass communication—the radio, the press, the movies—were in the hands of the enemy. Religious news was banned from the general press and the church could make no effective reply to the stream of attacks and misrepresentation. All youth, meanwhile, were forced into the Nazi youth organizations which were controlled by some of the more extreme proponents of the new paganism. With education and youth activities in Nazi hands, it was hard to see how Christianity could outlive the older generation.

But although Nazi indoctrination was perverting the generation who would come to the fore after the war, there was still fight in the Confessing Church. The Provisional Church Administration issued a proclamation against the pagan press and its "blood and soil." The Gestapo arrested seven hundred pastors and warned five thousand more. A Reichsminister for Church Affairs, named Kerrl, was appointed, and he confiscated the funds of the Confessing group, forbade them to raise more, or to organize, or to train ministerial candidates. These things they continued to do, as best they could, underground.

In 1936 the anti-Comintern pact and Hitler's league with

Franco signalized the drift toward war which increasingly distracted attention from the church conflict. A last dramatic flare-up occurred the following year. Kerrl had proclaimed that true Christianity was not that confessed by the creed, but was represented by the Nazi Party. In the resulting uproar Hitler ordered a new election, and then, apparently fearing its result, postponed it. Pastors were arrested all through the spring and, indeed, until practically the whole leadership of the Confessing Church, including Niemöeller, were behind bars. There were demonstrations, but the Gestapo held them down. In June came the Oxford and Edinburgh conferences, to which from Germany went only the Baptists, Methodists, and Old Catholics, who paid for their passage by testifying that there was freedom of religion in Nazi Germany. But the laity were wearied with the hopeless struggle and were, like all others, fascinated by the terrifying international situation, as Nazis fought in Spain and conspired in Poland and Czechoslovakia.

In 1938 Austria was annexed and in the fall millions of Germans thanked God for Chamberlain and Munich. Confessing Churchmen held services of confession for personal and also for *national* sins. The salaries of the ministers involved were cancelled. In the government, meanwhile, the extremists—Himmler, Ley, and Goebbels—came increasingly to the fore, and the murderous slaughter of Jews became brazen and open. Confessing Christians, such as Pastor Grüber of Berlin, labored for the rescue of Jews until they themselves were sent to concentration camps. In the war the witness of the Confessing Church merged with the Christian Resistance all over Europe against the Nazis. Perhaps one-eighth of the German people were already disaffected because of the religious issue when the war began. The vast majority still did not believe that it was the deliberate intention of the Nazi leaders to wipe out Christianity, and they could not face the bitter truth that the only hope for a Christian, or even an honorable, Germany was the defeat of Nazi Germany in war.

Chapter 30

GREAT BRITAIN AND THE COMMONWEALTH

Perhaps the most conspicuous general feature of British religious life between wars was the catastrophic acceleration in that decline of institutional Christianity which had been perceptible since the end of the nineteenth century. Social movements had much to do with it. As people left the countryside and rural parishes to camp as nomads in urban apartments, few of them established new ties with churches. New inventions radically transformed Sunday social customs. First the bicycle and then the automobile contributed to the week-end habit with all classes, and other diversions—soccer, the movies, the radio, the Sunday newspapers—offered alternative occupations for the day. The net result was that, whereas in 1850 probably at least half the population attended church regularly, by 1950 nine-tenths were quite emancipated from the custom. The bulk of them were not actively hostile to the church, as in several formerly Roman Catholic countries. A significant proportion evidently still listened with interest to radio presentation of the Christian perspective on various public questions. But only a tiny remnant still found any significance in what went on in church buildings on Sunday.

World War I was a terrible shock, wholly unexpected in its destruction, horror, and duration. One might have supposed that the war would have restored the credit of the Christian interpretation of the human situation as against the secular utopians, but the churches had so far shared the prewar optimism that they were in no position to offer intellectual guidance when the storms came. One of the most conspicuous theological currents of the prewar generation had been the attempt so

focused on ceremonies in worship, and there were still many complaints of priests imposing practices detested by congregations, and still scandalous outrages as services were interrupted. The Catholic minority had proved itself the most dedicated and militant, if often the most fantastically foolish, section of the Anglican clergy. This party also provided English Christianity with its boldest leadership in social ethics. One major controversy was occasioned by the attempt to gain parliamentary approval for a revision of the *Book of Common Prayer*. It was universally agreed that a revision was needed for many reasons, but the book proposed was twice rejected by Parliament, the last time in 1928. The notion of sacrifice set forth in the communion service, and the practice of reservation of the consecrated elements seemed offensive to the Protestant majority, who had been rendered suspicious by the conversations in the preceding years between Anglo-Catholics and Roman Catholics at Malines. Many Anglicans were offended that non-Anglicans should vote on such an issue in Parliament, but non-Anglicans pointed out that Anglican privileges rested on non-Anglican sufferance and raised questions about the honesty of Anglican bishops who encouraged disregard in practice of the decision of Parliament. Talk of disestablishment was for a time widespread. Bitterness subsided in the 1930's, however, and one heard less criticism of the establishment among Free Churchmen. A remarkable evidence of the increasing internal peace of the church was the co-operation on all sides to produce an "Agreed Syllabus" for the teaching of religion in the schools under the Education Act of 1944. Nothing comparable would have been conceivable in the United States at that time.

Attempts to meet the new missionary demands on the churches led to curious borrowings and crosscurrents. Free Churchmen and Anglo-Catholics shared in a revival of biblical authority and preaching and in a new sense of the church as a witnessing fellowship. "Let the church be the church" was the slogan of the 1930's and referred in Britain to this aspiration for a distinctly Christian common life within the congregation. The characteristically Baptist and Congregationalist "church meeting" found Anglican emulators, as also the actualization of the general priesthood in "cell groups." There was increasing unrest over the meaninglessness of Anglican baptism, and even proposals to defer baptism until adolescence after instruction. These ideas on the nature of the worshiping congregation found expression also in architecture. Hardly any of the new Anglican churches of this period were in the Victorian Gothic style with monastic chancels still favored in the United States. The new designs all sought to stress the corporate sense. Fonts and communion tables were moved from corners into the midst of the congregation. A new practice of regular weekly "parish communions" followed by church breakfasts spread rapidly. As the nation became a mission field, the church form of the first three centuries became a relevant model. Anglicans and Free Churchmen had an increasing sense of common concern and borrowed increasingly from each other.

DECLINE OF THE FREE CHURCHES. The changing situation of the English churches affected the several traditions in various ways. One of the startling phenomena of the second and third decades of the twentieth century was the decline of the English Free Churches. Nonconformity had seemed to be gaining on the state church all through the nineteenth century and had reached a triumph of power in the Liberal landslide of 1906, which put 157 liberal Free Churchmen into Parliament as well as many more on various local governmental bodies. But as we have already noted, liberal biblical criticism left the pulpit very uncertain when it was once off the topic of social reform. And precisely in the social and political area the Free Churchmen suffered another catastrophe. The labor movement had been largely nursed into power under Liberal auspices and Free Church influence. But now came a sharp split in both respects. The trade unions rapidly became the most notable political force in Great Britain after World War I. The Liberal Party found itself caught between organized labor and the Conservatives, with the interests of its propertied members largely inclining to the latter. In the 1920's the Liberals nearly disappeared from the political scene. And Free Churchmen were baffled as new political forces suddenly elbowed them from the national stage and made their traditional political orientation seem irrelevant.

In still another sense the Free Churches suffered. The increasing centralization of economic life in great corporations, and the increasing role of the state meant that for most Christians the critical social and political and cultural decisions were now made on a regional or national scale. Only a regionally or nationally organized church could address itself to these questions. The inherited localism and congregational autonomy of Congregationalists and Baptists now appeared as a crippling inhibition against doing the work of the Church in the modern world. All the Free Churches had been moving toward increased centralization with the use of moderators, superintendents, and synods. The National Free Church Council had as its unofficial archbishop in the second decade of the new century, the Baptist W. H. Shakespeare, who was convinced that the days of denominationalism were over and looked toward a "United Free Church" and even ultimate union with Anglicans. In this he could not carry the rank and file with him, but in the generation between world wars the Free Churches felt a widespread sense of frustration and ineffectiveness as a result of their ecclesiastical structure. Anglicanism and Roman Catholicism, by contrast, could take a lead on public questions and often did so in new and impressive ways.

One of the great advantages of Roman Catholicism and Anglicanism over many Protestant bodies in this period was that they were organized to embody a world perspective. In a generation when every informed and convinced Christian must think in world-wide terms, it was frustrating to be a Baptist or Congregationalist. To be sure, the chief Anglo-American denominations had organized world bodies in the nineteenth century—the Lambeth Conferences of Anglican bishops (1868), the Presbyterian and Reformed Alliance (1877), the Methodists (1891), the Congregationalists (1891), and the Baptists' World Alliance (1905). But of these only the Anglicans' really made much difference, for with an episcopal system the decisive group in the whole church was involved in the international enterprise in a continuing and responsible fashion. Overseas, Anglican bishops had increased from twelve in 1850 to a total of about four hundred in 1930, and the whole consciousness of English Anglicans was now changed. They were no longer merely members of the state church, but members of a world-wide communion, held together by the Prayer Book and episcopal order, but in most countries not established. This consciousness was stimulated by constant preaching to the theme in a way equaled in none of the Free Churches or the Church of Scotland. And under the leadership of two great churchmen, Davidson and Temple, the Archbishop of Canterbury came to occupy an unprecedented position in Christendom.

TEMPLE AND SOCIAL ETHICS. The greatest Anglican leader of the generation between wars was William Temple, successively bishop of Manchester, Archbishop of York, and Archbishop of Canterbury. He was the greatest popularizer of Christian social thought and the embodiment of the claim of the Church to have a significant judgment on public questions. Without him the two great church conferences on such problems—the Conference on Politics, Economics, and Citizenship (C.O.P.E.C.) at Birmingham in 1924 and that at Malvern in 1941—would not have been possible. He was also one of the major figures in the World Conferences held at Oxford and Edinburgh in 1937 and a chief architect of the World Council of Churches. It would be hard to think of a more significant churchman in non-Roman Christendom in his day, and certainly Anglican history in the period would have been infinitely less notable without him.

C.O.P.E.C. was the climactic expression of the "social gospel" movement of the whole English-speaking world. Built on four years of study and discussion groups of many sorts, it gathered together an extraordinary amount of materials on the baffling variety of social, economic, and political problems in the modern world and sought to formulate "Christian" answers to them. The problems were treated generally on the basis of humanitarian idealism, with little or no reference to Christian authority or Christian community as such. And the diversity of views on pacifism, divorce, and socialism at the Conference reflected the divisions among idealists generally in the 1920's. The labors and findings of the Conference were by far the most important preparation for the World Conference on Life and Work at Stockholm the following year, and they represented a level of competence and comprehensiveness never rivaled in comparable American enterprises.

Analysis of the social problem, however, accomplished little by way of remedy, and the preaching of social ideals and reforms from pulpits seemed to have no effect whatever on unemployment, crime, international anarchy, and the disintegration of marriage and the family. The bulk of the electorate and the government pinned their hope on the progress, if not the perfectibility, of man by applied science and legislation without benefit of clergy. In the thirties the breakdown of the League of Nations and the extension of the totalitarian state in Russia, Italy, Germany, and other Continental countries sobered many. The British churches, however, again gave no clear leadership in the interpretation of these new currents, but exhibited the same confusion as the general population. By the time of the Oxford Conference the churches were at least disillusioned enough about their public influence to place high on their agenda the need of putting their own house in order and of developing a pattern of relations and life within the church which might in itself be a testimony to the world. The Malvern Conference of 1941 developed further this concern for the character of the church and the theological bases for social decisions. The Conference was dominated by a group of Anglo-Catholics who had for some years been sponsoring an annual Summer School of Sociology and whose program emphasized a guild socialism based upon widespread private holdings. In the situation these views seemed highly academic and esoteric. But through World War II some of the best thinking in the world on the place of the church in the modern world was to be read in the pages of the *Christian News Letter*, edited by J. H. Oldham, Temple, and Kathleen Bliss.

ECUMENICAL EFFORTS. None of the churches, or at least their best leaders, felt that the divided character of institutional Christianity was justifiable in the twentieth century, and the sense of a common ecumenical reality grew steadily on all hands. The different traditions were variously affected by this leaven. The group least changed was that of the largest denominational family in the English-speaking world—the Baptists and Disciples. Their convictions that the church should be composed only of convinced adult believers and only of autonomous local congregations excluded them from participation in any projects looking toward more inclusive intercongregational organization and action.

There was more possibility of uninhibited development among Presbyterians and Methodists, and to some extent, Congregationalists. Before World War I a process of consolidation within these several denominational families was well under way. The merger in 1900 of the United Presbyterians of Scotland and the Free Church, as the "United Free Church," stimulated Presbyterian reunions around the world—in South Africa and India, in Australia and New Zealand. The English Methodists also followed suit, constituting in 1907 the United Methodists out of three minor Methodist bodies. Both in Scotland and in England still further plans of reunion continued through the war. In Scotland the proposed reunion of the United Free Church with the established Church of Scotland was complicated by the relation to the state. The Church of Scotland secured in 1921 an Enabling Act in which by sacrificing a sixth of its income it won formal recognition of its right to self-determination in church matters. And in 1929 the reunited Church of Scotland came into being, including the overwhelming majority of Scottish Presbyterians, and with a communicant membership of one quarter of the total population. No other Protestant national church included so large a proportion of its people. Shortly afterwards, in 1932, the three chief remaining Methodist bodies in England united. Comparable consolidations were under discussion among American Methodists and Presbyterians in the 1930's and bore results in the former case in 1939 with the creation of the Methodist Church out of the three chief Methodist bodies in the United States.

Within the English-speaking world generally, the process of institutional consolidation *across* denominational lines seemed promising in this period only within this group of traditions, the Methodist, Presbyterian and Congregationalist. In Australia and New Zealand negotiations were carried on among Presbyterians, Methodists, and Congregationalists. In Great Britain Presbyterians and Congregationalists failed in two attempts at merger, and in Ireland Presbyterians and Methodists explored closer relations. United States Methodists and Presbyterians agreed that they had no issue of principle keeping them apart, but that they should consolidate within their denominational families before attempting negotiations across families. These three denominations formed the main body of the Church of Christ in Japan, the United Church of Christ in the Philippines, and the Church of Christ in China. In North and South India and Ceylon, together with the novel participation of the Anglicans, they were the chief parties to the union negotiations.

UNITED CHURCH OF CANADA. The most instructive of the mergers actually effected in this period was that of the United Church of Canada of 1925. This merger consisted essentially of Methodists and Presbyterians, with a handful of Congregational churches, and came as a climax of negotiations begun twenty years before. The uniting churches represented a confluence of no less than forty originally distinct bodies gradually consolidating through nineteen previous mergers. The Basis of Union had been originally devised in 1908, was voted on by the churches, and was revised and approved in 1912-1914. But the interruption of World War I and the fact that about a quarter of the presbyteries of the Presbyterian Church opposed the merger led to a postponement of action until after the war. The greatest pressure for the merger came from the needs of the Canadian West, with its thin population scattered over immense distances. From the first publication of the Basis, union congregations had formed in the West, using the Basis as a constitution. Church leaders began to fear that a new denomination would have been created if the merger should not be completed. The objection from the Presbyterians was largely localized in the wealthier congregations of Ontario. Presbyterians were more churchly in feeling, definite in doctrine, dignified in worship, conservative on public questions, and more impressed by their own social distinction. The greatest difficulty in practice proved to be diverse conceptions of the ministry, as resting respectively on the "call" of the local congregation, with Presbyterians and Congregationalists, and as assigned by the "stationing committee" of the Methodist annual conference with no congregational meeting at all. The greatest bitterness at the moment arose over property questions, for the enabling legislation from the civil government let every congregation vote once again on the issue. About 30 per cent of the Presbyterians declined to enter the United Church. They found themselves long on property but short of ministers and active laymen, and in the following years the Presbyterian rump lost numbers, whereas the United Church prospered as the largest Protestant body in Canada. The worship of the United Church was assisted by a directory prepared by the scholars of Emmanuel College, Toronto, which was perhaps the best liturgical work of North American Protestants in the period.

ANGLICANS AND CHURCH UNITY. When Anglicans were actively engaged in such ecumenical ventures, discussion tended to focus about their view that the organ for more inclusive church fellowship must be of a specific sort, the historic episcopate. The discussion of this proposal took place in many parts of the world, between the Church of England and the Church of Scotland, American Episcopalians and Presbyterians, and most important of all, in connection with the proposed United Church of South India.

A major landmark in this latter group of negotiations and discussions was the "Appeal to all Christians" issued by the Lambeth Conference of Anglican bishops in 1920. The reunion committee of the Anglican bishops oriented itself primarily to their most pressing problem, that of relations with nonepiscopal denominations in the English-speaking world. They acknowledged this broken fellowship to be contrary to God's will and confessed an Anglican share in this guilt of schism. And in unprecedented breadth of view, they recognized the "spiritual reality" of nonepiscopal ministries, which had been "manifestly blessed and owned by the Holy Spirit as effective means of grace." They declared that they desired no repudiation by such ministers of their ordinations in any future union, but suggested that some type of mutual supplemental ordination or commissioning of ministers might be a means of bringing together the gifts of ministry contained in the Anglican and in non-Anglican traditions.

This "Appeal" was sent to the heads of all churches and

brought scores of replies from all over the world in the 1920's. In negotiations with English Free Churches, the Church of Scotland, the American Presbyterians, and other groups, the major difficulty soon appeared to be the lack of agreement within Anglicism as to what was meant by "the historic episcopate." Was it simply the oldest, the most widespread, and evidently the most practicable way of symbolizing and actualizing the community among Christian congregations? If so, there were many Presbyterians, Methodists, and Congregationalists who were ready to discuss a union based upon it, provided there were recognition of the full validity of the non-episcopal ministries by which they had been served for centuries. Or was the "historic episcopate," as many Anglo-Catholics urged, so essential to the very existence of a Church that non-episcopal churches never had been really true churches and could only become such by submission to episcopal churches? None of the non-episcopal churches could be interested in negotiations set upon this presupposition. But the Anglicans were not decided as to what was their view on this point. They opened negotiations with Scots and American Presbyterians by intimating the former basis and then broke off discussions when their Anglo-Catholic wing demanded the second position. The case was essentially the same with regard to the English Free Churches.

Two chief devices for bridging the gap between episcopal and non-episcopal ministries were debated in these years. One was the plan of mutual supplemental ordination or commissioning, by which each of two uniting churches would authorize ministers of the other to serve its people. This device, however, seemed to confuse ordination and installation, by overlooking the fact that ordination was by intention to serve the universal church. If all ministers had to be supplementarily reordained every time their church united with some other body, ordination in some parts of the world might come to be so frequent as to destroy its whole meaning. And the mutual aspect was in any case artificial, since the non-episcopal churches had raised no questions about Anglican ministers and did not suppose they had anything essential to add to their ordination.

UNITED CHURCH OF SOUTH INDIA. The other procedure was actually adopted in the most notable merger of the half-century, the formation of the United Church of South India, completed in 1947. In South India the chief bodies concerned were in origin Presbyterians and Congregationalists, who had already united, Methodists, and the Anglican Church in the area. It was thus a merger of the same traditions which had united in the United Church of Canada, which lacked the historic episcopate, with the Anglican Church, which claimed to possess it. And although other issues were raised, the problem of the episcopate was the central issue in the proposed merger. The South Indian proposal frankly recognized that this was not a matter for mutual supplementary ordination, but that non-episcopal churches would acquire by this merger something which they had hitherto lacked. But while all future ordinations in the United Church would be by bishops in the Anglican succession, along with presbyters, at the same time the existing non-episcopally ordained ministers of the Uniting Churches would be recognized as full and valid ministers, without reordination or supplemental ordination. This arrangement would continue for a period of thirty years, by which time very few non-episcopally ordained ministers would be left in the church. Then the church would decide on its rules for the future.

This proposal was the chief preoccupation of the Lambeth Conference of Anglican bishops in 1930. Old Catholic and Orthodox delegates were in attendance, and the delegation from the English Free Churches was snubbed. And with regard to South India, the bishops announced that if the basis were accepted they would be unable to hold communion with the United Church, although they would recognize it as in some sense part of the church universal. Anglo-Catholics were cultivating relations with various Catholic and Orthodox bodies, nearly all remote geographically—the Church of Rumania, the Russian Orthodox in Paris, the Old Catholics, as well as (for a brief period in the twenties) the Church of Rome. They had no sympathy with any overtures toward Protestants. It seemed clear that the "bridge church" was not long enough to reach from one shore to the other and could only be anchored firmly to either shore by relinquishing the other, or by being divided in the middle.

BRITISH ROMAN CATHOLICS. A word should be said finally about the Roman Catholics, who gained ground relatively throughout much of the English-speaking world in this period. The steady migration of the Irish continued to build up the Roman Catholic bloc in Scotland until it was about half the size of the Church of Scotland, and in England until it was about equal in constituency to the Church of England. Protestants were being driven from Eire meanwhile by organized economic and social pressures. The British Roman Catholics laid great emphasis on their school system, winning generous subsidies from the government. A number of converts made some of their most distinguished figures, Christopher Dawson, Shane Leslie, Ronald Knox, and Alfred Noyes. The international character of the Roman Church was one of its great strengths. Its authoritarian aspect was also a recommendation to many in the great pressures of the day.

Chapter 31

THE INSTITUTIONAL CONSOLIDATION OF AMERICAN EVANGELICALISM

In the generation between world wars, the urban trend which had been dominant in the United States since about 1890 gave a new face to the land. The characteristic social structure had now become the metropolitan area, with its suburbs, satellite cities, and dependent rural territory. Some ninety great cities held half the population of the nation, and these formed the centers of political and cultural power and influence. The older town and country culture of the nineteenth century still resisted the new metropolitan mentality, especially in the South and West, but could no longer hope to master it.

In a large number of these cities half or more of the population were foreign born or the children of foreign born, which meant that they were the deposit of the last great wave of immigration and were predominantly Roman Catholic. The Protestant church, meanwhile, remained in organization and mentality the most rural and least adapted to the new urban culture of all major American institutions. The prevailing Protestant outlook was still that of highly individualistic Evangelical pietism, denominationally, if not congregationally, autonomous. This is the pattern which had proved most successful on the frontier and which had raised the Baptists, Methodists, and Disciples to total a full half of American Protestants. However, the traditions of the "right wing"—the Lutherans, Episcopalians, and Presbyterians—along with that of the Roman Catholics—seemed better equipped for the changed situation. The history of the generation could be viewed as a struggle to develop Evangelical denominationalism toward a more corporate and institutional type of Christianity, amid a general contraction of Christian influence in the culture.

The decline of Christian influence generally in the national culture was not as marked as in European countries or Great Britain, but it was still noticeable. In America it was concurrent with a continuing extension of church membership and nominal adherence. Commenting on American social trends in 1933, the Hoover Commission observed, "Church and family have lost many of their regulatory influences over behavior, while industry and government have assumed a larger degree of control." One might take as an index of the culture its periodicals, newspapers, and popular literature. The circulation of such literature increased several times over in the first half of the twentieth century, in similar ratio to the expansion of secondary and higher education. But the Christian ingredient in this rapidly swelling flood grew ever smaller. The Protestant press declined catastrophically, both in circulation and in the scope of its subject matter. The proportion of articles on Christianity in general magazines also declined noticeably, and the tone indicated a general decrease of respect as well as of interest. "The most fundamental change in the intellectual life of the United States," commented an analyst for the Hoover Commission, "is the apparent shift from biblical authority and religious sanctions to scientific and factual authority and sanctions."

A similar trend could be observed with regard to the curriculum and tone of public education. Secondary education in America had been pioneered by the Protestant churches. But in the first thirty or forty years of the twentieth century the Protestant churches retired almost completely from this field, whereas public high schools multiplied ten times or more. In the curricula of these public schools, elementary as well as secondary, the Christian perspective steadily lost ground before that of a scientific humanism. Even in higher education, although the churches still supported and controlled about a third of the whole enterprise at mid-century, the Protestants had come perilously close to losing any sense of distinctive direction. The great growth was in state universities, and here the significance of Christian faith was minimal. The American people were to be nearly illiterate religiously in the second half of the twentieth century. The churches were still putting their trust in the nineteenth-century amateur enterprise of the Sunday Schools, in which about one-half hour a week of unevenly attended sessions, conducted by untrained volunteer teachers, was expected to supply the Christian perspective increasingly expurgated from the ever more extended work week of the public school. "Released-time" or "dismissed-time" religious instruction in connection with public schools was also experimented with, but proved difficult to organize effectively within what were understood to be the constitutional requirements of separation of the churches from public education.

OVER-CHURCHING AND UNTRAINED MINISTERS. This progressive loss of influence of Protestant thought in American life was heightened by a widespread anti-intellectual pietist obscurantism and the resentment this occasioned among educated people. The discrepancy was marked and increasing between the level of public education and of culture generally, and the level of the Protestant preacher and Sunday school teacher in the nineteenth-century pietist tradition, which put its trust in the communication of piety with a minimum of ideas. This anti-intellectualism, in turn, was strengthened by the prodigious over-churching in America. In the 1930's there were 164,000 white Protestant local churches in the country, of which at least 100,000 should have been closed or consolidated. In over thirty states, the rural population actually decreased. Only about 18,000 congregations had a membership of at least 350, which might be taken as the minimum size to support an effective program. Half of the total were served only on a part-time basis. And two-thirds of the men entering the Protestant ministry were in effect lay preachers, incompetent to give adequate intellectual and ethical guidance. The untrained ministry had proved its efficiency in evangelism and in money-raising. Where it could not compete with the trained minority was in the nurture and training of a congregation and its leadership in the witness to the larger community. A ministry adequately trained to cope with the rising cultural level and the increasingly complex social situation could have been secured only by a tremendous process of merger and consolidation of congregations, even across denominational lines. And, in fact, sectarian conviction was largely gone, save perhaps in the

South. Widespread transmigration of both clergy and laity, especially in the cities, where from a quarter to a half of transfers crossed denominational lines, signified an increasing approximation to a common type. But the denominational organizations remained tenacious of their autonomy and conveyed the general aspect still of "utter incoherence and colossal wastefulness." The greater parish efficiency of the Roman Catholic clergy and their markedly greater success in education, the press, and public issues demonstrated the price the Protestants were paying for their divisions.

FUNDAMENTALIST CONTROVERSY. We observed in an earlier chapter (see above, p. 273) how American revivalist Evangelicalism had produced a "fundamentalist" protest of proportions unknown in most European countries. Much of the popular fundamentalism is to be understood as the working theology of this great body of untrained lay-preachers who constituted the bulk of the Protestant ministry. World War I had postponed the great struggle between this popular pietist theology and the new currents in the seminaries and urban churches. Great fundamentalist conferences in Philadelphia in 1918 and 1919 now launched a campaign to capture the seminaries, mission boards, periodicals, and, in general, the administrative agencies of several denominations considered to be tainted with "modernism."

In the Presbyterian Church the General Assembly had twice affirmed the Five Fundamentals by a majority vote, and in 1924 an attempt was made to bind all ordinands to this program. The "liberal" presbytery of New York, meanwhile, was required by the General Assembly to regularize the preaching by the Baptist Harry Emerson Fosdick in the First Presbyterian Church of that city, and was reprimanded for ordaining two graduates of Union Seminary who declined to affirm belief in the Virgin Birth. The fundamentalist drive was blocked, however, by an "Affirmation" of ministers who refused to accept modification of the church's confession save by constitutional procedures. Dr. Fosdick declined the invitation of the Assembly to enter the Presbyterian ministry (and accept Presbyterian discipline). He left the First Church to become the most famous preacher of his generation from the pulpit of Riverside

Church in New York. The most distinguished of the Presbyterian fundamentalists, Professor Machen of Princeton, led a small secession which became known eventually as the "Orthodox Presbyterian Church" and founded Westminster Theological Seminary.

The Northern Baptists, similarly, were nearly split over the issue. The fundamentalists developed the deliberate policy of putting a "Bible school" beside each of the chief liberal seminaries of the denomination, whereby a larger number of ministers could be produced by shorter, less rigorous, strictly fundamentalist training. The Disciples were even more badly split; probably the only thing which saved them from actual schism was the fact that the denominational structure was already so loose and anarchic that it could accommodate what were in effect rival missionary, periodical, and religious education agencies.

In general the denominations of the East and North resisted the fundamentalist drive, but in the South and West the old revivalist Evangelicalism was still little alloyed with theological liberalism and the social gospel. The South was dominated by Baptists and Methodists. Southern Baptists, the largest single Protestant denomination, were overwhelmingly fundamentalist. This regional character of the theological parties is illustrated by the efforts to pass "monkey bills" outlawing the teaching of evolution in public schools. Four state legislatures —those of Texas, Tennessee, Arkansas, and Mississippi—actually passed such laws. Similar bills failed in seven other states. The Tennessee law was put to the test in the famous Scopes trial of 1925 at which William Jennings Bryan debated with Clarence Darrow. Thereafter interest rapidly waned. There were few heresy trials, and few efforts were made in the latter half of our period to capture denominational organizations. In their own region and in their own educational and social strata, however, the fundamentalists continued actively the Evangelical heritage, remaining a very substantial part of American Protestantism. It was notable also that they increasingly inherited the foreign missionary enterprise which, in the 1920's and 1930's lost ground rapidly in the liberal churches in terms of financial support, missionary personnel, and the vocation to missions.

PROHIBITION. If we now attempt to survey the social and political influence of the Protestant churches, their first conspicuous social expression after the war was their part in the passage of the Eighteenth Amendment. Along with the anti-evolution laws, this activity now gives the appearance of having been the last political revolt of rural and small-town Protestant America against the immigrant culture of the cities which was increasingly dominating the nation. "Temperance" had been from the beginning a characteristic feature of Anglo-American Evangelicalism and was established, for example, in the Methodist "Discipline." The Women's Christian Temperance Union (1874) and the Anti-Saloon League (1895) were virtually agencies of Evangelical Protestantism. In the new industrial age additional reasons were found for setting legal limits to the high-pressure marketing program of brewers and distillers. Gasoline and alcohol, many noticed, do not mix safely, either on the highway or in the factory. But the geographical extent of state prohibition prior to the national acts indicates that the chief support came from the farm states of the South and West, precisely the area which was to find the greatest support also for anti-evolution laws. Opposition, on the other hand, centered in the Lutheran states west of Chicago and was especially strong in the New England and Middle Atlantic states, particularly the big cities, which were now swamped with the most recent Roman Catholic immigration. New York City alone, it was observed, held more saloons than all the states south of the Mason-Dixon line. And particularly in these areas local officials did not seriously attempt to enforce the laws. The repeal of the Eighteenth Amendment in 1933, in addition to its other effects, dealt another blow to the declining political strength of this nineteenth-century backbone of the nation.

INTERNATIONALISM. In the urban congregations, where virtually all the trained Protestant ministers were stationed, the recovery of a sense of Christian responsibility for the structure of society which had begun with the prewar "social gospel" continued to establish itself. The war proved only a temporary shock to the idealistic optimism of the school of Rauschenbusch. These optimists really believed that it was a "war to end war," and they provided the chief political support for Wilson's dream of a federation of nations and a parliament of the world. Especially in the prosperity of the 1920's, this preoccupation with international relations largely displaced industrial relations as the primary concern of the "social gospel." The main current of internationalist opinion in the United States was very closely related to the Protestant churches—supporting the League, disarmament proposals, the World Court, and the Kellogg-Briand Pact. Widespread discussion of the intrigues of "munitions-makers," as exposed about 1930, increased the sense of shame which many churchmen felt for their uncritical support of World War I. In the early 1930's a number of major denominational assemblies "repudiated" war, or defined it as "sin." A considerable number of Protestant ministers declared that they would never support another war. Student Christian groups were especially affected by this pacifist sentiment. Its core was faith in humanitarian democracy and idealism, the belief that war was unnecessary and wasteful and could be stopped if men of good will would put their minds to it. Those who were of this opinion were increasingly disillusioned by the belligerent totalitarians of the 1930's, and the majority of ministers were ready to support World War II as a grim necessity. But the sense of international responsibility remained particularly strong in this Protestant tradition, and its ministers were among the first and most persistent in attempting to direct the thinking of the nation to the issues of postwar reconstruction. The Conference at Delaware, Ohio, in 1942 on a "Just and Durable Peace" was influential in the shaping of the United Nations. The theological rationale of this political tendency, meanwhile, had become more sophisticated and realistic in the 1930's. At the time of World War II no other major nation was still so much influenced in its foreign policy by church opinion.

SOCIAL AND ECONOMIC ETHICS. On the matter of industrial relations and "social service," meanwhile, the chief center of leadership in the "social gospel" after World War I was no longer in the several denominational commissions but was the newly strengthened Federal Council. Most significant, perhaps, were the reports occasionally released of critical controversies, often when the newspapers were conspicuously unfair, and the annual "Labor Sunday" encyclicals, which gradually

won a substantial hearing. The work of the social service commission of the Federal Council in the former type of activity
was often the only evidence of Protestant concern for groups
which felt themselves unjustly treated. Owing to the denominational and congregational anarchy of the Protestant churches,
the denominations with the best-trained ministers—for example,
Congregationalists, Presbyterians, and Episcopalians—were
generally the most privileged, politically conservative, and unsympathetic to labor. The literature of the "social gospel"
leaders, consequently, represented a movement on behalf of,
rather than by, the underprivileged, on the part of a minority
group regarded with little enthusiasm by many of their own
laity. Probably their chief effect was on the ministry itself.

From the beginning the Federal Council had urged a code of
industrial relations asserting the right of labor to organize, at
the same time deprecating violence and rejecting all theories of
class war. The influence of this propaganda can be gauged,
however, from the fact that immediately after World War I a
group of employers organized an "Open-Shop Movement" to
break labor unions, and most were amazed to find themselves
opposed by ministers. About the same time the Methodist
Bishop McConnell, on behalf of the Interchurch World Movement, released a study of the steel strike which condemned the
then-current twelve-hour shift in the mills. The Federal
Council joined with the National Catholic Welfare Conference
and the leading rabbis to oppose both this practice of the steel
industry and the union-breaking campaign. As a result some
employers' associations attempted to organize a financial boycott of the Federal Council. Then began an intermittent
stream of books and articles attacking the Council as subversive,
socialist, or communist.

The Great Depression did far more to undermine general
American confidence in progress and the soundness of the social
order than the war had done. There was abroad, especially in
the churches, a mood of "national repentance" analogous to
that preached in Great Britain in World War I. After three
years of widespread suffering, the Federal Council adopted in
1932 a revised version of the Social Creed. In addition to the
familiar recommendations on the control of child and woman

labor, protection in dangerous occupations, a Sunday rest, social insurance, and a "fair wage," two new emphases were significant. The "profit motive" was identified, as in the classic Christian tradition, with avarice, and appeals to other motives, such as pride in creative work and service to the group, were urged. And the old scruples against government in business were definitely abandoned, as state control and planning of financial and economic processes for the common good were commended. The ideal of "industrial democracy," in which workers would insofar as possible share in management, was set forth, and actual government ownership and control of economic enterprises were viewed without objection. Many of the early endeavors of the New Deal in these directions were commended, although by the end of the thirties the traditional Republicanism of the upper-class denominations in the North again asserted itself vigorously.

The terrifying race riots during World War I, especially the one in Chicago, awoke leaders of the "social gospel" to this whole problem which had been little considered previously. At the beginning of the century over three-fourths of American Negroes had been living in semi-serfdom in the rural South. A great migration to the Northern cities, however, was soon under way, and was much accelerated by World War I. The American Negro was launched on the transition from peasant to industrial worker. The Christianity of the Southern Negro was generally revivalistic, other-worldly Evangelicalism in tangible continuity with the great "spirituals" of slave days. But the general cultural and intellectual level of the urban Northern Negro rose rapidly. Although the new Negro professional class tended to leave the church, a better-trained ministry also grew up in Negro churches. At the end of the period under discussion there were probably about 8,300,000 Negro church members. The 300,000 were Roman Catholic, the 8,000,000 Protestant. Of the latter, 7,500,000 were in separate Negro denominations, the largest of these being the Negro Baptists and the three Negro Methodist denominations (nine-tenths of all Negro church members are Baptists or Methodists). The remaining half-million Negro Protestants were in congregations of predominantly white denominations, such as the Meth-

ever ambiguous, to the power as well as the hope of a transformed humanity. In the specifically theological realm all this implied also a much heightened sense of the sovereignty of God. Much less was heard of the limited "democratic" God of the twenties. And with the new sense of deep-rooted sin and guilt the classical doctrines of sin, grace, forgiveness, and new life took on fresh actuality. All these new emphases were apparent in the reports of the Oxford Conference of 1937 on Church, Community, and State, in which the outlook of the American delegates stood in startling contrast to that of Americans at the Stockholm Conference a decade earlier.

MODERNIST RELIGIOUS EDUCATION. Perhaps the most dramatic indication of the major religious and theological reorientation of the early 1930's was the collapse of the modernist religious education movement. A group of educators largely influenced by the theories of John Dewey and similar "progressive" theorists had in the twenties developed a concept of religious education based on a Rousseauistic doctrine of human nature. They preferred "social experience" in the classroom to the "authoritarian indoctrination" of the pulpit, and they regarded the church as merely one of several "character-building agencies." The whole enterprise was hard hit by the depression, and when religious education slowly recovered in the churches at the very end of our period and during the War, it was increasingly shaped by a consciously Christian perspective arising from the theological revival.

In worship the new orientation was slower to manifest itself. From the beginning of the century the pietist type of worship had been in decline, in private and family worship, in the "prayer meeting," and in the regular Sunday service. It was generally replaced, however, by more aesthetically pleasing but archaistic and theologically uncertain forms involving less congregational participation. Not until after the outbreak of World War II were there any significant signs of a liturgical movement with religious and theological substance such as the Roman Catholics of Europe were experiencing.

Perhaps the most pervasive tendency of this whole generation was toward the institutionalization of Christianity. As it had not for half a century or more, American Protestantism turned to a developed theology, to more formal worship, and to a new kind of political and social responsibility requiring a higher degree of organization in the churches. The trend to the growth of centralized institutions and control was visible in every denomination, even those, such as the Baptists and Disciples, who could with difficulty justify it theoretically. There was also a great proliferation of interdenominational agencies for co-operation in specific functions, such as religious education. The Federal Council had become indispensable by the end of World War I, even while it was jealously limited in resources and powers by the denominations and widely misinterpreted and distrusted by laymen. A certain limited progress in outright denominational merger was perceptible. Opinion in the churches, especially among the ministers, generally approved this trend and was indeed ready for more radical moves.

UNIONS AND FEDERATIONS. Of organic mergers there were a dozen or so. Among the more important ones were the Lutheran consolidations, which produced the United Lutherans in 1918 and the American Lutherans in 1921. The Lutherans had been divided among themselves by the diversity of their Continental points of origin, and by their different rates of adjustment to the American scene—most significantly to the English language. They had lived apart from the main currents of American church life and had made little impact on the society about them. Throughout the generation between wars, however, Lutherans discussed consolidation, and a process of unification seemed well under way even though there were still a score of distinct Lutheran denominations at the end of the period. As they realized increasingly their common strength of five or six million, and as they became increasingly Americanized culturally, Lutherans gave signs of beginning, like the Roman Catholics in this generation (see p. 374), to play a role proportionate to their numbers on the American scene and in church life generally.

Of other organic mergers, the final reunion of the Methodists, North and South, in 1939 made the "Methodist Church" the largest and most widely distributed Protestant denomination in the country. This last reunion succeeded only after several attempts, and the comparable Presbyterian efforts in this period were not successful. Although a substantial reduction in the numbers of denominations by merger seemed desirable, there was no prospect of organic union of more than a minority of American Protestants. Of the larger denominations the two which were in the strategic position to form nuclei of consolidations of related groups were the Methodists and Presbyterians. These were also the two of the larger denominations which had the greatest possibility of uniting with each other across confessional lines. Such a union was explored in the 1920's, but action was postponed until the denominational families should be separately consolidated. If this project were to be carried through, somewhat on the pattern of the United Church of Canada, it would result in a church more than half the size of the American Roman Catholic Church. The larger part of American Protestants would still need to be related through co-operative and federating agencies.

Co-operative and federating agencies progressed more rapidly than did the movement for organic merger. In 1908 the denominations had for the first time committed themselves to continued co-operation as ecclesiastical bodies. In the postwar inflation the Federal Council budget soared to $300,000 a year, and was then cut in half by the depression. It held together at the top more than a score of denominations comprising three-fourths of American Protestantism. The only large bodies which refused to co-operate were the Southern Baptists and the Missouri Synod Lutherans. But the recognition and support of the others were minimal. The denominations jealously retained sovereignty on all policy decisions, and their financial contribution to the Federal Council was a barely visible item in their budgets, totaling only 14 per cent of its income.

There were also state and city federations with no structural ties to the Federal Council. In 1936 about fifty cities had federations with paid executives, a number which increased rapidly in the following years. These city federations usually operated on a budget equivalent to that of a local congregation of moderate size. There were scores of other city federations without staff, but their effectiveness was limited. The difficulty with all city federations, and even more with state federations, was that local churches were generally bound to denominational programs, patterns, campaigns, and the like, and were unable to co-operate effectively across denominational lines on related matters. The stronger denominations were generally unwilling to give local federations real responsibility. The chief function of these federations was to moderate by "comity" conversations the prevailing practical denominational attitude of each against all. At least in new urban areas and among some of the leading home mission boards, "comity" was realized to a substantial degree.

THE NATIONAL COUNCIL. A major landmark in this whole process of consolidation should be noted, even though it carries us past World War II. In 1950 the National Council of Churches of Christ came into existence. It was based on a co-ordination of the chief interdenominational functional agencies, such as those for home and foreign missions, for religious education, and for women's work, with the Federal Council which united the denominations as such. This large and complicated organization marked a tremendous advance from the beginning of the century in attitude and practice, bringing into one focus, even if very indirectly and loosely, almost the whole range of activities of the Protestant Church. In this organization were focused all the hopes that denominational anarchy could be subdued to genuine co-operation without waiting for the even more painful and tortuous process of organic merger.

Finally, the whole relation of the Protestant community, generally, to the state took on a new aspect with the decline of pietism in the church and the development of the welfare state. It had been generally supposed in America that the church-state issue had been definitively settled early in the nineteenth century, and very little had been written on the subject in the first three decades of the twentieth. But by the thirties the state was expanding rapidly into many forms of social welfare and philanthropy which had hitherto been the preserve of the church. Public education was tending to monopolize the effective energy of the child with a program which was frankly a training in ideals and character (and thus in theology) and yet was not Christian. Church and state shared concerns and responsibilities in an increasing number of areas, and soon a lively debate arose over the meaning of the constitutional separation of the two. The jurists of the Supreme Court exhibited as much confusion as the common man as, in a series of postwar cases, they fumbled for an interpretation of the Constitution in this regard.

Chapter 32

THE YOUNGER CHURCHES

The quarter-century beginning in 1914 was a generation of revolution around the world. In these highly unsettled conditions Christianity still continued its rapid growth outside Europe and the United States. In Asia and Africa the Christian communities more than doubled in the generation, the most marked gains coming in Indonesia, China, India, and Africa below the Sahara. Eastern Christianity made little or no gains, but Protestantism and Roman Catholicism were both very active. The former still led, but a new surge of Roman Catholic activity closed most of the gap in initiative. About 1940 the total strength of the Younger Churches was about forty million, equally divided between Protestants and Roman Catholics. The non-Christian populations, however, were growing with equal or greater rapidity, so that although Christianity was becoming more widely established, it was not gaining as rapidly as rival faiths.

Nearly everywhere in Asia and Africa and the islands of the Pacific there were a marked rise of self-conscious nationalist feeling and increasing resentment against British, French, Dutch, and American imperialism and racism. Christianity was variously affected by this tendency. In many cases the nationalism tended to reinterpret and support the older non-Christian faiths as a part of national culture. This was true of Ceylonese, Burmese, and Thai nationalists as regards Buddhism; of Japanese Shintoists; of Indian Hindus; and of Javanese Moslems. But on the other hand, the nationalism was more or less secularist and tended to revise or even, occasionally, to break down the other religions also, as with Islam in Turkey and Persia. In any case Christianity was always under suspicion of being an agency of Western imperialism, and its Western associations, hitherto an advantage, now became a hindrance. A nearly universal phenomenon of missions was to hasten the process of devolution of control to national Christian leadership. Often this process of transfer resulted in an increase of evangelistic activity, as in Japan and Indonesia. Sometimes, as in some parts of Africa, the nationals did not seem to have been ready for the responsibility thrust upon them.

ROMAN CATHOLIC MISSIONS. The Vatican encouraged missions actively in this period. In 1919 Benedict XV issued a missions encyclical, *Maximum illud*, urging especially the development of indigenous clergy. Pius XI, his successor, enjoyed the title the "missionary Pope" as well as that of "the Pope of Catholic Action." Cardinal van Rossum headed Propaganda in the 1920's and spurred missionary activity. In 1925 a missionary exposition in Rome proved a great success. In 1926 six Chinese priests journeyed to Rome to be consecrated by the Pope himself. And in *Rerum ecclesiae* Pius summoned the whole church to a more active participation in missions, noticing also the need of developing indigenous priests and prelates. In 1927 Propaganda established the *Fides* news agency for publicity. Movies were also used. Chairs in "missiology" appeared in the universities. One Sunday of the year was assigned to money-raising for missions.

The largest societies were the Jesuits, the Paris Society for Foreign Missions, and the Franciscans. France still supplied the largest contingent of personnel but no longer had an actual majority. Italy, Germany, and the Low Countries showed a marked increase in missionary interest. United States Roman Catholics also began to play a part. By 1941 there were nearly three thousand American Roman Catholic missionaries, 45 per cent of them in China. Their best-known center was Maryknoll, where Father James Walsh was superior. The Society for the Propagation of the Faith was still the chief fund-raising agency. It was moved to Rome in 1922. In the next five years its income doubled, the American contributions quadrupling. Then in the depression from 1929 to 1933, gifts fell off 45 per cent, a drop especially noticed in the American contributions.

Thereafter the program steadily recovered until the onset of World War II.

Protestant Missions.   On the Protestant side the disasters which had overtaken the Continent, and especially Germany, left the missionary enterprise more than ever in the hands of the Anglo-Saxons.   At the end of the thirties the United States and Canada were carrying half the total load, and seven-eighths of that load were in the hands of the English-speaking peoples as a whole.   Protestant Younger Churches thus bore the stamp of Anglo-American Evangelicalism, rather than of the European right-wing of the Reformation.   And the whole enterprise felt the violent fluctuations in funds and personnel, owing to the American financial crash and the theological humanism of the end of the twenties.   This fluctuation affected Protestants more than Roman Catholic missions.

As with the Roman Catholics the Protestants' process of devolution was marked.   It was much more difficult, especially in the Far East, to build up a married middle-class professional ministry than to develop a celibate body of religious leaders. The organizational freedom of Protestantism, on the other hand, permitted the formation of autonomous churches, and in this way was more amenable to "indigenization."   At the end of the period 90 per cent of the personnel in Protestant mission fields were nationals, but the new churches were still able to raise only about half their financial support.   In line with this emphasis, the use of non-European music, painting, and architecture was experimented with in many places.   The comparison was sometimes made with the first three centuries of the Christian era, where the faith had been made indigenous at once, with no protracted period of tutelage.

Another phenomenon peculiar to the Protestants was the in-creasing co-operation, federation, and organizational consolida-tion of the many churches and agencies.   Most important in this respect was the work of the International Missionary Coun-cil, founded in 1921.   Under the leadership of A. L. Warnshuis and J. H. Oldham, affiliated regional and national councils were organized, reaching a total, in 1944, of twenty-six bodies. Among them were those of India, Burma, and Ceylon (1922); China (1922); Japan (1923); Mexico (1928); Brazil (1934);

and South Africa (1936). Here was a network holding these various churches together and restraining the nationalist tendency from breaking Christian unity.

In the United States, which was now the main support of Protestant missions, a major sag in religious morale coincided with financial crisis to make the decade 1925-1935 a low ebb in missions. A group of businessmen who had long supported foreign missions initiated a "Laymen's Foreign Missions Inquiry." Some seven volumes were published from the results in 1931-1932, and Professor Hocking of Harvard published an interpretation, *Rethinking Missions.* His point of view was far more liberal than that of most supporters of missions and was generally repudiated by them. Among liberals one found a disposition to minimize the differences between higher religions and to regard missions as a means of exchanging ideals and cultural values. Neither personnel nor funds, however, seemed to be evoked by a summons to missions couched in such terms.

In direct refutation of *Rethinking Missions*, a study volume was written for the next great missions conference at Madras in 1938. Professor Kraemer's *Christian Message in a Non-Christian World* asserted uncompromisingly the uniqueness and authority of the revelation of God in Jesus Christ. Probably most of the Continental supporters of missions would have agreed with Kraemer's position. At Madras, however, where the Younger Churches supplied a full half of the delegates, liberal Evangelicalism was the mean position and Kraemer stood at the extreme right.

NORTH AFRICA AND THE NEAR EAST. We may begin a rapid survey of missions with the region where Christianity made the least progress. That area is the Moslem Near East and North African littoral. There was little change in North Africa, except that rising Egyptian nationalism strengthened Islam slightly. In Syria, similarly, now under French mandate, Western missions continued their work as before. The Protestant university of Beirut, renamed the American University in 1920, was matched by a similar American University in Cairo. Both Protestants and Roman Catholics gained in Syria more than elsewhere. Palestine was increasingly a focus of Zionist immigration and saw little Christian advance. The Western

churches reorganized their work in the area. Rome detached
a new Congregation for Oriental Churches from Propaganda
in 1917. And a Protestant United Missionary Council for
Syria and Palestine was strengthened five years later to a unit
of the International Missionary Council (I.M.C.), and was
called the "Near East Christian Council."

The startling changes were the result of nationalism in Turkey, Persia, and, to some extent, Iraq. The Young Turks made
a religion of secular nationalism, as had the Jacobins of the
French Revolution. Their release of the state from the Moslem
control aided Christians in part. But the Turks murdered tens
of thousands of their national minorities, especially the Armenians. In Persia (now Iran), similarly, Armenians and Nestorians were slaughtered during and after World War I, and in
Iraq the Nestorians suffered similarly. It was estimated that a
third of the Iraq Chaldeans and of the Turkish Roman Catholic
community were killed. The Armenian Gregorian Church
suffered most of all from massacre and deportation.

"Near East Relief" was a remarkable rescue work initiated
largely by American Protestant missionaries to save the Armenians of Turkey from total extermination. Probably a million
lives were saved, and some 132,000 orphans were rescued and
educated. By 1930 over $100,000,000 had been contributed to
the cause. The Eastern churches, however, never recovered
from their terrible losses. And although both Roman Catholic
and Evangelical communities gained somewhat through the
Near East, they were very weak and dependent upon Western
energies for their maintenance.

AFRICA. In contrast to the African countries on the
Mediterranean, with their almost imperceptible gains for Christianity, Africa south of the Sahara was the area of the most
sensational success in the world mission. Christians increased
more than five times in one generation. The economic and
cultural revolution was a major factor. Western economic
penetration progressed rapidly, with its gold, diamond, and cop-
per mines, its plantations and lumbering, its railroads and air-
planes. Black laborers were assembled in mass concentrations.
Everywhere the tribal structure and tribal religion disintegrated
and Africans were in danger of complete atomization and derac-

ination. Christianity might provide a community and a sense of meaning, and gave hope of yielding some clues to the problem of adjusting to the new economic and technological world. Most of what schools and medical care were available to the blacks were also maintained by Christian missions. Africans came to Christianity in such masses that it was often difficult to instruct them adequately. A number of African-led movements and semi-Christian prophets arose out of the general ferment.

As before 1914 Protestant work was especially strong in British areas, such as the Union of South Africa, the Rhodesias and Nyasaland, Kenya and Tanganyika. Roman Catholic missions, as before, prospered especially in the Belgian Congo, Portuguese Angola, and French Africa. Roman Catholics put on a larger staff (10,000 to the 7,500 Protestants in 1936) and increased their constituency seven times to the Protestants' fourfold gain. The earlier concentration of African Christians in South Africa was now matched in the Belgian Congo, which raised a Roman Catholic community of 70,000 in 1912 to 2,-580,000 thirty years later. In this last case, to be sure, as in Portuguese Angola, the government subsidized Roman Catholic and hindered Protestant work. In several areas, especially the Gold Coast and Nigeria, Christian missionaries were competing with aggressive Moslem propaganda, not always successfully. The Jehovah's Witnesses also raised difficulties in some areas, preaching the Second Coming and denouncing missions as works of the devil.

The peculiar problems of South Africa require mention. Here blacks outnumbered whites four to one and were increasing somewhat more rapidly, while the white minority desperately fought to maintain political, economic, and social control. The Boers advocated "Afrikaans" nationalism and a rigid caste system. The Dutch Reformed Church, which included over half the whites, was closely related to the Boer program. The British community supported Anglicanism, the second largest church of the Dominion, and other British churches. Presbyterians, Methodists, and Congregationalists were engaged in negotiations for merger. Roman Catholics were weaker than anywhere else in the British dominions, less than 5 per cent of the total. There were tensions between Briton and Boer as well as between black and white. One result of the latter conflict was the rapid proliferation of independent sects, sometimes by tribes, among the Bantu, about half of whom were Christian. Over a million supported these independent black churches. And in the worst areas of exploitation, the festering black slums, the church may even have lost ground altogether. In any case these sharp cleavages made the career of the Christian Council of South Africa a stormy one, and relations with the World Council were slow in developing.

Among famous personalities was Albert Schweitzer, who came out to French Equatorial Africa in 1913. Though his mission station was not particularly notable in itself, the man became a symbol of missionary devotion, partly because of the distinguished careers in music and scholarship which he had sacrificed for service in Africa. J. E. K. Aggrey of the Achimota higher school on the Gold Coast was one of the finest of the African leaders. Some of the African "prophets," for example William Wadé Harris and Garrick Braid in World War I, were colorful and powerful religious leaders. Braid, who announced himself as the "Prophet Elijah," was strongly anti-white and was finally jailed by the British, as was Simon Kabangu by the Belgians in the Congo. Some of the missionaries also made efforts to adapt the Gospel to African traditions, utilizing initiation and marriage rites, or native architecture and vestments. In many cases, however, second-generation Christians slipped back into pagan customs and concepts.

LATIN AMERICA AND THE PHILIPPINES. In the old Spanish and Portuguese colonial area of Latin America and the Philippines, the churches gained, with certain exceptions. Here was the largest concentration of professed Roman Catholics outside Europe and probably the area of least religious vitality. In Latin America the Roman Catholic Church was financially tied to the large landed interests and found its chief support among women. The intellectual leaders and socially-minded citizens, who had traditionally been indifferent or hostile to the church, began to find here and there a point of contact, with Catholic social action in Brazil or Chile perhaps, or neo-Thomist philosophy in Argentina or Mexico. But on the whole the obscurantist reactionary type was dominant and the Roman clergy proved in the 1930's to be a chief vehicle of the Nazi and Fascist penetration of Latin America. A high proportion of Latin American clergy came from a Fascist background in Spain and Italy. The Protestants, on the other hand, who were strongest in Mexico and Brazil, were based on the lower classes but were rapidly creating of them a new middle class. In Brazil, in particular, many congregations were wholly self-supporting and active in lay evangelism. Protestantism was making more converts in these countries from nominal Roman Catholics than Roman Catholics were from Protestants anywhere, although Protestant Christianity was still regarded as something exotic. Much of the work among the Indians was done by undenominational "faith missions." The majority of the Protestant groups were joined to the I.M.C. through half a dozen national councils.

Mexico suffered a church struggle comparable to that of Spain. In pursuit of its program of popular education and agrarian reform, the revolution of 1911 had been forced to challenge the landholding and obscurantist church. Out of the conflict came in 1917 the most anticlerical constitution Mexico had known. Among a variety of similar provisions were restrictions on religious orders, on religious education, the secularization of marriage, and disfranchisement of the clergy. These restrictions were not enforced until 1926. Calles' efforts then led to violent reactions. Conflict flared up even more bitterly in the early 1930's, evoking an encyclical from Pius XI in 1932. Priests were arrested and church buildings secularized. No aliens were permitted to serve as clergy, nor any clergy to teach. There was some antireligious teaching in the state schools. In 1935 fourteen of the Mexican states had forbidden celebration of the sacraments and seven were without any priests at all. The Apostolic Delegate was deported. The latter half of the thirties saw a relaxation of the struggle and some religious recovery, but the heritage of bitter intolerance and violence remained on both sides.

The Philippines provided a contrasting picture. The islands were 90 per cent nominally Christian. Although nationalism had produced the large Aglipayan schism before World War I, that schism did not hold its ground. The Roman Church, meanwhile, hastened the development of indigenous clergy. In 1936 seven of the ten bishops were Filipinos and over half of the parishes were under Filipino priests. In 1935 the Commonwealth Government was set up, and there was much less trouble over clerical politics than in Latin America. The tiny Protestant community was growing by leaps and bounds, was united in a National Christian Council related to the I.M.C., and witnessed the merger of the Congregationalists, Presbyterians, and United Brethren into the United Evangelical Church of the Philippines (1929). A Protestant missionary to the Moros, Frank Laubach, here developed the techniques of teaching literacy on a mass scale which were later used in several other countries.

SOUTHEAST ASIA. Further to the south and west in the islands of Indonesia was the greatest concentration of Protestants in the Far East. World War I embarrassed the missions, which were chiefly Dutch and German, but the mass movements to Christianity in the German fields in Sumatra and Nias continued. Indonesian nationalism increased in the 1920's and was sometimes associated with a Moslem revival. Indonesian Christians were restive under European clergy, and where they enjoyed autonomy, as in the Batak Church, they displayed increased evangelistic energy. In 1935 the Church of the Netherlands Indies was at last separated administratively from the state. The church was related to the I.M.C. and later to the World Council. By 1940 Protestants in Indonesia numbered nearly two million. The smaller Roman Catholic missions, meanwhile, had been growing more rapidly than the Protestant, owing, perhaps, to increased Roman Catholic strength in Holland.

The Roman Catholic Church increased in Indochina from nearly one million to nearly two million, in this generation, with an overwhelmingly indigenous clergy. Nationalist feeling was stronger among the Christians than among the general populace. A plenary council was held in 1934. Protestant work was also begun in Indochina during this quarter-century.

INDIA. In the subcontinent of India national feeling grew rapidly, finding its leadership in Gandhi and the Indian National Congress, and demanding Indian autonomy in or out of the Commonwealth. British rule was rapidly liquidated, although there were fears of civil war between the Hindu and Moslem communities once the *raj* should be removed. The population was also growing, from 315,000,000 in 1911 to 388,000,000 in 1941, thus increasing the danger of famines and of social unrest by driving down living standards. The "untouchable" sixth of India's population was developing new aspirations and becoming a political force. Among the young intellectuals, meanwhile, secularism (and especially Communism) found many adherents.

In these circumstances Indian Christianity more than doubled its strength in this generation, becoming the third chief religion of India with nearly eight million adherents. The Hindu nationalists, however, generally opposed conversions as changing the social structure. There were attempts to reclaim converts. And Christians were conspicuously snubbed in the nationalist discussions of the future of India. The Indian Christians generally supported the movements for political autonomy, although missionaries were inhibited by the government. In 1943 the All-India Conference of Indian Christians called on the British to promise full freedom to India within two years of the end of the war.

The rate of growth of the Roman Catholic Church in India was somewhat more than that of the population in this period, although nearly all its efforts were devoted to its own constituency into the 1930's. The *padroado* issue (see above, p. 326) was largely settled at last by another Concordat with Portugal in 1928. The great majority still were located south of Goa and Madras, where they constituted 5 per cent of the population. The staff was substantially increased, although not as much as in China and Africa, and devolution was pursued. By 1931 over a quarter of the Indian Roman Catholics were in entirely Indian care, and half a million were being served by indigenous clergy (save for their bishops). The church was still divided by racial and caste lines, however, and dependent on the West for funds and personnel. Catholic Action of various sorts was initiated. A considerable educational program was maintained, although there were fears that Indian independence would eventuate in restrictions on Christian schools. A large group of the Syrian Jacobites became Uniates. By the time of World War II the Roman Catholic community was approaching four million.

Indian Protestantism was more actively missionary in its program and grew more rapidly, nearly tripling in size in the generation. There were more mass movements to Christianity than before 1914, especially from the untouchables. Some Indian Christians feared a lowering of the religious, moral, and cultural level of the church, especially since the staff was sharply cut in the 1930's, owing to the falling off of missionary funds from the United States. The number of Indian ministers increased, however, and their quality improved. As denomination after denomination passed over large areas of control to Indians, there was a startling development of leadership and initiative in a constituency hitherto poverty-stricken and psychologically depressed. The first Indian Anglican bishop, Azariah, was vigorous in promoting evangelism.

The Indian National Christian Council (1923), led by K. T. Paul and William Paton, proved to be the most successful of all such councils. The sentiment for union produced also significant mergers. The United Church of North India (1924) was constituted chiefly of Presbyterians and Congregationalists. The United Church of South India, formed in 1908 by Presbyterians, Congregationalists, and Reformed, engaged after World War II in merger discussions with Wesleyan Methodists and Anglicans. These negotiations were to attract world-wide attention before their successful culmination in 1947 in the Church of South India. In 1932 the "Mission of Fellowship from the Churches of India and Burma to the Churches of Great Britain and Ireland" dramatically demonstrated the vitality of the Indian Younger Christians.

Especially after the Jerusalem Conference (1928) new attention was directed to the fact that 93 per cent of Indian Protestants were villagers. Most of the missions' education had hitherto presupposed urban conditions. In the 1930's progress was made in training for a Christian rural society, with its credit banks, schools, medical care, and recreation. Sam Higginbottom's rural work in Allahabad was influential. Some missionaries also attempted to adapt their Western habits in order to live more nearly on Indian standards. C. F. Andrews, the friend of Tagore and Gandhi, was particularly successful in finding an Indian Christian way of living. Indian architecture, hymns, and painting were also increasingly used. E. S. Jones adapted the Indian *ashram* for Christianity. Sundar Singh was a famous instance of a Christian form of the traditional Indian *sadhu* or holy man. And millions outside the churches were affected by the influence of Christianity against caste, child marriage, polygamy, and toward the improving of health, education, and morals generally.

CHINA. Across the "hump" of the Himalayas in China lived four hundred million people, a quarter of the human race. Here since the 1890's a vast revolution had been in progress, substituting the "Republic" of 1911 for the ancient Confucian empire, shattering the family structure, the civil service, the religions, and the literary language and culture of China. No other part of the world, save perhaps Russia, was being so profoundly transformed. Sun Yat Sen, the leading figure of the Republic, died in 1925 amid political confusion. The next year, however, his Kuomintang army, now led by Chiang Kaishek, began a campaign which had nearly won China by the 1930's. There was still, however, a substantial Communist resistance. And with the "Mukden Incident" in 1931, the Japanese began their imperialist campaign. After setting up "Manchukuo" in defiance of the League of Nations, in 1937 they launched an attempt at conquest of all China against both the Kuomintang and the Communists. Various local warlords added to the civil strife throughout.

Despite all these difficulties, and others, both Protestants and Roman Catholics approximately doubled their constituency in the course of the generation. The Roman Catholic gains in China, indeed, were equaled in this period only in Equatorial Africa and in the United States. The missionary staff was reinforced much more heavily in China than in India, and rapid progress was made in building a unified indigenous Roman Catholic Church. The first Apostolic Delegate, Constantini, was appointed in 1922. He was particularly concerned to relate Christianity to Chinese art and customs. In 1926 six Chinese were consecrated bishops in St. Peter's, and in 1940 there were fourteen vicariates under Chinese bishops. There were more orphanages, hospitals, and dispensaries than in any other Roman Catholic mission area save Africa. Schools were also emphasized more than formerly. In 1935 the first National Congress of Catholic Action was held. In general, however, the Roman Catholic prelates disavowed any desire to influence the country as a whole as the Protestants were doing, and concentrated on building the church. By 1941 that church numbered 3,250,000. Over half its funds came from China, chiefly from land endowments.

Largely through Protestantism, meanwhile, Christianity was affecting China more profoundly than any other major Asiatic country. While numbering less than 1 per cent of the population, Protestants had pioneered in medicine, surgery, and public health. Nine-tenths of the nurses in China were Christians. Most of the constructive social work of the 1930's was done by Christians. Christians might be one in a hundred in the total population, but in *Who's Who* they were one in six. And half of all listed had been educated in Christian schools or colleges. The Kuomintang "New Life Movement" was of Christian inspiration. A group of the most influential leaders, Sun Yat Sen, Chiang Kai-shek, Kung, and the wives of these three leaders (all from the Soong family) were Christians. Many generals, educators, and statesmen had arisen from the thousands of Chinese who had studied abroad and become Christian. The Y.M.C.A. and churches pushed Jimmy Yen's devices for mass education in literacy. A considerable section of the Protestant workers in China were consciously out to remake all Chinese life, and they were having appreciable influence in that direction. There was a question, on the other hand, as to whether they were not spreading themselves too thin. The middle schools and universities increasingly lost their Christian character. Where Christianity was interpreted largely as social reform, Communism won many of the ablest students by its greater precision and apparent realism. And the American religious education movement made its ambiguous impact.

There was also a sharper split than on any other field save Latin America between "fundamentalists" and "liberals."

Partly because of their social activity Protestant missions were also more attacked than those of the Roman Catholics. There was a strong antireligious movement in the 1920's, partly Communist-inspired, directed especially against British Protestants. Missionaries were choice prizes for kidnapings by bandits. Western extraterritoriality, leaseholds, and the like aroused nationalist resentment which found expression sometimes against missions. Kuomintang policy was nationalist and secularist with regard to Christian schools. The Protestants also suffered from fluctuations in staff and funds, owing to sudden changes in the United States from which so much of the missionary effort came. It was peculiarly difficult to get Chinese to enter the ministry. Able teachers, executives, Y.M.C.A. secretaries, and the like were to be found, but China had no precedent for the role of the pastor and it was hard to produce local support for it. There were more Chinese Protestant clergy than Roman Catholic, to be sure, but the latter had the hurdle of seminary training in Latin.

The Chinese National Christian Council was founded in 1922. In 1927 came what was then the most inclusive union of any in the world, the Church of Christ in China. The nucleus was Presbyterian and Reformed; to it were joined Congregationalists, United Brethren, and even Baptists. Over half of the Protestant ministers in China belonged to this church in 1934. Its chief leader, Cheng Ching-yi, made it well known in the West by his travels. Ties were maintained with the I.M.C. and the World Council. The Chinese delegation to the Madras Conference in 1938 was particularly able.

By this time Japan was launched in full-scale war on China and the reconciling bonds of the Christian Church were strained between the two churches. Deputations were exchanged by the National Christian Councils of Japan and China. There were some pacifists in Japan, but most of the Japanese Christians took Japan's idealist justification of the war at face value and sought simply to help relieve the suffering in China.

JAPAN. Japan had led the Asiatic nations in the acquisition of Western technology, and Japanese Christianity was the first to achieve full self-support and self-government. Protestant-ism, largely founded by Americans, was more active and larger than the Roman Catholic Church, under the care chiefly of the Paris Society for Foreign Missions. Indigenization pro-ceeded rapidly. In the 1920's Kagawa's "Kingdom of God Movement" had sought to bring the Christian news to the whole nation. An Overseas Evangelistic Association was cre-ated in 1931 to care for Japanese in Latin America, the Philip-pines, Formosa, the mandated islands, and Manchukuo. There had been a National Christian Council since 1923. Partly un-der government pressure, to be sure, the Church of Christ in Japan (1941) brought to a culmination the tendencies to a unified and indigenous Protestant church. The union was made up of forty-one denominations and was the most inclusive in the world. Only the Seventh Day Adventists and the Angli-cans refused to enter.

Japanese Protestantism was less rural than any other Asiatic church and appealed especially to the professional and civil service classes. The great feudal masses were scarcely touched by it. Kagawa was the representative best known in America. Living by choice in a slum, he endured beatings and contracted trachoma. He promoted social settlements, co-operatives, folk schools of the Danish type, (see above, p. 152) and fought prostitution and alcoholism. He was imprisoned for support-ing labor in industrial conflicts. In addition to this kind of en-terprise, there were the usual educational and medical programs.

War psychology made missions difficult in this generation. Americans particularly were under suspicion because of Jap-anese resentment at the actions of the Washington Naval Conferences and because of American immigration legislation. American missionaries in Korea and Formosa were also regarded as opponents of the Japanization of these territories. As partic-ipation in Shinto ceremonies was more and more made the test of patriotism, Protestants resisted much more often than Roman Catholics. While many Protestants considered these rites to be exact parallels of the emperor-worship of the early church, Rome authorized participation in them (1930). From the out-break of the war in 1937, American Protestant missionaries were withdrawing from Japan and Korea, finding that their presence was often an embarrassment to native Christians. Roman Catholic missionaries, on the other hand, being largely French, escaped much of the pressure. All administrative heads of churches and schools, of all branches of Christianity, were required to be Japanese by government action in 1940. In the war the Japanese tried to assimilate Protestant churches within the conquered countries to the Church of Christ in Japan. And in 1939-1940 a nation-wide United Evangelistic Campaign was at work in the home islands.

As the war became well-nigh universal, the cohesion of the world-wide missionary enterprise was dramatically illustrated. Many mission fields were cut off from their supporting countries. Japan alone swept over a quarter of the territory of world missions. The I.M.C. now set up a central reservoir, the "Orphaned Missions Fund," from which resources were distributed to some forty countries. For this fund the churches of India and China contributed $100,000. And not a mission station was closed or missionary withdrawn for lack of finances in one of the most striking instances of mutual help in Christian history. The progress of federations and mergers also continued in the war years at an even faster rate than before.

Chapter 33

THE ECUMENICAL MOVEMENT

In its most comprehensive sense the ecumenical movement is generally conceded to be the most important development in the church history of the twentieth century. It is a groundswell which has found expression in hundreds and thousands of organizations and institutions, sometimes apparently working at cross-purposes. Of these we must single out those few which seem most significant, the Student Christian Movement (S.C.M.), the International Missionary Council, the Life and Work and the Faith and Order movements, with their offspring, the World Council of Churches.

The first two of these tributaries represent perhaps the most important contribution of American Protestantism to world Christianity in the last two generations. Although dependent on Germany for theological scholarship, and on England and Scotland for ethical pioneering and the understanding of the Church itself, American Protestantism has taught the world much about missions and Christian youth movements.

STUDENT CHRISTIAN MOVEMENT. The world-wide student Christian movement developed from the first international Christian student conference at D. L. Moody's Mt. Hermon center in 1886. The missionary vocation of Evangelical Protestantism was there proclaimed with revivalistic urgency and 100 of the 250 students registered their intention to become foreign missionaries. The conference sent messengers such as Robert Wilder to circulate around the colleges. In one year 2,200 students volunteered. John R. Mott was the administrative genius who organized this enthusiasm into the "Student Volunteer Movement," of which he was chairman from 1888 to 1915. With its traveling secretaries the movement soon spread to Britain, Scandinavia, Germany, Holland, and Switzerland. Membership was based on the declaration, "It is my purpose, if God permit, to become a foreign missionary." The watchword was "the evangelization of the world in our generation." These volunteers vitalized student Christian work with their demand of absolute commitment, at the same time that they easily bridged denominational differences. The Student Volunteer Movement (S.V.M.) quadrennial conventions have had a unique influence on colleges and universities. As for the mission fields themselves, three-fourths of the men and 70 per cent of the women who have sailed from North America since 1890 have been "volunteers."

A comparable, if less specific and more comprehensive student Christian movement grew out of the international and interdenominational Y.M.C.A. Wishard had long dreamed of such a development, but it was John R. Mott again who brought it to birth. At a Y.M.C.A. conference in Amsterdam in 1891, Mott gathered delegates from various countries to discuss an international student Christian fellowship, and in 1895 at Vadstena, Sweden, the World Student Christian Federation was organized. The W.S.C.F. varied from country to country in its theological and ecclesiastical character, but in it hundreds and thousands of future professional people learned to think, worship, and work for the glory of God across denominational lines, yet without compromising their convictions. By training men in this context, and by building all kinds of personal ties across denominational and national lines, the W.S.C.F. became the most important, and probably the indispensable, nursery of the personnel of the ecumenical movement. It is significant that of the five persons who probably made the greatest individual contributions to the ecumenical movement in this period—Mott, Oldham, Söderblom, Temple, and Visser 't Hooft—every one came into it through the student Christian movement.

The student movement has been perhaps the most prophetic organ of Protestant Christianity in the twentieth century, more responsive to new biblical, theological, and ethical insight than the parish ministry and congregations. Large numbers have been brought to the Gospel in the student Christian movement who were never challenged in their home churches to take the faith seriously. And so far as international ties are concerned, the W.S.C.F. was the only student group which held across the battle lines in World War I, when both Communist and socialist student internationals split open. In the postwar despair, again it was the W.S.C.F. which alone mustered faith to undertake the task of rebuilding. Out of this effort came the great International Student Service Organization (I.S.S.O.). In the same period between wars in the United States, however, the student Christian movement made less of a contribution than in Europe. The theological liberalism of the 1920's and the denominational fractioning which succeeded it have alike weakened its ecumenical contribution. World Youth conferences of the W.S.C.F., as at Amsterdam (1938), and Oslo (1948), paralleled the conferences of the other contributary streams of the ecumenical movement.

EDINBURGH 1910: MISSIONARY CO-OPERATION. If the interdenominational student movements were the chief nurseries for the leadership of the ecumenical movement, its strongest continuing thrust has been the concern for the apostolicity of the church in the sense of mission. The Edinburgh World Missionary Conference of 1910 marked both the climax of the missionary enthusiasm of British and American Evangelical Protestantism and the first great landmark in the development which produced the International Missionary Council and the World Council of Churches. It was significant that the Edinburgh Assembly was constituted by Americans and British up to three of every four delegates, and that it was the third in a series of Anglo-American missionary councils at ten-year intervals. In this tradition the word "ecumenical" had meant simply the world-wide character of the missionary task and the need to conceive it as a totality. The Edinburgh Conference also spoke out of prewar optimism, Western complacency, and faith in progress. The difficulties discussed were chiefly tactical; the character of the Christian message was generally taken for granted. And although anxiety was expressed as to the implications for missions of the rising nationalism in Asia and the colonial world, the full depth of the problem to be revealed after the war was not yet dreamed of. A startling glimpse into he prevailing temper of Western missions at that time is opened y the speech which Azariah of India was prevailed upon to 1ake, pleading that the gift of the Gospel should be conveyed 1 a fellowship of missionaries and nationals in social equality ather than in a spirit of "condescending love."

But other aspects of Edinburgh looked forward in new di-ections. The predominant type of Anglo-American Evan-elical Protestantism was complemented in two directions. 2ontinental Protestantism with its more theological temper was lso drawn into the movement at Edinburgh. And only two nonths before the Assembly the hesitant Archbishop of Can-erbury was persuaded to attend and to bring the Anglican ommunion with him. It was the S.C.M. leaders and inter-lenominational contacts which finally overcame Anglican re-istance. The Anglicans stipulated that doctrine and order 1ust be scrupulously avoided, a regulation which they them-elves broke more than did any others, and they kept Latin \merica off the agenda on the theory that it was not properly nissionary territory. But full Anglican participation in the cumenical movement since Edinburgh has meant a very sub-tantial gain and a main key to the co-operation of Orthodox nd Old Catholics.

Edinburgh also opened a new era in its technique. It was riginally conceived simply as a great demonstration. But, argely at the prodding of John R. Mott, its character was hanged into a study and planning conference. International ommissions involving hundreds of correspondents prepared cholarly materials on each of eight main areas, and the resulting urvey of missionary conditions and problems was published nd widely circulated. This study volume technique was o be repeatedly used thereafter by ecumenical conferences, which thus became the foci of innumerable seminars and study roups involving thousands all over the world who never attend he actual sessions.

I.M.C. Another aspect of the Edinburgh Conference which proved to be a precedent was the setting up a continua-ion committee. The Edinburgh Committee was thus in a po-ition to care for "orphaned missions" during World War I. \fterward (1921) it launched the first of the permanent ecumenical bodies, the International Missionary Council, with Mott as chairman. Dozens of national or regional conferences have since been held by the I.M.C., and it has become related to some twenty or thirty "National Christian Councils." In this way a world organization has come into being, in some ways parallel to the Roman Catholic Propaganda. The "Younger Church" constituency of the World Council was to be composed of the structures created by the I.M.C. And it was also the I.M.C. which first worked out the principle now fundamental in the World Council, that only the members make policy; the ecumenical body cannot become a "super-church."

The I.M.C. has held a series of world conferences at ten-year intervals which have reflected the same theological developments as the other ecumenical meetings which we are to mention. At Jerusalem (1928) there was perceptible the contrast between Continental and Anglo-American views on eschatology and social action which were conspicuous at Stockholm. Madras (1938) found its focus in the recovered sense of the centrality of the Church as a community which marked the other great ecumenical conferences of the thirties. Other emphases, however, have been peculiarly characteristic of the situation of the "Younger Churches." At Jerusalem the race problem was first faced seriously on Christian grounds. The study preparations for Madras raised questions about the economic bases of missions and the Younger Churches, and their increasing difficulties with rising nationalism and governments. The necessity of adjusting the program to the overwhelmingly rural constituency of the Younger Churches has been increasingly stressed. And ever since Edinburgh there has been unremitting emphasis on the need for "indigenization" and the scandal of denominational division. This last concern has also been expressed in the series of denominational mergers, such as the Church of Christ in China, the Church of Christ in Japan, the Church of South India, the Church of North India, the United Church of the Philippines. "For you union may be a luxury," it was said at Madras, "but for us it is a necessity."

STOCKHOLM: LIFE AND WORK. While only the missionary program of the church gave to the ecumenical movement an enduring association with continuous activity on a large scale, two other aspects of the church's life were given institutional ecumenical form. A concern for co-operative ethical witness had been widely felt before World War I. It was a primary motive, for example, in the organization of the American Federal Council of Churches in 1908. Similar currents were to be found in Britain, France, Switzerland, Germany, and Scandinavia, and had resulted, in many cases, in comparable federations. Regional conferences of churchmen on social issues were also held, as in France at Besançon, and most impressively of all, in Birmingham, England. The latter Conference on Politics, Economics, and Citizenship (C.O.P.E.C.) was to prove the most substantial preparation for the Stockholm World Conference in 1925, which launched the ecumenical "life and work" movement.

Before the war most advocates of the Christian social witness were interested in the problems of industrial conflict, capitalism and socialism, poverty, drink, slums, and sexual vice. Both the definition of the problems and their urgency, however, were modified by the war itself, with its appalling destruction and spiritual demoralization and its aftermath of hysterical nationalism, revolution, and bolshevism. Was Christianity just irrelevant to this kind of world? Was it not possible for Christians to speak and act together at least with regard to some of the most undeniable evils? "The world," said Bishop Brent, "is too strong for a divided church," and the burden of proof lay on those who wished to continue in denominational isolation. Archbishop Söderblom of Sweden, who had urged peace negotiations during the war, became the leading figure afterward in the effort to hold a world conference of Christians on social and political issues.

The great problem of such a conference, of course, was the bitterness of former combatant nationals. It proved necessary to leave aside the English, French, and Germans in the planning and preparation, most of which was carried by Söderblom and MacFarland of the American Federal Council. And when the conference did convene in Stockholm seven years after the Armistice, the Germans came in bitter resentment from out of the intellectual blockade. They came chiefly to testify that the Versailles thesis of Germany's "sole guilt" was a damnable lie, whereas with the French and Belgians it was equally a matter of honor to insist that the thesis was true. The German reception of American, British, and French schemes to outlaw war and to set up a League of Nations to ensure the position of the victor nations was not enthusiastic. That they remained without provoking an incident was itself some demonstration of the power of reconciliation.

Beneath the political issues of the League, the World Court, disarmament, pacifism, and immigration laws, a deep theological divergence as to the basis and scope of Christian ethics became apparent. The Americans talked of the Golden Rule in international relations, of "Christianizing" business, and sometimes came close to identifying the Kingdom of God with prohibition. Bishop Brent hoped to outlaw war within a generation. The Lutherans and Barthians, on the other hand, argued, in the words of Bishop Ihmels, "peace and war follow their own laws which we cannot change," and that no human effort could hasten the coming of God's Kingdom. Here for the first time the Continental and American theological traditions met on a broad range of issues, and both were shocked. And the possibility of a common ethical witness without raising theological presuppositions began to fade in the minds of churchmen. As with Edinburgh, however, the actual gathering of the conference and the network of personal relations established, and the subtle shifts in attitudes effected were more significant than any official findings. And as at Edinburgh, the significant action taken was the setting up of a continuation committee to co-ordinate the study and actions of the several churches in "life and work."

OXFORD. At Oxford in 1937 a successor conference to Stockholm was held on "Church, Community, and State." The title indicates how the rise of the new totalitarian movements had posed the question of Christian ethics in a new way. No longer was it a matter of enlisting Christian support behind various specific reform within an accepted framework, but the very nature of the framework was now in question. Totalitarianism, with its claim to control the whole of man's private and intellectual life as well as his politics, threatened the very existence of the church and reawakened the sense of the Church itself as a total community life embodying the way of the Gospel. The Americans and Continentals found themselves closer together than at Stockholm or Jerusalem. At Oxford the various aspects of the common life which Stockholm had tended to treat in isolation were usually related explicitly to Christian theology and in the context of the Church as a community with an ethos of its own. The very existence of an ecumenical Christian community was a challenge to the new political religions. The major German churches, as well as the Russian, were prevented from sending delegates. Representatives of at least ten nations warned of possible difficulties with home governments. But the findings of Oxford won a recognition and influence, if without authority, comparable to those of papal encyclicals on similar issues in the Roman Church. And from the Oxford Conference came the initiative to invite the "Faith and Order" movement to join in the formation of a World Council of Churches.

LAUSANNE: FAITH AND ORDER. "Faith and Order" was the enterprise of facing head-on those issues of doctrine and church order which the Anglicans had ruled out of bounds at Edinburgh. Charles Brent, the American Episcopalian bishop to the Philippines, had been convinced by the experience of Edinburgh itself that the *caveat* was unjustifiable. It was not honorable for Christians to meet and not discuss these matters. And it was unnecessary to avoid them. Actual church unity, thought Brent, was a real possibility within a century. And he led the American Episcopalians in preparing a world conference on doctrine and polity to meet at Lausanne two years after Stockholm. Lausanne was to avoid, on the one hand, any premature constitution for a world church, and on the other, mere irresponsible debate. The churches were to discover precisely where they stood in relation to each other within a common perception that a congeries of sects was no adequate witness to Christ's intention in the Church. The scandal lay, not so much in administrative division, but in the lack of mutual recognition, fellowship, and co-operation. Brent's own formulation of the goal of the Faith and Order movement was put in the metaphor of the British Commonwealth of Nations, politically autonomous and with separate customs, but effectively united by acknowledgment of one common king.

Lausanne disproved the fears of the timid. Nothing exploded. As was remarked, it was the first time in church history that the churches had considered together the deepest grounds of their divisions and had parted without anathemas or excommunications. There were important absentees, of course. Of the Americans the Southern Baptists and the Missouri Synod Lutherans would not touch such an enterprise. The Bishop of Rome responded to the overtures which had been made to him by the encyclical *Mortalium animos*, which defined the Roman Catholic attitude toward the ecumenical movement as benevolent nonparticipation. And the Greek Orthodox delegates at Lausanne stated their exceptions to the findings of the conference. But on the whole, success was so much greater than anticipated that a continuation committee was launched in a mood of surprised gratification. Bishop Brent was its chairman, and on his death in 1929 Archbishop Temple succeeded him. Unlike the I.M.C., or even Life and Work, however, Faith and Order had no staff or activity of its own, other than the interests of individual churchmen in its problems.

The discussions at Lausanne had helped to identify areas of agreement and disagreement. As an agenda for the next period of study were taken those issues so crucial since the Reformation—the doctrines of grace, and those involved in ministry and sacraments. Suggestions for closer association with Life and Work were received with some coolness, although it was at length agreed that the next two conferences of the two movements should be held in nearby cities within one month. The constituency of Faith and Order was inclined to suspect Life and Work of theological liberalism and indifferentism. Several of the churches involved had not reckoned beforehand on any continuation of the efforts culminating at Stockholm and Lausanne. Some had almost made it a condition of their participation that no permanent body should be organized. Time and again in this ecumenical movement the churches have ratified after the fact steps which they might have debated for a century beforehand could they have been asked for an opinion.

EDINBURGH 1937. The Edinburgh Conference on Faith and Order met immediately after the Oxford Conference in 1937. To the surprise of many, it succeeded in drafting a statement on grace acceptable to Orthodox and Reformed, thus repeating the achievement of the Conference of Regensburg at the Reformation. But ministry and sacraments proved more intractable and were seen to rest upon divergent conceptions of the nature of the church itself. A direct consideration of the doctrine of the church, consequently, provided the central agenda for the third Faith and Order Conference at Lund, Sweden, in 1952, which marked the last independent enterprise of Faith and Order before integration into the World Council. That integration had first been proposed at Edinburgh, where it had resulted in a "battle royal." The proposal was at length accepted, with the provisions that Faith and Order matters in such a council must always be considered on a Trinitarian basis. The next year a joint committee met at Utrecht to draw up a constitution for the World Council. There was unanimous agreement to accept such a basis not only for Faith and Order deliberations, but also for the Council as a whole. Thus the World Council acquired the old Y.M.C.A. formula of faith in Jesus Christ "as God and Savior" as its constitutional foundation. The chief constitutional engineer was William Temple, who had also been the main force in bringing Life and Work and Faith and Order together in 1937.

But the World Council was still some distance from organization. The joint committee which had drafted the constitution enlarged itself into a "Provisional Committee" and in 1939 appointed as executive secretaries W. A. Visser 't Hooft, William Paton, and H. S. Leiper. The constituent Assembly for the new World Council was planned for 1941. In September 1939, however, the Germans invaded Poland and all international meetings were precluded by the consequent world war. And for nearly a decade more the secretariate of the Provisional Committee was to function on behalf of the World Council "in process of formation." Through that war the I.M.C. and the World Council skeleton staff were able to care for orphaned missions, prisoners of war, refugees, and other pressing needs on behalf of the churches. And the sense of an international and ecumenical reality of the One Church deepened among laity as well as ecclesiastics.

AMSTERDAM: THE WORLD COUNCIL. In contrast to the protracted delay after World War I, as early as February 1946 church representatives from the former combatants were able to meet together to make arrangements for the organization of the long-planned World Council. And when they did meet there was much less of a theological gap between Continentals and Americans than had been the case in the 1920's. The first Assembly convened at Amsterdam in 1948, representing 147 churches from 44 countries, who pledged each other "to stay together." With slight modifications the Utrecht Constitution of 1938 was adopted, making it explicit that the World Council could have no constitutional authority over its member churches. It was noteworthy that it seemed necessary to hold no less than four separate communion services. And the Central Committee two years later explicitly defined that membership in the World Council in no way implied recognition of other member churches as *churches* in the full sense. The continuing organization was to consist of a Central Committee of ninety to meet annually, and an Executive Committee elected from this to meet two or three times a year. There were six presidents and a small staff. Representative Assemblies like that at Amsterdam would be convoked periodically. And the following year a kind of Asiatic sequel was held at Bangkok, Thailand, to compensate in some measure for the necessarily slight Asiatic representation at the Amsterdam Assembly. The most comprehensive institutional expression of the ecumenical movement thus began its work in the devastation left by World War II.

A question in the minds of many was how far the World Council could be expected to maintain the vision of the ecumenical pioneers. It had been a growing conviction that the churches could not profitably draw together as they then were, that the unity to be desired was a unity which would require radical reformation of all constituent members. As Dr. Visser 't Hooft put it, "The ecumenical movement is a movement of repentance." The task of the ecumenical movement was more to relate the churches to the One Church and its Lord than simply to each other. Amsterdam reflected much of this insight. But as the ecumenical movement passed into the official hands of ecclesiastical bureaucracy, how much could be hoped of such a vision?

EVANSTON 1954. Great abstentions from the World Council were still to be noted. The Pope reaffirmed his official ban on Roman Catholic participation in *De motione ecumenica*. And in the same summer as Amsterdam, the Russians assembled a counterdemonstration in Moscow, a pan-orthodox synod, which condemned World Council and Vatican alike as kindred imperialist and antidemocratic agencies. The political tension between the Communist and Western liberal states continued to threaten the integrity of the World Council in the following years, especially with the Communist conquest of China and the Korean war. But the second Assembly, held at Evanston in the United States in 1954, was attended by a dozen or so "Iron Curtain" delegates from Europe, although the Chinese churches were now cut off. Outside the Communist orbit the World Council seemed at Evanston to be solidly established as an indispensable agency of an ever larger number of churches. The greater part of the staff and budget were devoted to the practical tasks of "Inter-church Aid and Service to Refugees," while other departments carried on the concerns of faith and order, evangelization, and political, social, and economic ethics. Dr. Visser 't Hooft was continued as executive secretary at Evanston, while Bishop G. K. A. Bell was succeeded as chairman of the Central Committee by Dr. Franklin Clark Fry of the United Lutherans (U.S.A.).

In the long perspective the ecumenical councils of the twentieth century sometimes recalled those of the fifteenth. In that earlier age the prelates and theologians of the Western church had struggled to reorganize church institutions which had ceased to meet the problems of the day. Thomas Aquinas, a century and a half before, had rationalized a "secularization" of many areas of the common life, and from his day the medieval synthesis had swiftly disintegrated. Scholastic theology was widely despised as irrelevant; nationalism had broken the unity of Christendom, the economic ethic of the church seemed unable to keep up with the rise of finance, commerce, and industry. General respect for ecclesiastical leadership was very low. The fathers of Pisa and Constance and Basel labored in these circumstances for an "ecumenical reformation."

The synthesis which had broken down in the twentieth century was more complicated and had not involved all divisions of Christendom equally. Since the eighteenth century, if not earlier, this largely Protestant synthesis had been the dominant moral force in Western culture, but, by the middle of the nineteenth century it was visibly losing momentum. Bourgeois Protestantism seemed increasingly unable to provide meaning and direction for an industrial society, and a widespread desire was felt for a more direct theonomous relation between Christian faith and political, economic, and cultural practice than was provided by the Evangelical appeal to the "moral law." There was a widespread sense that an age was past and that Christians must seek new ways of recovering genuine Christian community and an integrity of personal life. The conviction was general that all were in schism and that all were outrageously unfaithful to Christ in the common life. It remained to be seen whether the ecumenical movement of the twentieth century would have more success than its predecessor of the fifteenth.

Chapter 34

WORLD WAR II AND AFTER

The state of the churches in the last decade or so may be surveyed quickly with particular reference to the main themes we have been tracing. The missionary expansion of Christianity had left it a genuinely global religion by the mid-twentieth century. It existed nearly everywhere as a minority movement. But the population dynamics seemed to indicate that it would be a progressively smaller minority in the decades to come. The inner dynamic of Christianty also seemed at this period less vital than that of some of its rivals, especially nationalism and Communism. The missionary enterprise was nearly immobilized by its own prodigious investment in educational and medical institutions. In the "mission compound" in Asia and in the "bourgeois ghetto" in Europe, the Christian church seemed to be increasingly withdrawn from the new movements and the new groups remaking society. The war seemed to have accelerated the tendency over the generations to constrict the cultural influence of Christianity. "Post-Christian society" was a frequent expression in Europe. Only the United States fell outside this general tendency, but here the prosperity of organized religion assisted a great mixture of incompatible if apparently amicable faiths, and it was difficult to estimate how the Christian faith was competing with its rivals within the churches.

Our survey begins with the Younger Churches, proceeds to the great Communist-controlled areas, then returns to Western Europe—Protestant and Roman Catholic—and concludes with the English-speaking world.

Asian and African Christianity. In one sense the Younger Churches fell outside the constellation of forces we have followed throughout, but on the other hand, the history of modern Asia and Africa is the story of their penetration and disruption by modern Western civilization. Western technology, industrialism, imperialism, nationalism, and Communism were the revolutionary powers which set the problems of life both for Christians and non-Christians in these regions. And as in the West, the increasingly non-Christian or anti-Christian impact of these powers provided the main themes of church history.

The most striking aspect of the life of Asia and Africa in the twentieth century was the ever accelerating rise of nationalism in these lands. This nationalism was both imitation of and opposition to the West. For most of the Asiatic world it has meant the breaking down of merely local or family loyalties, provincial and, to a degree, religious communities, and the substitution for these of the overarching goal of a political state based on cultural, linguistic, and historical affinities, as in Europe. Such a nation-state and national consciousness are radically new in India and China, for example, and in large measure exhibit the influence of nineteenth-century European ideas. In part the movement is economic anticolonialism, but increasingly it is a spiritual matter, the assertion of communal pride against the arrogance and patronizing of the West and the "whites."

Japan's role in the war illustrated vividly how quickly Asiatic nationalism could emulate and even outstrip that of the West in aggressive imperialism. And even though Japan was at last defeated, her demonstration that an Asiatic nation could deal on equal terms with Americans and Europeans in war quickened hopes in Indonesia, Indochina, Malaya, Burma, and India, as well as in much of Africa. In the short-lived occupation there was a definite church policy which in some ways resembled that of postwar Russia. In the Religious Bodies Law of 1940 Christianity was officially recognized for the first time in Japan and was given the position of the third religion beside Shintoism and Buddhism. There was also strong pressure to unite all the diverse denominations from the West in one Church of Christ in Japan (1941) and to sever ties with the English-speaking churches. Christian ministers were sent with the armies overseas, and in Korea, the Philippines, Indonesia, and North China, the same attempt was made, insofar as possible, to unite the churches and to separate them from the West. With the withdrawal of Japanese troops nearly all of these countries were left with collaborationist-resistance hostilities in the churches and with the problem of how far the enforced church unions could and should be retained. In Japan itself church contacts with the West were re-established within a few weeks after the surrender, and the church regained lost ground during the American occupation. Several bodies, such as the Episcopalians and Salvation Army, withdrew from the United Church, the Kyodan, which still held about four-fifths of Japan's Protestants.

After the war Asiatic nationalism continued its course with undiminished tempo. Seven new nations came into existence within five years. Social and technological revolutions accompanied or followed the political revolution. The religious consequences of the general movement of nationalism have been twofold. On the one hand, the rise of national consciousness and pride has strengthened the position of the older religions against Christianity. The Younger Churches were, in most cases as yet, poorly assimilated. Culturally, as well as economically, they still bore many signs of missionary planting from the West and thus gave the impression of cultural and religious imperialism. In many cases the Christians held back from the nationalist movements in greater or less degree. Hinduism in India, Buddhism in Burma, Islam in Indonesia, in contrast, rode on the wave of nationalism while the Christian gains slowed down. Pakistan saw an illustration of a renascent Islam nourished by nationalism. Even the older religions, on the other hand, suffered the corrosion of Western secularism. The new national, political, and economic hopes, and the technology by which they were to be realized, turned men from *all* religions. In the colleges and universities where the nationalism was strongest, the great body of the students were agnostics or atheists in most Asiatic countries. Confucianism collapsed the most dramatically of all, and there was some evidence that Christianity was better able to withstand the impact of industrial technology than any of the other great world religions.

But in any case the real rivals now seemed often to be the new political religions—nationalism and Communism.

Whereas the "Christian nations" of the West, whose traditions might have led them to contribute to the liberalizing of Asian nationalism, were inhibited by racism and colonial interests, Communism exploited the universal surge of the underdeveloped areas. The totalitarianism of the Soviets could not terrify peoples who had never known personal liberties, and Russian imperialism seemed much more remote than the British, Dutch, and French imperialism under which they smarted daily. The most dramatic consequence of this situation, of course, was the conquest of China by Communism and the consequent expulsion of Western influences (including the missionaries) from what had been the greatest single mission field in the world.

All through the thirties the Chinese had struggled against Japanese conquest in Manchuria, and then after 1937, in the coastal provinces generally. They found it hard to understand the apparent indifference of the Western nations up to the time when Pearl Harbor (1941) also involved the Americans. Soon most of China was occupied, and in the greatest migration in Chinese history, one hundred million moved to the free areas of the interior. There, as in the occupied countries of Europe, the Church won unprecedented contacts and respect from the larger community. While Christianity grew rapidly in Free China, there was very little religious activity in the Communist northwest. At the Japanese defeat the Communists were in a position to take over the military stocks of Manchuria, while the nation as a whole revolted against Chiang Kai-shek. In the Civil War that followed, the collapse of the Nationalists was more conspicuous than the victories of the Communists, and resentment against the Americans was more apparent than enthusiasm for the Russians. The Roman Catholics actively supported Chiang, while the Protestants tried for a time to be more or less neutral. By the 1950's both Protestants and Roman Catholics had been cut off from other churches, their schools and hospitals were all taken over by the Communists, and numerous official church statements had appeared condemning Western missions as forms of imperialism. The Reign of Ter-

or in China reached dimensions unknown in European history, and Chinese "brain washing" seemed the most thorough and ruthless form of Communist converting technique.

COMMUNIST AREAS. This Communist revolution in China meant that a full third of the world's population, some eight hundred million men and women, were under the control of this passionate and ruthless atheist religion. In one generation Communism had expanded as no other religion in world history. This was the really "ecumenical" movement of the mid-twentieth century, easily maintaining the moral initiative over Christianity and a dynamism far superior to that of the largely secularized religion of formerly Christian Europe and America. Church history had known no comparable losses or threats since the rip tide of Islam in the seventh and eighth centuries. Communism was gaining rapidly elsewhere in Asia and Africa, indoctrinating millions in a militantly antireligious faith.

One consequence of this development, together with other persecuting movements, was that persecution again became a normal part of Christian experience in great areas of the world, even while in some places, as in America, this still seemed incredible. But millions of European and Asiatic Christians were tried under terrific pressures to deny their Lord. Many were the martyrs, and many more, no doubt, the *traditores*. Many aspects of the New Testament, from its unpolitical ethic to its eschatology, took on startling actuality under these circumstances.

In Russia itself, as we have seen in an earlier chapter, World War II brought a notable moderation in the administration of the anti-Christian campaign. The masters of the country could not afford to alienate further that large body, perhaps half of the population, who still "believed." The appeal of the Moscow radio at the time of the Nazi invasion of 1941 to "all God-loving inhabitants" amazed the world. Antireligious periodicals and demonstrations lapsed. Sunday and the seven-day week were restored. A Sobor was convened in 1943 and permitted to elect a patriarch, Sergius. The *Journal of the Moscow Patriarchate* began to appear, and Bibles and Prayer Books could once again be printed. Some religious education was even permitted. Two theological academies and ten seminarie were soon functioning. And in 1945 an Orthodox Sobor as sembled forty bishops, four other Oriental patriarchs, and rep resentatives of other Eastern sees.

This last gathering illustrates one of the most notable aspect of the government's change in policy. The expansion of Com munist influence in Eastern Europe gave the government a new use for Orthodoxy in foreign policy. In the war itself the con cessions to the church were in part designed to counteract Hit ler's appeals to Christians, and those of the emigré Orthodo₃ who supported Hitler. Now the Moscow Patriarchate could be used as a point of attraction for Orthodox Rumanians, Bul gars, Serbs, and other groups. Russian bishops suddenly were permitted and encouraged to visit Orthodox churches outside Russia. The Orthodox of the areas of occupation in the Baltic states, Bulgaria, and Yugoslavia were put under Moscow' jurisdiction. Uniate churches, under some pressure, returned again to the Moscow orbit, as in Rumania. Russia once again made a bid to be the protector of Christians in the Holy Land For a time even the emigré church centered in Paris accepted the jurisdiction of the Moscow Patriarchate, while retaining connections also with Constantinople. Even some four par ishes of the Russian Orthodox in the United States acknowl edged the Moscow Patriarch.

A climax in this development was reached in 1948 when the five hundredth anniversary of the independence of the Russian Church was celebrated in Moscow. The affair drew repre sentatives of ten autocephalous churches and became in effec a Pan-Orthodox Congress and a rival demonstration to the meeting of the World Council at Amsterdam that year. Both the World Council and the Vatican were fiercely denounced The Orthodox world was caught between two poles of attrac tion on opposite sides of the "Iron Curtain," each tending to view the other as hopelessly entangled in political activities.

Protestant and Roman Catholic Churches in the areas o Soviet occupation, on the other hand, were submitted to a grea variety of pressures. When the Russians invaded the Baltic countries at the beginning of the war, they nationalized the churches and hindered their life in many ways. Over one hun red thousand Balts were deported. Then came the Nazis, who turned the persecution from the Christians to the Jews. As they withdrew again they took thousands of Balts with them some voluntarily), and the Russian return meant new deportations. In all, probably only half the original population remained, carrying on church life with great difficulty. Of those deported to Russia little or nothing is known.

The countries which became Communist satellites were prevailingly Roman Catholic. The Vatican had seemed so involved with the Nazi conquest and policy in Poland, Hungary, Yugoslavia, and in some cases the Roman Catholic church had been so blatantly collaborationist, that a reaction was natural. The Russians were hailed as liberators in Hungary. Poland denounced its Concordat in 1946. Tito turned fiercely on the Roman Catholic Croats, who had played Hitler's game.

In Poland, the new boundaries cut off about four million Orthodox on the Russian side, while three million Jews had been exterminated, and about a million Protestants were driven out to Germany. Poland was thus left more exclusively Roman Catholic than she had ever been. A Concordat was signed in 1950, whereby the Catholic clergy swore to accept the political frontiers and the Communist social revolution in Poland. This Concordat marked a lull in the struggle between the church and the state which had been proceeding since the end of the war.

In Hungary, Czechoslovakia, and Yugoslavia the most outright initial resistance to the Communists came from the Roman Catholics. But in every case this was beaten down and isolated from the Vatican and any Western contacts. In Hungary and Yugoslavia, particularly, the problem was complicated by the interest of the churches in the land-holding system, which was in obvious need of reform. These lands were the chief financial basis of the church schools in these countries, and these, too, the Communist rulers were determined to nationalize and secularize. In Hungary Cardinal Mindszenty and Lutheran Bishop Ordass were both imprisoned in this controversy. In Yugoslavia the Roman Church suffered especially because of its implication with the pro-Axis Croat dictatorship of Pavelich in the war. Tito's break with the Cominform led to some relaxa-

tion of pressure, first on the Orthodox, and later, as Wester
contacts increased, also on other churches.

Protestantism in the areas of Soviet occupation did not gen
erally attempt such uncompromising political resistance as th
Roman Church at first exhibited. Except in Eastern German
the Protestants were everywhere weaker and less politically or
ganized. The vigorous Lutheran churches of East Prussia
Pomerania, and Silesia were destroyed, probably forever, whe
the Poles incorporated these areas and drove the German popu
lation west of the Oder and Neisse. The refugees were scat
tered over Germany in camps. The zone of Soviet occupatio
was the most solidly Protestant portion of Germany. Her
the churches followed the policy of accepting the Communis
rule as a necessity and of bearing a Christian witness so far a
possible in daily life. The church was not silent when Com
munist ideology was taught to Christian children. In 195
Bishop Dibelius issued a courageous pastoral letter and pro
tested directly to the premier against indoctrination, even whil
making clear that the church was not seeking to interfere i
political decisions. In 1953 the East German Protestant youth
suffered severe pressure for a time. In Czechoslovakia on
found a positive attitude toward the socialist revolution withi
one wing of the Czech Brethren, led by Professor Hromadka
While maintaining the Christian faith without qualification i
theology and ethics, Hromadka was ready to accept the revolu
tion with all its attendant suffering and cruelty, as the necessar
correction of great historical injustices. In Hungary a signifi
cant section of the church held similar views. Great number
behind the Iron Curtain, both Protestants and Catholics, hear
nothing of international affairs save the Communist view an
came to share that interpretation of the aggressiveness of th
capitalist imperialist West.

EUROPE. West of the Iron Curtain on the European Conti
nent one found no longer militant and persecuting anti-Chris
tian movements in the seats of political power, but the memor
of Fascism and Nazism was everywhere alive. Their triumph
short-lived as it had been, had shown how thin and weak th
Christian tradition in Europe had become, and how great masse
could let it go without serious resistance. France, the tradi

tional seat of Roman Catholic culture and thought, had now become for many the type of de-Christianization. Three-fourths of the nation acknowledged no religious ties, and of these many lived in a real post-Christian paganism. Some of this continued the nineteenth-century anti-clericalism; much of it was Marxist atheism. Just in proportion as they felt themselves a minority, meanwhile, the churches of France intensified their corporate sense and raised the quality of their life. Many of the most striking experiments in evangelism within the world of pagan industrialism were made in France.

Elsewhere in the Roman Catholic world where the church retained its public position, its hold on the people was little more impressive. The one area where Fascism survived the war was in Spain and Latin America, and here the governments continued their religious persecution of Protestants in return for Roman Catholic support at the polls. Under such condi-tions, however, the Protestants generally multiplied, popular disaffection from the Roman Catholic Church was conspicuous, and there was little of the religious vitality of a humbled church, as in France. The large majority had no time for God or his Church.

The Italian situation fell between that of France and Spain. The masses were not as secularized as in France, but their Chris-tianity was of a lower order, often little more than a matter of superstition about observances which could easily be combined with a vote for Communism. The Vatican succeeded in main-taining the privileged position it had secured by its Concordat with Mussolini, and the victors in the war permitted the main-tenance of disabilities on religious minorities. Immediately after the war the Roman Catholic Church had provided a nucleus for political reorganization in many countries, and there was hope that this might be a focus for democratic, socially progressive groups. Catholic parties were dominant in Italy, West Germany, Belgium, and France. But the general tend-ency was for these parties to become increasingly clerical and increasingly the organs of the relatively privileged.

In Northern, Protestant Europe one consequence of the war was to build new bridges for the churches to reach the rest of the community. Under the Nazi occupation the churches had generally been the voice of the people, as in Norway, Denmark, Holland, or Germany itself, for that matter. Here were heard the chief and often the only protests against the treatment of the Jews, the denial of civil rights, and the immoralities of Nazi policy. There was unprecedented co-operation of the different confessions under such pressures, which left many ties, as between Protestants and Roman Catholics, after the war. But the end of the war saw a general falling off from the churches of the new supporters gained in the occupation. Here as in France, the general tendency was for an increasing movement away from the Church among the people generally, and for an increasing core of really practicing Christians within the church. The conquest of the Nazis had been a sensational revelation to the church of how far the process of de-Christianization had gone throughout the whole structure of society. The church was newly conscious of the great inadequacy of its work in religious education, with youth, with industrial labor, and with professional people. One of the most striking postwar developments was the organization of Christian centers for the training of laymen in conceiving their tasks as Christian vocations. Sigtuna in Sweden, Driebergen in Holland, the various "Evangelical Academies" in Germany, and the World Council Institute at Bossey were all consequences of this consciousness that modern Western society was no longer Christian in any significant sense and that the church must begin from the beginning to see if and how the Christian life could be lived in such a context. One other common experience was that precisely in the forced isolation of occupation the sense of ecumenical fellowship became most intense and significant, something for the layman as well as the ecclesiastic. Yet everywhere merely confessional loyalties seemed also quickened, and the legacy of the collaborationist-resistance bitterness hindered reconstruction.

GREAT BRITAIN. In Great Britain many of the same consequences of the war were apparent. There was the same heightening of consciousness of the world Church, together with a hardening of denominational lines. The sense of the de-Christianization of society and the concern to rediscover Christian vocation were here expressed in 1945 by a Church of

ngland commission report on the *Conversion of England*,
which noted a "wholesale drift from organized religion" and
the "present irrelevance of the Church in the life and thought
of the community." There was still a fairly widespread respect
or certain aspects, at least, of Christian ethics, but little or no
ense of the meaning of Christian community or Christian worship among the people generally. As in France, it was urged
that the conversion of England must be considered in the terms
and methods of foreign missions. And while the Education
ill reflected the general concern over religious education
n all state schools, nevertheless the religion so taught was valued
enerally rather as part of a cultural heritage than as a matter of
saving truth.

UNITED STATES. Of all Western peoples, those of the
United States were probably the least divorced from the Chris-
an heritage in public life. Nowhere else did politicians con-
der it so necessary to include prayers in appeals for votes or
to make such play of religious feelings. The churches claimed
numbers and wealth in proportions rivaled nowhere else, and
while attendance at worship seemed to be declining, it was still
probably higher than elsewhere. Probably three-fourths of the
world-wide activities of Roman Catholicism as well as of Protestantism were now financed from the United States. But
while American religion was generous and humanitarian, it was
theologically confused and uncertain of its direction. There
were new currents of undeniable Christian conviction, but they
owed in a broad stream composed also of many less healthy
elements. The prevailing drift of the nation as a whole was to
a more radical secularization. Probably the most prevalent
aspect of it was a technological humanism, a confidence that
man alone could discover and achieve the good life by means of
scientific method. Such confidence was almost gone in Europe, where one no longer found hope that the difficulties of
humanity could be materially improved by science. But curi-
ously enough, this was also the hope of the communist third of
the world. In the U.S.A. and the U.S.S.R. the religion of technology and the engineering mentality seemed the most success-
ul rivals to Christian faith. And the world watched fascinated
while the scientists of these rival powers brought ever nearer

that war which could leave most or all of the earth uninhabitable by man.

* * *

Keeping in mind the long sweep of Christian history, we may conclude our account in these terms. The modern Christian churches inherited the great new enterprise of medieval and Reformation Christianity, the endeavor to penetrate and "Christianize" civilization. For three hundred years they continued this attempt, yet, on the whole, with ever less success. There are, one might guess, as great a proportion of convinced and practicing Christians as ever. But the great forces and structures of modern civilization have increasingly eluded Christian guidance and have pursued new gods, tribal or utopian. In recent years Christians have become increasingly aware of the width of the chasm between the tone of the industrial West and anything that might be called Christian. It does not yet appear how they will adjust to this situation. Will they return to the policy of the church in the Ancient Roman Empire, in which, whether persecuted or recognized by the state, the church entertained no serious hope of transforming state and society, but sought rather to manifest another quality of life within its own community? Or will the church continue to seek, and perhaps find, some way of humanizing and rendering responsive to Jesus Christ a militarized, technological mass civilization?

SUGGESTED READINGS

GENERAL

Encyclopedias:

Hauck-Herzog. *Realencyclopedie der protestantischen Theologie und Geschichte*, 3d ed. 24 vols. Leipzig: J. C. Hinrichs'sche Buchhandlung, 1896-1913.

Schiele, F. M., and Zscharnack, L. *Religion in Geschichte und Gegenwart*. 5 vols. Tübingen: Mohr, 1909-1913.

Ward, A. W., Prothero, G. W., and Leathes, S. (eds.). *The Cambridge Modern History*. 13 vols. and atlas. New York: The Macmillan Co., 1903-1912. (Hereafter cited as *C.M.H.*)

Manuals:

Stephan, H. *Kirchengeschichte der Neuzeit*, 2d ed. Tübingen: Mohr (Paul Siebeck), 1931.

Veit, L. A. *Die Kirche im Zeitalter des Individualismus*. 2 vols. Freiburg i. B.: Herder, 1931-1933.

CHAPTER 1

Becker, Carl L. *The Heavenly City of the 18th Century Philosophers*. New Haven: Yale University Press, 1932.

Gabriel, Ralph H. *The Course of American Democratic Thought*. 2d ed. New York: The Ronald Press Co., 1956.

Groethuysen, B. *Origines de l'esprit bourgeois en France*. 2 vols. Paris: Librairie Gallimard, 1927-1930.

Grützmacher, R. H. *Alt- und Neuprotestantismus*. Erlangen: A. Deichert, 1920.

Hazard, Paul. *The European Mind (1680-1714)*. London: Hollis & Carter, 1953.

Hall, T. C. *The Social Meaning of Modern Religious Movements in England*. New York: Charles Scribner's Sons, 1900.

Halperin, S. W. *Separation of Church and State in Italian Thought from Cavour to Mussolini*. Chicago: University of Chicago Press, 1937.

Hayes, C. J. *The Historical Evolution of Modern Nationalism*. New York: R. R. Smith, Inc., 1931.

——. *Essays on Nationalism*. New York: The Macmillan Co., 1926.

461

Kühn, J. *Toleranz und Offenbarung.* Leipzig: F. Meiner, 1923.

Macmillan, K. D. *Protestantism in Germany.* Princeton: Princeton Unive sity Press, 1917.

Nichols, J. H. *Democracy and the Churches.* Philadelphia: Westminist Press, 1951.

Niebuhr, H. R. *The Social Sources of Denominationalism.* New Yor Henry Holt & Co., 1929.

——. *The Kingdom of God in America.* New York, Chicago: Wille Clark & Co., 1937.

——. *Christ and Culture.* New York: Harper & Bros., 1951.

Perry, R. B. *Puritanism and Democracy.* New York: Vanguard Press, 194

Ruffini, F. *Religious Liberty.* New York: G. P. Putnam's Sons, 1912.

Schaff, P. *The Progress of Religious Freedom.* New York: Charles Scri ner's Sons, 1889.

Tawney, R. H. *Religion and the Rise of Capitalism.* New York: Harcou Brace and Co., 1926.

Troeltsch, E. *The Social Teaching of the Christian Churches.* New Yor The Macmillan Co., 1931, and Glencoe, Ill.: Free Press, 1949.

——. *Die Trennung von Staat und Kirche.* Tübingen: Mohr (Paul Siebec 1907.

——. *Protestantisches Christentum und Kirche in der Neuzeit,* in Hinnebe *Kultur der Gegenwart,* I, iv, 1, Berlin, Leipzig: Teubner, 1909.

Weill, G. J. *Histoire du catholicisme libéral en France,* 1828-1908. Par F. Alcan, 1909.

CHAPTER 2

Adeney, W. F. *The Greek and Eastern Churches.* New York: Charl Scribner's Sons, 1908.

Bolshakov, S. *Russian Nonconformity.* Philadelphia: Westminister Pre 1950.

Conybeare, F. C. *Russian Dissenters.* Cambridge: Harvard University Pre 1921.

Frere, W. H. *Some Links . . . of Russian Church History.* London: Fai Press, 1918.

Kliuchewski, V. *History of Russia.* 5 vols. London: Dent, 1911-1913.

Koch, H. *Die Russische Orthodoxie im Petrinischen Zeitalter.* Breslau: Pri batsch, 1929.

Kyriakos, A. D. *Geschichte der Orientalischen Kirchen von 1453-18* Leipzig: A. Deichert (G. Boehme), 1902.

Leroy-Beaulieu, A. *The Empire of the Tsars.* 3 vols. New York: G. Putnam's Sons, 1893-1896.

Miliukov, P. *Outlines of Russian Culture.* 3 vols. Philadelphia: Universi of Pennyslvania Press, 1942.

Palmer, W. *The Patriarch and the Tsar.* 6 vols. London: Trübner, 187 1876.

Papadopoulos, T. H. *Studies and Documents Relating to . . . the Gre Church . . . under Turkish Domination.* Brussels: Librairie Scaldis, 19

Pascal, P. *Avvakum et les débuts du Raskol.* Paris: H. Champion, 1938.

Tondini, R. P. C. *Le Règlement ecclésiastique de Pierre le Grand.* Paris: I brairie de la société bibliographique, 1874.

CHAPTER 3

Dézert, G. M. *L'Espagne de l'ancien régime*. 3 vols. Paris: Soc. française d'impr. et de libr., 1897-1904.

Gazier, A. L. *Histoire générale du mouvement janséniste*. 2 vols. Paris: E. Champion, 1922.

Geffcken, F. H. *Church and State*. 2 vols. London: Longmans, Green & Co., 1877.

Jervis, W. H. P. *History of the Church of France (1516-1789)*. 2 vols. London: J. Murray, 1872.

Lafitau, P. T. *Histoire de la constitution Unigenitus*. 2 vols. Maestricht: Impr. de. P. L. Lekens, 1791.

Maass, F. *Der Josephinismus*. 3 vols. Vienna: Herold, 1951, 1953, –.

MacCaffrey, J. *History of the Catholic Church from the Renaissance to the French Revolution*. 2 vols. Dublin and Waterford: M. H. Gill & Son, Ltd., 1915.

Moss, C. B. *The Old Catholic Movement*. London: S.P.C.K., 1948.

Nielsen, F. K. *History of the Papacy in the XIXth Century*, Vol. I. London: J. Murray, 1906.

Palmer, R. R. *Catholics and Unbelievers in 18th Century France*. Princeton: Princeton University Press, 1939.

Sicard, A. *L'ancien clergé de France*. 3 vols. Paris: V. Lecoffre, 1899-1905.

CHAPTER 4

Drews, P. *Der evangelische Geistliche in der deutschen Vergangenheit*. Jena: E. Diederichs, 1905.

Drummond, A. L. *German Protestantism Since Luther*. London: Epworth Press, 1951.

Geffcken, F. H. *Church and State*. 2 vols. London: Longmans, Green & Co., 1877.

Hagenbach, K. R. *History of the Church in the XVIIIth and XIXth Centuries*. 2 vols. New York, Charles Scribner's Sons Co., 1869.

Holl, K. "Die Bedeutung der grossen Kriege," *Ges. Aufsätze*, III. Tübingen: Mohr (Paul Siebeck) 1928-1932.

Macmillan, K. D. *Protestantism in Germany*. Princeton: Princeton University Press, 1917.

Rocholl, R. *Geschichte der evangelischen Kirche in Deutschland*. Leipzig: A. Deichert (G. Boehme), 1897.

CHAPTER 5

Colligan, J. H. *Eighteenth Century Nonconformity*. London, New York: Longmans, Green & Co., 1915.

Haller, W. *Liberty and Reformation in the Puritan Revolution*. New York: Columbia University Press, 1955.

Jordan, W. K. *Development of religious toleration in England*. 3 vols. Cambridge: Harvard University Press, 1932-1940.

Legg, J. W. *English Church Life, 1660-1833*. London: Longmans, Green & Co., 1914.

McNeill, J. T. *History and Character of Calvinism.* New York: Oxfor University Press, 1954.

Moorman, J. R. H. *A History of the Church in England.* London: A. and (Black, 1953.

Overton, J. H. *Life in the English Church* (1660-1714). London: Longman Green, & Co., 1885.

———, and Relton, F. *The English Church* (1714-1800). London, New Yorl Macmillan & Co., 1906.

Sykes, N. *Church and State in England in the XVIIIth Century.* Cambridg England: Cambridge University Press, 1934.

Troeltsch, E. *The Social Teaching of the Christian Churches.* New Yorl The Macmillan Co., 1931; Glencoe, Ill.: Free Press, 1949.

CHAPTER 6

Baldwin, A. M. *The New England Clergy and the American Revolution* Durham, N. C.: Duke University Press, 1928.

Cobb, S. H. *The Rise of Religious Liberty in America.* New York: Th Macmillan Co., 1902.

Gewehr, W. M. *The Great Awakening in Virginia, 1740-1790.* Durham N. C.: Duke University Press, 1930.

Greene, E. B. *Religion and the State.* New York: New York Universit Press, 1941.

Humphrey, E. F. *Nationalism and Religion in America, 1774-1789.* Boston Chipman Law Publishing Company, 1924.

Koch, G. A. *Republican Religion.* New York: Henry Holt & Co., 1933.

Maxson, C. H. *The Great Awakening in The Middle Colonies.* Chicago University of Chicago Press, 1920.

Miller, P. *Jonathan Edwards.* New York: W. Sloane Assoc., 1949.

———. *Orthodoxy in Massachusetts, 1630-1650.* Cambridge: Harvard Univer sity Press, 1933.

———. *The New England Mind, the 17th Century.* New York: The Macmil lan Co., 1939.

———. *The New England Mind, Colony to Province.* Cambridge: Harvar University Press, 1953.

———, and Johnson, T. H. *The Puritans.* New York: American Book Co 1938.

Morais, H. M. *Deism in 18th Century America.* New York: Columbia Uni versity Press, 1934.

Perry, R. B. *Puritanism and Democracy.* New York: Vanguard Press, 1944

Stokes, A. P. *Church and State in the United States.* 3 vols. New York Harper & Bros., 1950.

Sweet, W. W. *The Story of Religion in America,* rev. ed. New York: Har per & Bros., 1939.

———. *Religion in Colonial America.* New York: Charles Scribner's Sons 1942.

Trinterud, L. J. *The Forming of an American Tradition, . . . Colonial Pres byterianism.* Philadelphia: Westminister Press, 1949.

Chapter 7

Addison, W. G. *Renewed Church of the United Brethren, 1722-1930*. London: S.P.C.K., 1932.

Edwards, M. *John Wesley and the 18th Century*. New York, Cincinnati, Chicago: The Abingdon Press, 1933.

Hagenbach, K. R. *History of the Church in the XVIIIth and XIXth Centuries*. 2 vols. New York: Charles Scribner's Sons, 1869.

Heppe, H. L. J. *Geschichte des Pietismus und der Mystik in der Reformierten Kirche*. Leiden: E. J. Brill, 1879.

Knox, R. A. *Enthusiasm*. Oxford: Clarendon Press, 1951.

Piette, M. *John Wesley in the Evolution of Protestantism*. New York: Sheed & Ward, 1937.

Ritschl, O. *Geschichte des Pietismus*. 3 vols. Bonn: A. Marcus, 1880-1886.

Seeberg, E. *Gottfried Arnold*. Meerane i. Sa.: E. R. Herzog, 1923.

Sessler, J. J. *Communal Pietism Among Early American Moravians*. New York: Henry Holt & Co., 1933.

Townsend, W. T., Workman, H. B., Eayrs, G. *New History of Methodism*. London: Hodder & Stoughton, 1909.

Chapter 8

Becker, Carl L. *The Heavenly City of the 18th Century Philosophers*. New Haven: Yale University Press, 1932.

Groethuysen, B. *Origines de l'espirit bourgeois en France*. 2 vols. Paris: Librairie Gallimard, 1927-1930.

Hagenbach, K. R. *History of the Church in the XVIIIth and XIXth Centuries*. 2 vols. New York: Charles Scribner's Sons, 1869.

Hirsch, E. *Geschichte der neueren evangelischen Theologie*. 5 vols. Gütersloh: C. Bertelsmann, 1949-1954.

Masson, P. M. *La religion de J. J. Rousseau*. 3 vols. Paris: Hachette et c^{1e}, 1916.

McGiffert, A. C. *Protestant Thought before Kant*. New York: Charles Scribner's Sons, 1911.

Palmer, R. R. *Catholics and Unbelievers in 18th Century France*. Princeton: Princeton University Press, 1939.

Stephen, Leslie. *History of English Thought in the 18th Century*. 2 vols. New York: G. P. Putnam & Co., 1876.

Chapter 9

Aulard, F. O. *Christianity and the French Revolution*. London: E. Benn, Ltd., 1927.

Debidour, A. *Histoire des rapports de l'Eglise et l'Etat en France de 1789 à 1870*. Paris: F. Alcan, 1898.

Gazier, A. *Etudes sur l'histoire religieuse de la Révolution française*. Paris: A. Colin et c^{1e}, 1887.

Geffcken, F. H. *Church and State*. 2 vols. London: Longmans, Green & Co., 1877.

De la Gorce, P. *Histoire religieuse de la Révolution française.* 5 vols. Paris Plon-Nourrite et cⁱᵉ, 1921-1924.

Jervis, W. H. P. *The Gallican Church and the Revolution.* London: Keegan Paul, Trench & Co., 1882.

Latreille, A. *L'Eglise catholique et la Révolution française.* Paris: Hachette et cⁱᵉ, 1946.

Ledré, C. *L'Eglise de France sous la Révolution.* Paris: R. Laffont, 1949.

Leflon, J. *Histoire de l'Eglise. La crise révolutionnaire, 1789-1846.* Paris Bloud et Gay, 1949.

Mathiez, A. *La Révolution et l'Eglise.* Paris: A. Colin, 1910.

———. *La théophilanthropie et le culte décadaire 1796-1801.* Paris: F. Alcan 1903.

Nielsen, F. K. *History of the Papacy in the XIXth Century.* Vol. I. London: J. Murray, 1906.

Phillips, C. S. *The Church in France, 1789-1848.* Milwaukee: Morehouse Publishing Co., 1929.

Sciout, T. *Histoire de la constitution civile du clergé (1790-1801).* 4 vols Paris: Firmin Didot frères, fils et cⁱᵉ, 1872-1881.

Seché, L. *Les derniers Jansénistes (1710-1870).* 3 vols. Paris: Perrin et cⁱᵉ 1891.

Sicard, A. *L'ancien clergé de France.* 3 vols. Paris: V. Lecoffre, 1899-1905

Sloane, W. M. *French Revolution and Religious Reform 1789-1804.* New York: Charles Scribner's Sons, 1901.

Chapter 10

Debidour, A. *Histoire des rapports de l'Eglise et l'Etat en France de 1789 à 1870.* Paris: F. Alcan, 1898.

Geffcken, F. H. *Church and State.* 2 vols. London: Longmans, Green & Co., 1877.

Goyau, G. *L'Allemagne religieuse. Le Catholicisme 1800-1870.* 4 vols Paris, Perrin et cⁱᵉ, 1909-1910.

Latreille, A. *L'Eglise Catholique et la Révolution française.* Paris: Hatchette et cⁱᵉ, 1946.

Leflon, J. *Histoire de l'Eglise. La crise révolutionnaire, 1789-1846.* Paris Bloud et Gay, 1949.

MacCaffrey, J. *History of the Catholic Church in the 19th Century.* 2 vols St. Louis: B. Herder, 1910.

Nielsen, F. K. *History of the Papacy in the XIXth Century.* Vol. I. London: John Murray, 1906.

Phillips, C. S. *The Church in France, 1789-1848.* Milwaukee: The Morehouse Publishing Co., 1929.

Schmidlin, J. *Papstgeschichte der neuesten Zeit,* 2d ed. München: Verlag Josef Kösel & Friedrich Pustet, 1933.

Wickham-Legg, L. G. "The Concordats," *C. M. H.,* IX, Chap. 7.

Chapter 11

Craig, J. (trans.) *History of the Protestant Church in Hungary . . . to 1850* Boston: Phillips, Sampson & Co., 1854.

Félice, G. de. *Histoire des Protestants des France*. Toulouse: Société des livres religieux, 1895.

Fleming, J. R. *History of the Church in Scotland, 1834-74*. Edinburgh: T. & T. Clark, 1927.

Geffcken, F. H. *Church and State*. 2 vols. London: Longmans, Green & Co., 1877.

Good, J. I. *History of the Reformed Church of Germany, 1620-1890*. Reading: D. Miller, 1894.

——. *History of the Swiss Reformed Church*. . . . Philadelphia: Reformed Church in the U. S., 1913.

Groen Van Prinsterer, G. *Le parti anti-révolutionnaire . . . dans l'Eglise réformée des Pays-Bas*. Amsterdam: H. Höveker, 1860.

Holl, K. "Thomas Chalmers," *Gesammelte Aufsätze* III, Tübingen: Mohr, 1928.

Koehler, A. *Die Niederländische Reformierte Kirche*. Erlangen: A. Deichert, 1856.

Laski, H. J. *Problems of Sovereignty*. New Haven: Yale University Press, 1917.

Chapter 12

Geffcken, F. H. *Church and State*. 2 vols. London: Longmans, Green & Co., 1877.

Gerhardt, M. *Ein Jahrhundert Innere Mission*. 2 vols. Gütersloh: C. Bertelsmann, 1948.

Hermelink, H. *Das Christentum in der Menschheitsgeschichte*. . . . Stuttgart: Metzler und Wunderlich, 1951.

Kissling, J. B. *Der deutsche Protestantismus 1817-1917*. 2 vols. Münster i. W.; Aschendorff, 1917-1918.

Macmillan, K. D. *Protestantism in Germany*. Princeton: Princeton University Press, 1917.

Schnabel, F. *Deutsche Geschichte im neunzehnten Jahrhundert*. Bd IV. Freiburg i. B.: Herder, 1929.

Seeberg, R. *Die Kirche Deutschlands im neunzehnten Jahrhundert*, 2d ed. Leipzig: A. Deichert (G. Boehme), 1904.

Shanahan, W. O. *German Protestants Face the Social Question*. Notre Dame, Ind.: University of Notre Dame Press, 1954.

Tischhauser, C. *Geschichte der evangelishen Kirche Deutschlands*. . . . Basel: R. Reich, 1900.

Chapter 13

Barth, K. *Die protestantische Theologie im 19. Jahrhundert*. Zollikon/Zürich: Evangelischer Verlag, 1947.

Creed, J. M. *The Divinity of Jesus Christ*. Cambridge: Cambridge University Press, 1938.

Dilthey, W. *Leben Schleiermachers* 2d ed. Vol. I. Berlin and Leipzig: Walter de Gruyter & Co., 1922.

Elert, Werner. *Der Kampf um das Christentum*. Munich: C. H. Beck'sche Verlagsbuchhandlung, Oskar Beck, 1921.

Hirsch, E. *Geschichte der neueren evangelischen Theologie.* 5 vols. Gütersloh: C. Bertelsmann, 1949-1954.

Kattenbusch, F. *Die deutsche evangelische Theologie seit Schleiermacher,* 5th ed. Giessen: Toepelmann, 1926.

Lichtenberger, F. A. *History of German Theology in the 19th Century.* Edinburgh: T. & T. Clark, 1889.

Mackintosh, H. R. *Types of Modern Theology.* . . . New York: Charles Scribner's Sons, 1937.

Pfleiderer, O. *Development of Theology in Germany since Kant* . . . , 3d ed. London: Sonnenschein, 1909.

Chapter 14

Brilioth, Y. T. *The Anglican Revival.* New York: Longmans, Green & Co., 1925.

Carpenter, S. C. *Church and People, 1789-1889.* London: S.P.C.K., New York: The Macmillan Co., 1933.

Church, R. W. *The Oxford Movement.* New York: The Macmillan Co., 1892.

Faulkner, H. V. *Chartism and the Churches.* New York: Columbia University Press, 1916.

Halévy, E. *History of the English People in 1815.* Bk. III. London: Penguin, 1937.

Hall, T. C. *The Social Meaning of Modern Religious Movements in England.* New York: Charles Scribner's Sons, 1900.

Klingberg, F. J. *Antislavery Movement in England.* New Haven: Yale University Press, 1926.

Laski, H. J. *Problems of Sovereignty.* New Haven: Yale University Press, 1917.

Mathieson, W. L. *English Church Reform 1815-40.* London: Longmans, Green & Co., 1923.

Raven, C. E. *Christian Socialism, 1848-54.* London: Macmillan & Co., 1920.

Stewart, H. L. *A Century of Anglo-Catholicism.* London: J. M. Dent & Sons, Ltd., 1929.

Storr, V. F. *Development of English Theology in the XIXth Century.* London: Longmans, Green & Co., 1913.

Taylor, E. R. *Methodism and Politics 1791-1851.* Cambridge: Cambridge University Press, 1935.

Tulloch, John. *Movements of Religious Thought in Britain during the 19th Century.* New York: Charles Scribner's Sons, 1885.

Ward, B. N. *The Eve of Catholic Emancipation.* 3 vols. New York: Longmans, Green & Co., 1911-1912.

Wearmouth, R. F. *Methodism and the Working Class Movements of England, 1800-1850.* London: Epworth Press, 1937.

Willey, B. *Nineteenth Century Studies.* London: Chatto & Windus, 1949.

Chapter 15

Barnes, G. *The Antislavery Impulse.* New York: Appleton-Century-Crofts, 1933.

Bates, E. S. *American Faith.* New York: W. W. Norton Co., Inc., 1940.

Bestor, A. E., Jr. *Backwoods Utopias*. Philadelphia: University of Pennsylvania Press, 1950.

Billington, R. A. *The Protestant Crusade, 1800-1860*. New York: The Macmillan Co., 1938.

Cleveland, C. C. *The Great Revival in the West, 1797-1805*. Chicago: University of Chicago Press, 1916.

Cross, W. R. *The Burned-over District . . . Western New York, 1800-1850*. Ithaca: Cornell University Press, 1950.

Elsbree, O. W. *Rise of the Missionary Spirit in America, 1790-1815*. Williamsport, Pa.: Williamsport Printing and Binding Co., 1928.

Jenkins, W. S. *Pro-Slavery Thought in the Old South*. Chapel Hill: University of North Carolina Press, 1935.

Keller, C. R. *The Second Great Awakening in Connecticut*. New Haven: Yale University Press, 1942.

Mead, S. E. *Nathaniel William Taylor, 1786-1858*. Chicago: University of Chicago Press, 1942.

Mode, P. G. *The Frontier Spirit in American Christianity*. New York: The Macmillan Co., 1923.

Parrington, V. L. *Main Currents in American Thought*. 3 vols. New York: Harcourt, Brace and Co., Inc., 1930.

Sweet, W. W. *Story of Religion in America*, rev. ed. New York: Harper & Bros., 1939.

———. *Revivalism in America*. New York: Charles Scribner's Sons, 1944.

———. *Religion on the American Frontier*, 4 vols. Vol. 1, New York: Henry Holt & Co., 1931; Vol. 2, New York: Harper & Bros., 1936; Vols. 3 and 4, Chicago: University of Chicago Press, 1939, 1946.

———. *Religion in the Development of American Culture 1765-1840*. New York: Charles Scribner's Sons, 1952.

Tewksbury, D. G. *The Founding of American Colleges and Universities*. New York: Teachers College, Columbia University, 1932.

Tocqueville, A. de. *Democracy in America*. 2 vols. New York: A. A. Knopf, 1945.

Tyler, A. F. *Freedom's Ferment*. Minneapolis: University of Minnesota Press, 1944.

CHAPTER 16

Acton, Lord. "The Vatican Council," *Essays on Freedom and Power*, Glencoe, Ill.: Free Press, 1948.

Aubert, R. *Histoire de l'Eglise. Le pontificat de Pie IX (1846-1878)*. Paris: Bloud et Gay, 1952.

Blennerhassett, Lady. "The Papacy and the Catholic Church," *C.M.H.*, X, Chap. V.

Butler, E. C. *The Vatican Council*, 2 vols. New York: Longmans, Green & Co., 1930.

Collins, R. W. *Catholicism and the Second French Republic*. New York: Columbia University Press, 1923.

Debidour, A. *Histoire des rapports de l'Eglise et l'Etat en France de 1789 à 1870*. Paris: F. Alcan, 1898.

Fawkes, A. A. "Rome and the Vatican Council," *C.M.H.*, XI, Chap. XXV.

Goyau, G. *L'Allemagne religieuse. Le Catholicisme 1800-1870.* 4 vols. Paris: Perrin et cᶦᵉ, 1909-1910.

Guérard, A. L. *French Prophets of Yesterday.* London: T. F. Unwin, 1913.

Haag, H. *Les origines du catholicisme libéral en Belgique 1789-1839.* Louvain: Bibl. de l'Univ., 1950.

"Janus" [Doellinger]. *The Pope and the Council,* 3d ed. rev. London: Rivingtons, 1870.

Laski, H. J. *Authority and the Modern State.* New Haven: Yale University Press, 1919.

Leflon, J. *Histoire de l'Eglise. La crise révolutionnaire, 1789-1846.* Paris: Bloud et Gay, 1949.

MacCaffrey, J. *History of the Catholic Church from the Renaissance to the French Revolution.* 2 vols. Dublin and Waterford: M. H. Gill & Son, Ltd., 1915.

Moss, C. B. *The Old Catholic Movement.* London: S.P.C.K., 1948.

Nielsen, F. K. *History of the Papacy in the XIXth Century.* Vol. II. London: J. Murray, 1906.

Phillips, C. S. *The Church in France, 1789-1848.* Milwaukee: Morehouse Publishing Co., 1929.

———. *The Church in France 1848-1907.* New York: The Macmillan Co., 1936.

Salmon, G. *The Infallibility of the Church.* London: J. Murray, 1923.

Schmidlin, J. *Papstgeschichte der neuesten Zeit,* 2d ed. Munich: Verlag Josef Kösel & Friedrich Pustet, 1933.

Vidler, A. R. *Prophecy and Papacy* [Lamennais] New York: Charles Scribner's Sons, 1954.

Weill, G. J. *Histoire du catholicisme libéral en France, 1828-1908.* Paris: F. Alcan, 1909.

Woodward, E. L. *Three Studies in European Conservatism.* London: Constable & Co., Ltd., 1929.

CHAPTER 17

Acomb, E. M. *The French Laic Laws, 1879-1889.* New York: Columbia University Press, 1941.

Binchy, D. A. *Church and State in Fascist Italy.* London: Oxford University Press, 1941.

Bodley, J. E. C. *The Church in France.* London: Constable & Co., 1906.

Briand, A. *La séparation des églises et de l'état. . . .* Paris: Cornély, 1905.

Brodhead, J. M. N. *The Religious Persecution in France, 1900-1906.* London: Keagan Paul, Trench, Trübner & Co., Ltd., 1907.

Debidour, A. *L'eglise catholique et l'état sous la troisième république (1870-1906).* Paris: F. Alcan, 1906-1909.

Geffcken, F. H. *Church and State.* 2 vols. London: Longmans, Green & Co., 1877.

Gladstone, W. E. and Schaff, P. *Vatican Decrees.* New York: Harper & Bros., 1875.

Goyau, G. *Bismarck et l'Eglise: Le Kulturkampf 1870-1887,* 4 vols. Paris: Perrin, 1911-1913.

Gwynn, D. R. *The Catholic Reaction in France.* New York: The Macmillan Co., 1924.

Halperin, S. W. *Italy and the Vatican at War 1870-1878.* Chicago: University of Chicago Press, 1939.

Kissling, J. B. *Geschichte des Kulturkampfes im Deutschen Reiche,* 3 vols. Freiburg: Herder, 1911-1918.

Lecanuet, E. *L'eglise de France sous la troisième république,* 2 vols. Paris: J. de Gigord, 1910.

Lüttge, W. *Die Trennung von Staat und Kirche in Frankreich und der französische Protestantismus.* Tübingen: Mohr, 1912.

Mecham, J. L. *Church and State in Latin America.* Chapel Hill, N.C.: University of North Carolina Press, 1934.

Phillips, C. *The Church in France, 1848-1908.* New York: The Macmillan Co., 1936.

Schmidlin, J. *Papstgeschichte der neuesten Zeit,* 2d ed. Munich: Verlag Josef Kösel & Friedrich Pustet, 1933.

Schrörs, H. *Deutscher und französischer Katholizismus in den letzten Jahrzehnten.* Freiburg: Herder, 1917.

Soderini, E. *Leo XIII, Italy and France.* London: Burns, Oates & Washbourne, Ltd., 1935.

Weill, G. *Histoire du catholicisme libéral en France, 1828-1908.* Paris: F. Alcan, 1909.

CHAPTER 18

Barbier, E. *Histoire du catholicisme libéral.* . . . 6 vols. Bordeaux: Y. Cadoret, 1924.

Bergstraesser, L. *Der politische Katholizismus,* 2 vols. München: Drei Masken Verlag, 1921-1923.

Gurian, W. *Die politischen und sozialen Ideen des französischen Katholizismus, 1789-1914.* München: Gladbach, Volksvereins Verlag, 1929.

Husslein, J. *Social Wellsprings: Fourteen Documents by Pope Leo XIII.* Milwaukee: Bruce, 1940.

Lecanuet, E. *L'eglise de France sous la troisième république.* 2 vols. Paris: J. de Gigord, 1910.

McEntee, G. P. *The Social Catholic Movement in Great Britain.* New York: The Macmillan Co., 1927.

Michon, G. (ed.). *Les documents pontificaux sur la démocratie et la société moderne.* Paris: Rieder, 1928.

Moon, P. T. *The Labor Problem and the Social Catholic Movement in France.* New York: The Macmillan Co., 1921.

Nichols, J. H. *Democracy and the Churches.* Philadelphia: Westminister Press, 1951.

Nitti, F. S. *Catholic Socialism.* New York: The Macmillan Co., 1908.

Soderini, E. *The Pontificate of Leo XIII.* London: Burns, Oates & Washbourne, ltd. 1934.

Weill, G. *Histoire du catholicisme libéral en France, 1828-1908.* Paris: F. Alcan, 1909.

CHAPTER 19

Drummond, A. L. *German Protestantism Since Luther.* London: Epworth Press, 1951.

Gerhardt, M. *Ein Jahrhundert Innere Mission.* 2 vols. Gütersloh: C. Bertelsmann, 1948.

Hermelink, H. *Das Christentum in der Menschheitsgeschichte,* Bd. III. Stuttgart, Metzler, Tübingen: R. Wunderlich, 1955.

Macmillan, K. D. *Protestantism in Germany.* Princeton: Princeton University Press, 1917.

Means, P. B. *Things That Are Caesar's.* New York: Round Table, 1935.

Ragaz, L. "Von der schweizerischen religiös-sozialen Bewegung zur dialektischen Theologie," *Reich Gottes, Marxismus, Nationalsozialismus,* ed. Wünsch. Tübingen: Mohr, 1931.

———. *Der Kampf um das Reich Gottes in Blumhardt, Vater und Sohn.* Zurich: Rotapfel-verlag, 1922.

Révész, E., Kováts, J. S., and Ravasz, L. *Hungarian Protestantism.* Budapest: Bethlen Gábor Literary and Printing House Co., Ltd., 1927.

Siegmund-Schultze, F. (ed.). *Ekklesia-Eine Sammlung von Selbstdarstellungen der Christlichen Kirchen.* Gotha: L. Klotz, 1934-1938. Vol. II, *Die Skandinavischen Länder;* Vol. III, *Die Mitteleuropäischen Länder* [Switzerland, Netherlands]; Vol. IV, *Die Evangelische Kirche in Österreich;* Vol. V, *Die Osteuropäischen Länder* [Czechoslovakia, Poland].

Wuensch, G. *Evangelische Ethik des Politischen.* Tübingen: Mohr, 1936.

CHAPTER 20

Beck, G. A. (ed.). *The English Catholics, 1850-1950.* London: Burns, Oates & Washbourne, 1950.

Binyon, G. C. *The Christian Socialist Movement in England.* London: The Macmillan Co., 1931.

Clark, H. W. *History of English Nonconformity,* Vol. II. London: Chapman & Hall, Ltd., 1913.

Cornish, F. W. *English Church in the 19th Century.* London: The Macmillan Co., 1910.

Elliott-Binns, L. E. *Religion in the Victorian Era.* London: Lutterworth, 1936.

———. *The Development of English Theology in the later Nineteenth Century.* London: Longmans, Green & Co., 1952.

Figgis, J. N. *Churches in the Modern State.* London: Longmans, Green & Co., 1913.

Fleming, J. R. *History of the Church in Scotland, 1875-1929.* Edinburgh: T. & T. Clark, 1933.

Henderson, G. D. *Claims of the Church of Scotland.* London: Hodder & Stoughton, 1951.

Lloyd, R. B. *The Church of England in the 20th Century,* 2 vols. New York: Longmans, Green & Co., 1947.

Reckitt, M. *Maurice to Temple.* London: Faber & Faber, 1948.

Spinks, G. S. *Religion in Britain since 1900.* London: Dakers, 1952.

Stewart, H. L. *A Century of Anglo-Catholicism.* London: Dent, 1929.

Wagner, D. O. *The Church of England and Social Reform since 1854.* New York: Columbia University Press, 1930.

Webb, C. C. J. *A Study of Religious Thought in England from 1850.* Oxford: Clarendon Press, 1933.

CHAPTER 21

Abell, A. I. *Urban Impact on American Protestantism, 1865-1900.* Cambridge: Harvard University Press, 1943.

Atkins, G. G. *Religion in our Times.* New York: Round Table, 1932.

Dombrowski, J. *Early Days of Christian Socialism in America.* New York: Columbia University Press, 1936.

Gabriel, R. *Course of American Democratic Thought.* 2d ed. New York: The Ronald Press Co., 1956.

Garrison, W. E. *The March of Faith.* New York: Harper & Bros., 1933.

Guilday, P. "The Church in the U.S.A., 1870-1920," *Catholic Historical Review,* 1921. Vol. VI, 533-547.

Hammar, G. *Christian Realism in Contemporary American Theology.* Uppsala, Sweden: A.-b. Lundequistska bokhandeln, 1940.

Hofstadter, R. *Social Darwinism in American Thought.* Philadelphia: University of Pennsylvania Press, 1945.

Hopkins, C. H. *History of the Y.M.C.A. in North America.* New York: Association Press, 1951.

————. *Rise of the Social Gospel in American Protestantism.* New Haven: Yale University Press, 1940.

May, H. F. *Protestant Churches and Industrial America.* New York: Harper & Bros., 1949.

Maynard, T. *The Story of American Catholicism.* New York: The Macmillan Co., 1941.

Parrington, V. L. *Main Currents in American Thought.* Vol. III. New York: Harcourt, Brace & Co., Inc., 1930.

Schlesinger, A. M. "A Critical Period in American Protestantism, 1875-1900," *Mass. Hist. Soc. Proc.* LXIV (Oct. 1930).

Sellin, T. (ed.). "Organized Religion in the United States," *Annals of the American Academy of Political Science* (March, 1948).

Shedd, C. P. *Two Centuries of Student Christian Movements.* New York: Association Press, 1934.

Sperry, W. L. *Religion in America.* Cambridge: Cambridge University Press, 1945.

Stokes, A. P. *Church and State in America,* 3 vols. New York: Harper & Bros., 1950.

Sweet, W. W. *Story of Religion in America,* rev. ed. New York: Harper & Bros., 1939.

Thompson, E. T. *Changing Emphases in American Preaching.* Philadelphia: Westminister Press, 1943.

CHAPTER 22

Barth, K. *Die protestantische Theologie im 19. Jahrhundert.* Zollikon/Zürich: Evangelischer Verlag, 1947.

Creed, J. M. *The Divinity of Jesus Christ.* Cambridge: Cambridge University Press, 1938.

Kattenbusch, F. *Die deutsche evangelische Theologie seit Schleiermacher,* 5th ed. Giessen: Töpelmann, 1936.

Lichtenberger, F. A. *History of German Theology in the 19th Century.* Edinburgh: T. & T. Clark, 1889.

Mackintosh, H. R. *Types of Modern Theology.* . . . New York: Charles Scribner's Sons, 1937.

Oman, L. W. *The Problem of Faith and Freedom.* New York: A. C. Armstrong & Son, 1906.

Pfleiderer, O. *Development of Theology in Germany since Kant* . . . , 3d ed. London: Sonnenschien, 1909.

Stephan, H. *Geschichte der evangelischen Theologie.* Berlin: Töpelmann, 1938.

Webb, C. C. J. *A Study of Religious Thought in England from 1850.* Oxford: Clarendon Press, 1933.

CHAPTER 23

Buonaiuti, E. *Le modernisme catholique.* Paris: Rieder, 1927.

Fawkes, A. *Studies in modernism.* London: J. Murray, 1913.

Hocedez, E., S.J. *Histoire de la théologie au XIXᵉ Siècle.* 3 vols. Paris: Desclée de Brouwer, 1947-1953.

Holl, K. "Der Modernismus," *Gesammelte Aufsätze,* III. Tübingen: Mohr, 1928.

Houtin, A. *Histoire du modernisme catholique.* Paris: Chez l'auteur, 1913.

Lilley, A. L. *Modernism.* New York: Charles Scribner's Sons, 1909.

Loisy, A. F. *Mémoires pour servir à l'histoire religieuse,* 3 vols. Paris: E. Nourry, 1930-1931.

Petre, M. D. *Autobiography and Life of Tyrrell,* 2 vols. London: Ed. Arnold, 1912.

———. *Modernism, its Failure and its Fruits.* London and Edinburgh: T. C. & E. C. Jack, Ltd., 1918.

Sabatier, P. *Modernism.* New York: Charles Scribner's Sons, 1909.

Tyrrell, (trans.). *The Programme of Modernism.* New York: G. P. Putnams Sons, 1908.

Vidler, A. R. *The Modernist Movement in the Roman Church.* Cambridge, England: Cambridge University Press, 1934.

CHAPTER 24

Latourette, K. S. *A History of the Expansion of Christianity.* New York: Harper & Bros. Vol. IV, *The Great Century 1800-1914 Europe and the U.S.A.* (1941); Vol. V, *The Great Century in the Americas, Australasia and Africa 1800-1914* (1943); Vol. VI, *The Great Century in Northern Africa and Asia 1800-1914* (1944).

Richter, J. *Die evangelische Mission in Fern-und Südost-Asien, Australien, Amerika.* Gütersloh: L. Bertelsmann, 1908-1932. *Die evangelische Mission in Niederländisch-Indien* (1931); *Geschichte der evangelischen Mission in Afrika* (1922); *Indische Missionsgeschichte,* 2d ed. (1924); *Mission und Evangelisation im Orient,* 2d ed. (1930).

CHAPTER 25

Arens, B., S.J. *Handbuch der katholischen Missionen*. St. Louis: Herder, 1920.

Descamps, Baron E. *Histoire Générale Comparée des Missions*, Paris: Librairie Plon, 1932.

Latourette, K. S. *A History of the Expansion of Christianity*. New York: Harper & Bros. Vol. IV, *The Great Century 1800-1914 Europe and the U.S.A.* (1941); Vol. V, *The Great Century in the Americas, Australasia and Africa 1800-1914* (1943); Vol. VI, *The Great Century in Northern Africa and Asia 1800-1914* (1944).

Lecanuet, E. *L'église de France sous la troisième république*. 2 vols. Paris: Gigord, 1910.

Piolet, J. B. *Les Missions Catholiques Françaises au XIX⁰ Siècle*, 5 vols. Paris: A. Colin, 1900-1903.

Schmidlin, J. *Katholische Missionsgeschichte*. Kaldenkirchen: Missionsdruckerei Steyl, 1924.

CHAPTER 26

Berdiaev, N. *Origin of Russian Communism*. New York: Charles Scribner's Sons, 1937.

Bolshakoff, S. *Russian Nonconformity*. Philadelphia: Westminister Press, 1950.

Conybeare, F. C. *Russian Dissenters*. Cambridge: Harvard University Press, 1921.

Curtiss, J. S. *Church and State in Russia, 1900-1917*. New York: Columbia University Press, 1940.

Losskii, N. O. *History of Russian Philosophy*. New York: International Universities Press, 1951.

Miliukov, P. N. *Outlines of Russian Culture*. 3 vols. Philadelphia: University of Pennsylvania Press, 1942.

CHAPTER 27

Anderson, P. B. *People, Church and State in Modern Russia*. New York: The Macmillan Co., 1944.

Attwater, D. *The Christian Churches of the East*. 2 vols. Milwaukee: Bruce, 1947-1948.

Bates, M. S. *Religious Liberty*. New York: International Missionary Council, 1945.

Curtiss, J. S. *The Russian Church and the Soviet State*. Boston: Little, Brown & Co., 1953.

Fedotov, P. P. *Russian Church Since the Revolution*. New York: The Macmillan Co., 1928.

Spinka, M. *Church and the Russian Revolution*. New York: The Macmillan Co., 1927.

Timasheff, N. S. *Religion in Soviet Russia 1917-42*. New York: Sheed & Ward, 1942.

Chapter 28

Bates, M. S. *Religious Liberty*. New York: International Missionary Council, 1945.

Binchy, D. A. *Church and State in Fascist Italy*. London: Oxford University Press, 1941.

Brenan, G. *The Spanish Labyrinth*. New York: The Macmillan Co., 1943.

Dark, S., and Essex, R. S. *The War against God*. New York, Cincinnati, Chicago: The Abingdon Press, 1938.

De la Bedoyère. *Christian Crisis*. New York: The Macmillan Co., 1942.

Guilday, P. (ed.). *The Catholic Church in Contemporary Europe 1919-1931*. New York: P. J. Kennedy & Sons, 1932.

Gurian, W., and Fitzsimons, M. A. *The Catholic Church in World Affairs*. South Bend, Ind.: University of Notre Dame Press, 1954.

Gwynn, D. *The Catholic Reaction in France*. New York: The Macmillan Co., 1924.

Halperin, S. W. *Separation of Church and State in Italian Thought from Cavour to Mussolini*. Chicago: University of Chicago Press, 1937.

Howard, G. P. *Religious Liberty in Latin America?* Philadelphia: Westminister Press, 1944.

Manhattan, Avro. *The Vatican in World Politics*. New York: Gaer Associates, 1949.

Mendizabal, A. *Martyrdom of Spain*. New York: Charles Scribner's Sons, 1938.

Micklem, N. *National Socialism and the Roman Catholic Church*. London: Oxford University Press, 1939.

Neuhäusler, J. B. *Kreuz und Hakenkreuz: der Kampf des Nationalsozialismus gegen die Katholische Kirche und der kirchliche Widerstand*. 2 vols. Munich: Katholische Kirche Bayerns, 1946.

Peers, E. A. *Spanish Tragedy 1930-36*, 2d ed. London: Methuen & Co., Ltd., 1936.

———. *The Persecution of the Catholic Church in the Third Reich, Facts and Documents*. New York: Longmans, Green & Co., 1942.

Salvemini, G. and La Piana, G. *What To Do with Italy?* New York: Duell, Sloan, & Pearce, 1943.

Simon, Y. *The Road to Vichy 1918-1938*. New York: Sheed & Ward, 1942.

Sturzo, L. *Church and State*. New York: Longmans, Green & Co., 1939.

Teeling, W. *Crisis for Christianity*. London: Religious Book Club, 1939.

Chapter 29

Beckmann, J. *Kirchliches Jahrbuch für die Evangelische Kirche in Deutschland, 1933-45*. Gütersloh: Bertelsmann, 1948.

Duncan-Jones, A. S. *The Struggle for Religious Freedom in Germany*. London: V. Gollancz, Ltd., 1938.

Frey, A. *Cross and Swastika*. London: Student Christian Movement, 1938.

Gerhardt, M. *Ein Jahrhundert Innere Mission*. 2 vols. Gütersloh: C. Bertelsmann, 1948.

Gunz, J. *Sozialismus und Religion in Deutschland der Nachkriegszeit*. Munich: Duncker und Humblot, 1933.

Herman, S. W. *It's Your Souls We Want*. New York: Harper & Bros., 1943.

Hermelink, H. (ed.). *Kirche in Kampf. Dokumente des Widerstands und des Aufbaus in der Evangelischen Kirche Deutschlands von 1933 bis 1945.* Tübingen: R. Wunderlich, 1950.

Horton, W. M. *Contemporary Continental Theology.* New York: Harper & Bros., 1938.

Keller, A. *Church and State on the European Continent.* Chicago: Willett, Clark & Co., 1936.

———. *Christian Europe Today.* New York: Harper & Bros., 1942.

———, and Stewart, G. *Protestant Europe: Its Crisis and Outlook.* New York: Doubleday, Doran, 1927.

Leiper, H. S. (ed.). *Christianity Today.* New York: Morehouse-Gorham, 1947.

Means, P. B. *Things that Are Caesar's.* New York: Round Table, 1935.

Niemoeller, W. *Kampf and Zeugnis der Bekennenden Kirche.* Bielefeld, Evangelische Presse Verband, 1948.

Chapter 30

Beck, G. A. *The English Catholics 1850-1950.* London: Burns, Oates & Washbourne, 1950.

Bell, G. K. A. *Randall Davidson.* 2 vols. New York: Oxford University Press, 1935.

Fleming, J. R. *History of the Church in Scotland, 1834-74.* Edinburgh: T. & T. Clark, 1927.

Horton, W. M. *Contemporary English Theology.* New York: Harper & Bros. 1936.

Iremonger, F. A. *William Temple.* New York: Oxford University Press, 1948.

Leiper, H. S. (ed.). *Christianity Today.* New York: Morehouse-Gorham, 1947.

Lloyd, R. B. *The Church of England in the 20th Century.* 2 vols. New York: Longmans, Green & Co., 1947.

Reckitt, M. *Maurice to Temple.* London: Faber & Faber, 1948.

Silcox, C. E. *Church Union in Canada.* New York: Institute of Social and Religious Research, 1933.

Spinks, G. S. *Religion in Britain since 1900.* London: Dakers, 1952.

Sundkler, B. *The Church of South India.* London: Lutterworth, 1954.

Chapter 31

Cavert, S. M. and Van Dusen, H. P. *The Church Through Half a Century.* New York: Charles Scribner's Sons, 1936.

Douglass, H. P. "Religion: The Protestant Faiths," in Stearns, H. E. (ed.), *America Now.* New York: Charles Scribner's Sons, 1938.

———, and Brunner, E. de S. *The Protestant Church as a Social Institution.* New York: Institute of Social and Religious Research, 1935.

Fry, C. L. *The U. S. Looks at its Churches.* New York: Institute of Social and Religious Research, 1930.

Hammar, G. *Christian Realism in Contemporary American Theology.* Uppsala: A.-b. Lundequistska bokhandeln, 1940.

Hopkins, C. H. *History of the Y.M.C.A. in North America.* New York: Association Press, 1951.

Hutchison, J. A. *We Are Not Divided.* New York: Round Table, 1941.

May, M. A. *The Education of American Ministers.* 4 vols. New York: Institute of Social and Religious Research, 1934.

Maynard, T. *The Story of American Catholicism.* New York: The Macmillan Co., 1941.

Nash, A. S. *Protestant Thought in the Twentieth Century.* New York: The Macmillan Co., 1951.

Schneider, H. W. *Religion in 20th Century America.* Cambridge: Harvard University Press, 1952.

Sellin, T. (ed.). "Organized Religion in the United States," *Annals of the American Academy of Political and Social Science* (1948).

Chapter 32

Davis, J. *The Economic and Social Environment of the Younger Churches.* London: Edinburgh House Press, 1939.

Goodall, N. (ed.). *Missions under the Cross.* New York: Friendship Press, 1953.

Grubb, K. G. and Bingle, E. J. (eds.). *World Christian Handbook.* London: World Dominion Press, 1949.

Latourette, K. S. *A History of the Expansion of Christianity.* New York: Harper & Bros., Vol. VII, *Advance Through Storm* (1945).

Leiper, H. S. (ed.). *Christianity Today.* New York: Morehouse Gorham, 1947.

Parker, J. I. *Interpretative Statistical Survey of the World Mission.* New York: International Missionary Council, 1938.

Paton, W. *Christianity in the Eastern Conflicts.* Chicago: Willett, Clark & Co., 1937.

Petty, O. A. (ed.). *Laymen's Foreign Missionary Inquiry. Fact-Finder's Reports.* 7 vols. New York: Harper & Bros., 1933.

Ranson, C. W. *Renewal and Advance.* London: Edinburgh House Press, 1948.

Van Dusen, H. P. *World Christianity—Yesterday, Today, Tomorrow.* Nashville: Abingdon-Cokesbury, 1947.

———. *For the Healing of the Nations.* New York: Charles Scribner's Sons, 1940.

Chapter 33

Bell, G. K. A. *Documents on Christian Unity, 1920-1924.* London: Oxford University Press, 1924.

———. *Documents on Christian Unity, Second Series.* London: Oxford University Press, 1930.

———. *Documents on Christian Unity, 1930-1948.* London: Oxford University Press, 1948.

———. *The Kingship of Christ.* Baltimore: Penguin Books, 1954.

Brown, W. A. *Toward a United Church.* New York: Charles Scribner's Sons, 1946.

Douglass, H. P. *A Decade of Objective Progress in Church Unity, 1927-1936.* New York: Harper & Bros., 1937.

Hogg, W. R. *Ecumenical Foundations: A History of the International Missionary Council.* New York: Harper & Bros., 1952.

Horton, W. M. *Toward a Reborn Church.* New York: Harper & Bros., 1949.

Neill, S. *Towards Church Union, 1937-1952.* London: Faith and Order Commission, Papers No. 11, 1952.

Rouse, R. *The World's Student Christian Federation.* London: Student Christian Movement Press, 1948.

———, and Neill, S. *History of the Ecumenical Movement 1517-1948.* Philadelphia: Westminister Press, 1954.

Tatlow, Tissington. *Story of the Student Christian Movement of Great Britain and Ireland.* London: Student Christian Movement Press, 1933.

CHAPTER 34

Beckmann, J. (ed.). *Kirchliches Jahrbuch (1945-48).* Gütersloh: Bertelsmann, 1950.

Bingle, E. J., and Grubb, K. G. *World Christian Handbook,* (2d ed.) London: World Dominion Press, 1952.

Devanandan, P. D., and Thomas, M. M. (eds.). *Communism and the Social Revolution in India.* Calcutta: Y.M.C.A. Pub. House, 1954.

Herman, S. W. *Report from Christian Europe.* New York: Friendship, 1953.

Ranson, C. W. *That the World May Know.* New York: Friendship, 1953.

Shuster, George N. *Religion Behind the Iron Curtain.* New York: The Macmillan Co., 1954.

INDEX